Love, Friendship, and Narrative Form After Bloomsbury

Love, Friendship, and Narrative Form After Bloomsbury

The Progress of Intimacy in History

Jesse Wolfe

BLOOMSBURY ACADEMIC
LONDON • NEW YORK • OXFORD • NEW DELHI • SYDNEY

BLOOMSBURY ACADEMIC
Bloomsbury Publishing Plc
50 Bedford Square, London, WC1B 3DP, UK
1385 Broadway, New York, NY 10018, USA
29 Earlsfort Terrace, Dublin 2, Ireland

BLOOMSBURY, BLOOMSBURY ACADEMIC and the Diana logo
are trademarks of Bloomsbury Publishing Plc

First published in Great Britain 2023
Paperback edition published 2024

Copyright © Jesse Wolfe, 2023

Jesse Wolfe has asserted his right under the Copyright, Designs and
Patents Act, 1988, to be identified as Author of this work.

For legal purposes the Acknowledgments on p. x constitute
an extension of this copyright page.

Cover design: Rebecca Heselton
Cover: *America* (2008), by Bo Bartlett. 80 × 116 inches. Oil on linen.
Courtesy Bo Bartlett Studio.

All rights reserved. No part of this publication may be reproduced or transmitted
in any form or by any means, electronic or mechanical, including photocopying,
recording, or any information storage or retrieval system, without prior
permission in writing from the publishers.

Bloomsbury Publishing Plc does not have any control over, or responsibility for,
any third-party websites referred to or in this book. All internet addresses given
in this book were correct at the time of going to press. The author and publisher
regret any inconvenience caused if addresses have changed or sites have ceased
to exist, but can accept no responsibility for any such changes.

A catalogue record for this book is available from the British Library.

Library of Congress Cataloging-in-Publication Data

Names: Wolfe, Jesse, 1970- author.
Title: Love, friendship, and narrative form after Bloomsbury : the progress
of intimacy in history / Jesse Wolfe.
Description: London ; New York : Bloomsbury Academic, 2023. | Includes bibliographical
references and index. | Summary: "Exploring how the Bloomsbury Group's cutting-edge thinkers-Virginia
Woolf, Sigmund Freud, and E. M. Forster-understood the intimacy of friends, lovers, spouses, and families
as historically unfolding phenomena, this book offers a compelling account of modernism's legacies
in contemporary fiction and demonstrates the myriad ways in which intimacy was a guiding and
persistent idea explored by writers across the 20th-century and up to the present day. Often modernists
have been celebrated for their insights into social and civilizational sickness but this book unearths a strain
of modernist thought that is more complex and inspiring than this. It discusses how Bloomsbury's
thinkers wrestled with the question "Does intimate life improve?" as sexual egalitarianism expands, as
taboos against same-sex love, interracial love, and singlehood wane, and as parents and children relate
less formally and often more warmly toward one another. And it discusses how many of today's major
novelists, such as Salman Rushdie, Zadie Smith, Ian McEwan and Rachel Cusk, look to Bloomsbury's
thematic and formal examples when they reformulate this question for our time"– Provided by publisher.
Identifiers: LCCN 2022031198 | ISBN 9781350328822 (hardback) | ISBN 9781350328860 (paperback) |
ISBN 9781350328839 (ebook) | ISBN 9781350328846 (epub) | ISBN 9781350328853
Subjects: LCSH: Intimacy (Psychology) in literature. | English fiction–21st century–History and criticism. |
English fiction–20th century–History and criticism. | American fiction–21st century–History
and criticism. | American fiction–20th century–History and criticism. | Bloomsbury group–Influence. |
Modernism (Literature) Classification: LCC PR890.I64 W65 2023 | DDC 820.9/0091–dc23/eng/20221006
LC record available at https://lccn.loc.gov/2022031198

ISBN: HB: 978-1-3503-2882-2
PB: 978-1-3503-2886-0
ePDF: 978-1-3503-2883-9
eBook: 978-1-3503-2884-6

Typeset by Integra Software Services Pvt. Ltd.

To find out more about our authors and books visit www.bloomsbury.com
and sign up for our newsletters.

I dedicate this book to my father, Thomas P. Wolfe.

Contents

List of Plates	viii
List of Tables and Appendices	ix
Acknowledgments	x
Introduction: Historical Despair and Bloomsbury's Enlightened Modernism	1
1 Do Things Get Better?—Bloomsbury, Private Lives, and Dreams of Progress	25
2 Woolfian Pessimism: Rachel Cusk's Vision of Paralysis	49
3 Post-Freudian Skepticism: *Atonement* in an Age of De-Conversion	75
4 Post-Freudian Hope: *Regeneration* in an Incredulous Milieu	97
5 Forsterian Skepticism: Transcontinental Eros in *The Satanic Verses*	127
6 Forsterian Optimism: Zadie Smith's Post(?)-Realist Homage	151
7 Woolfian Optimism: Michael Cunningham's Modernist Homage	175
8 Bloomsburian Horizons: Intimacy in a Polyamorous Light	195
Appendices	219
Bibliography	227
Index	245

Plates

1. *The Walled Garden at Charleston* (1916), by Vanessa Bell. 46 × 35.5 cm. Oil on canvas. Courtesy Artists Rights Society
2. Monk's House, dining room. Photograph courtesy of Howard Grey
3. *The Sampling Officials of the Drapers' Guild* (1662), by Rembrandt van Rijn. 191.5 × 279 cm. Oil on canvas. Courtesy Rijksmuseum, Amsterdam
4. *A Woman Bathing in a Stream* (1654), by Rembrandt van Rijn. 61.8 × 47 cm. Oil on panel. Courtesy National Gallery, London
5. *The Hours*. Film. 2003
6. *The Hours*. Film. 2003
7. *The Hours*. Film. 2003
8. *The Hours*. Film. 2003
9. *The Hours*. Film. 2003
10. *The Hours*. Film. 2003
11. *The Hours*. Film. 2003

Tables and Appendices

Tables

1	Comparison of Freud's to McEwan's techniques	83
2	Comparison of what Rivers thinks to what he may unconsciously mean	117

Appendices

A1	Percentage of adults ever married (currently married, widowed, or divorced)	220
A2	Married couples as percentage of adult population (age 16 and over)	220
A3	Illegitimacy rates (England and Wales)	220
A4	Divorce rates through Edwardian times and today	221
A5	Divorces granted by sex: England and Wales, 1900–2010	222
B1	Growth of the South Asian population of Great Britain, 1951–2011	223
B2	Timeline of post-Second World War immigration legislation and cultural events	224
B3	Estimated number of Black-white US marriages, 1980–2010	225
B4	US attitudes toward interracial marriage, 1972–2002	225
B5	US laws and culture pertaining to interracial marriage, 1664–1967	226

Acknowledgments

This book was years in the making, and I owe thanks to many. The National Endowment for the Humanities funded nine months of full-time study. My home institution of California State University, Stanislaus, provided support in numerous forms, including sabbatical funding; travel funding; course releases under the auspices of Research, Scholarship, and Creative Activity; and Graduate-Assistant Fellowships funded by the Center for Excellence in Graduate Education (CEGE). I had the pleasure of working with Angela Liesching, Jenny Hamby, and Trevor Jackson on the CEGE fellowships. I was graciously assisted at Stanislaus's library by Tim Held, Laura French, and others. My classroom discussions with master's students, including Danae Zevely, Heather Simmons, and Tara Dybas, enriched my thinking and improved the quality of the manuscript. My colleague Arnold Schmidt provided advice and encouragement. I thank Glenn Pillsbury for his technical expertise.

Fellow scholars, especially in the Modernist Studies Association, have helped in numerous ways. John McGuigan, Matt Brown, Randi Saloman, and Doug Mao have read chapters, providing feedback and votes of confidence. I am grateful to Elsa Högberg for organizing the 2015 "Intimate Modernism" conference in Uppsala, Sweden, and to the conference's other attendees for our stimulating exchange of ideas.

My wife, Alex Block, and my father, Thomas Wolfe, have given generous editorial feedback. My dissertation director, Richard Begam, has continued to provide counsel, even through the completion of this, my second book, long after my graduate studies ended.

Thank you to the Bo Bartlett Studio; Artists Rights Society; Howard Grey; Rijksmuseum, Amsterdam; and the National Gallery, London, for permission to use images.

Introduction

Historical Despair and Bloomsbury's Enlightened Modernism

For decades, thanks largely to modernist legacies, four forms of historical pessimism and philosophical skepticism have been common in the humanities and *de rigueur* in some bastions of literary theory. One does not logically entail another, but they share family resemblances, and when two or more combine, they capture a complex attitude of non-complicity in a stultifying status quo, disillusionment that yields intellectual liberation.

First, disbelief in historical progress—the steady improvement of public-sphere life—was a major symptom of the First World War and an impetus to modernist originality across the arts. The Second World War, the social unrest of 1968, wars in Vietnam and elsewhere, the gathering threat of anthropogenic climate change, and in the last half decade, the global rise of ethnonationalism have been among the many reasons why this modernist-inflected form of skepticism has retained cachet.

Second, disbelief in love, whether in the restricted forms that social norms permit, or in *any* form, has been a recurrent theme in literature by modernists and their legatees. While the "era of mandatory marriage" persisted, roughly through 1960, critiques of love often focused on its normative conventions; with the commencement of the era of "mass divorce" *c.* 1970,[1] such critiques have often focused on the fragility and impermanence of intimacy. But in each case, critics have linked public- and private-sphere woes. If civilization is ailing, then it makes sense that love relations would suffer—and vice versa.

Third, a disbelief in the coherence of the human subject has been among modernism's philosophical legacies. E. M. Forster said in "What I Believe" that "Psychology has split and shattered the idea of a 'Person,' and has shown that there is something incalculable in each of us, which may at any moment rise to the surface and destroy our normal balance."[2] From Lacan's linguistically inflected readings of Freud, down through poststructuralism, this intuition has been revisited. It is not surprising that Foucault admired Beckett's subject-dissolving formulation from the third of his *Texts for Nothing* ("What matter who's speaking, someone said what matter who's speaking?"): Beckett's linguistic experiments foreshadow an array of French theories. When *Women in Love*'s

Ursula attempts to extract a confession of love from Birkin, he resists this conventional emotion with the claim that her selfhood—even if it is real—is not what allures him. "I want to find you, where you don't know your own existence," he explains, "the you that your common self denies utterly."[3]

However annoying a lover Birkin makes, with his lapses into weariness and cynicism, he might seem like an astute reader of Forster's theory—were the portion of "What I Believe" quoted above taken out of context. If the "I" that people present to the world and the "you" by which they know their lovers, friends, parents, children, etc. are reductive—perhaps inaccurate—presentations of a dynamic and unstable core, then, Birkin in effect asks, aren't intimacies based on the pledge "I love you" made in bad faith, and always in peril? Shouldn't he and Ursula strive for a more adventurous bond, one that is truer to their changeable and unknowable natures?

Forster cagily embeds his talk of a "split and shattered" person within a pragmatic Pascalian defense of this same humanist concept. As if he were reassuring his inner Birkin—his own doubts about subjecthood and hence intimate bonds—Forster asserts his "faith" in "personal relationships ... something comparatively solid in a world full of violence." Although "Psychology" has taught us that "in theory" we cannot put trust in them, "in practice we can and do." Although "A is not unchangeably A, or B unchangeably B," he maintains, "there can still be love and loyalty between the two."[4] Forster's and Lawrence's doubts are sometimes appeased by this reassurance and sometimes not. Birkin's skepticism always threatens to undermine Ursula's Forsterian faith in the love between (more or less) coherent subjects, and Ursula's love always threatens to contain and normalize Birkin's radical modernist quest to transvalue the terms on which bourgeois men and women construct lives together.

Finally, a mistrust of realist narrative techniques—those relics of Victorian intellectual confidence that modernists so delighted in revaluing—has for a century provoked poets, novelists, and other artists to "remake it new," in the words of Lynn Keller. (But modernists so effectively made so many things new that in their wake, avant gardism has passed through phases of exhaustion and replenishment.[5])

Why shouldn't literary realism seem anachronistic? If civilization is unstable—with world wars and totalitarian states threatening to emerge—if love feels like a cage to those who have it and like a fairytale to those who don't, and if the coherent self is a mirage, then how could a storyteller *not* dispense with the techniques appropriate to a more epistemologically naïve and sedate epoch? Virginia Woolf famously opined in "Modern Fiction" that "if a writer were a free man and not a slave ... there would be no plot ... in the accepted style."[6] Some of her works, such as *The Waves*, test this hypothesis severely, while her more popular efforts, including *Mrs Dalloway*, balance the demands and rewards of radical post-realism with fiction's familiar comforts. Forster's ruminations on Gertrude Stein (he said that her attempt to "abolish time" in her fiction was an instructive "failure"[7]) suggest not merely his personal ambivalence toward avant-garde extremes. They suggest modernism's general uncertainty about how far it should go, in what directions, toward dismantling novels and short stories as they have been known and training readers of literary fiction to develop new epistemological habits.

Modernist Legacies and the Limits of Disbelief

To study modernism is to feel the excitement of Lawrence's skepticism, the horror of Conrad's heart of darkness, the discontent at the heart of civilization that Freud diagnosed, the civilizational despair that animates *The Waste Land* and *Guernica*, the disenchantment with "culture itself" that Lionel Trilling saw as a modernist trademark,[8] the creative possibilities enabled by formal experimentation in an atmosphere of radical uncertainty. To read the works of Bloomsburian legatees, from Rachel Cusk through Pat Barker and others, is to see how modernists' skepticism toward progress and love, their doubts about subjecthood and representation, and their admiration for avant-garde epistemologies continue to spur creativity.

But this volume aims to loosen the association of modernism with uncompromising disbelief in each of these areas, and thus to honor the spirit of questioning—and even historical optimism—that enlivens many of modernism's and Bloomsbury's finest works. Rather than solely emphasizing those modernist legatees who channel pure-minded pessimism or incredulity regarding progress, love, subjecthood, or representation, this study instead focuses on how six contemporary Anglo-American novelists respond to the uncertainties and the capacity for troubled hope expressed by three major Bloomsbury-related figures.

Between extreme despair and comfort with the status quo—concerning the state of society or the state of intimacy—Bloomsburians and their legatees have often articulated ambivalent critiques. They have expressed alienation from mainstream values, such as monogamy and marriage, qualified by a sense of benefitting from those values. They have expressed disillusionment with both the dead weight of Victorian habits of mind and explosive modern ways of thinking—while feeling implicated in each of these things. Between a complete disbelief in the solidity of the "Person" and a stubborn clinging to pre-Freudian assumptions about the mind, they have sought new bases on which to forge authentic—or at least workable—interpersonal relations. Between the stylistic extreme of Woolf's *The Waves*, Stein's *Tender Buttons*, or Cusk's *Outline* trilogy on the one hand, and the precedents of Jane Austen and George Eliot on the other, they have forged narrative tools, as refined as possible, as innovative as needed, for the tasks of representing individual cogitating minds and the interplay within couples or between friends who are trying to understand their feelings for one another.

Bloomsburians devised numerous ways to pursue such inquiries, from stream-of-consciousness narration (with its sensitivity to a wife's fluctuating thoughts and feelings about her husband) to the use of doppelgängers like *Mrs Dalloway*'s Clarissa and Septimus, who, though mutually unacquainted, share common predicaments and feelings. Sarah Ahmed argues that these characters "who do not meet ... achieve an odd intimacy: the not-just-private suffering of the housewife and the not-quite-public suffering of the returned soldier are interwoven ... proximate but not contagious."[9] In their commitments to honor the non-realist dimensions of Woolf's aesthetic, other critics such as Elsa Högberg also value how she "defamiliarizes and even dislocates habitual connections of intimacy."[10]

The coming chapters will discuss doppelgängers in works by James Joyce, Woolf, and Salman Rushdie, all of whom use this device to defamiliarize and dislocate a single character's selfhood (what Forster calls a "Person") and hence that character's relationship both with himself and with other people. Coming chapters will also discuss how Bloomsburian legatees broaden the doppelgänger device, developing (in Barker's case) three or (in Cusk's case) five characters as aspects of a composite self. Such many-sided men or women provide chances to explore a society's evolution through time, or a social class's paralysis within historical time, with the multi-angular insight with which Picasso's analytical cubism regards an object of portraiture. They provide chances not only to *depict* intimacy literally but also to *evoke* it figuratively, in a suburban woman's longing to know and be known by her neighbor or an analysand's longing for his therapist's understanding and approval. I will strive in additional ways—beyond attention to two-, three-, or five-part composites—to honor the *avant-garde* spirit in Bloomsbury and Bloomsbury-legatee works, as critics including Högberg do. After all, these stylistic innovators have revealed that intimacy is not a self-evident category, but one open to reconsideration from new narrative and philosophical angles, from the non-linear to the non-humanistic.

But my analyses will focus on how these authors *represent* intimacy, not on such "odd" figurative *evocations* as Ahmed deftly limns. The three Bloomsburians and six legatees I discuss often (not always) follow Forster's humanistic determination to see the "Person" as a comparatively solid man or woman seeking intimacy with other men and women, prone to neurosis as they all, and in danger of psychic disintegration as some of them, may be. These authors also sometimes follow Forster's historically sanguine moods in imagining that personal relations will grow *more* solid, more varied, and healthier as society evolves.

But Forster, like Woolf and Freud, was self-divided. These writers express both hope and apprehensiveness concerning the future for same-sex or interracial love, or literature that depicts such love, or psychotherapy's ambition to heal neurotic individuals. Their ambivalence—their varied tonal register—is crucial to their philosophical and aesthetic legacy, as I explain below.

The coming chapters will elaborate upon the titular concept of "intimacy in history," which neither Bloomsburians nor their legatees employ, but which aims to capture their shared sense of intimate feelings and relationships as effects of historical forces to which people are subject but over which they have some creative control. Bloomsburians' sense of themselves as (partial) authors of their own erotic and romantic destinies, and as trailblazers for the future, links them to melioristic-minded Victorians from whom in some ways they strove to distinguish themselves. *Do things improve* over time, Bloomsburian modernists wondered, for friends, lovers, spouses, and families? Their legatees wonder: have late twentieth- and early twenty-first-century citizens, on balance, been happier than their forebears because they have been freer to love whom, how, and if they want to? As contraception has facilitated family planning; as sexual pleasure has been affirmed as part of a good life; as more spaces have opened for interracial love, same-sex love, intersexual fraternization, divorce, and singlehood; and as polyamory has made tentative inroads into respectable society, are people finding more satisfaction within and beyond coupledom? As "new dads" replace absent authoritarian fathers; as women make gains in struggles for workplace equity; as men contribute more housework and childcare;[11] and as parents and adult children relate to one another on less hierarchical terms and more like friends, are people improving (as should happen in an enlightened culture) their crucial life-skills as each other's intimates? Bloomsburian modernists made it easier to formulate such questions and to discern their interrelations. They also made it easier to answer such questions affirmatively, or at least ambivalently; I hope that recovering this strain of sanguinity from their works can illuminate modernism as the period of hope and renewal that it always was—in addition to being a period of despair, disillusion, and expansive skepticism.

Ongoing Sources of Despair

Admittedly, for at least the four decades since Jean François Lyotard's 1979 diagnosis of "incredulity toward metanarrative," it has been difficult for literary critics to take seriously the Enlightenment ideal of progress or to close read literary texts in its light. There are powerful reasons why historical despondency continues to make the most alienated expressions of high modernism seem profound and relevant. For decades, a loneliness epidemic has battered the working class and underclass in America and elsewhere, with people unmoored from marriage, faith communities, well-paid jobs (or any jobs), and educational opportunities. In addition to large numbers of suicides, "deaths of despair"[12] have resulted, with deracinated individuals slowly killing themselves with drugs and alcohol. Communal anxiety and rage have scapegoated immigrants and fueled ethnonationalism. Mistrust of the ethnic (or sexual) other menaces past decades' progress toward peaceful coexistence, racial equality, interracial intimacy, and appreciation of queer sexualities. Political polarization divides families along epistemic lines, with the private sphere reproducing the public sphere's pathologies. The MeToo movement has exposed how pervasive and violent the sexual hierarchy remains. Antiblack police violence offers harrowing evidence of a persistent racial caste system.

As if this news weren't grim enough, Covid-19 has disproportionately battered working classes and communities of color, while Zoom-connected professionals (though not unscathed) have shared Margaret Schlegel's experience of privilege. "You and I and the Wilcoxes," the heroine of *Howards End* tells her sister, "stand upon money as upon islands."[13] The long-term impacts of quarantines and social distancing on familial, personal, and cultural relations can only, as of yet, be speculated about.

While vaccines can combat a pandemic, anthropogenic climate change poses a more harrowing civilizational threat. A warming planet and meteorological apocalypses threaten to exacerbate economic inequities and erode the chances for personal relations—the friendships, family bonds, and erotic attachments that Forster treasured—to bridge divisions among classes, races, and cultures.

Can There Be Progress in the Private Sphere?

With all these reasons to doubt that public-sphere life has yet or will ever vindicate the Enlightenment's promises, it might seem especially Pollyannaish to entertain ideas of progress in the private sphere—to imagine that more humane British or American or European societies will yield more fulfilling relationships between lovers, among friends, or within families—or more happiness for people who avoid toxic intimacies. Not surprisingly, just as high modernism—and its legatees in contemporary literature and theory—offers fulsome support for *public-sphere* despair, it likewise critiques *private-sphere* life. Eliot's *Waste Land* depicts a "young man carbuncular" raping a typist—one of its many images of sexual sterility or depravity. A character from Joyce's *Dubliners* concludes that "Love between man and man is impossible because there must not be sexual intercourse and friendship between man and woman is impossible because there must be sexual intercourse."[14] Lawrence's *Sons and Lovers* worries, perhaps with insufficient evidence, that Oedipal attachments stunt a generation of young men emotionally and sexually. *Women in Love*'s Birkin rails against the "egoïsme à deux"[15] that he believes normative love encourages.

The conclusion of *A Passage to India* casts questions of sexual and interpersonal unfulfillment in queer and postcolonial terms. Aziz and the protagonist Fielding, each partnered (perhaps unfittingly) with a woman two years after they were intimate with one another, argue passionately. Aziz says that only when India drives every English colonizer into the sea can the men "be friends" again. Fielding asks "Why can't we be friends now?" The earth, birds, and sky respond "not yet ... not there," reinforcing Aziz's bitter appraisal of the present and dashing Fielding's hope—in Mau, India, circa 1922—for inter-civilizational same-sex intimacy. The novel's concluding words are at once heartbreaking and open-ended, given that they do *not* say "not ever ... not anywhere."

Whereas *The Waste Land* and "A Painful Case" from *Dubliners* evoke the despair of the unmarried, other high modernist works reinforce *Passage*'s picture of unfulfilled homoerotic possibilities and evince despair among those who are partnered. *Mrs Dalloway* and *To the Lighthouse* probe the narrow horizons of women born (as Woolf was) into the Victorian world, who remained married through the modernist era, perhaps harboring long-dormant Sapphic passions. "Professions for Women" discusses how women internalize narrow conceptions of their intellectual capacities and must slay imaginary "angels" to free themselves. *A Room of One's Own* indicts higher education for its complicity, a quarter of the way into the twentieth century, in the sexual hierarchy. *Three Guineas* draws connections among English families' and schools' differential treatment of boys and girls, the military pomp and vanity to which men of many nations are endeared, and Nazi Germany's overt totalitarianism. In combination these texts expose how a social paradigm of sexual inequality mars numerous intimate relations: those between spouses denied the stimulation of intellectual parity, those between parents and children whose sexes of each generation are siphoned into constricted roles, and those among grown men and women denied the chance for intersexual fraternization that Bloomsbury helped to normalize.

Contemporary theorists have channeled this modernist spirit of radical dissent in formulating "pure critiques."[16] In 2011, Lauren Berlant lamented that "lively, durable intimacy," like "upward mobility, job security," and social justice, was an increasingly tenuous "fantasy."[17] Hence, according to Berlant, "optimism" can be "cruel"—though she acknowledges the value of utopian thought.[18] Likewise, according to Ahmed, the "promise of happiness" is often deceptive, especially for queer, female, and non-white subjects.

In formulating new concepts—"antirelationality" and "negativity"—queer theorists including Leo Bersani and Lee Edelman have plumbed the skepticism and despair born from marginalization. Bersani's 1995 *Homos* sees ongoing evidence of homophobia amid ostensible signs of inclusivity and codes gay male sexuality as anticommunal. As suggested by its title, Edelman's 2004 *No Future: Queer Theory and the Death Drive* associates the future with the Child and thus the repronormative and antiqueer. "Futurism," he says, is "always purchased at our expense."[19] Admittedly, Edelman links negativity and the death drive to irony and *jouissance*, but his feeling of exclusion from mainstream society and from the future that it shapes casts a pall over these ostensibly reparative attitudes.

Widening the scope of "negativity," Ashley Shelden's 2017 *Unmaking Love* asserts that mainstream culture has long suppressed an important truth; that modernists including Joyce, Freud, Woolf, and Lawrence ambivalently articulated it; and that their contemporary legatees including Ian McEwan and Smith embrace it. "Love has failed," Shelden proclaims.[20] She distinguishes modernists' naïve clinging to the love ideal from contemporaries' turn toward the "negative"—a term that for her evokes "discontent," "inequity," and "divorce."[21] On her end-of-intellectual-history account, perspicacious contemporaries recognize that all hopes of romantic "union" are "fantasmatic" and that the self, the couple, and time are all fragmented.[22] Her critique draws together the four forms of modernist-inflected skepticism with which I opened—regarding progress, love, subjecthood, and narrative style. Modernists and their legatees, she asserts admiringly, do not merely question received concepts but demolish them.

A Turn against Radical Dismay

But theorists in numerous specialties, queer studies included, have been reacting against negativity and oppositionality as critical standards. Their efforts to reanimate a spirit of open questioning, and their receptivity to hopefulness and enchantment, recall Bloomsbury and some of its successors. Bloomsburians entertained ideas of the public and private spheres evolving, not hand in hand, but roughly in solidarity, as British colonialism ended, or as the middle class's dominance over public life waned, clearing space in which healthier intimacies might thrive. Sometimes, when they or their legatees express *intellectual* incredulity toward such a hopeful vision, they also evince *emotional* attachment to it—an ambivalence that enriches their aesthetics.

Rita Felski summed up this scholarly push back against doctrinaire disenchantment in *The Limits of Critique* (2015), which asserts that a romance with critique has long led critics to privilege a hermeneutics of suspicion over other styles of reading. Felski was preceded by, among others, Eve Kosofsky Sedgwick, whose *Touching Feeling* (2003) complained that paranoid reading practices have become so common in queer studies that they have lost critical power.[23]

Questioning the value of critiques unleavened by appreciation for past social progress or hope for further gains, José Muñoz and others have theorized time and futurity in hopeful veins.[24] Muñoz argues that a "romance [with] negativity" leads many queer critics—including Edelman, whom he admires—to jettison the utopian energies that he sees as necessary to a flourishing resistance.[25] He credits some theorists, including Sedgwick, with thinking flexibly about "negativity" and not foregoing hope in the process. His own project turns toward the future, toward "queer utopianism," in language strongly reminiscent of Forster.

The subtitle of Muñoz's *Cruising Utopia: The Then and There of Queer Futurity* recalls *Passage*'s final words ("not yet ... not there"). Reiterating Forsterian motifs of deferral and longing, Muñoz asserts that "queerness is not yet here" and that "we must vacate the here and now" and look toward "openings" and "horizons."[26] It may seem disheartening that *Cruising Utopia* (2009) still postpones the dream that the conclusion of *Passage* (1924) held in such poignant suspense almost a century earlier. As Muñoz acknowledges, "disappointment is a big part of utopian longing."[27] But he values the longing. He does not see negativity as necessary to rigorous dissidence, nor as the best route to *jouissance* for the sexually dispossessed. Instead, as Judith (Jack) Halberstam says in praise of *Cruising Utopia*, "for some queers, particularly for queers of color," hope and futurity are not luxuries to be dispensed with.[28]

Robyn Wiegman and Elizabeth Wilson broaden critiques of historical pessimism into a wide-ranging meditation on oppositionality in an essay entitled "Antinormativity's Queer Conventions." These co-authors describe "antinormativity" as a tendency in queer theory to adopt narrowly oppositional stances with regard to "norms" that—in the eyes of such radicals—are themselves fixed and narrow. Wiegman and Wilson conceive of norms as broad constellations, not wholly oppressive, whose boundaries can be difficult for dissidents to step "outside" of.[29]

With their Derridean approach to containment, subversion, and social change, Wiegman and Wilson represent a strain in queer and feminist theory akin to Bloomsbury's ambivalent, insider/outsider spirit.[30] Woolf's father and his library gave her an insider's access to great men of letters, yet her sex barred her from Oxbridge. Her bisexual curiosity, including her passionate, erotic bond with Vita Sackville-West, gave her an outsider's perspective on a world emerging from Victorian proprieties. But her long and stable partnership with a patient and caring spouse ensconced her in the bourgeois redoubt of marriage. Forster's fear of having his sexual orientation exposed likely motivated his remaining a virgin until he was nearly thirty-eight, and his ninety years of unmarried life (the latter of which may have suited his temperament). But his academic talents; his early brilliance as a prose fiction writer; his inheritance from his great-aunt, combined with his widowed mother's finances; and his sane, ambivalent, liberal, not exactly middle-of-the-road politics—an object of Smith's admiration—all helped to ensconce him in English privilege. Bloomsburians had footholds from which to experiment in their personal lives and advocate for social reform, and their attachments to national traditions, including progressive traditions, ran deep.

Woolf and Forster, like Wiegman and Wilson, advocated pluralistic freethinking, psychosexual boundary testing, feminism, and anti-homophobia. These four thinkers draw on common pre-Bloomsburian sources and point toward common post-Bloomsburian horizons. But—to adopt a psychoanalytic concept—each pair of thinkers understands interpersonal or political progress on the model of *working through*, not in terms of sudden illumination or being guided by a fixed star into a promised land. Forster and his successor Smith are fond of the term "muddle." Their muddles do not preclude progress, though they may impede the propulsive force of utopian ambitions or erotic passions that tempt lovers—á la Tristan and Isolde—with the promise of deliverance from ordinary life.

Seeing Bloomsbury in this light can clarify its value to our era of democratic decline. Forster was a non-magical thinker willing to entertain the capitalized figure of a "Beloved Republic." He and Woolf were beset by self-doubts and avoided violent radicalisms, but they thought often about how the future might improve on the present—in both the public and private arenas. Forster could feel old-fashioned, musing that he belonged to the "fag-end of Victorian liberalism" in a world riven by radicalism and war.[31] "I do not believe in Belief," he proclaimed in a savvy rhetorical construction, a slogan in defense of a non-sloganistic approach to thinking and living.[32] His despair at the state of public affairs could drive him to seek refuge in "personal relations"—only to acknowledge that they too are fragile.[33] His faith in the future was not unshakeable, when he saw progress under assault by reactionary forces, any more than our faith in the durability of progress can be unshakeable when we see it under assault today.

Bloomsbury's Reception: Civilization, "Becoming Together" and the Polyamorous Horizon

I am not the first reader to appraise Bloomsbury in light of such political, historical, and perhaps metanarrative questions. Raymond Williams influenced subsequent scholarship with his ambivalent assessment of the group's "civilized individualism," which he both admires and critiques as a rebellion against, and expression of, upper-class values. On the one hand, he quarrels with leftist critics who cast Bloomsburian individualism as retrograde, but on the other hand he criticizes Bloomsbury for failing to offer "any alternative idea of a whole society."[34]

Objecting to what she sees as Williams's insinuations of the group's disengaged aestheticism, Christine Froula situates Woolf, the group, and its multidisciplinary writings within modernity's "permanent" post-Enlightenment revolution. Froula admires Bloomsbury's commitment to "civilization"—not merely as something to sustain but as something to bring into being, to wrest from war, empire, and the patriarchy.[35] Her conjoining of Bloomsburian-modernist concerns to Enlightenment values provides an important precedent for this study.

Christopher Reed promotes Bloomsburian values in less heroic terms than Froula. He shares Williams's frustration with formulaic Marxist indictments, but he demurs from Williams's call for a comprehensive "alternative idea"—which is, after all, another formulaic standard of evaluation.[36] Reed distinguishes subculture from utopia, seeing Bloomsbury as a shining example of the former. Unlike utopian schemes, he argues, subcultures oppose dominant norms "without the promise of eventually becoming, themselves, normative." While interior design is not my primary focus, as it is for Reed, his valuation of Bloomsbury's "domestic avant garde" informs this study. Modernist creators such as Le Corbusier and theorists such as Clement Greenberg would have seen this label as oxymoronic, given their associations of domesticity with feminine artistry and avant gardism with masculine heroism. But Reed values Bloomsburian "housework" in contrast to Corbusian "heroism." Although he admires Bloomsbury's dissidence, he recognizes—pace Wiegman and Wilson—that "counter-hegemonic movements ... are never completely outside the mainstream cultural forms they challenge."

Todd Avery also discusses Bloomsbury's dissident individualism in examining their experiments in art and life.[37] Avery asks, in a Bloomsburian spirit, whether it is more important to write a great novel or paint a church mural than to achieve blissful intimacy with a friend or lover. The group had a "foundational, self-defining understanding of sexuality," he explains, "as a private psychophysical capacity with public implications." Sexuality was central to their way of being, Avery says, and he quotes Virginia Woolf's description in her memoir "Old Bloomsbury" of how there was "nothing that one could not say, nothing that one could not do, at 46 Gordon Square. It was, I think, a great advance in civilization."

There may be playful hyperbole in this assertion, but not much. For Woolf, the word "civilization" had no taint of the Victorian high diction that Paul Fussell lampoons.[38] "Civilization" did not ring to Woolf's or Bloomsbury's ears with the hollowness of the word "empire," for example.[39] Instead, Clive Bell employed it as a book title, and group members including John Maynard Keynes and Lytton Strachey use it as a standard against which to measure contemporary society's shortcomings. That Woolf speaks of "advance" is also noteworthy: it underscores this volume's theme of progress: Bloomsbury's belief in progress already achieved and the hope of more progress in the future.

Brenda Helt and Madelyn Detloff's 2016 *Queer Bloomsbury*[40] shares Avery's interest in the public implications of the "psychophysical" phenomena of "sexuality." The editors acknowledge the impossibility of imagining an "unqueer" Bloomsbury, but they nonetheless reanimate the group's dissident queerness for readers a century later, when the term "queer" may have lost its edge, given the LGBT community's focus on mainstream acceptance. In Helt and Detloff's telling, the group courageously pushed beyond families as units of cohabitation, living with friends in the city and countryside. They pursued sexual intimacy with friends of either gender, which they saw as a "rich source of intellectual, artistic, and philosophical affinity." Helt and Detloff honor the group's "conviviality," a term borrowed from Paul Gilroy: he employs it in a post-imperial sense and they employ it in a post-heteronormative sense. They argue that conviviality enables the "becoming together" of multiple people, whereas a focus on "identity" tends to fix concepts. This volume's focus on intimacy has a similar rationale.

As illuminating as their collection is, however, it leaves one legacy of Bloomsbury's conviviality largely unexamined—namely, polyamory. This emerging subculture—a form of relationship modernism—pushes Bloomsburian-modernist life experiments and theories of intimacy in directions that the group itself never fully articulated. As Chapter 8 discusses, Bloomsbury anticipated poly practices of the last half century, although poly literature rarely mentions the group, let alone celebrates it as an inspiration. One contributor to *Queer Bloomsbury*, Regina Marler, admires the group's "love triangles." In so doing, she begins to link Bloomsbury to contemporary poly practices, which expand from romantic threesomes into "quads" and "moresomes."

Poly transvaluations of values have multiple ramifications for this study— and for likely future studies of intimacy and its literary treatments. From a sociological point of view, polyamory challenges not only heteronormativity and mononormativity, but also amatonormativity—the assumption that an exclusive amorous relationship should be preferred over other forms of becoming together. From a literary critical point of view, poly concepts shed new light on texts by Bloomsbury and its legatees, from their alienation from amatonormative values (in *Mrs Dalloway*) to their conservative investments in monogamous values (in *Howards End* and *On Beauty*). Because they pertain to contemporary, poly-inflected culture, these discussions will be deferred until Chapter 8—after discussions of Bloomsbury's life and thought and their impact on six novels of the late twentieth and early twenty-first centuries.

Queer Bloomsbury is not alone in offering multi-angular views of the multifarious collective. Other valuable edited collections, including Victoria Rosner's *Cambridge Companion to Bloomsbury* and Derek Ryan and Stephen Ross's *Handbook to the Bloomsbury Group*, examine its life practices, politics, philosophy, and the waxing and waning of its cultural cachet. But the group's novelistic heirs are more important to this study of intimacy in history and its literary treatments than its many distinguished critics. The six novelists discussed herein respond to Bloomsbury's exempla in both historical and *literary*-historical ways: they contemplate how intimacy has evolved since Bloomsbury's time, and they adapt Woolfian, Forsterian, and Freudian forms in order to understand this evolution.

Woolf, Forster, and Freud each preside as *genius loci* in multiple chapters. The first two of these figures were core group members, and the third strongly influenced Bloomsbury's development. As publishers, Leonard and Virginia Woolf brought Freud to the English-speaking world. As translators, James and Alix Strachey rendered his elegant German in elegant English; and as practicing therapists, each of whom was psychoanalyzed by Freud, these two Bloomsburians disseminated his therapeutic techniques. Freud's cultural and intellectual importance also derives from his influence, *qua* writer, on authors from the modernist era until today. As I discuss in chapters on McEwan and Barker, these savvy respondents to modernism understand the movement as a dense network of ideas and institutions in which Freud played important roles, from therapeutic strategies for treating neurotic housewives or traumatized soldiers to narrative strategies for depicting such traumatized minds in the process of being psychoanalyzed. That McEwan and Barker each wrestle simultaneously with the influence of Freud *and* Woolf suggests that they grasped the overlapping and mutually illuminating pursuits of Freudian and Bloomsburian literature.

In addition to examining Woolf, Forster, and Freud as influences on contemporary novelists, I also ruminate on two other major modernists. Neither Joyce nor Lawrence features in upcoming chapters as a primary modernist legator, but each connects Bloomsbury's concerns to the movement's psychosexual and aesthetic zeitgeist. Joyce's formal genius, polymorphous perversity, feminism, pacifism, and socialism qualify him (in spirit) as a Bloomsbury cousin. *Ulysses* anticipates *Mrs Dalloway*'s one-day format, stream of consciousness, and blending of Stephen's and Bloom's minds into Blephen and Stoom. (An irreverent revision of *Mrs Dalloway* might turn Clarissa and Septimus into Sarissa and Cleptimus.) Joyce plays supporting roles in two upcoming chapters, one of which discusses *Ulysses* and "The Dead" as forerunners of Cusk's *Arlington Park* and the other of which discusses the inspiration that Rushdie drew from *Ulysses*.

Lawrence, already a presence in this Introduction, was of course a famous (or infamous) Bloomsbury scourge.[41] His disdain for the group is marred by the stereotypes of masculine effeminacy that have persisted for decades in what Reed calls "Bloomsbury bashing." But as the foregoing citations of him illustrate, this disdain masks his and Bloomsbury's commonalities—shared concerns with sexual selfhood, authentic intimacy, and their relation to middle-class mores. Cusk sees Lawrence as a visionary dissident, profoundly insightful about sexual oppression and liberation. Her oeuvre, as I discuss in Chapter 2, channels both Woolf and Lawrence—influences that enrich her work and, by virtue of their distinction from one another, underscore the complexity of modernism's ongoing importance.

Meta-Bloomsbury

Contemporary novelists like Cusk (haunted as she is by Woolf and Lawrence), Smith (with her debts to Forster and other modernists), and Cunningham (whose most popular novel, *The Hours*, might not emerge from Woolf's shadow) evince Bloomsbury's part in a passionate scholarly and literary engagement with "the central experiments and debates of twentieth-century modernist culture." I borrow this language and adapt this section title from David James and Urmila Seshagiri's seminal 2014 essay "Metamodernism."[42] At a time when scholars are widening the geographical and temporal scope of modernism[43]—witness the *New Modernisms* Series from Bloomsbury Academic—James and Seshagiri argue that innovative contemporary authors have been provoked by an "era, aesthetic, and archive" of innovative late nineteenth- and early twentieth-century works. They see these contemporary authors, among whom they include McEwan and Smith, engaging with this temporally and culturally bound modernism in two ways: by pushing forward modernist aesthetics (discontinuity, perspectivalism, etc.) and/or by plotting fictions around "the very creation and reception of modern arts and letters."[44]

For aesthetic, biographical, and historical reasons, Bloomsbury and its legatees claim a major role in such "metamodernist" phenomena. Aesthetically, the Bloomsbury locale and coterie belong to a small set of modernist epicenters—along with the Rive Gauche, Greenwich Village, and Harlem.[45] Twenty-first-century scholars and novelists who see modernism as the self-conscious, collective creation of artists in a shared milieu are naturally drawn to these epicenters. Biographically and historically speaking, these twenty-first-century legatees are fascinated not only by art produced in modernist networks, but by the producers themselves. *Who were the Bloomsburians,* some legatees ask—anew—for contemporary purposes, *how did they live, and how did their lifestyles impact their artistic legacies?* In the language of this study, legatees including Cunningham wonder *how did group members' experiences of intimacy in history affect their depictions of it? How, therefore, can contemporary writers who experience intimacy as an historical process learn from Bloomsbury?* To return to James and Seshagiri's language, Chapters 2–7 discuss how contemporary novelists appraise Bloomsburian "aesthetics" and (in McEwan's and Cunningham's cases) "the creation and reception" of Woolfian "letters."

Because Bloomsbury was a varied collective whose legatees vary aesthetically and temperamentally, my meta-Bloomsbury narrative emphasizes the multiplicity of their responses. Where aesthetic form is concerned, I treat three kinds of responses to Bloomsburian precedents: positive ones (homages), negative ones (disavowals of palpable influence), and one example of indifference (a lack of explicit engagement with a Bloomsburian precedent that nonetheless looms large).[46] Where conceptual content is concerned, I stress that Bloomsburians themselves had different feelings about intimacy in history—ranging from pessimistic to optimistic, both among writers and within a single writer's *oeuvre*—and thus that they inspired legatees who also have a range of ideas about how love, friendship, and sexuality are progressing (or not) in tandem with social justice.

In sketching this rhizome of Bloomsburian exempla and responses, this volume broadens the investigations of my previous book, *Bloomsbury, Modernism, and the Reinvention of Intimacy*. In the early twentieth century, *Reinvention* argues, Bloomsburians reconceived intimacy in a modernist spirit, both in their complex living experiments and in daring literary texts that worked through their feelings toward a Victorian inheritance they partly valued and partly strove to transvalue. They understood their rapidly changing milieu in relation both to their recent Victorian past and to near and more distant futures they hoped to help shape. The complexity of the exempla to which they responded informed their ambivalence, and this ambivalence was an aesthetic asset. *Reinvention* proposes two large categories to explain how six Bloomsburian texts dramatize social changes to which their authors contributed. On the one hand, works including *Mrs Dalloway* and *Dora* espouse *anti-essentialist accommodations*, challenging the essentialist gender categories and heteronormative values of their authors' parents and grandparents, but nonetheless remaining invested in marriage, monogamy, and even a bit of hypocrisy—pillars of the same "middle-class social order"[47] whose ideas about sexual selfhood they found so hidebound. On the other hand, I argued, works including *Howards End* issue *essentialist rejections*, excoriating the Victorian marriage paradigm despite remaining invested in the gender typologies (and flirting with the homophobia) that undergirded it.

Each of these kinds of self-divided thought helped Bloomsburian novels to transcend the easy self-confidences of both conservative and radical thinkers. Conservatives such as Coventry Patmore—Woolf's target of critique in "Professions for Women"—envisioned a natural fit between what they believed were men's and women's *innate natures* on the one hand and the sexes' *social roles* on the other hand. For its part, the Freudian Left[48] envisioned an equally logical fit, though one that would disrupt the monogamic social order, between men's and women's innately polymorphous perversities and the sexually freer and more promiscuous society they desired. Lacking faith in any model that proposed such consistency between people's psychic endowments and society's ideal structure, Bloomsbury's novels depict self-divided characters (who aren't sure who they are or what they want) who both rebel against and embrace the psychosexual norms of a society that is also self-divided and in the process of transforming. Neither the protagonists of these novels nor their societies are ever perfected, any more than a Freudian analysand is cured. Instead, Bloomsbury makes ambivalence and irresolution a basis for its philosophical wisdom and aesthetic form—and yet frequently maintains hope for a future in which lovers and friends on the one hand, and society on the other hand, will make strides toward more perfect unions. This commitment to ambivalence, irresolution, and (in many cases) dogged hope as not only philosophical but also aesthetic principles is central to the legacy that this volume sees Bloomsbury bequeath to its varied successors.

In addition to working through philosophical ambivalences, Bloomsburians also searched for sentence styles and narrative forms appropriate to their epistemological ambitions. New ways of writing, new ways of seeking personal happiness and authenticity, and progressive ways of thinking about social organization did not present themselves in simple analogies, although Bloomsbury's excursions in each realm were mutually fructifying. A virtuous circle carried Bloomsbury from aesthetics to intimacy to politics and back to aesthetics. The group's curiosities bled from making art and decorating their homes into making love and friendship, informing their searches for beauty in exterior and interior living spaces. (Plate 1, *The Walled Garden at Charleston* (1916), is one of many paintings by Vanessa Bell of the garden at the farmhouse that she and Duncan Grant made their country home. They shaped the garden after designs by Roger Fry. A place for essentials during wartime—vegetables and hens—it transformed in the '20s into an aesthetic laboratory combining Mediterranean and cottage-garden elements bursting with color and texture. Plate 2 shows the dining room at Monk's House, where Virginia and Leonard Woolf lived, a few short miles from Charleston. The furniture was designed by Vanessa and Duncan and includes Virginia's initials—"VW"—in the foregrounded chair.) Bloomsbury's boundary testing in their intimate lives enriched their thinking about society and justice, including the roles of women in politics and the degree to which queer sexualities could win tolerance and respect beyond the group's charmed circles in London and Sussex. These knotty social questions supplied their literary art with new quandaries and productive tensions.

The Sociological Bloomsbury: Progress in the Public and Private Spheres

Some of these tensions concerned relations between the public and private spheres. At times, Bloomsburians and their modernist peers sharply distinguish between the two. Forster's essay "What I Believe" contrasts the "world of business relationships" with "the world of personal relationships." The former, he says, depends on the "reliability" of "contracts," whereas the latter depends on the "heart, which signs no documents."[49] Lawrence grumbles in his essay "Democracy" that politics are "just another, extra large, commercial wrangling over buying and selling—nothing else."[50] In another essay he swipes at "henny" women who lay votes and ink bottles rather than eggs.[51] Lawrence might have appreciated the antifeminist strain in Woolf's 1919 novel *Night and Day*. The suffragette character Mary Datchett's commitment to politics likely damages her personal life, for example in prompting her rejection of a marriage proposal.

But even Lawrence recognized the instability of his wonted dichotomy between public and private values. In *Women in Love*, Birkin recalls Forster's devaluation of "documents" in favor of the "heart," and echoes Lawrence's essays, when he denies the relevance of equality and individual selfhood to his and Ursula's erotic bond. Ursula, however, calls Birkin's—and by extension Lawrence's—bluff when she accuses his mystical anti-individualism of masking his fear of vulnerability and his reliance on male privilege.

In Ursula's spirit, speaking generally, Bloomsbury's fiction repeatedly invites readers to see private- and public-sphere struggles unfolding in the same direction. In *Howards End*, Henry Wilcox's coupling with the more intellectually independent Margaret after the death of his more Victorian wife, Ruth, raises questions about the evolution of marital roles, even if none of these three characters is strictly allegorical. In *Mrs Dalloway* and *To the Lighthouse*, the middle-aged heroines' marriages—as Clarissa Dalloway mulls over the unfulfilled same-sex longings of her youth, and Mrs. Ramsay's homemaking artistry evokes Lily Briscoe's painterly artistry—raise questions about how matrimony shaped women's emotional and creative horizons as the Victorian world gave way to the modern world.

In imagining commonalities between the public and private spheres, Bloomsbury anticipated late twentieth- and early twenty-first century thinking within and beyond literary studies. Sociologist Anthony Giddens's 1992 *The Transformation of Intimacy* includes a chapter entitled "Intimacy as Democracy." On Giddens's telling the "meaning of democracy" applies to marital and/or parent-child relations in four ways that it also applies to state-citizen relations. First, democracy enables people to "develop their potentialities and express their diverse qualities." Second, it protects people from the "arbitrary use" of "authority and coercive power." Third, it enables individuals to determine the "conditions of their association" and asks that they "accept the authentic and reasoned character of others' judgements." Finally, it expands people's economic opportunities.[52]

As this study unfolds, with Bloomsbury and its legatees thinking through the evolution of erotic love, friendship, and familial camaraderie, the parallels that Giddens suggests between progress in the public and private realms will serve as reference points. But how clear can such reference points be, if they purport to span two spheres of life and decades of history? Supposed north stars for progressive politics—even those limited to public-sphere questions—can prove to be wandering bodies. (Lyotard exposes how much aura has been drained from Marxist utopian dreams.) Forster awarded only "two cheers" to democracy, the arena governed by documents. He reserved "three cheers" for "Love the Beloved Republic," where the heart rules.[53] If Giddens labors to draw the two together, then surely his sweeping history will collapse under the burden of its own hubris.

But perhaps there are good-faith forms of credulity toward metanarratives of progress in personal and social life. I refer not to a Pollyannaism nor to a mythopoetry untethered from historical paradoxes, ambiguities, or reversals, but instead—among other things—to the aesthetic and philosophical value of ambivalence. Building on *Reinvention*'s treatment of Bloomsbury's ambivalences, this study traces a thread from Bloomsbury's self-divided thoughts to those of six legatees and to their philosophical kindred spirits such as Wiegman and Wilson.

Chapter 1: On Post-Enlightenment Intimacy

Before Chapters 2–7 link contemporary novels to Bloomsburian precursors, Chapter 1 discusses intimacy in history—particularly as it has progressed since the Enlightenment. On the one hand, this term refers to how lovers, friends, and families spontaneously make worlds, and on the other hand, it invokes the process of reflexivity—including the "reflexive project of self"—which Giddens sees as a hallmark of post-Enlightenment modernity.[54] Reflexive modern citizens critique artificial or unjust social mores, imagine how their collective future can improve upon their past, and compare themselves to their parents and their own younger selves in seeking happy and meaningful relationships.

My historiography shares Bloomsbury's troubled faith in progress and its valuation of self-doubt and formally daring fiction as epistemological paths toward progress. The sexological-Freudian-Bloomsburian experiments of the late nineteenth and early twentieth centuries grew from the feminism, individualism, and pursuit of happiness by which Enlightenment modernity set itself against tradition, inherited authority, and dogma. As early as the post-revolutionary years in eighteenth-century France, Britain, and America, social conservatives lamented that marriage could not withstand women's demands for equality or men's and women's demands for personal fulfillment. Their warnings could be shrill, and in many cases they were premature. But they were also prescient. Love and intimacy, as now popularly understood—as organic processes that must satisfy lovers rather than their parents, churches, or societies—have proven threatening to marriage. The end of mandatory marriage and the commencement of mass divorce; the commonality of fatherless families, especially among lower classes; and the banality of singlehood, even for women—all these developments vindicate counter-Enlightenment fears.

Or do they? As organic intimacies have undermined prejudice and hierarchy—fostering intergenerational comity, interracial eros, and female emancipation—they have argued against counter-Enlightenment gloom. If Bloomsburian modernism threatens—not marriage itself, nor social cohesion *per se*, but limited conceptions of what they mean—then it remains a welcome threat. Modernism has counter-Enlightenment qualities, including the anti-realism that Woolf helped to theorize. But Bloomsbury's feminism, queer politics, and pursuit of friendship as an end in itself—which it felt to be anti-Victorian gestures—reanimate the Enlightenment's promise of freedom. The group's patron philosopher, G. E. Moore, exalted friendship and art as life's two greatest goods. Elaborating on this intuition helped Bloosmburian civilization define its opposition to vulgar materialism, war, and sexual prejudice and repression.[55]

Chapters 2–7: Legatees' Historical Moods, Bloomsburian Sources, and Intertextual Modes

In a meta-Bloomsburian spirit, Chapters 2–7 limn the historical moods and aesthetic modes of six novels. Regarding *historical moods*, this chapter sequence aims to propel my discussion of intimacy in history from Cusk's pessimism, treated in Chapter 2, to Cunningham's ambivalent optimism, treated in Chapter 7. This journey unearths a modernist legacy (troubled hopefulness) from beneath a more frequently trumpeted mood (tough-minded alienation).

These chapters explore meta-Bloomsburian *intertextual modes* according to a different rhythmic principle. They begin and end by examining positive responses: contemporary novels that emulate their precursors' formal achievements. In different ways, Cusk's homage to Woolf (Chapter 2) and Smith's and Cunningham's homages to Forster and Woolf (Chapters 6 and 7) pay such tribute. Along the way, Chapters 3–5 explore McEwan's and Barker's ostensible disavowals of Freud that disguise their debts to him, and Rushdie's engagement with Forsterian questions but limited interest in Forster's stylistic precedents.

Chapter 2: Woolfian Pessimism

A reading of Arlington Park

Arlington Park, Cusk's pessimistic homage to Woolf, premises its satire of suburban ennui, stultification, and triviality on a *lack* of progress in intimacy. Cusk teases out of *Mrs Dalloway*, as she transposes it onto the present, a paralysis akin to that depicted in *Dubliners*. Cusk adapts Woolf's techniques when her characters explode in rage and bitterness, sometimes from no proximate cause. *Mrs Dalloway*'s "caves"[56] connect Clarissa's present emotions to her past experiences, and *Arlington Park*'s women suffer from "nameless dissatisfaction,"[57] recalling Betty Freidan's "problem that has no name." Woman by woman, they might seem more culpable for their frustrations were their complaints not so common.

But *Arlington Park*'s five main female characters combine to make a general point. In "Shakespeare's daughters," a *Guardian* article published three years after *Arlington Park*, Cusk remarks that, while "women's lives have altered in some respects" over the last generation, in others they have not, and that "oppression, being a type of relationship, can never be resolved, only reconfigured."[58] *Arlington Park* suggests that *Mrs Dalloway*'s patriarchal world has changed little in eight decades. Hence Cusk employs Woolfian motifs (mentions of oppressive "hours" throughout *Arlington Park*[59] recall *Mrs Dalloway*'s working title) and techniques, including the one-day narrative structure and the use of dinner parties as stages on which to expose the failures of contemporary community. Cusk exceeds Cunningham's dexterity as a Woolfian stylist, but his indication that the politics of sex and intimacy have *not* been paralyzed since the 1920s pays greater tribute to Woolf's attitudinal complexities than Cusk's darker vision enables her to.

Chapters 3–4: Freudian Skepticism and Hope

Readings of *Atonement* and *the Regeneration* Trilogy

Cusk's homage to Woolf illustrates a positive mode of response to a Bloomsburian precursor. Chapters 3 and 4 illustrate a negative mode, examining how McEwan and Barker *disavow* Freud yet betray debts to him. Each novelist exploits the case history's formal and epistemological potential, exemplified in *Dora*, but consigns Freud to the margins: one of McEwan's characters briefly ponders Freud while another thinks deeply about Woolf, and Barker makes Freud's contemporary psychologist W. H. R. Rivers her protagonist. Each chapter addresses the potentially terrifying Freudian question: does therapy cure, or is it circular and interminable?

As Chapter 3 discusses, *Atonement* (2001) represents the moment in McEwan's career when his Freudian tools were sharpest and when he most deftly blended his interest in psychoanalytic and historical themes. *Atonement* follows the more explicitly psychoanalytic *Enduring Love* (1997) and precedes the explicitly political *Saturday* (2005) and *Solar* (2010), which move from psychotherapy into hard sciences, treating neuropathology and climate change—as well as the fate of civilization.

In *Enduring Love*, a supporting character, Jed Parry, suffers from de Clerambault's syndrome, which causes the deluded sufferer to believe someone to be in love with him. Jed stalks his love-object, the protagonist Joe Rose, straining Joe's marriage. One of the novel's appendices, labeled "Case History," explains that, three years subsequent to the tale's conclusion, Jed remains uncured (as Freud's "Dora" was never cured) and that Joe's marriage has recovered. Even before *Atonement*, in other words, McEwan exploited Freudian motifs such as troubled romances, etiological detective stories, and inconclusive treatments.

Saturday, a Woolfian one-day novel,[60] extends McEwan's examinations of psychopathologies into neuropathology. Written in response to 9/11, it features the privileged Perowne family, menaced by Baxter, whose condition, Huntington's disease, has no more cure than do Dora's or Jed's conditions. Whereas *Mrs Dalloway*'s mention of Septimus's suicide darkens the Dalloways' party, *Saturday*'s Baxter is more imposing than a figure in a psychiatrist's anecdote. He breaks into the Perownes' home, holds Perowne's wife at knifepoint, and threatens to assault their daughter. More disturbingly, the comforts of present-day Western life may be as precarious as those of the Perowne family, if Baxter's intrusion and the exploding plane in *Saturday*'s opening scene are synecdoches for social and inter-civilizational strife.

In *Solar*, McEwan replaces terrorism with climate change as a portent that Western progress may have begun to reverse. Its protagonist, the scientist Michael Beard, lives in denial about the harm caused by his womanizing, about the lesion on his wrist (which proves cancerous), and about a "swelling sensation" in his heart (which presages a heart attack). His obtuseness about intimate matters is a loose allegory for the contemporary world's failure—as global temperatures rise—to address threats that imperil it as gravely as Beard is imperiled.

Although *Atonement* doesn't contemplate a possible end of civilization as *Saturday* and *Solar* do, it does look back to the Second World War as a catastrophe that almost destroyed Europe and did help to destroy the protagonist's family. *Atonement* focuses less on civilizational than on personal catastrophe, and on how an individual, equipped with novelistic and Freudian tools, might understand and recover from devastation. The author-protagonist, Briony, like Freud's pseudonymous "Dora," is thirteen. Each protagonist's poor self-understanding leads her to harm herself and others, and each suffers hysteria as a result—if we can assume that Briony's spending sixty-four years writing *Atonement* is symptomatic. That Briony's therapy continues for six decades gives it the look of interminability. But en route to the dispiriting thought, *Atonement* metafictionally celebrates the fruits of (Briony's) self-analysis, which are nothing less than this novel itself—McEwan's masterpiece.

As Chapter 4 discusses, although Barker's *Regeneration* trilogy (1991, 1993, 1995) honors Rivers's analytic labors, his starring role thinly disguises Freud's formal and thematic centrality to all three novels. *Dora*'s critics have noted that the patient may reveal much about herself through transference, but that the analyst also reveals much about himself (including his erotic fascination with the patient) through countertransference.[61] But Freud fails to notice—though his astute readers *do* notice—what therapy reveals about him. Because "Dora" breaks off analysis before completion, both she and Freud remain in a state of suspended insight. Barker exploits all these features of the case history in depicting Rivers's interactions with multiple patients and his struggle with the admonition "Physician, heal thyself."

But Freud's intertextual value to Barker is not exhausted by these formal features of the case history. Across Freud's career, his belief in the efficacy of therapy waned, and he was drawn to fatalistic concepts like the "death instinct"—as is Barker's war-haunted and anthropologically informed trilogy.

Even while examining the death instinct and compulsive violence, however, Barker envisions how things can *get better*. Rivers and his patients, the historical Siegfried Sassoon and the fictional Billy Prior, are all gay or bisexual—and closeted to others and perhaps themselves. All once supported Britain's involvement in the First World War and later come to oppose it—though they participate in the war effort after their changes of heart. In a composite manner, they evoke British society as it develops an anti-war conscience and overcomes homophobia and sexual repression. Therapy is essential to their shared growth. Thus, Barker extends the salvific metanarrative ambitions of psychoanalysis beyond the patient's life, into the analyst's and into subsequent decades of history—as though individual psychotherapy might begin to heal society.

Chapter 5: Forsterian Skepticism

A Reading of *The Satanic Verses*

Whereas Chapters 3 and 4 examine McEwan's and Barker's Freudian-themed skepticism, Chapter 5 plumbs Salman Rushdie's Forsterian-themed skepticism. *The Satanic Verses* tests the capacities of transcontinental love, secularism, and Western freedom to dissolve misogyny and racism—in other words, the power of progress to overcome theocracy and colonialism. But whereas Freud's successors *disavow* his importance to them, *Verses* adopts an indifferent, or *neutral*, attitude toward a major precursor text: *A Passage to India*.

Rushdie has commented on the stylistic gulf between his and Forster's prose.[62] But he effuses respect for Forster's grasp of intimacy in history, explaining that "occasionally, a work of literature offers its readers a clearer, deeper understanding of the opaque events being reported in the press." *Passage* "taught us that the great public quarrels of history can make it impossible for individuals to construct a private peace," that Fielding and Aziz cannot be friends "while imperialism's great injustice stands between" them.[63] As a tale of intimacies between Britons and Indians, *Verses* asks Forsterian questions about how the lingering injustices of post-imperial society affect the "private peace" sought by interracial friends and lovers.

Passage has a structural motif of posing questions, proffering answers, and then withdrawing those answers in favor of further questions, giving a provisional cast even to the novel's concluding words ("not yet ... not there") in response to Fielding's question "Why can't we be friends now?" As if Forster had handed Rushdie a baton, *Verses* asks *What about now and here*? in 1980s' multicultural London. Now that the official barriers of British colonialism have come down, Saladin's and Gibreel's romances compel readers to wonder, what psychic legacies of colonialism—including white Britain's exotic fascination for Indian migrants—remain obstacles to successful intimacies? The novel returns sadder answers than one might expect from so vocal a champion of freedom and hybridity as Rushdie.

But *Passage* parallels *Verses* in more than thematic ways: it anticipates Rushdie's post-realist narrative pyrotechnics. As Bart Moore-Gilbert explains, much literature produced "as a consequence of the long history of Britain's rule in India"[64] shares a discursive field. *Passage* helps to shape this field: its epistemological multiplicity anticipates avant-garde novels about Anglo-India, including *Verses*. *Passage* puts multiple styles of knowing into conversation and conflict, including Fielding's rationalism and Godbole's mysticism. Their unresolved dispute foreshadows *Verses*' more radical post-realism.

Chapters 6–7: Forsterian and Woolfian Optimism

Readings of On Beauty and The Hours

Around the turn of the twenty-first century, Smith and Cunningham despaired less at the obstacles to traditionally taboo forms of intimacy than Rushdie did in the 1980s. In thematic terms, *On Beauty* and *The Hours* ask, with some sanguinity, *Are the kinds of love that were risky in Forster's and Woolf's time—cross-class, interracial, and/or same-sex—more likely to flourish today? Does this historical trajectory suggest that future lovers and friends will be even freer—and thus happier?* In aesthetic terms, these two relatively optimistic novels—unlike *Verses*—embrace their formal Bloomsburian precedents. Smith sees Forster as a pivotal figure in post-Austenian realism. She credits him with avant-garde techniques and disillusioned attitudes that his critics overlook—in other words, she sees in texts like *Howards End* paths out of the cul-de-sacs of realism. But at the same time, she affirms Forster's and Bloomsbury's humanistic ethos, which she connects both to moral realism and to literary realism—because these values offer the best hope for intimacies in a fluid twenty-first-century world.

Smith paves the way for our journey through six post-Bloomsburian novels to conclude with Cunningham's homage to Woolf. *The Hours* thinks more hopefully about same-sex intimacy and historical progress than *Mrs Dalloway*, and much more hopefully than Cusk's *Arlington Park*. But it does so in a tough-minded way. Cunningham braids together three tales of sadness in intimacy that leave readers to infer when the sadness arises *because of* or *in spite of* the intimacy. The connections among Virginia Woolf (as she writes *Mrs Dalloway*, while living unhappily in a London suburb in 1923), the fictional Laura Brown (as she reads *Mrs Dalloway*, while living unhappily in a Los Angeles suburb in 1949), and Clarissa Vaughan, who lives openly (but not entirely happily) as a lesbian in 1990s New York, imbue a sober treatment of love's disappointments with hints of metanarrative optimism. Both by interweaving these three stories (in a nod toward non-linear narration, though each storyline is linear) and by having them take place on a single day (á la *Ulysses* and *Mrs Dalloway*), Cunningham honors modernist poetics.

Chapter 8: Polyamory—and Bloomsbury's Implications for Intimacy and Art in the Future

With their discussions of six meta-Bloomsburian novels, Chapters 2–7 interlace modernist and contemporary experiments in light of a century of intimacy in history. Chapter 8 carries this volume's discussion into the future of intimacy by focusing on polyamory. I contend that this movement, with its richly elaborated concepts and ethical precepts, retrospectively clarifies Bloomsbury's life-experiments. It does so in two ways: first by helping us to understand Bloomsburians' innovations as lovers and friends—as precursors of poly culture—and second by helping us to see the limitations of both their lifestyles and their thought. The group was ahead of its time, but only to a point. Understanding—with polyamory's help—what Bloomsbury was unable to articulate about itself does not devalue the group's daring or originality. Instead, delineating differences between the past and present underscores the continually evolving—i.e., historical—nature of intimacy.

The polyamorous critiques of several sexual and social norms—heteronormativity, mononormativity, and amatonormativity, all of which will be discussed below—reveal how revolutionary the Enlightenment's love revolution has been and continues to be. As Chapters 1 and 8 will both elaborate, the eighteenth century's assertion of lovers' prerogatives over the dictates of their parents, churches, and communities has morphed, over the last several hundred years, in ways that Mary Wollstonecraft could not have predicted—from the life-experiments of Bloomsbury in the early twentieth century to the ethical ideals of polyamorists in the early twenty-first century. Bloomsbury has precursors and successors in the history of intimacy who have been every bit as transformative as they, if not more so.

Chapter 8 revisits Bloomsbury's place in this volume's sweeping account of how post-Enlightenment intimacy has *progressed*. Progress is a titular term in this study, and while being wary of historical mythopoetry, the coming chapters return, with Bloomsbury's help, to questions of what progress looks like in the private sphere, i.e. to why we might claim that *things are getting better* in relationships among friends, family members, and lovers as societies democratize over time.

Just as Bloomsbury was prodded—by thinking about intimacy in new ways—also to develop new literary forms, likewise future poly authors might be prodded by their life-experiments to think of new ways to tell stories and write poems about intimacy. Such aesthetic innovations cannot, of course, be predicted by any formula. But as my concluding chapter muses, future poly writers might look back on Bloomsbury as a forerunner—an archive of past lifestyles and artistic styles that point hopefully toward *their* future yet to be written.

Notes

1. Gillis 229–304, Roderick Phillips 185–223.
2. "What I Believe" 65.
3. *Women in Love* 147: 32–3.
4. "What I Believe" 66.
5. See Matz, *The Modern Novel*, discussing John Barth's evaluation of the state of fiction in the 1960s and '80s (127–8).
6. "Modern Fiction" 150.
7. Aspects of the Novel 41.
8. Trilling, "On the Teaching of Modern Literature" 3.
9. *The Promise of Happiness* 72.
10. Högberg 12–13.
11. The US Bureau of Labor Statistics still records discrepancies, for the year 2015, between time spent by men and women on household chores. See https://www.bls.gov/tus/charts/household.htm. Accessed June 10, 2021.
12. Case and Deaton.

13 *Howards End* 58.
14 *Dubliners* 92.
15 *Women in Love* 352: 5.
16 Illouz (89–95) discusses the danger of this methodology and the virtues of "immanent critiques."
17 *Cruel Optimism* 2–3.
18 Berlant, *Cruel Optimism*, "'68 or Something." In 1998, Berlant edited a special issue of *Critical Inquiry* entitled *Intimacy* and published in book form in 2000. Many contributors examine both the public and private dimensions of intimacy, and many take a jaded view of the phenomenon, examining its structuring fantasies, its complicity in social inequality, and/or its failure to provide people the lives they hope for.
19 Edelman 4.
20 Shelden 57.
21 Ibid. 3, 5, 5.
22 Ibid. 16.
23 See Muñoz 12.
24 Drawing from a current movement in environmental sociology, Jesse Matz advocates "time ecology," a form of consciousness attuned to the fullness of the past, present, and future—unlike the time-schemes of urban capitalism (*Modernist Time Ecology* 1–7).
25 Muñoz 12. Other queer theorists also make investments in critical futurity, including Castiglia and Reed.
26 Ibid. 185, 91.
27 Ibid. 188.
28 Ibid. back cover.
29 Wiegman and Wilson 18.
30 Wiegman and Wilson engage with a large and diverse body of queer scholarship dating back to Foucault's foundational 1978 *History of Sexuality*, much of which shares their spirit of resistance to conformism within the field. In 1994 Edelman exhorted scholars to resist the institutionalization of queer theory (4), in 2003 David Halperin lamented that this was happening (4), and in 2005 David Eng and others expanded Halperin's critique of "queer liberalism." Wiegman and Wilson also discuss the foundational impacts of Eve Sedgwick's 1990 *Epistemology of the Closet*, with its counterhegemonic readings of canonical literature, and Judith Butler's 1990 *Gender Trouble*, with its innovative concept of gender performativity, drawn from Foucaultian and speech act theories. Wiegman and Wilson's archive of queer theorists expands from there, including critiques of nationalism and "cisnormativity" (7, 9).
31 "The Challenge of Our Time" 54.
32 "What I Believe" 65.
33 Ibid. 66.
34 Williams 148–69.
35 See especially Froula's Introduction 1–32.
36 The discussion of Reed draws from throughout the Introduction to *Bloomsbury Rooms* (1–17).
37 See "Bloomsbury and Sexuality," especially 17–20.
38 Fussell 23–4.

39 Moffat discusses Forster's fluctuating attitude toward "civilization," from that of an ironic dissident to that of an engaged partisan (90, 102, 131, 136, 243, 245).
40 See their Introduction 1–12.
41 For a discussion of Lawrence's insight into the limits of Bloomsbury's wisdom, see Keynes.
42 James, David and Urmila Seshagiri, "Metamodernism: Narratives of Continuity and Revolution." *PMLA* 129.1 (2014). 87–100.
43 See Friedman, Mao, and Walkowtiz's 2008 PLMA article "The New Modernist Studies," and their Introduction to their 2006 book *Bad Modernisms*.
44 James and Seshagiri 89.
45 Latham and Rogers 9.
46 See Begam and Valdez Moses's Introduction to *Modernism, Postcolonialism, and Globalism* (9, 15) for a useful discussion of allied intertextual modes. They speak of "affiliation," "indifference," and "antagonism" in linking the temporally expanding "modernist" epoch (which extends as far as the Second World War, encompassing late modernism) to a subsequent epoch that is both dependent upon modernism and distinct enough from modernism to *respond* to it.
47 Freud, "The Sexual Enlightenment of Children" 132.
48 See Paul Robinson.
49 Forster, "What I Believe" 66.
50 Lawrence, *Reflections* 67: 39–40.
51 Lawrence, *Sex, Literature, and Censorship* 49–50.
52 Giddens 184–5.
53 Forster, "What I Believe" 67.
54 Giddens 28–32, 39, 180, 189.
55 See Froula and Goldman.
56 *The Diary of Virginia Woolf, Vol. 2* 263.
57 *Arlington Park* 181, 189.
58 Cusk, Rachel. "Shakespeare's Daughters." *The Guardian*. December 11, 2009. https://www.theguardian.com/books/2009/dec/12/rachel-cusk-women-writing-review. Accessed October 18, 2020.
59 22, 79. Also see 76 ("time going on and on") and 188 ("had they ever been expected for dinner at a time other than eight o'clock?"), etc.
60 Critics have discussed how each novel has a "political" setting (given *Saturday*'s plane crash and Richard Dalloway's political connections) and narrates one day culminating in a social gathering including family, intruded upon by threats. Anne Marie Adams explains that *Saturday* "reimagines" *Mrs Dalloway* to "recalibrate the focus of 'modern fiction' for contemporary times" (548). Richard Brown describes both Septimus and Baxter as "pathological outsiders who pose a threat to the [main character's] upper-class domestic security" (86).
61 See Racker 105–26 for a discussion of countertransference. *Dora* critics who discuss this phenomenon and Freud's antipathies for his patient include Moi.
62 *Joseph Anton* 56.
63 Rushdie, "May 2000: J. M. Coetzee" 297.
64 Moore-Gilbert 1.

1

Do Things Get Better?—Bloomsbury, Private Lives, and Dreams of Progress

In 1979, Lyotard identified "incredulity toward metanarrative" as crucial to the "postmodern" sensibility.¹ Since then, even as scholars have questioned the value of "postmodernism" as a cultural-historical marker,² they have largely retained Lyotard's association of intellectual rigor with a refusal of historical Pollyannaism. In a secular milieu (a label that applies more to the literary intelligentsia than to all contemporary culture), the limited appeal of historical *telos*—with its trace of magical thinking—is not surprising. Even during promising times, the proclamation that President Obama had woven into an Oval Office carpet—"The arc of the moral universe is long, but it bends toward justice"—can ring hollow to incredulous ears.³ The "pure critiques" of recent high theory, such as Berlant's, recall not only radical modernism's incredulous attitude toward Victorian meliorism, whether in its secular versions (e.g., *Middlemarch*) or its sacred ones (e.g., *In Memoriam*). These critiques also recall radical modernism's quest to transvalue common sense and defy a stultifying status quo.⁴ Caught between a desire to imagine a very different future and a sense that historical optimism of any kind is naïve, many theorists since Lyotard have revisited the paradoxes and ambivalences that animated modernist thought.

A careful examination of High Modernism, especially in the wake of the First World War, reveals that skepticism about progress—with its accompanying feelings of unease, paralysis, and frustration—is far from a late twentieth- or early twenty-first-century invention. Henry James despaired that the Great War exposed the naivety of the "whole long age" during which nineteenth-century thinkers believed the world was "gradually bettering."⁵ The Second World War led John Maynard Keynes to call civilization a "thin and precarious crust" maintained by "guilefully preserved" rules and conventions.⁶ Modernism's prestige derives in part from the rigor of its cultural critique (which often shades into despair), even amid placid pre-war conditions like those endured by Joyce's lonely Dubliners.

However, the radically critical, anti-teleological, and pessimistic strains in modernist literature and contemporary theory tell only part of a multifaceted story about how intimacy and progress have been viewed since the modernist era—a story in which Bloomsbury plays key roles. Bloomsburians retained, amid their incredulity, the capacity to think optimistically about the future (for women writers, for women's rights, for same-sex love, for civilizational health, for personal self-transformation) and even to craft rather *grand récits* in doing so.

The forms of their provisional optimism are central to their legacies. Critics have included such avant-garde techniques as free indirect style and non-linear narration among modernism's strategies for rethinking selfhood and time, and admired how Bloomsburians employ such techniques to rethink intimacy.[7] But scholars have devoted less attention to the relationship between the history of intimacy and metanarrative forms of thought, from *In Memoriam*'s invocation of "one far-off divine event/To which the whole creation moves"[8] to narrative or poetic juxtapositions of a benighted and repressed past with a liberated, wiser, and more loving future. The coming chapters address this oversight, tracing connections among novelists' ideas about the direction of history, their narrative handling of time, and their depictions of love and friendship.

Stories of Progress (Public and Private): Condorcet, Hegel, Marx, Carpenter, Freud

When Bloomsburians and their legatees imagine things *getting better* for same-sex or interracial lovers, they might not articulate a systematic view of historical change, as Marquis de Condorcet did from a non-revolutionary perspective and Marx did from a revolutionary one. Nevertheless, Enlightenment theories of social change inform their ideas about what historical optimism looks like and how social critique—*A Passage to India*'s exposé of imperial oppression, *Howards End*'s and *Mrs Dalloway*'s examinations of wives' marital dissatisfactions—can serve long-term struggles to liberate both the public and private spheres. Closer in spirit to Condorcet than to Marx, Forster and Woolf argued for the value of tolerance, supported non-violent change, and (with reservations) channeled eighteenth-century *philosophes*' faith in historical meliorism,[9] as they critiqued residual Victorian attitudes toward femininity, sexual freedom, and aesthetic form.

Condorcet's optimistic metanarrative appears in the posthumously published *Sketch for a Historical Picture of the Progress of the Human Mind* (1795), which denounces slavery and advocates equality for women and all races. Condorcet believed that injustice does not spring inevitably from human nature but is a symptom of ignorance, prejudice, and unexamined traditions. What Giddens, at the end of the twentieth century, would term "reflexivity"[10]—the capacity to control nature, to correct compulsive behaviors, to reform social practices—Condorcet touted as a fundamental human virtue.

Whereas Condorcet's eyes were set on the future (he composed his *Sketch* in prison, where he died after a flight from revolutionary authorities), Hegel's divinized account of historical progress legitimated his present. According to Hegel, man—or Absolute Spirit, a pure self-consciousness—grows freer throughout history, when he realizes himself *as* free spirit. From this self-recognition, improved forms of government emerge: the material plane reflects the achievements of the intellectual plane.[11]

Marx and Engels de-divinize Hegel in *The German Ideology* (1845–6).[12] Unlike Hegelian theories that descend from heaven to earth, their dialectical-materialist approach ascends "from earth to heaven ... [O]n the basis of their real life-process we demonstrate the development of the ideological reflexes and echoes of this life-process." They see ideologies as "phantoms" in the brain, determined by past societies' structures of labor. Though the compositions of ruling and producing classes shift, "the ideas of the ruling class are in every epoch the ruling ideas, i.e., the class which is the ruling *material* force of society, is at the same time its ruling *intellectual* force."

Such a metanarrative makes human freedom seem doubtful. What kinds of intimacy can a woman develop with members of her own class or not even imagine having with members of other classes? Are all her intimacies—though they feel like organic unfoldings of her personality—merely "reflex" responses to, or "phantoms" of, her society's structures of ownership? Do divisions *within* her class bar her—as daughter, wife, and mother—from other forms of productive labor and from certain kinds of intimacy? Is sex itself a class? Marxian vocabularies, adapted to the private sphere, have generated such questions, from Engels's *The Origin of the Family, Private Property, and the State* (1884) to Shulamith Firestone's *The Dialectic of Sex: The Case for Feminist Revolution* (1970).

Condorcet has not been alone since the Enlightenment in envisioning non-revolutionary transformations in the public and private spheres. The radical Victorian Edward Carpenter—an inspiration for Forster—moderated Marx's and Engels's revolutionary fervor in a Ruskinian socialism imbued with rural nostalgia. He identified interests shared by women, working people, and sexual "Intermediates" (his term for gays and lesbians); and he saw intimate life as a creative sphere, not merely an epiphenomenon of economic processes.

While Carpenter's feminism and economic radicalism impressed Forster and other modernists, he influenced them most profoundly as a pioneer of gay consciousness. In many pamphlets and essays written between 1870 and 1925, building on writings by German sexologists, Carpenter argued that Intermediates have existed throughout history and have unique contributions to offer to civilization. So inspiring was his pride that Millthorpe Cottage—the rural residence that he constructed and called his "Thoreau ideal"—became a pilgrimage site for gay men. Carpenter and his working-class lover, George Merrill, embodied Walt Whitman's ideal of male "comradeship" as a vital force bridging social divisions in a democratic culture. Siegfried Sassoon wrote to Carpenter as a "leader" and a "prophet" before visiting him in 1911—an event that *Regeneration* imagines the young Sassoon discussing with his therapist Rivers.[13] A year later, Forster traveled to Millthorpe "as one approaches a savior."[14] Carpenter and Merrill provided the basis for the cross-class romance at the heart of *Maurice*, Forster's only openly gay novel.

Male "comradeship" was not the only context in which Carpenter pondered the intersections of sexuality and class. In analyses that blend sexual psychology with a critique of England's economic structure, his 1896 essay collection *Love's Coming of Age* decries the roles of "lady," "drudge," and "prostitute" available to Victorian middle-class, working-class, and underclass women.[15] *Howards End*'s Margaret Schlegel recalls Carpenter when she wonders, "Are the sexes really races, each with its own code of morality?"[16] But Carpenter's categories are more varied than Margaret's: he suggests that socioeconomic strata have segregated women into three "races," just as his own and Merrill's different backgrounds might have divided them, in the absence of erotic affection.

Despite his sensitivity to social fissures, Carpenter's belief in the value of Intermediacy undergirded his critique of Victorian gender roles and inspired his melioristic attitude toward history. As suggested by his volume's title, *Love's Coming of Age*, he foresaw a not-distant future in which men and women would mature out of the stunted Victorian stage in which they were mired. He uses words like "evolution," "drift," and "tendency" to anticipate, for example, the increasing frequency of a benevolent form of monogamy, spiritually more than physically motivated and free of coercion by Church and State.[17] Carpenter saw his partnership with Merrill—lifelong though not monogamous, and rooted in a community of fellow manual laborers—as a model toward which many love-relations strove, hampered though they might be by bourgeois gender codes.

Carpenter, however, was determined *not* to denigrate the group-marriage paradigm or other alternative forms of intimacy. He argues that "practices of former races and times" express "needs and desires" still present in "human nature." As life evolves "from confusion to distinction," a "rational" society will permit radically different practices, from monkish asceticism to Bacchanalian festivals, from "a woman's temporary alliance with a man for the sake of obtaining a much-needed child" to the ethically preferable "permanent spiritual mating" of two people.[18]

Carpenter had faith in men's and women's power to transcend gendered personality types. Their tenacious repressiveness is evident in Henry Wilcox's insensitivity, as well as in Margaret's reversion to an angelic domestic role at the conclusion of *Howards End*. But people's freedom to renegotiate these roles is evident in Kiki Belsey's decision, near the end of *On Beauty*, to separate from her insensitive husband, Howard. The many qualities that Kiki shares with Margaret testify not only to Forster's influence on Smith, but also to Carpenter's indirect influence on her, by way of Forster.

As I discuss elsewhere, Carpenter affected both the form and content of many of Forster's writings, from his novels' plot constructions, to his psychosexual character types, to the "double turns" of his novels and essays, which distinguish his ambivalent sensibility from Carpenter's more historically optimistic one.[19] A range of Forster's characters give flesh and blood to Carpenter's categories, including "Intermediates" (*Howards End*'s Tibby, *Maurice*'s titular hero, and others), the "lady" (*Howards End*'s Ruth Wilcox, and to a lesser degree Margaret, after she marries Henry), and the "drudge" (*Howards End*'s Jacky).

Carpenter was more suggestive than many thinkers, Freud included, about the impact of society and history on psychosexuality. Nonetheless, modernists and their legatees have found no richer resource for narratives of the heart, including teleological ones, than the Austrian psychoanalyst. Like Carpenter and the sexologists, Freud renounced Victorian prudery and accepted human sexual variety as a fact of life. He sought to understand it scientifically, not to condemn its atypical expressions on religious grounds (although psychoanalysis has a history of pathologizing nonconforming sexualities on dubious medical grounds).

Freud brought a new vocabulary and epistemology to bear on the study of intimate relations. In his case studies and essays, patient-therapist intimacies can be elaborate dramas, fraught with love, resentment, and exciting plot twists. Additionally, they function as textual doubles, illuminating struggles that brought the analysand to Freud's office: her feelings toward her parents, her lover, or herself. Freud's concepts—repression, neurosis, repetition compulsion, death instinct, transference—function like miniature personalities housed within individuals. Freud's epistemology appealed to many thinkers, with its scientific and humanistic warrants and its combination of hermeneutic and narrative elegance. The analysand and the analytic process move inward (hermeneutically) to move forward (narratively) toward cure, decoding utterances and dreams, tics and pregnant pauses. All of this appeals to the Freudian-minded novelist who wants every detail to signify.

The forward-driving Freudian quest for at-one-ment sometimes strained for both narrative closure and metanarrative scope. At its most basic, the metanarrative included

* neurosis and repression,
* analysis with the help of transference,
* *and cure,*

and had the power of universality: it applied to every suffering person (and everyone suffers), as, in a previous epistemic era, all Christian wayfarers could endure temptation, stray from god, and then achieve metaphysical cure in reunifying with god. The Freudian tale also had more fine-grained iterations, such as the eight-point template of neurosis and cure discussed in Chapter 3. This template had an ambitious reach both vertically, into the recesses of a patient's infancy, and horizontally, aiming to codify universal processes of suffering and possible maturation.

These Freudian templates, with their ambition to understand and improve the entire person through a lifetime, compete with Marxian metanarratives for intellectual daring and hubris. One explains how *things might—or will—get better for society*, and the other can seem to explain, according to a different determinism, how *things will get better for the individual*. Marx's fable of economic history, with the proletariat contending against the bourgeoisie on the way to a classless society, finds its match in Freud's fable of the psyche, with the unconscious being made conscious. But Freud's programs for self-improvement have numerous progeny of less epistemological ambition. Twelve-point, nine-point, and five-point programs abound for addiction recovery, weight loss, getting rich, etc. Many of them employ no Freudian vocabulary but nonetheless recall Freud's decades-long struggle to impose narrative order on the sprawl of a mind's career, to control what might be uncontrollable.

Whether social or personal history is in question, people in our largely post-Freudian and post-Marxist environment tell stories with various attitudes toward freedom and perfectibility. Some thinkers are confident that things will improve, for either deterministic or probabilistic reasons. Some sense that history is directionless—as it applies to society or to themselves personally—with progress and reversals occurring unpredictably. (Rushdie's magical realism, as discussed in Chapter 5, evokes such wonders and terrors.) Sometimes, people sense fatalistically that things have devolved since the good old days, or that the repressed is bound to return, whether in the form of violent pornography and violence against women (according to Giddens's account of male sexuality[20]) or in the form of war (in Barker's anthropologically inflected treatment of the human compulsion to violence). Texts are often hybrids; attitudes toward history mix and mingle; sometimes they coalesce from attitudes or feelings into theories; sometimes theories dissolve, less in the face of conclusive counterevidence than in the face of a countervailing mood.

The six novelists discussed in the coming chapters express *a range of attitudes toward Bloomsbury* just as they express *a range of attitudes toward progress*. It can be tempting to seek affinities between their attitudes in these two areas. For example, the stringent, tough-minded *avant gardists* McEwan and Rushdie treat both Bloomsbury and the idea of progress in iconoclastic ways, seeing the former as somewhat passé and the latter as potentially naïve. Moreover, the tender-minded homagists Smith and Cunningham treat both their precursors and the idea of progress more credulously, unembarrassed by their admiration for Forster and Woolf, their desire to see Black women and lesbians love more freely, or their pleasure in the gains such citizens have already won. But any attempt to reduce Bloomsbury's varied and complex legatees to a formula would be foolhardy. Cusk, for example, could be seen as tender-minded for her unembarrassed adulation of Woolf (not only in *Arlington Park*) but tough-minded to the point of bleakness in her vision of contemporary love. Hence this study leaves open the question of how and whether these legatees' visions of a social future relate to their visions of their literary past.

Bloomsbury's Melioristic Musings

In both formal and informal writings, Bloomsburians test drove a variety of ideas about how intimacy will evolve. In an April 1906 letter, Lytton Strachey wrote to Keynes about public attitudes toward homosexuality. "Our time will come about a hundred years hence," Strachey mused, "when preparations will have been made, and compromises come to, so that at the publication of our letters, everyone will be, finally, converted."[21]

Forster's feelings about the future rose and fell with changing circumstances. *Howards End*'s Schlegel sisters discuss whether men will ever understand women. Helen thinks they never will, but Margaret says that in "two thousand years" they will,[22] which doesn't leave readers breathless with anticipation. *Passage* shortens this timeframe—somewhat. Fielding wants friendship "now," but Aziz says that it will only be possible in "fifty or five hundred" years, once Indians drive their colonizers into the sea.[23] Forster's 1926 essay "Notes on the English Character" shortens the timeframe radically, foreseeing a "change of heart" in the next twenty years, into something more "lovable," as the middle class loses its dominance over English education and national character formation.[24] Sadly, though, twelve years later, this Carpenterian hope gave way. In the wake of German expansionism, Forster's 1938 essay "What I Believe" doubts the likelihood of public- or private-sphere progress. "No millennium seems likely to descend … no form of Christianity and no alternative to Christianity will bring peace to the world or integrity to the individual," Forster writes. He adds, quoting his own earlier essay, "No 'change of heart' will occur."[25]

Woolf was not averse to playing with dates. Her quip about human character changing "on or about December 1910"—Roger Fry mounted a Post-Impressionist exhibition at London's Grafton Gallery in November 1910—conveys her sense that human relations are transforming and that novelists need new methods for depicting character.[26] Her fondness for thinking in terms of historical epochs, concerning both art and sexuality, is evident in the structures of *Between the Acts* and *Orlando*. But unlike Forster, she didn't offer twenty, fifty, or five-hundred-year timeframes for her desired social transformations. Instead she mused on unspecified moments when Chloe's "liking" for Olivia would be a fit topic for literature and when women writers could transcend Elizabethan constraints on Shakespeare's hypothetical sister, dispense with Charlotte Brontë's "indignation," and dissolve the Victorian domestic angel.[27]

By fashioning open endings and by withholding timeframes, Bloomsburians demurred from espousing hopefulness or pessimism. *Women in Love* ends on a stalemate similar to *Passage*'s, when Fielding wants "now" what Aziz puts off for fifty or five hundred years. In a voice not unlike Fielding's, Birkin laments "I wanted eternal union with a man too: another kind of love," and in a voice not unlike Aziz's, Ursula retorts "You can't have it because it's false, impossible."[28] Each novel shares its protagonist's desire for sexual freedom, while not discounting the beloved's point of view. Each novelist would hasten the day when the sentence "Cyril liked Dr Aziz" or "Rupert liked Gerald" is as natural as "Chloe liked Olivia." Nonetheless, each leaves readers unsure what future to expect for nonconforming lovers.

Even before Strachey, Forster, or Woolf offered timeframes of decades or centuries, or before *Women in Love* left Birkin and Ursula's dispute hanging, Bloomsburians weighed the risks and benefits of challenging taboos against same-sex love. The Apostles, a secret Cambridge undergraduate discussion society, dated to 1820. Over the decades, its members included Tennyson, Alfred North Whitehead, and Rupert Brooke, and by the turn of the twentieth century, it supplied Bloomsbury's nucleus.[29] In Saturday-night discussions, the young men in this group—poised to become adults in a homophobic (or uncomprehending) Victorian society—explored their sexuality. Those who might have been, or who decided that they were, what we now call "gay" expressed or hid this orientation. The reticence—and perhaps the internalized homophobia—of some such Victorian men led Bloomsburians later to joke about their "higher sodomy": intense mutual affection that was too pure for sexual contact.[30] Under G. E. Moore's leadership, the Apostles retained some delicacy in their sexual self-expression. But when Strachey inherited Moore's leadership in February 1902, politeness and indirection gave way to ribald homoerotic banter. Apostles became irreverent and insolent toward Mrs Grundy.

Almost like the Apostles at their most explicit, Forster treats same-sex affection directly in *Maurice*, a novel that combines qualities of a Bildungsroman and fairytale, in which two men disappear into the woods to live together. But the price for this relative openness about male-male attachment is threefold. First, Forster suppressed

Maurice's publication. Written in 1913, the novel did not appear until 1971, the year after its author's death. Second, the fairytale ending indicates that, by 1913, Forster could only envision men living together happily ever after in a Neverland. Third, as poignant as this love story is—and even though it was circulated only among Forster's friends during his lifetime—it stops short of naming anything as vulnerable to charges of "gross indecency" as sodomy. Its titular character initially rebuffs the advances of his fellow Cambridge student, Durham, before finally acknowledging his homosexuality to himself (a "storm" that "had been working up … for six years"). The young men tell one another "I love you," then kiss, "scarcely wishing it." They ditch school to spend a day together "perfectly," bike riding and swimming. But a dean notices them leaving campus and, resenting Maurice's insolence, suspends him from school pending a letter of apology. The narrator explains that the dean "always suspected such friendships," leaving readers to deduce whether he infers sexual misconduct. The narrator suggests that the young men's two-year romance never progresses beyond kissing into sexual intercourse, thus avoiding the extremes of the "saint or sensualist."[31] Instead, *Maurice* almost shows its hero doing what *Passage* dares not have Fielding and Aziz do. In their silences, hesitations, and deferrals, these texts express the longing for a sexually tolerant future that Bloomsbury also invoked in twenty, fifty, one-hundred, five-hundred, and two-thousand-year horizons.

Optimism and Pessimism since Bloomsbury's Time

Bloomsburians' ideas about sexual selfhood, personal happiness, and social justice emerge from a dense prehistory and have yielded rich legacies. They contemplated intimacy in history in complex moods, from Freud's increasing skepticism about the possibility of psychoanalytic cure, to Forster's doubts about the viability of his liberal-humanist dreams, to Woolf's bitterness against the patriarchy, struggles with despair and mental health, and hope for future women artists. Forster and Woolf represent strains of modernism alternative to Eliot's and Lawrence's apocalypticism and sweeping denunciations of modernity. Though each was a sexual dissident, though one killed herself, and though *Three Guineas* is hardly sanguine about the state of civilization, these Bloomsburians offer tonic correctives to the sometimes dubious profundities of their more pessimistic modernist peers.

Woolf's and Forster's ambivalent attitudes toward history, including intimacy in history, enable us to ask of Eliot's and Lawrence's more radical cultural despair, "What does it mean to us now? How valuable is it, among modernism's legacies?" Just as Lawrentian despair is echoed in some theory, so too is Bloomsburian hope. Numerous popular and academic writers on post-Enlightenment social history, including Steven Pinker, recuperate Condorcet's optimism about public-sphere progress. Likewise, numerous writers on post-Enlightenment intimacy recuperate Carpenter's optimism about the private sphere. Though not direct legatees of *Howards End* or *A Room of One's Own*, this latter group of writers helps to explain what Forsterian "friendship" and Woolfian "liking"—such as Chloe's for Olivia—have come to mean.

From the 1968 Paris riots, through the 2008 global economic meltdown, and into recent ethnonationalist paroxysms, the Enlightenment, liberal democracy, and the idea of progress have all had critics. But their champions multiplied after the passage of Brexit and the elections of Trump and Boris Johnson. To sample a recent array of apologies, a 2018 *Foreign Affairs* issue asked, "Which world are we living in?"[32] and offered six *grand-récit* options: a world driven by great-power rivalries, by the resilience of the liberal order, by the persistent oppressions of capitalism, by tribal identities, by technology, or by climate change. The authors who argue on behalf of a "liberal world" say that, whereas realists see history as cyclical, liberals are "heirs to the Enlightenment project of technological innovation, which opens new possibilities both for human progress and for disaster."[33] Liberalism's enshrinement of tolerance, individual dignity, and freedom makes its appeal universal, with champions from Gandhi to Mandela to Gorbachev. Although its history has been marred by imperialism, slavery, and racism, "liberalism has always been at the forefront of efforts—both peaceful and militant—to reform and end these practices."[34]

Beyond the confines of foreign policy disputes, and as a counterweight to the despair undergirding ethnonationalist movements, champions of liberal-Enlightenment heritage have poured forth encomia to modernity. In 2018, multiple books argued that the current state of the world is far healthier than is commonly known, including Gregg Easterbrook's *It's Better Than It Looks: Reasons for Optimism in an Age of Fear* and Hans Rosling's *Factfulness: Ten Reasons We're Wrong about the World—and Why Things Are Better Than You Think*. Perhaps the most widely discussed of these 2018 volumes, Pinker's *Enlightenment Now: The Case for Reason, Science, Humanism, and Progress* argues that the last three centuries have witnessed huge worldwide gains in human flourishing, thanks to the first three Enlightenment values listed in his subtitle. Scientific medicine and agriculture, brainchildren of Western Europe's turn away from superstition, vastly reduced deaths from disease and starvation, sending life expectancy on an upward trajectory that continues to this day. Humanistic values have inspired democracy, human rights, and international norms of cooperation such as Kant advocated. This moral progress has driven down death rates in several large ways. Great powers continually fought between 1500 and 1800, but even accounting for the two world wars, have done so much less frequently in the last two hundred years. Homicides—historically more lethal than war—have claimed fewer victims in established European nations since the fifteenth century, in New England since the seventeenth century, and in the southwestern United States since the nineteenth century. Because of both legislation and behavioral changes, since the early twentieth century the United States has seen a decrease in death rates by less melodramatic causes, such as motor vehicle accidents, fires, drowning, lightning strikes, and occupational hazards. Laws have grown more enlightened regarding child labor and education (most notably for girls); European literacy rates have climbed since 1550, global literacy has skyrocketed since the early nineteenth century, and global IQ rates have risen steadily since the early twentieth century.[35]

These governmental, scientific, and technical advances have gone hand in hand, on Pinker's triumphalist account, with expanding liberal attitudes. As they grow wealthier, nations allocate a greater percentage of their GDP to social programs.

Racism, sexism, and homophobia have declined in the United States since the mid-1980s, Pinker claims, and this heartening trend is global: social attitudes among today's young Middle Eastern Muslims are comparable to those of young Western Europeans in the early 1960s.[36]

Pinker is so convinced of the *significance* of these data points that he correlates them with people's states of mind. (His use of quantitative data to support qualitative judgments and his application of general concepts to particular cases are among the major sources of contention for his book's many vociferous critics.[37]) Life satisfaction, he argues, tracks with income gains—though a dollar in the bank buys less satisfaction as people get richer—a hopeful sign for a world continuing to produce more plenty. Pessimists who link social-media use or singlehood to atomization overlook studies that demonstrate, for example, declining rates of self-reported loneliness among American college students between 1978 and 2010. Studies of suicide (available only from Switzerland, the United States, and England) show a slight downward trend during the last century and a half.[38]

A non-magical thinker, Pinker offers no guarantee of continual progress. The only certainty is that there will be (at least) temporary setbacks, as appear on many graphs he provides, in the forms of spiking violence or declining prosperity, along diagonal lines that document long-term improvement. He eschews heroic military accounts of progress, as well as dialectical explanations, theodicies, or other teleologies. His picture of social improvement is prosaic, emphasizing trial-and-error problem solving—tinkering with legislation, manners, and technology—that accrues benefits over time.[39] And yet, even in the wake of Trumpism, he tells a sweeping tale, with repeated allusions to Parker's metaphor of a moral "arc,"[40] but with reason and sympathy replacing god or historical laws, and probabilistic thinking replacing abstract certainties.

Pinker does not focus on intimate life. But his narrative cries out for completion by the non-quantifiable insights of storytellers including Lawrence, Woolf, and Forster, and formalized by literary theorists. Where is society (that of the modernist era or of today) broken, unjust, inhumane? How do novelists evoke its pathologies in depicting spousal intimacies or a character's inwardness? Can sexual dissidents resist a repressive status quo, as Herbert Marcuse believed they might? Or, as Foucault suspected, will they inevitably reinforce an individualistic ethos and fuel the commodification of sex? If societies grow more humane as they prosper through "gentle commerce,"[41] then how does this progress tell in men's and women's love lives? Such questions flow into the gaps of quantitative, public-sphere-centered accounts of post-Enlightenment progress.

A combination of recent academic and popular literature about intimacy, marriage, and sexuality fills these gaps. Combining methods from sociology, anthropology, and self-help, some of this literature supports—with caveats—the idea that *things are improving* in the intimate sphere, as they have been improving in social and economic spheres since the American and French Revolutions. With an additional century of post-Enlightenment hindsight that Bloomsburians did not have, Giddens in *The Transformation of Intimacy* (1992), Stephanie Coontz in *Marriage: A History* (2005), and Eli Finkel in *The All-or-Nothing Marriage: How the Best Marriages Work* (2017) tell largely congruent tales about the eighteenth century's revolutionary ideals concerning love and marriage. Only now, these writers say, is the Enlightenment's internal logic—with its destabilizing implications for families and communities—working toward its (perhaps ineluctable) conclusion.

Several themes link these writers' accounts of post-Enlightenment intimacy. First, speaking roughly, post-1700 Western history has seen three periods of sexual boundary-pushing and expansion: one at the end of the eighteenth century (with roots earlier in the century), another during the sexological-modernist-Bloomsburian period, and a third after 1970 (a "turbulent" period from which we might not have emerged). Second, as mentioned, since the Enlightenment, traditionalists have lamented the "love revolution": a paradigm that has subordinated communal needs to couples' happiness, and since the 1960s sexual revolution to individual erotic pleasure. Liberals have shared their general understanding of this "revolution" but reversed their evaluation of it, seeing gains in sexual freedom and egalitarianism outweighing losses in social and familial cohesion. Third, to understand early twentieth-century sexual radicalism as the least convulsive of these three expansive periods is humbling and salutary for enthusiasts of modernist culture. Without overlooking Freud's, Lawrence's, and Bloomsbury's daring insights, we can recognize the late-eighteenth and late-twentieth centuries as more radically transformative eras in the history of intimacy.

As the following sections discuss, intimacy did not follow a straight path, from the late-eighteenth to the early twenty-first century, with regard to spouses enjoying equality and friendship, parents treating children less formally and harshly, society countenancing sexual freedom (including homosexual freedom), or the mandate of lifelong monogamy growing less oppressive. In some ways, intimate practices behave like a network of streams, converging and coming apart, diving underground and resurfacing. During some periods, the intimate sphere expands more than it contracts—either for a few or for many social groups—accommodating new varieties of love and sexual exploration. During other periods, gender roles retrench, the nuclear family consolidates, and nonstandard forms of sexual expression go underground.

Expansions and Contractions in the (Social) Life of the Heart: Eighteenth-Century Progress

Although smooth *grand récits* of social progress, or the progress of love, are simplifications, nonetheless the post-revolutionary late-eighteenth century makes for a stirring origin point in a narrative of intimate life. Mary Wollstonecraft's *Vindication of the Rights of Man* (1790) expresses its era's emancipatory fervor, and her *Vindication of the Rights of Woman* (1792) follows the first treatise's premise to a logical conclusion (what are democracy and equality without feminism?). In conjunction, these two works extend public-sphere principles to the private sphere, discouraging couples from seeing marriages as "little monarchies."[42] Wollstonecraft nudged Western love toward the present moment, when many men and women look to coupledom not merely to meet basic needs but to satisfy what Abraham Maslow termed "higher-order" needs—a dangerous aspiration. Rather like modernism, on some accounts, sought a replacement for religion in literature and culture,[43] Finkel argues that marriage, for some contemporary couples, fills a void left by religion,[44] freighting it with unmanageable burdens.

But even apart from the contradictions inherent in what Giddens terms the "pure relationship"—a bond entered into "for its own sake," for as long as it provides each person enough "satisfactions"[45]—this journey toward "higher-order" intimacies was arduous. It defied centuries of male authority, dogma, and tradition during which people didn't marry for love. They did, admittedly, fall in love, sometimes with their spouses. But the social pressures that shaped marriage answered communal existential concerns. Marriages could have sexual rationales when populations were sparse ("Be fruitful and multiply"), or in other circumstances, be conceived in puritanical terms. ("It is better to marry than to burn," but sexual passion is dangerous, and marriage can only curtail and channel it, without eliminating it.) Pre-moderns tied sexuality to reproduction and death in ways difficult to conceive today, when few mothers die giving birth and infant-mortality rates are low. (In the 1980s, AIDS re-linked sex to death, with the difference that it threatened men as well as—in fact, more than—women.) Because pre-moderns had not *socialized nature*, they succumbed to diseases and famine. In lamenting humankind's "self-imposed nonage,"[46] Kant eschews a nostalgic view of life in intimate contact with the earth. (Elizabethan puns on orgasms as "little deaths" can mislead, if they suggest that the only pre-modern connection between sex and death concerned ecstatic transport, not syphilis.) Even pre-moderns who survived infancy and childhood could expect shorter lifespans than can twenty-first-century citizens throughout much of the world. This colored the meaning of life-partnerships: "till death do you part" means one thing if you live to be thirty, forty, or fifty, and another if spouses expect to live for eight decades or be wed for three decades like the protagonists of Smith's *White Teeth* and *On Beauty*.

For many reasons, before the late seventeenth century at the earliest, and even then only in pockets of Western Europe, marriages were rarely justified in terms of love or sexual fulfillment, as Coontz explains.[47] The *interests* of neighboring farms might motivate their son and daughter to wed (pooling interfamilial resources), as the interests of royal families might lead a prince and princess to wed, but conventional wisdom did not anchor their union in undying affection and attraction. Finkel associates the pre-Enlightenment era with "pragmatic marriage," which would be displaced by "love marriage" circa 1850. He locates the transition during the Industrial Revolution, rather than after the French Revolution, tying it to economic and technological forces more than ideological ones.

By contrast, with the emergence of what Giddens terms "plastic sexuality"—sex divorced from reproduction[48]—couples begin to author their own destinies. Before modern contraception, and even before the American and French Revolutions, couples limited family sizes, illustrating how the development of reproductive technologies answers to preexisting needs and is not entirely their cause.

Even if eighteenth-century people's feeling of authoring their own love lives was partly illusory—as contemporary theory argues that many ideas about freedom are illusory—it still marks a watershed in the way people *experience* their emotional careers. It is no accident that couples' feeling of romantic self-fashioning coincided with the rise of the novel. In *Howards End*, the masculinized Wilcox family sees life as a "battle" and suffers from excess "preparedness"; the feminized Schlegel family sees life as a "romance" and would avoid being too "cautious" about having their umbrella filched. The practical Wilcoxes excel at the "outer life" of "telegrams and anger"; the impractical Schlegels value the "inner life."[49] Whereas Forster uses the men of a nationalistic, business-oriented family as a synecdoche for stunted masculinity, Giddens and Coontz suggest that pre-modern husbands generally lacked the tenderness that educated classes increasingly value in men, and the capacity for introspection that novels are designed to sharpen.

The Enlightenment love revolution may have had an internal logic from its inception, pointing toward something like today's "uncharted territory,"[50] with high divorce rates, destigmatized same-sex and interracial love, friendships between parents and adult children, and transgender politics unsettling assumptions about sexual selfhood. Nonetheless, four impediments delayed its arrival: women's dependence on men (economic and otherwise), poor birth-control technologies, social penalties for sexual nonconformity (e.g., the 1950s' stigmatization of singlehood), and ideas about innate differences between the sexes, widely held since the Victorian era.[51] These impediments have added a cyclical element to the history of intimacy, complicating the march of progress touted by thinkers like Finkel, who—for all the caveats he offers—believes society is on the cusp of "the most successful period of marital well-being that the world has ever seen."[52]

Expansions and Contractions: Retrenchments in the 1800s and 1950s

Modernists, considering themselves enlightened about sex and passion, often used Victorians as a foil when articulating their own values. Likewise, sexual liberationists since the '70s have often used the '50s as a foil: a model of staid conformism and female subjection. But neither period that is broadly defined by retrenchment lacked elements of dissent. As important as Enlightenment rationalism and the pursuit of happiness were to the move away from the pragmatic marriage paradigm, Victorian sentimentality was required to complete the articulation of "love" as the moral ideal now—still—so widely embraced. The nineteenth century's separate spheres were an accomplishment: they made possible childhood as we now know it: a period of innocence and play to be protected from the demands of labor and the cruelty of a merely disciplinarian father. Nineteenth-century factories did exploit child workers (consistent with pre-Victorian agricultural traditions), but Victorian reformers combated and greatly reduced this practice. The existence of separate spheres afforded some men chances for *dexterity of self*: showing a more competitive face to the public sphere and a tenderer one in the private sphere, they learned Wildean lessons about psychic fluidity and anticipated the insights of queer theorists. The separation of the spheres also entailed the invention of motherhood, admittedly a role with fewer opportunities for self-dexterity than that of working fathers. But in a flash of dialectical analysis, Giddens argues that, from within the cages of angelic domesticity, Victorian women embodied values—patience, non-violence, and non-competitiveness—that have informed subsequent social movements, offered an alternative ethic to capitalistic acquisitiveness, and contributed to the feminization and egalitarianism of married life.[53]

Victoria reigned for sixty-four years, whereas the 1950s lasted only a quarter as long (perhaps from 1946 to 1962 or '64), but the '50s too embraced cultural currents and crosscurrents that defy a unitary label. In some ways, Coontz explains, gender roles quietly loosened, with men doing more housework amid the plethora of postwar appliances available to middle-class US families. With the wider availability of automobiles and the burgeoning pop-culture industry, the '50s were more hedonistic than the roaring '20s. And many '50s couples felt themselves to be autonomous, marrying in their early twenties as the husbands embarked on careers—though in hindsight such ostensible autonomy has the look of tightly scripted gender differentiation.

The constrictions of life in the 1950s—the Victorian age redux, with variations—include the stigmatization of singlehood and the reassertion of the holiness of motherhood. They include the four aforementioned impediments to the Enlightenment love revolution, among them poor birth control. (Enovid was mass marketed in the '60s.) They include pre-Stonewall homophobia, testified to in the 74-year-old Forster's 1953 article entitled "A Magistrate's Figures," which describes how easy it was for police officers to entrap gay men. But, Coontz argues, the victims of these constricted gender roles were not only women and gay men. Sloan Wilson's 1955 novel *The Man in the Gray Flannel Suit* and David Reisman's 1950 sociological study *The Lonely Crowd* show postwar corporate culture valuing other-directed men over inner-directed ones, leading many men to feel spiritually stultified. Looking back, we might imagine such texts being titled "The Masculine Mystique": they complemented *The Feminine Mystique*, Betty Friedan's landmark 1963 study of unhappy housewives. Friedan's book, often seen as initiating second-wave American feminism, also had popular forerunners where women's experiences are concerned. A 1956 *McCall's* article entitled "The Mother Who Ran Away" set a record for readership[54] and likely inspired the Laura Brown storyline in Cunningham's *The Hours*. A 1960 CBS documentary, *The Trapped Housewife*, repeated the premise of the *McCall's* article.

In other words, even in the '50s, in some cultural outlets people already confessed to malaise and unhappiness. Nonetheless, this was the least anxious decade about marriage since the Enlightenment. *Leave it to Beaver*, *Ozzie and Harriet*, and a range of other redoubts, including scholarly ones, defended the status quo. From an anthropological point of view, George Peter Murdock argued that marriage—understood as mixed-sex, economically cooperative, and sexually active—was a human universal. From a sociological point of view, Talcott Parsons argued that the male-breadwinner/female-homemaker marital model was perfectly suited to a mobile society. In a more elaborate version of Parsons's thesis, the sociologist William Goode drew on such statistics as the reversal of an eighty-year-old upward trend in divorce to predict that monogamy would become a worldwide norm. He comforted his peers with the assurance that it did not entail full sexual equality.[55] The blind spots in this metanarrative—optimistic and convinced that a present-day status quo was a wave of the future—are useful cautions against a complacent assumption that early twenty-first-century lovers, families, or sexual free agents are discovering durable solutions to the quandaries of friendship, sexual intimacy, and personal fulfillment.

Expansions and Contractions: Widening Horizons in Bloomsbury's Time and Ours

Bloomsbury's ambivalent explorations of sexuality gave fine texture to the dilemmas of modernist-era men and women in search of greater freedom in intimacy. *Mrs Dalloway*'s picture of a possibly bisexual wife married to a kind husband captured its author's mixed feelings about the marriage institution. The spectral possibility in *Howards End* of an unregenerate Henry Wilcox domineering over Margaret, his wife-to-be, as he had domineered over his first wife, Ruth, expresses Forster's fear of toxic masculinity. But Margaret's mystical, dissociated state of mind at novel's end, and Tibby's ineffectuality as an advocate for his family, suggest that Forster envisioned no easy way of transcending Wilcoxian masculinity. Woolf and Forster worked through these ambivalences, toward (sometimes faltering) visions of finer futures for lovers and platonic intimates.

For similar reasons, a new kind of ambivalence, combining incredulity with nostalgia for a kind of optimism that can no longer be innocently enjoyed, helps late twentieth- and early twenty-first-century writers to probe Bloomsburian themes. Lyotardian rejection of metanarratives partly characterizes our post-Marxist, decreasingly religious, and even post-Freudian age (i.e., one that doubts the likelihood of cures or full insights into the self, as Freud himself came more and more to do). But contemporary novels such as *The Hours* and *On Beauty* are enriched by residual utopian yearnings. Developing themes in their Bloomsburian precursor-texts, *Mrs Dalloway* and *Howards End*, they glimpse utopia not in a perfected society but in perfected love, and they wonder whether such loves will be more within reach in the future. Beneath the surface of such contemporary tales—or occasionally *on* their surface—lies the question, "Have our newly won freedoms in intimacy made us happier, and will they continue doing so?" In an age with so many divorces and with unprecedented numbers of singles, questions about freedom *in* intimacy lead naturally to questions about freedom *from* intimacy: "How happy are millions of non-cohabiting adults, and will the dignity of their autonomy characterize the lives of more citizens to come?" (Appendix A, Table 2 records the growing number of singles in England and Wales.)

Bloomsbury could not have anticipated the wide relevance of this question, and it is far from the only contemporary question that races ahead of Bloomsbury and its six heirs under discussion. Yearly and even monthly developments transform the landscape of transgender politics and show *Orlando*—Woolf's 1928 novel; Ulrike Ottinger's and Sally Potter's 1981 and 1992 film adaptations; subsequent stage performances in Illinois, Los Angeles, Paris, Edinburgh, and New York, plus two operatic adaptations—to have been both ahead of its time in 1928 and in constant need of updating to remain *with* the times. Avant-garde theater directors Robert Wilson and Sarah Ruhl, the experimental filmmakers mentioned above, and musical composers have all faced the question of how to make Woolf's text new while reanimating its gender-subversive and identity-blurring spirit. From Wilson's minimalist stage adaptation to Potter's film with its lush cinematography, with various kinds of musical accompaniment and with varied critical receptions, their efforts illustrate that Woolf's experimental text has neither been forgotten nor reified.[56]

Even as ethnonationalist movements strain to reconsolidate traditional identities, sexual dissidents and scholars take cues from *Orlando* in questioning essentialist categories. As mentioned, *Howards End*'s Margaret Schlegel worried that the sexes are "really races, each with its own code of morality."[57] Woolf addressed this fear in 1929 by praising the "androgynous mind,"[58] and subsequent psychological research has given empirical backing to her intuition. Sandra Bem associates "psychological masculinity" with assertiveness, and at its worst with destructive self-absorption and antisocial behavior. She associates "psychological femininity" with nurturance, and at its worst with destructive self-effacement. Bem's clinical language, that is, pathologizes traits that Carpenter ascribes to "extreme specimens" of each sex,[59] that Margaret Schlegel laments, and that Woolf imagines overcoming. Complementing this judgment, various psychological studies see "psychologically androgynous" individuals as well-adjusted and possessing high emotional intelligence.[60] The whole idea of "adjustment," of course, is relative to social norms, and it is logical that psychic androgynes should function well as separate spheres are softening—during our so-called "grand gender convergence."[61]

In a further proliferation of Bloomsburian inquiries, today's urbanites challenge inherited ideas about intimacy and selfhood. Books such as Elisabeth Sheff's 2014 *The Polyamorists Next Door*, Mimi Schippers's 2016 *Beyond Monogamy: Polyamory and the Future of Polyqueer Sexualities*, and Carrie Jenkins's 2017 *What Love Is: And What It Could Be*[62] argue that polyamorists are irrationally stigmatized—as gays and lesbians have long been—although they do openly what others do secretly. As I'll discuss in Chapter 8, Bloomsbury is due for scholarly attention as a forerunner of poly culture. To employ a poly term retroactively, Bloomsbury's romantic "vees"—such as Forster's long romance with the policeman Bob Buckingham, whose wife May eventually became Forster's dear friend—presage the vees formed by polys since the '70s. Furthermore, Bloomsbury's wider sexual and romantic groupings roughly parallel what poly theorists call "quads," "moresomes," and "intimate networks."[63]

Bloomsbury's bold experiments in living and loving occasioned joy, as they brought questions about sexual propriety, social permissiveness, and moral hypocrisy out of aristocratic culture and into middle-class culture. But their unconventional amours also caused pain, as attested to by Angelica Garnett's 1984 memoir *Deceived with Kindness*. Garnett complains about her parents' deceptiveness in leading her to believe herself Clive's, not Duncan's, biological daughter.

Neither Carpenter nor Bloomsbury employed the term "polyamory," and as mentioned he preferred a couple's "permanent spiritual mating"[64] to other intimate configurations. But his writings open up possibilities for love as it "comes of age." Partly anticipating the ethos of today's polys, he and Russell saw sexual jealousy as a symptom of private property—a social arrangement that treats wives and children as men's possessions. Carpenter and Russell distinguish "natural" from "artificial" jealousy, the former being transient and relatively non-violent, and the latter stemming from patriarchal habits.[65]

Today's proponents of ethical non-monogamy examine jealousy from various angles. Often they do not link it to capitalism, being more sexually radical and less economically radical than Carpenter and Russell. Often they do not downplay the emotion as transient, but see it as useful for self-exploration and necessary to manage in healthy relationships. Nonetheless, polys strive to transcend jealousy and have even coined a term, "compersion," for lovers' pleasure in their beloveds' enjoyment of a third party. Quantitative psychological data and testimonies from polys associate consensual non-monogamy with high relationship quality and low jealousy levels.[66]

Post-Bloomsburian citizens in our age of gender convergence renegotiate interpersonal relations in dimensions beyond dyadic and non-dyadic romances. As Joyce's lonely bachelor testifies, intersexual fraternization in Bloomsbury's time was rare. Hence, meetings at Gordon Square were breakthroughs, even before Strachey asked if a stain on Vanessa's dress was semen.[67] But today such fraternization, and resultant platonic mixed-sex friendships, are common. So argues William Deresiewicz, who laments that the 1989 film *When Harry Met Sally* wrongly answers "no" to the question "can a man and a woman be friends?" because, as Harry claims—echoing Joyce's bachelor—"the sex part always gets in the way." Deresiewicz hopes that storytellers can catch up with social reality, depicting platonic male-female friendships.[68]

Families, too, transvalue old relationship protocols, including patriarchal hierarchies. "New dads" replace "absent authoritarian" fathers,[69] parents spend more time with their children than they did in the 1950s, they and their adult children see one another as friends, and large majorities of respondents tell pollsters that their current family is as close as the one in which they grew up, or closer.[70] Hence the intergenerational affections in *On Beauty* differ radically from those in *Howards End*: one cannot imagine Henry Wilcox joking with his sons or showing them the physical signs of love that Howard Belsey—for all his shortcomings—displays in Smith's homage. Whatever the potential problems of this new intergenerational intimacy—helicopter parents who smother their offspring, grown-up kids who live under the parental roof long into their twenties[71]—they are far outweighed by their benefits. At least, a sanguine *grand récit* of intimacy in history, perched on a twenty-first-century vantage, could say so.

In *The Conquest of Happiness* (1930), by contrast, Russell was not nearly so confident. He thought that, while parent-child relations could be "one of the greatest sources of happiness," at present they were "in nine cases out of ten, a source of unhappiness to both parties, and in ninety-nine cases out of a hundred a source of unhappiness" to at least one party. Without lamenting the spread of democracy, he saw it as a source of familial despair. It upsets long-established roles and hierarchies, leaving career-minded women burdened by childcare without adequate domestic service, and wage-earning men so career-driven that their only time for their children is at night (when the children sleep) and on weekends, when they develop merely superficial relations with them. With children no longer respectful and obedient, and educated parents terrified by psychoanalysis with the thought of doing unwitting harm, parenthood is beset by anxiety, he claims.[72]

Russell's popular works are rife with sweeping and sparsely supported assertions. But notwithstanding such empirical shortcomings, his writings on marriage and sexuality have inspired current taboo-busters such as Jenkins. His precursor-relation to her parallels Woolf's relation to Cusk: each contemporary draws on the earlier radical in decrying the terms on which men and women love one another today.

Russell's pessimism about intergenerational and marital relations stems from his lack of faith in men's capacity to transcend their habitual mindsets: their obsession with status and emotional disconnection from their spouses and children. In Carpenter's buoyant view, Victorian Intermediates, combining radical democratic values with homoerotic open-heartedness, anticipate an early twentieth-century gender convergence. But there were no "new dads" on Russell's radar. Thus, it has been left to subsequent thinkers, from the late-twentieth and early twenty-first centuries—inspired by Russell's critiques of bourgeois love-protocols—to recuperate Carpenter's optimism and see the human male as more psychically flexible than Russell gave him credit for being.

The high divorce rates since the sexual revolution have complicated this task. As mentioned, Goode and other 1950s commentators cited declining divorce trends in defense of their time's status quo, and they valued how breadwinner marriages seemed to decelerate the march toward equality in intimacy. But the '50s seem now to have been an aberration; the Enlightenment love revolution rolls on, needed and liberating or deadly and destabilizing, depending on the commentator's political sensibility. Russell's sense that democracy contributes to familial unhappiness echoes what the love revolution's critics had been saying since the eighteenth century. In Giddens's terms, the "pure relationship" harbors contradictions: to develop a shared history, people must give themselves to a relationship. But without the prop of male authority, the compulsion of economic necessity, or the sense that lifelong partnership is "natural," lovers have less reason to gamble on such a commitment—and they know that their partner faces the same quandary.[73] Nonetheless, today's optimists can point to a decline in divorce rates from their peak in the early 1980s[74] as a sign that lovers have found new ways of "containing" instabilities, to invoke a Cold War metaphor.

Perhaps the very forces of enlightened self-interest that have partly dissolved the Victorian marriage model have also produced—or could produce—a new equilibrium. Neither Giddens, Coontz, nor Finkel refers to the marketplace in their book titles, but all three employ commercial metaphors to describe contemporary intimacy. We live in a sexual free market, which is positively or negatively connoted depending on whether one resists seeing relationships in instrumental terms. Finkel, as mentioned, thinks we're on the cusp of a golden age of marriage—but only for some couples. As the "all-or-nothing" tag in his title indicates, he thinks that wealthy and culturally adjusted couples can enjoy "all" that marriage has to offer, ascending Maslow's hierarchy. But economically and culturally dispossessed couples often break up, enjoying "nothing" of their fortunate contemporaries' blessings. The many couples between these extremes weigh imperfect options according to a "supply and demand" calculus. Are they, Finkel asks, "investing enough resources" to achieve their marital goals? If not, they can strategize about how to "(1) get more mileage out of available resources, (2) invest additional resources ... or (3) recalibrate expectations."[75] While the Enlightenment love revolution has, on the one hand, raised spouses' ambitions above base material considerations, on the other hand Finkel's pragmatic metaphors suggest that intimate relations remain conditioned by economic concerns. *Homo sentimentalis* turns out to be—or he *should* be, if he navigates his post-Victorian world wisely—*homo economicus*, after all. This principle would apply to unmarried as well as to married people, to friends as well as to lovers, between families and within them.

But the free market can be cruel in interpersonal as well as economic terms. Whatever optimists like Pinker think about the march of progress and the dividends it pays in intimate life, disciplines including psychology and epidemiology have documented pervasive atomization in today's societies and its toxic effects. With growing numbers of people living alone and/or reporting no close confidantes, with marriage and childbirth rates falling in many demographic groups, and with volunteerism and religious affiliation declining, all as lifespans lengthen, comorbid factors such as diabetes and suicide increase.[76] Of course, Covid-19 has caused further atomization, with attendant pathologies that scholars are only beginning to comprehend.

Recalling the disenchantment of radical modernists from both the left and right, today's theorists—drawing on remnants of Marxist traditions—critique the culture of love and intimacy under late capitalism. Because neither today's global economy nor its gender taxonomies reproduce those of the early twentieth century, analogies between the eras are imprecise. But just as Lawrence worried that instrumental reason threatens interpersonal life, that normative life scripts oppress sexual nonconformists, and that psychoanalysis can abet these forces, current theorists including Berlant, Ahmed, and Eva Illouz see similar dangers in contemporary culture.[77]

Radical Theory and Intimacy Today

Whereas popular writers such as Finkel evoke intimacy (un-anxiously) with economic metaphors, others mistrust such formulations. Illouz's 2007 *Cold Intimacies: The Making of Emotional Capitalism* argues that twentieth-century psychology has laudable roots as a force for sexual and economic equalization but that it has drifted from this foundation into a status symbol for the well to do. She strikes a Lawrentian note, seeing psychology as allied with instrumental reason, hence a crude compass for navigating unconscious and erotic terrain.[78]

Freud's legacy, she argues, has been coopted by capital, which posits sicknesses to sell cures: psychodynamic therapy, pharmaceutical products pegged to the DSM, and self-realization on the model of the humanist movement. Expert guidance in emotional self-management, couples counseling, and numerous therapies for children are available primarily to those who can afford them and who benefit from them to preserve their social advantages.

Illouz contends that the ethos of "communication," while salutary for corporate culture, has been transferred with only minor modifications to the therapeutic jargon of feminism and relationship therapy, where it flattens out the individual and irrational dimensions of love and desire. As psychology approximates a *lingua franca*, it becomes dehumanizing.

Ahmed makes related claims about the tension between conventional wisdom and nonstandard forms of love and desire. Her *Queer Phenomenology* (2006) and *The Promise of Happiness* (2010) employ feminism, queer studies, and affect theory to critique the "happiness turn" of the last decade and a half, which draws on self-help and Buddhism in advising readers about how to find happiness. Ahmed says that such advice "redescribe[s] social norms as social goods." When slaves or housewives are depicted as happy, or when heterosexual coupledom is sentimentalized, the happiness meme "justifies oppression."[79] Ahmed sees normative trappings of happiness much as Illouz sees therapeutic know-how—as forms of cultural capital.

Ahmed strives to uncover archives of unhappiness buried in normal (and even privileged) life, much as *Arlington Park* does. As Chapter 2 discusses, when Cusk's character, Juliet Randall—mother of two, resident of a comfortable suburb, and part-time teacher at a high school for privileged girls—repeats the refrain that her amiable husband Benedict has "murdered" her,[80] she might seem melodramatic, an object of satire rather than sympathy. (Cusk frequently satirizes upper-middle-class women, and none of the five focalized women characters in *Arlington Park* escapes her scathing wit.) But Juliet—an exceptional student in her day—has traded her professional promise for subordinate roles as wife and mother. She is uncongenial, and the bitterness, nastiness, and apparent pettiness of mothers like her reflect the subservient roles to which they remain confined, eight decades after *Mrs Dalloway*. Juliet's "murder" metaphor grows more compelling upon subsequent readings of *Arlington Park* and attention to its Woolfian resonances.

Ahmed's *The Promise of Happiness* footnotes Cusk's novel during an admiring discussion of Cunningham's *The Hours* in which Ahmed explains that "to inherit feminism can mean to inherit sadness."[81] The scene she admires in *The Hours* has a close parallel in a scene from *Arlington Park*, which also involves a trapped housewife. Cunningham's novel, like its precursor-text by Woolf, helps Ahmed to build her critique of the happiness industry, with its valuation of typically "happy families." Dan and Laura Brown's marriage is tailor-made to suit such a critique; it could be objected that Cunningham crafts this couple too transparently in the service of unmasking a false ideal—that in depicting their marriage he puts his thumb in the pan, as Lawrence wanted novelists not to do.[82]

Such oppositional theories as Illouz's and Ahmed's do not invalidate the idea of progress in the public or private sphere, but they do plunge it into radical doubt. Who defines "progress" (or related terms such as "happiness," "cure," or "self-realization")? Whose interests does the definition serve, and whose exclusion or suffering does a given formulation of progress obscure?

Ahmed dexterously curates archives of disappointment and frustration in texts by Bloomsburians and their legatees. But a fuller reading of these works finds that they also express hope and envision finer futures. Woolf's and Forster's art was not an autotelic defiance of a fallen (or worse, an irredeemable) world, but an active engagement with a world that was changing, in some ways for the better. Their legacy is larger than one of protest (though they did this, in expository and fictional writings), lament (though they expressed this feeling eloquently), or a defense of aesthetic autonomy (though this was a Bloomsburian—and modernist—value).[83] This volume detects Bloomsbury's legacies partly in the resonances of Woolf's, Forster's, and Freud's *moods*—sanguine and despairing—in successors' writings.

Notes

1. *The Postmodern Condition* xxiv.
2. See Hungerford, Huyssen. Also see the Fall 2007 issue of *Twentieth-Century Literature*, especially Andrew Hoberek's introduction, "After Postmodernism."
3. Theodore Parker, a nineteenth-century Unitarian minister and abolitionist, was paraphrased by Martin Luther King before Obama paid him tribute. For a critique of how Obama adapts the precept for secular purposes, see Matt Lewis.
4. Illouz 89–95.
5. Lubbock 384.
6. Keynes 447.
7. For selfhood and time, see Matz, *The Modern Novel* 57–8 and Kern, *The Culture of Time and Space*. For intimacy, see Hillis Miller.
8. *In Memoriam*, Epilogue, lines 143–4.
9. See Froula for a discussion of Woolf's thought in the context of the long Enlightenment struggle for democracy, human rights, and peace.
10. Giddens 28–32, 90–4, 180–1.
11. He developed these ideas in *Elements of the Philosophy of Right* (1820) and *Lectures on the Philosophy of History* (published posthumously in 1837, first delivered as lectures in 1822, 1828, and 1830).
12. The following summary derives from pages 39–64.
13. Moeyes 25, Barker, *Regeneration* 53–4.
14. *Maurice* 249.
15. *Love's Coming of Age* 30.
16. *Howards End* 172.
17. *Love's Coming* 65, 68, 74, 99.
18. Ibid. 98–9.
19. I discuss Carpenter's influence on Forster in "Case Study."
20. Giddens 119–23. He qualifies an otherwise essentialistic link between male sexuality and violence at the end of this cited section.
21. Qtd. in Holroyd 92.
22. *Howards End* 211, Armstrong, 295.
23. *A Passage to India* 312.
24. "Notes on the English Character" 13.
25. "What I Believe" 69.
26. *Mr. Bennett and Mrs. Brown* 4, 5, 13–19.
27. *A Room of One's Own*. Chloe and Olivia appear on 82, Shakespeare's sister on 46–8, and Brontë on 68–9.
28. *Women in Love* 481: 27, 33.
29. Regan 33–6.
30. Helt and Detloff 8.
31. *Maurice* 62, 74, 82, 79.
32. *Foreign Affairs* July/August 2018, Volume 97, Number 4.
33. Deudney and Ikenberry 17.
34. Ibid. 18.
35. Pinker 156–8, 170–1, 176–8, 182, 189, 187, 236, 240–1.
36. Ibid. 216–28.

37 Admirers of *Enlightenment Now* include Bill Gates, who calls it his "favorite book of all time" (quoted in David Bell, 31); Shermer, who calls it "the most uplifting work of science I've ever read" (58); Fontana, who calls it a "tour de force" (55); and Brooks, who admires its optimistic political centrism but faults it for overvaluing Cartesian reason and underrating the severity of the current loneliness epidemic. Gopnik gives it a more mixed but largely positive review, admiring its articulation of modern cosmopolitan values, but faulting its disrespect for traditional small-town values. The book's critics, who fault its shallow treatment of eighteenth-century thinkers as well as its technocratic sensibility, include Frim and Fluss, Moyn, Williamson, Bell, Szalai, and Gray ("The Limits of Reason").

38 Pinker 269, 276, 279. For an account of current precarity and despair, especially in the United States, see Brooks, "Moral Convulsion." For an account of current despair and suicide among US whites, see Case and Deaton.

39 Pinker 11.

40 Ibid. 208, 213, 223.

41 Ibid. 162.

42 Finkel 52.

43 See Pericles Lewis. In his essay "In God We Trust," Rushdie—an atheist since age fourteen—says that "perhaps I write, in part, to fill up that emptied God-chamber with other dreams" (377). In *Midnight's Children*, Aadam Aziz's loss of faith makes "a hole in him, a vacancy in a vital inner chamber, leaving him vulnerable to women and history" (4).

44 Finkel 75, 80–3.

45 Giddens 58.

46 "What Is Enlightenment?" 203.

47 Coontz 15–23.

48 Giddens 2.

49 *Howards End* 104–5, 25, 296.

50 Coontz 281–301.

51 Ibid. 307.

52 Finkel 26.

53 In Chapter 8 (page 212), I discuss how recent theorists mistrust the "philogyny" of thinkers like Giddens.

54 Coontz 242.

55 Finkel 5, 59, Coontz 242–3.

56 For a discussion of intertextuality in Potter's film, see Hoyle. For discussions of gender and desire in the film, see Ruth Martin, Craft-Fairchild, Ferris and Waites, and Ciecko. For a discussion of Ottinger's film, see Castaneda. For a discussion of *Orlando*'s theatrical adaptations, see Jonathan Brown. For a discussion of an operatic adaptation, see Barone.

57 *Howards End* 172.

58 *A Room of One's Own* 98.

59 *Love's Coming of Age* 88–9.

60 See Finkel 70–1, 106 for discussions of Bem, et al.

61 Economist Claudia Goldin makes this case. Others disagree, including Elisabeth Sheff, who sees "conformity" to traditional gender roles even among polyamorists (119).

62 Jenkins was featured in *The Chronicle of Higher Education*'s February 2017 article "I Have Multiple Loves," by Moira Weigel.

63 Sheff 13–17.
64 *Love's Coming of Age* 88–9.
65 Ibid. 116–17, *Marriage and Morals* 25–8.
66 In a study comparing long-term monogamous to long-term consensually non-monogamous relationships, respondents in the latter category reported slightly higher relationship quality with their sole or primary partner and significantly lower jealousy (Finkel 250–5). Literature advocating alternative sexual and romantic arrangements is robust, including the aforementioned Jenkins, Sheff, and Schippers, as well as O'Neill and O'Neill, and Easton and Hardy. Adam Phillips's 1996 *Monogamy* offers short meditations on the topic, intended to raise questions more than to supply answers.
67 Woolf, "Old Bloomsbury." *Moments of Being* 195–6.
68 Dereseiwicz.
69 Schwartz (79) connects this kind of father to the classical Oedipal triangle.
70 See Pinker 256. Coontz cites a Pew Research Center poll according to which more than 80 percent of Americans say this about their current family. ("The Not-So-Good Old Days.")
71 See Arnett.
72 *Conquest of Happiness* 169, 174, *Marriage and Morals* 179–82.
73 Giddens 134–56. See especially page 137.
74 Anderson represents the divorce rate as the number of divorces per 1,000 married women aged fifteen and older. She shows it reaching a forty-year low in 2015.
75 Finkel 181.
76 See Russo.
77 Jennifer Cooke has examined the cultural functions performed by theorists like these three, in two collections that she edited: a 2013 issue of *Textual Practice* and a book from the same year entitled *Scenes of Intimacy*. Her introductory article to the *Textual Practice* issue argues that, under the dominance of global capitalism since the modernist era, radical critique and robust counterculture have been largely dormant.
78 Illouz 34, 19, 37.
79 Ahmed *The Promise of Happiness* 2.
80 *Arlington Park* 25.
81 Ahmed *The Promise of Happiness* 75.
82 Lawrence, "Morality and the Novel" 110.
83 For a Bloomsburian defense of aesthetic autonomy, see Clive Bell's *Art*. See Begam, "Rushdie and the Art of Modernism," on modernism and autonomy.

2

Woolfian Pessimism: Rachel Cusk's Vision of Paralysis

As I discuss in the Introduction, Bloomsburians' varied legatees take cues from various aspects of their art. In exploring whether *things get better* for lovers and friends, Michael Cunningham adapts Woolf's non-linear techniques for rendering women's experiences of time present and time past. Salman Rushdie renews Forster's questions about intimacy in history (e.g., what kinds of love or friendship are possible under what conditions), while Ian McEwan and Pat Barker elaborate on Freud's storytelling techniques even as they question Freudian diagnostic orthodoxies. In responding to signs of progress, hope, or despair in our time, these and other writers take cues from Woolfian or Forsterian moods about the early twentieth century, ranging from guarded optimism about the future to melancholic regret over a compromised past and present. Chapter 7 details Cunningham's "metamodernist" strategies:[1] his historiographic incorporation of Woolf herself into *The Hours* and his stylistic tribute to her, with techniques that recall hers without recapitulating them. But perhaps he wears Woolf so much on his sleeve (though of course that is what homages do) that her influence cannot work subtly on his text and its Woolf-savvy readers.

Rachel Cusk has not written a self-declared "hommage," as Smith's *On Beauty* labels itself vis-à-vis Forster,[2] and as Cunningham's *The Hours* as good as labels itself vis-à-vis Woolf. Nonetheless, many of her works betray deep influences of modernist experimentalism in general and of Woolfian and Lawrentian techniques in particular. Her admiration for D. H. Lawrence glows in her introduction to the 2011 Vintage edition of *The Rainbow*. She says that the Brangwen sisters "give voice to themselves out of the long silence of femininity," groups *The Rainbow* with Joyce's *Ulysses* as being "more or less without literary antecedent," and calls Lawrence "subversive, transformative, life-altering."[3]

Her fiction evokes Lawrence repeatedly, whether to endorse his ideas about intimacy or to test their applicability to her sexually and emotionally frustrated characters. *The Bradshaw Variations* (2009) chronicles the havoc wrought on Thomas Bradshaw and Tonie Swann's marriage when they switch gender roles, with him quitting work to care for their eight-year-old daughter while she becomes head of her university's English Department and works late. (Cusk and her second husband conducted a similar failed experiment, described in her 2012 divorce memoir, *Aftermath: On Marriage and Separation*.) Their daughter contracts near-fatal meningitis under Thomas's care, while

Tonie is having an affair and hence not answering her husband's desperate calls. But it is not in this Sophoclean plot device—with the spouses belatedly learning the folly of their experiment—that *The Bradshaw Variations* channels Lawrence's mistrust of feminist idealism and rationalism most recognizably. Cusk evinces stylistic debt to the author of *Women in Love*, for example, when her narrator describes Tonie, after years of enervating marriage, missing Thomas's masculinity. "Each thing had its necessary opposite—this is what she had forgotten," Cusk writes. "And suddenly she craved it, her opposite, masculinity. She craved it not of Thomas or of any other man, but of herself. She wanted her own duality. She did not want to grow and grow, a branching tree of femininity: she wanted her own conflict of female and male, her own synthesis."[4] Cusk owes the uniqueness of her vision in large part to her blending of influences— Lawrence's and Woolf's—that might not seem compatible. *The Bradshaw Variations* and other novels of Cusk's punctuate extended meditations on the disappointments of marital and familial life, largely in a poetic Woolfian vein, with passages of pulsing Lawrentian philosophy and sexual psychology, such as when Tonie's mother—who is terminally ambivalent toward Tonie—has a "dark feeling" about Thomas. "She would like to take him; she would like to have him for herself," the elder Mrs Swann temporarily thinks of her son-in-law, before the feeling passes through her and liberates her of its burden.[5] Such shocking upsurges of Lawrentian feeling have their place in a novel that combines cruelly satirical treatments of complaining women, such as Thomas's sister-in-law Claudia, with the piercing observation of Tonie's one-night lover: "I know what [women's] resentment is. It is the ubiquitous consequence of sexual inequality."[6] In the early twentieth century, the Bloomsburian universe—with its inner-circle members including Woolf and its detractors including Lawrence—comprised a range of sensibilities, all committed to rethinking intimacy and sexuality. The polyphony in Cusk's fiction recaptures some of this dynamic variety.

But her fiction depicts many people who *fail* to flower in the ways Lawrence would like lovers (and individuals) to do, and few if any characters who succeed. In *Arlington Park*, Solly Kerr-Leigh, suffering physically and mentally seven months into her lonely pregnancy with her fourth child, sympathizes with Katzmi, the second in a series of boarders whom she and her husband take in to supplement their income. She knows that Katzmi also suffers, far from her home in Japan, because she hears her cry in bed at night. "Blindly, dimly, their natures touched," remarks the narrator,[7] invoking the unconscious understanding for which Birkin longs in *Women in Love*. But while the narrator reports what Solly would *like* to believe, it is unclear that the women's natures actually "touch." Later in Cusk's post-Lawrentian novel, Christine Lanham laments that, when with her husband, she "had to think with the front of her brain. She didn't think with her body. It all happened at the front of her brain." Christine's "terror of her expulsion from the light" recalls Lawrence's conviction that intellectualized consciousness destroys spontaneity and authenticity. The repetitive nature of her thinking (the phrase "front of her brain" recurs six times in two pages)[8] recalls Lawrence's penchant for repetition, defended in *Women in Love*'s Foreword as the "frictional to-and-fro" of "every natural crisis in emotion or passion or understanding."[9]

But as much as Cusk admires his stylistic signatures, courageous iconoclasm, frank treatments of sexuality, and distinctive insights into people's yearnings for intimacy,

Lawrence punctuates her narratives rather than supplying their deepest rhythms. Thematically and technically, Cusk draws deeper inspiration from Woolf. She extends Woolf's inquiries into privileged women's disappointments in intimacy—still largely private matters, even after multiple waves of feminism and in a confessional culture. And across her oeuvre, Cusk extends modernism's search for new ways of posing such questions. Recent years have seen her trilogy: *Outline* (2014), *Transit* (2017), and *Kudos* (2018). Faye, the narrator of *Outline* whose name is revealed only in the penultimate chapter, has been described as "a cipher who inspires other people to confess."[10] An English novelist who teaches a summer creative writing course in Greece, she elicits lengthy, self-revelatory dialog (or monologs) from people she sits next to on an airplane, teaches in a classroom, or dines with. But other than the fact that she is a divorced mother (like Cusk), readers discover little about her—directly. She is not a developed "character," in the traditional sense of that concept which Woolf found limiting. But she is, as the title indicates, richly suggested in outline: she is a kind of negative space, befitting someone who at least *claims* to seek "a life as unmarked by self-will as possible."[11] This narrative strategy both recalls and diverges from that of *Jacob's Room* (1922), Woolf's third novel and the one that—following upon the more realistic *Night and Day* (1919)—set her novel writing on post-Victorian trails from which it never returned. Woolf develops her titular character based largely on the impressions other people have of him. (The word "room" in Woolf's title suggests a void where Jacob might be more directly depicted, much like the sole word in Cusk's title evokes a missing essence, or selfhood, within the outline of Faye.) Whereas we learn about Jacob from what others think of *him*, we learn about Cusk's speaker—or fail to do so—from what others tell her about *themselves*. Cusk's adjustment to Woolf's parallaxes tells us two things about her artistry: first, that Woolf is a profoundly important formal model, and second, that Cusk is an ingenious successor, capable of taking something that was new to begin with and making it new again.

The focus of this chapter, then—2006's *Arlington Park*—represents one moment in a lengthy and fruitful literary successorship that lacks the marks of discipleship evident in Cunningham's deft homage and that serves as a test of high modernism's unspent innovatory energies. Like other contemporary novelists, Cusk asks how provocative Woolf's treatments of gender politics, psychological distress, and mental illness remain at a point in economic history (globalized late capitalism) and sociocultural history (after the collapse of Marxism; after third-wave feminism; in the midst of mass divorce, heightened awareness of climate change, and persistent sexual inequality) that Bloomsbury could only have imagined vaguely.

Cusk and her post-Bloomsburian peers arrange four textual and extratextual elements in various relations to one another: Bloomsbury's society; their aesthetic techniques for depicting it; our society; and aesthetic techniques, indebted to Bloomsbury, useful for depicting it. One pleasure of reading Cusk—as of reading McEwan—owes to her dexterity at adapting Woolfian (and other) forms. Cusk's *Arlington Park* and McEwan's *Atonement* each dazzle with their originality, despite their debt to Bloomsburian precursors. By contrast Smith's and Cunningham's tribute-novels can seem (willingly, self-consciously) modest. It is one thing to tell a new story with Woolfian, Forsterian, or Freudian flavors; it is another thing to re-tell a

Woolfian or Forsterian story with updated period costumes. Frederic Jameson was right—to continue this line of thinking—to decry postmodern pastiche.[12] Nothing reveals a decadent literary phase more than fawning tributes to the techniques, ideas, or sensibilities of a bygone milieu.

But rigorous avant gardism supplies only one criterion for gauging the value of a modernist-legatee text. This study proposes that Bloomsbury's searching treatments of intimacy in history, and their questions about whether intimate relations *progress* over time, supply precedents for their legatees that are as suggestive as their stylistic experiments. In light of these criteria, *On Beauty* and *The Hours* channel an important component of Bloomsburian thought—historical hopefulness—that *Arlington Park* does not. Their formal properties as homages aid them in this project.

Cusk's, Smith's, and Cunningham's novels each wonder how intimate relations have improved (or not), across the twentieth century, for spouses, lovers, friends, or parents and children. Smith and Cunningham explore whether any collateral damages have offset the gains of increased tolerance for interracial marriage and homosexuality, whether too much freedom has produced new pathologies. Their homages pose these questions effectively *because* they are homages. The jarring experience of seeing Margaret Schlegel's or Clarissa Dalloway's quandaries rebooted in a contemporary setting highlights how different our world is from that of 1910 or June 1923. Chapter 7 discusses how Cunningham's plan for *The Hours* was to "place Clarissa Dalloway in the world today, where women have more freedom than she had, and see what her life would be like."[13] That women have more freedom is a premise of his homage; the extent of this social progress adds poignancy to his characters' disappointments. Richard Brown's desertion by his mother Laura leaves him grieving a half century later in a world where housewives (particularly in New York) have wider horizons than Laura did in 1949; she was born out of time, by a generation or two. In a different storyline, notwithstanding her freedom and wealth, Clarissa Vaughan remains (to some degree) unhappy in her intimacies with her partner Sally, her friend and long-ago lover Richard, and her daughter Julia. How much social and political progress has been made, and how much can this progress enrich intimate life? Homages like Cunningham's and Smith's crystallize these questions, and their recognition of the gains won by progressive movements anchors them in twentieth-century history.

A Loss of Faith in Progress

It is less clear whether Cusk's novel, for all its stylistic virtuosity, is as well-anchored. "This is what it boiled down to, all of history," remarks *Arlington Park*'s narrator, indirectly rendering the character Juliet Randall's thoughts. "A place of purely material being, traversed by private thoughts."[14] Does Cusk endorse this evocative notion, or is it a symptom of Juliet's alienation? A counterclaim might run: "History—in particular when social justice advances—is a place of only *partly* material being, *transformed* (not merely traversed) by private thoughts that have been shared and made public." When Woolf expresses desire for a day in which the sentence "Chloe liked Olivia" is possible,[15] she hastens its arrival, according to my counterclaim. But *Arlington Park* is pointedly *not* about such transformation.

Juliet's despairing claim, which severs the "purely material" from the "private," might be savvier than my Whiggish counterclaim allows. When she first appears in the novel, Juliet awakens from a Kafkaesque nightmare in which a cockroach is embedded in her scalp and her husband Benedict doesn't help her. The dream provokes her epiphany (with which readers might not agree) that "she and Benedict were separate."[16] The previous night at dinner—apparently cowed by their boorish, chauvinistic host—Benedict had made a degrading remark about Juliet's breasts. The nightmare extends the motif of his abandoning her in the face of a menacing threat. As the novel elaborates, the spouses' "separateness"—their fraying intimacy—is a casualty of social and historical forces that influence, e.g., whose career their marriage prioritizes, and how they divide child-care duties. But these material facts are "traversed," to employ Juliet's parlance, by the most private matters: Juliet's dream and her interpretation of it. Cusk's depiction of Juliet's moment-by-moment experience (and that of other wives and mothers) enables readers to ask when historical forces move inward to enrich or impoverish intimacies. It also enables readers to ask whether intimacies can radiate outward to influence history, if lovers craft their relationships self-consciously (or fail to do so), either reenacting or revising gender scripts. Finally, Cusk's detailed depictions of inner life enable readers to ask when private thoughts "traverse" public events without affecting them. Such questions knit together the chapters of this volume that limn the shifting moods in which contemporary novelists, in dialog with Bloomsbury, conceptualize intimacy in history.

Modernist "Paralysis" and the "Stretched-Out" Twenty-First-Century Present

In the four decades since Lyotard's 1979 report on postmodernity, other prognosticators have also sensed a waning of metanarrative sanguinity. As discussed in Chapter 5, Salman Rushdie's 1985 essay "In God We Trust" laments that the "mechanization of society has created a mechanical politics" that unfortunately leaves questions of ultimate meaning to religious movements. Such politics promises only a narrow, economic "progress"—an "ever-expanding cake"—for the future, and even in this regard it disappoints. "Western political systems," Rushdie concludes, "both of the liberal-capitalist and communist variety, have simply failed to deliver progress."[17] (Rushdie's 1988 *Satanic Verses* explores whether an Anglophilic Indian man, Saladin Chamcha, tastes the fruits of Western progress in his transplantation to England, either in his marriage to an Englishwoman or in his professional life as a minority actor—and it returns a largely negative answer.)

Other theorists, anticipating or echoing Cusk, have combined analyses of late capitalist society with analyses of affect and intimate life. Lauren Berlant's 2011 *Cruel Optimism* and Sarah Ahmed's 2010 *The Promise of Happiness* each offer not-quite-Marxist accounts of false consciousness. Each volume's title names the form of consciousness under critique: "optimism" for Berlant and conventional ideas of "happiness" for Ahmed. At the material level, the realities belied by these ideological formations include a fraying social-democratic safety net (for Berlant), and social or familial systems that marginalize queer, female, or non-white subjects (for Ahmed). At the affective level, Berlant describes people's "incoherent mash"[18] of attitudes, feelings, and behaviors when the desiderata of their socially conditioned optimism fail to materialize. Ahmed argues that the concept of "happiness" serves normalizing, disciplinary functions, shaping "what coheres as a world" in ways that "justify oppression." In recent years, as a "happiness turn" has influenced scholarship, conventional wisdom has associated happiness with privilege: happy people tend to live in developed countries, to be wealthy, to belong to majority groups, and to be married. Critiquing the association of privilege with psychic well-being, Ahmed expresses the political unconscious—the "unthought"—of the "promise of happiness." She decries the figures of the "happy housewife," "happy slave," and heterosexual "domestic bliss," assembling in their place an "unhappiness archive."[19]

These theories of contemporary affect illuminate how *Arlington Park*'s largely unsympathetic female characters advance a social critique that runs through Cusk's oeuvre, even as she satirizes these same women. Embittered and rarely kind, *Arlington Park*'s wives and mothers are (in many cases) at once beneficiaries of class privilege and victims of systemic sexual bias. The novel's feminist critique is sharpened by their unattractive character traits, which—to invoke Tonie's lover from *Bradshaw Variations*—stem from "inequality." Berlant laments an "impasse" since the Reagan-Thatcher years. Drawn to fantasies of the good life even as they prove either unattainable or unfulfilling once attained, people experience the present as an "ongoing crisis:" a series of exhausting and irresolvable challenges from financial strain to elusive work-life balance and faltering intimacies.[20]

In *Arlington Park*, Juliet's marriage is an ongoing crisis. She can never be happy as long as she and Benedict move from house to house in service of his highly successful career as a high school teacher while she feeds on the crumbs of part-time labor and a monthly Literary Club meeting that she feels to be her sole chance for self-actualization. She can never be happy as long as, in her words, she has to "spend her life looking after Benedict, buying food for him, washing his clothes." She cannot help being bitter as long as Benedict shirks the task of disciplining their children, distracting himself by listening to CDs of early English composers. And the toxic dynamic of male privilege seems destined to reproduce itself when Juliet reprimands her son Barnaby, "In this house … we don't have servants" and he retorts, "We do. You're our servant."[21] In Juliet's experience, marriage falls far short of the ideal of "intimacy as democracy" (see the Introduction, page 15). It does not enable her to "develop her potentialities," nor grant her a full share in "determining the conditions of [spousal] association," nor fully to "expand" her individual "economic opportunity."[22]

Admittedly, Juliet can be self-dramatizing: her decision to cut all her hair off, for example, has a touch of the juvenile. And readers might question whether she was destined for greatness before marriage ground her down; in fact, she herself wonders if her success as a student and career as a teacher prove "merely" that she was "good at going to school."[23] Nonetheless, the novel's design supports her many variations on the thought "All men are murderers." Ruminating on her unfulfilled promise, she elaborates upon the metaphor. "My husband, Benedict, murdered me. He was very gentle about it; it didn't really hurt at all. In fact, I hardly knew it was happening."[24]

Clarissa Dalloway, by contrast, never formulates such a thought about her husband Richard, though some critics see her marriage as imprisoning.[25] Nor does Clarissa characterize Peter Walsh as a murderer, though she does compare his interruption of her kiss with Sally to "running one's face against a granite wall in the darkness."[26] Cusk's wives have more insurgent affects, in contrast to Clarissa's relative quiescence—her "false consciousness," to read *Mrs Dalloway* from a radical angle—though their insurgent energies have no collective outlet and often express themselves in outbursts of personal nastiness.

Juliet's "present" promises to remain "stretched out," to proceed with Berlant's terminology, for as long as her children remain young, if not indefinitely. *Arlington Park*'s many resonances with *Mrs Dalloway* encourage readers to ask what else—in intersexual relations for post-Victorian Britons—remains stretched out. Clarissa's June 1923 day does not, for the most part, belong to Juliet's "present," nor does Barnaby's possible future marriage—during which one hopes he will not see his wife as a "servant." But sexual inequality has extended long beyond Queen Victoria's death, despite modernist critiques of gender essentialism (such as *Mrs Dalloway*'s) and multiple waves of feminism. When Juliet vaguely justifies her haircut to her Literary Club students by saying of her boredom with life, "You realize you're waiting for something that's never going to happen,"[27] readers can extrapolate a larger message: that many women have spent decades waiting for something that hasn't happened yet. If they have been optimistic that marriage and parenthood would be more fulfilling—not to mention more "democratic"—then their optimism has been cruel.

As a *Mrs Dalloway* legatee, *Arlington Park* handles form more deftly than does *The Hours*. But Cusk's novel expresses such severe disbelief in progress that Cunningham's novel might seem wiser, given how it balances its assumption that progress has transpired with depictions of problems that progress has not (perhaps cannot) solved, and others that progress might *create*. (Clarissa gets to live with Sally in *The Hours*, rather than with a Richard or Peter isotope, but it's not clear that this fulfilled opportunity makes her happy. Richard Brown has lived his adult life as a gay man—a freedom of which his 1950s childhood offered scant promise—but his freedom has led to his contraction of AIDS. His mother struck out for freedom in a way that few '50s housewives did—abandoning her husband and child—and her choice burdened Richard with lifelong sadness.) *Arlington Park* might seem guilty of thematic decadence: modernist masters including Joyce have been celebrated for depicting alienation and paralysis,[28] but what can a twenty-first-century novelist contribute by tilling the same soil? Are London suburbanites, circa 2006, *paralyzed*, whether individually or collectively, as Dubliners were circa 1904? Praising Cusk, Jane Smiley claims that American novels of social critique often diagnose suburban despair, but "diagnostics ... imply a possible cure. Rachel Cusk is not as weak-minded as that. [*Arlington Park*'s] characters are stuck."[29] Its admiring tone notwithstanding, perhaps Smiley's review pinpoints how Cusk rehearses a theme that was fresher in early twentieth-century literature and more pertinent to early twentieth-century society.

Berlant's terminology suggests how Cusk might *not* re-till modernist soil, how her female characters are not constrained in exactly the ways that Clarissa Dalloway or Joyce's *Dubliners* were, but are unfree nonetheless. As mentioned, Berlant says that victims of ongoing crises suffer from an "incoherent mash" of depression, dissociation, and other attitudes.[30] The focal characters of *Arlington Park*'s five storylines are both distinct individuals and collective representatives of a middle-class female plight. On individual levels, their "mashes" of feelings are more or less coherent, and their "crises" take different forms, some of which could strike readers as trivial. But as a collective psyche they are affectively "incoherent"—or at least varied and partly unknowable—in illuminating ways, and they reveal a crisis in spousal relations and sexuality as pitched as anything depicted by Lawrence. The crisis extends beyond the bourgeois couple: fathers' intimacies with their small children are attenuated at best; mothers' intimacies are riven with ennui, bitterness, and tension; and women fail to develop satisfying friendships with one another during their long stretches of unemployed hours.

Worse yet, pathologies are so "ongoing" that they extend through generations—albeit with variations—and not only in the case of Barnaby aggressively claiming the male privilege that his father Benedict enjoys more passively. Christine, a focal character in three of *Arlington Park*'s eight chapters, reproduces the cynicism that informs her mother, Viv's, pathologies concerning class, race, and gender. First, in an inebriated phone conversation with her daughter, the self-pitying Viv complains, clearly not for the first time, about growing up in an orphanage.[31] Being her mother's daughter, Christine is terrified of slipping into a lower class, she is jealous of her acquaintance Maisie and determined to "neutralize" her because Maisie comes from London,[32] and she trumpets the virtues of Arlington Park. (But whereas Clarissa Dalloway's internal pep talk—"What a lark! What a plunge!"—may succeed in lifting her mood, neither Christine's companions nor Christine herself believes her claim that Arlington Park's residents "may not be the wealthiest people you've ever met, or the most famous and important, but believe me, the people I see here every day are the most diverse, interesting, courageous group of people you'll find anywhere!"[33])

Next, Viv makes a racist complaint about Asians, to which Christine responds with banter (perhaps, in her defense, because she is busy preparing food and lacks the energy to confront her difficult parent). Soon later, Joe one-ups the two women, extending the motif of the prejudiced and bullying husband introduced with the character of Matthew Milford, Juliet's chauvinistic host. With pride, Joe shows the male guests a wooden knickknack of a military figurine decapitating a kneeling dark-skinned man.[34] Christine not only reincarnates some of her mother's prejudices, but she seems habituated to them in a cohabitant and perhaps attracted to them in a man.

Finally, Viv anticipates her daughter's unhappiness within her marriage and nuclear family, as well as her jaded attitude toward families in general. Viv complains that her deceased husband Larry "took" most of her time from her (echoing Juliet's complaint about "looking after" Benedict) and never let her on his boat. She blames his selfishness on his having been an only child, but the novel depicts many men as selfish, whether or not they have siblings: Larry is like Benedict, Barnaby, and Matthew Milford in doing as he likes. After Christine gets off the phone with her mother, Joe echoes Viv's description of Larry by accusing Viv of being "completely selfish," talking only about herself, and nagging Larry about his boat, and he says that Christine "isn't like that" because she values his and her "separate lives." But Christine's reply—that "separate lives" means him surfing for the weekend while she cares for the children—suggests that Joe exploits the same prerogatives that Larry did.[35] (The maritime motif linking Larry's boat to Joe's surfing reinforces the men's commonality.) No wonder the grieving Viv tells her daughter "I always imagined that families were loving things," prompting Christine's cynical reply "You could be forgiven for imagining that" and Viv's admonition "It's all one way in a family, Christine. It's all selfishness and greed. Don't let it happen to you."[36]

Viv is intoxicated enough that it's unclear what she wants not to "happen" to Christine: a family of any kind or merely its "selfishness and greed." But in either case, the warning is late, hence ineffectual. Christine is joined to a selfish man (not that she is a model of altruism). Cynicism is the common affect among Christine's "mash" of inheritances from her mother: racial prejudice, class insecurity, and sexual grievance. Through portraits of families like the Lanhams, *Arlington Park* has a lot to say about broken intimacies and the ongoing crises and pathologies they precipitate, but little to say about healthier, more democratic intimacies.

Woolf complains in *A Room of One's Own* about a "jerk" in *Jane Eyre* when the narrator interrupts the story with the phrase "Anybody may blame me who likes" and proceeds to lament women's homebound lives devoid of "action." Woolf says that such "indignation" prevents Brontë from expressing her genius "whole and entire."[37] But indignation was not foreign to Woolf: no reader can miss it in *Mrs Dalloway*'s treatments of Drs Holmes and Bradshaw. Is Woolf's genius not "whole and entire" in these depictions? *Arlington Park* confronts readers with similar questions about a writer's "genius" and her "indignation." (Cusk has earned critical plaudits throughout her career and such intense praise for her *Outline* trilogy that she seems to have secured a place in the canon.[38]) Notwithstanding the conspicuous flaws in the mothers and wives who inhabit Arlington Rise, it is difficult to discern authorial distance from their rage at the patriarchy. Just as Cusk's evocation of "ongoing crises" extends and renews modernist legacies, so too her handling of tone in *Arlington Park* tests how Woolfian feminism can be reconfigured six and a half decades after Woolf's death. If progress for middle-class women has been chimerical and suburbs in the early twenty-first century remain a hellscape, then the tone linking *Arlington Park*'s various narratives—the cast of mind linking its protagonists—may be Cusk's best way to express her embittered genius "entire." The Woolfian art of indirection and the Woolfian ideal of incandescence can enrich Cusk's novel in other ways, even if its narrator does not aspire to the "androgynous mind" that is "resonant and porous" because it "does not think specially or separately of sex."[39]

While there is no "jerk" in *Arlington Park* between descriptions of events and an intrusively editorializing narrator, Maisie Carrington's dissociative states punctuated by fits of rage do indicate deep wells of feeling that can only be expressed imperfectly and at inopportune times. Maisie and her husband Dom have moved from London to Arlington Park at her prodding, and she finds herself "more frightened" in their new locale than in the City, although there's "nothing in their situation ... she could say she hadn't chosen."[40] Thus the narrator comments ironically on women's culpability in their own unhappiness, or the impossibility of happiness, in keeping with Christine's rhetorical question "Don't you think we all just want to have it both ways? We want our secure homes and our husbands and our lovely holidays ... and yet sometimes ... I think, God, I could just bring all this down." (In a Lawrentian repetition, she goes on, "I could just bring it all down around me."[41]) Maisie's conflicting desires, if they parallel Christine's, might explain why she can be so dissociative as not to respond during Christine's rant against political correctness, then scream "stupid fucking bitch" at a parking-lot driver whom she feels has endangered Stephanie's small son.[42] Such conflicting desires can partially explain the "fundamental sadness," the lost "power of renewal," and the "nameless dissatisfaction"[43] that she lyrically diagnoses in herself—in language that could apply to other women in *Arlington Park*, not to mention those in *The Hours*. (Like Juliet, Maisie works part time—in her case, three days a week at a postproduction company. Like Benedict, her husband Dom works full time and—perhaps for this reason—expects Maisie to do most of the childcare.) But deeper causes are needed to explain why Dom feels it necessary to tell her, on their way to dinner at the Lanhams', "just don't get angry with everyone," and why she responds "I *am* angry with everyone. I worry that if I don't get angry I'll die. So maybe I should just die. Maybe you want me to die."[44]

Such deeper causes likely lie in the history of abuse that she feels she has endured from her parents. The descriptions of this maltreatment are vague enough to leave readers uncertain whether Maisie is self-pitying or if her grievance is just. (Like Christine's mother, Viv, Maisie's parents are cruel, but how abusive they were is unknowable to the reader.) Maisie's behavior toward her own six- and four-year-old daughters, however, is not left vague, for example when she throws her six-year-old, Elise's, lunch box at the kitchen wall, "where it burst like a firework," then screams at her daughters "You're ruining my life."[45] Regardless of how abusive Maisie's parents were, the novel's pictures of intergenerational familial pathologies are among its strongest expressions of incredulity toward the idea of progress for women, families, and romantic intimacy. Neither Berlant nor Ahmed, despite their skepticism about progress, paints pictures as harrowing as *Arlington Park*'s depictions of Christine's and Maisie's unhappiness following on the heels of their parents' unhappiness.

Like overlapping circles in a Venn diagram, *Arlington Park*'s five focalized women (Juliet, Solly, Christine, Maisie, and Amanda Clapp) share enough affect, and in some cases recall Clarissa Dalloway in similar enough ways, to illuminate one another. But they are also distinct from one another, and they also recall Woolf's heroine each in their own way. Amanda ponders "her heart that had no love in it"[46]—as well she might. When her son Eddie says "I love you, Mummy," she can only call him a "silly boy." He makes her think of "failure and meaninglessness," though he's never depicted being disobedient or mean-spirited. Similarly, when Maisie's daughter, with a trembling hand, gives her a note reading "I love you Mummy love Elsie," all she can do is rebuke the child for not being dressed. Amanda's self-scrutiny also recalls Juliet, to whom it was "unclear ... whether she could love anybody."[47] Taken individually, each of these three women of *Arlington Park* seems blameworthy for her lack of love: Amanda and Maisie are bad moms, and Juliet is an ineffective parent to her male child. But taken collectively, their shortcoming indicts their social milieu as well, including its low parenting expectations for fathers. Especially in the case of Amanda, whose Gran accuses her of being "cold," this purported failure to love—partly an excessive self-critique, partly a just accusation—recalls Clarissa Dalloway, who for decades recalls Peter Walsh's claim that she is "cold, heartless, a prude"[48] and who worries that she has failed her husband (perhaps especially in a sexual sense). Like Cunningham's novel, *Arlington Park* archives women's "coldness," much as Ahmed archives women's unhappiness: as an index of the exclusion and inequity entailed in roles that remain so gendered as to seem almost Victorian.

Love is not the only transcendent force from which Amanda is alienated. Death, too, largely eludes her powers of intuition. When Amanda's sister Susannah informs her on the phone that Gran has died, Amanda thinks that "death had entered her kitchen"—inconveniently, as she's preparing for her guests—recalling how news of Septimus's passing leads Clarissa to feel death "in the middle" of her party.[49] But Clarissa's intimation highlights her sensitivity, her powers of intuition. By contrast, when Eddie says that he saw Granny in the garden, Amanda tells him that "Granny can't have been in the garden [because] she died this morning."[50] Amanda's lack of imaginative sympathy for her sensitive son typifies her unkindness.

Even Amanda, though, can garner sympathy when her plight is seen in conjunction with that of other women. She had won a Manager of the Year award at her recruiting firm, before marrying and relocating to the suburbs—recalling Juliet and Maisie, who also sacrificed their careers. When Susannah addresses her as "Mandy," Amanda thinks of her lost maiden name, Mandy Clapp, much as Woolf's heroine ponders the subsumption of her old identity in the appellation "Mrs Dalloway."[51] Marriage seems to have swallowed Amanda. Hence, even when she attains an object of her fantasy—a large house with a gaudily large kitchen—its promise of happiness proves dubious; her optimism proves to have been cruel. (One guest calls her kitchen "enormous," another says "you could fit a jumbo jet in here," and "in that moment Amanda knew that her kitchen was too large."[52] As Ahmed remarks, "There can be nothing more terrifying than getting what you want, because it is at this moment that you face what you want."[53]) Even having gotten her house, and even though she spends portions of each day driving her clean spacious silver Toyota—triggering fantasies of grandeur and control—Amanda frequently plunges into panic attacks, driving around "weeping, sweating ... her feet shaking on the pedals,"[54] recalling Maisie's abrupt transitions from dissociation into rage.

From worries about emotional "coldness" to intuitions of death, from a wife's lost maiden name (and identity) to dinner parties where attendees might not connect with one another, does *Arlington Park* borrow too much from *Mrs Dalloway*? In spite of whatever variations it plays on modernist motifs of alienation and paralysis, such as the important point that middle-class twenty-first-century women have more cause for alienation than men, does it lapse into a comfortable derivativeness? Paradoxically, *Arlington Park*'s best defense against such a charge lies in a further elaboration of its intertextuality. The foregoing paragraphs have discussed its thematic dialog with *Mrs Dalloway* (though not exhaustively); the following ones will focus on its technical similarities to and distinctions from other modernist precursor-texts. Modernist newness, after all, lay more in its form than in its content; in order to "remake it new,"[55] *Arlington Park* would have to do what I explain above Cusk's *Outline* trilogy doing: learn from Woolf's techniques without repeating them.

Post-Woolfian Technique: Twenty-First-Century Forms of (Dis)Connection

Assuming such a challenge hardly marks Cusk as unusual among her contemporaries. In the decade prior to 2006, the literary world paid frequent tribute to *Mrs Dalloway*'s and *To the Lighthouse*'s form and content. Writers including Cunningham, McEwan (in both *Saturday* and *Atonement*, with its one-day first section), Robin Lipincott, and Jeanette Winterson honored Woolf with allusions and arguably critical revisions.[56] *Arlington Park*'s critics have diligently examined its relations to *Mrs Dalloway*; I draw on their work in assembling the following five-part list of its "neo-modernist" techniques, to borrow Monica Latham's label.[57] First, Cusk's novel can also be classified as a short-story cycle—a form more suited than a linear tale to evoking social atomization. Second, *Arlington Park* employs weather—non-divinized but, teasingly, almost transcendent—as a structuring motif. In so doing, it dialogs with Joyce, Lawrence, and multiple novels by Woolf. Third, it counterposes clock time—all too human and a reminder of our mortality—to the weather, perhaps to deflate any hope that wind and rain offer paths to transcendence. Next, its one-day structure mediates between hints of transcendence and reminders of constraints, on the one hand underscoring a day's mundaneness and on the other hand excavating a day's richness. Joyce and Woolf had demonstrated how one-day tales can be plotless by the lights of Victorian realism but can contain capacious backstories, endowing twenty-four ordinary hours with the archetypal weight of a whole life, or (in *Ulysses*' case) with the mythical weight of lives past and present. Finally, *Arlington Park* culminates with a dinner party, an ideal vehicle for expressing disillusionment with current mores. By experimenting with multiple subgeneric precedents, Cusk carves a niche for her individual talent within several modernist traditions.

I borrow the "short-story cycle" categorization from Elke D'hoker, who sees the form as suited to exploring the "tension between commonality and difference." The "gaps," "non-sequitirs," and "ironic juxtpositions" among the stories, D'hoker believes, underscore this tension without resolving it either into the feeling that all upper-middle-class housewives think alike or into the feeling that meaningful collective experience is untenable.[58] D'hoker's label distinguishes *Arlington Park* from a short story *volume* like *Dubliners*. Joyce's stories also explore commonality and difference; they link characters across stories with the help of motifs like paralysis; but readers expect gaps between stories in a volume more than between chapters in a novel, even one featuring an ensemble cast. Like an adventurous film editor, Cusk cross cuts among subplots, underscoring how alienation can (symbolically) link people who live in proximity to one another.

Such a "cycle," with gaps and connections among its storylines, and a loosely linear handling of time, might appeal to a novelist who follows Woolf's suggestion in

"Modern Fiction" that "if a writer were a free man and not a slave, if he could write what he chose, not what he must ... there would be no plot ... in the accepted style."[59] Nonetheless, with its variations on other modernists' weather motifs, *Arlington Park* resembles a sort of "accepted style" for modernists. Joyce, Lawrence, and Woolf provide models of how weather can, variously, symbolize a transcendent and benevolent force, symbolize an amoral and perhaps destructive force, or offer a screen onto which fallible characters project their changeable moods.

The snow in Joyce's "The Dead," like the rain and wind in *Arlington Park*, is "general."[60] Arguably, it provides a scalar contrast to individual human predicaments: Gabriel's disappointments look less significant from a broad meteorological perspective. But alternatively, the snow symbolizes human predicaments, from the coldness of Gabriel's marriage (given Gretta's passion for Michael Furey) to the general decline of Irish culture. Likewise, *Arlington Park*'s dynamic weather initially seems to provide a scalar contrast to the paralysis suffered by many characters, almost mocking their torpor by virtue of its superhuman energy. But ultimately it becomes all too human, either emblematizing their depression or externalizing the passion that they would like to unleash in themselves.

Lawrence offers, in part, a more Romantic model of nature as a life-giver than Joyce does. Cusk's aforementioned Introduction says that *The Rainbow*'s "evocation of the cyclical harmony of man and beast and land" in its opening pages is "among the most memorable in English literature." But this "harmony" is not wholly benign: Cusk quotes the passage in which the Brangwen sisters "looked out from the heated, blind intercourse of farm life, to [the wider horizons of] the spoken world beyond." Whereas the farm imprisons these sisters, bourgeois civilization imprisons the residents of Arlington Rise. In the face of suburban ennui, it is doubtful that Cusk can long entertain a Romantic conceit of nature as life-restoring.

More than Joyce or Lawrence, Woolf provides models, from *To the Lighthouse* (1927) to *The Waves* (1931) to *The Years* (1937)—of how Cusk can use weather for a range of tonal and stylistic purposes.[61] *To the Lighthouse*'s "Time Passes" section disrupts linear time, mentioning Mrs Ramsay's death after it happens, and mentioning Prue and Andrew Ramsay's deaths in brief, bracketed sentences. With its "nights ... full of wind and destruction," its "stray airs, advance guards of great armies" that "blustered" into the Ramsays' summerhouse, and with its brisk mention of the war blowing up twenty or thirty young men, "Time Passes" subordinates human aspirations and architecture to larger, non-anthropomorphized, perhaps amoral forces.[62]

Woolf had several provocative designations for *The Waves*, her most radically experimental novel.[63] In a diary entry, she called it "an abstract mystical eyeless book: a playpoem." The term "eyeless" suggests that it lacks both the concrete social observation often associated with the novelist's documentary "eye," and any discernible centering consciousness (or "I"), whether first- or third-person, omniscient or limited in perspective. While *The Waves* contains little that is traditionally associated with the novel form, it does resemble a play in that it contains six "speakers" (a term its critics use in place of "characters"),[64] each of whom delivers soliloquies. It resembles a poem thanks to the recurring sound of its titular waves. (Woolf said that she wanted to write "to a rhythm.") While the waves, by themselves, are not a direct isotope of the rain and wind in *Arlington Park*, in combination with the sun and other aspects of the climate in Woolf's playpoem, they do spur Cusk's imagination.

Woolf signals the importance of weather by using it as an archetypal framing device. *The Waves* contains nine sections (or chapters), each of which is introduced by a brief italicized scene beginning with the words "the sun" (e.g., "the sun had not yet risen" prior to the first section and "now the sun had sunk" prior to the final section). In service of rhythm and musicality, Woolf named these scenes "interludes"—a term that has been applied to *Arlington Park*'s similar use of weather.[65] *The Waves*' nine interludes describe a single day, with noon falling in the fifth interlude. As the day progresses, so do the speakers: the first chapter shows them as small children and the final one as older adults. The fifth interlude seems to track the sun's path not only in the six speakers' surrounds, but also in southern Europe, the Middle East, and the Far East. As the "Time Passes" section of *To the Lighthouse* demonstrates, Woolf liked to use meteorology to broaden narrative perspective, from intimate concerns to political ones, and even into something non-human. In fact, *Jacob's Room* (1922) had already done something similar, and the locales evoked in *The Waves*' fifth interlude call attention—however obliquely—to the spread of the British empire and the rise of fascism.

To the Lighthouse and especially *The Waves* are key precursors for *Arlington Park*'s use of weather. But *The Years*, which reprises numerous techniques from these earlier Woolf novels, may also have been suggestive to Cusk. *The Years* chronicles the Pargiter family; its eleven chapters are set from 1880 to the "present day" circa 1937; each chapter's opening sentence mentions weather and/or the time of year. The first chapter is set in an "uncertain spring,"[66] and the concluding one on a summer evening, roughly recalling *The Waves* in its archetypal temporality, with spring suggesting beginnings and evening suggesting endings. As Tonya Krouse explains, not only in the chapters' opening sentences, but within the body of each chapter, weather "intrudes upon the plot," linking episodes divided by time and place.[67] It challenges readers to apportion their attention in unfamiliar ways, and it eschews symbolic formulas. In the first chapter, for example, as the matriarch Rose Pargiter is dying, the rain temporarily evokes grief—especially that of Rose's daughter, Delia, whose point of view is focalized. But soon later, Delia detaches herself by "dispassionately" observing rain sliding down the windowpane.[68] Nor does Delia's perspective monopolize weather as *The Years* continues; rain and wind couple with and decouple from other characters' thoughts and feelings.

It is debatable what, if any, political significance inheres in *The Years*' weather. Krouse claims that, rather than using it as a strict contrast to human concerns (in a nature/culture binary), Woolf uses it to unsettle all binaries, a gesture consistent with her feminist and antifascist politics. Such an interpretation is tempting for readers seeking to link Woolf and Cusk, given the latter's feminism and anti-authoritarianism. But in order to understand Woolf's importance to her successor, it is less useful to fix a meaning for *The Years*' weather than to understand how ambiguous, broadly suggestive, and thematically crucial nature and the climate are in many of Woolf's works, with their interpersonal, political, and mystical dimensions.

Arlington Park builds on Joycean, Lawrentian, and especially Woolfian precedents in employing weather as a unifying (but partly opaque) motif. The novel opens with a "prologue" that poetically describes rain falling with inhuman, even superhuman force. Four human-centered chapters follow, then an "interlude"[69] in which "fresh wind" blows,[70] then four final human-centered chapters, before the wind returns at novel's end. In the prologue, says the narrator, rain falls "joyously" on parkland, without explaining the reason for its joy. Sleepers hear its "thunderous noise," which "penetrates their dreams" like "uproarious applause." Before the interlude, the narrator interrupts a storyline to repeat this motif, explaining, "A thunderous noise began to beat at [Solly's] window in the dark, a deafening, joyous, uncontrollable sound like the sound of applause."[71]

Such images offer powerful temptations to read weather positively, but its connotations shift in subsequent scenes. When Juliet stands by her sitting-room door, "the rain [falls] at the window. It was so grey, so grey and unavailing!" explains the narrator, in a mood opposite to the prologue's "joyous" storm. The rain "felt like sorrow: it seemed to preclude every possibility, every other shade of feeling."[72] Juliet makes this observation—not an omniscient narrator—but her grief is typical of many women in the novel: her simile applies collectively. There is much to grieve in *Arlington Park*, from spousal dissatisfaction to many women's sense of something "irretrievably lost," to describe Solly's feelings as her pregnancy nears its end.[73] Cusk's suburbanites need emancipation from their mind-forged shelters—unlike the Brangwen sisters, who live *too* nakedly under the sun—but it is not clear that the rain will do more than externalize their feeling of stultification.

The wind in *Arlington Park*'s interlude and final pages, like the rain in its prologue, teases readers with a promise of rejuvenation. A "cold, fresh wind" blows into the Lanhams' house, making "bits of paper fly off the table … They somersaulted, they made loop-the-loops as they glided to the floor."[74] But *Arlington Park*'s final two chapters are filtered through Christine's point of view; this sense of nature's restorative power is as unstable as anything she thinks, and liable to transform into its opposite when her mood shifts.

Christine's penchants for projection and radical mood swings fill the novel. At one point, she asks Maisie "What are you so worried for?" but the question seems self-directed, given her earlier (semi-rhetorical) questions "Why do we all *worry* so much?" and "What are we so frigging worried about?"[75] Her anxieties are multiple, from aging (with its "flabby tits"[76]) to losing the material comforts and social status of Arlington Park and reverting to the shabby insecurity of her Redbourne childhood. She recognizes how "lucky" she is to have escaped Redbourne[77] but doesn't want to feel "guilty" for her fortune, and when confronted with others' ghastly misfortune, she says she doesn't mind if "it's something people have brought on themselves."[78] She tries to allay this anxiety and guilt by insisting that she and her friends "have some fun"[79] or that she and her houseguests "push the table against the wall and dance,"[80] but these forced attempts at spontaneous joy don't prevent the return (within the same paragraph) of a violently bitter mood in which she "could just bring all this down."[81] In fact, far from *preventing* her misanthropy (reminiscent of Birkin in *Women in Love*), her bouts of mania may *enable* it. Christine's interwoven neuroses—her tendency to project her moods onto people or objects, and the radical instability of those moods—counsel readers against seeking too much cause for hope in somersaulting bits of paper. Even when *Arlington Park*'s weather seems to express energy and joy, it may do so only in the form of an unrealizable fantasy or the externalization of a character's brief mania. *Arlington Park* is not a tale of progress or rebirth, at least not manifestly.

Moreover, any teasing promises of transcendence held out by the weather, or by Eddie's mystical attunement to Gran's death (reminiscent of Clarissa's attunement to Septimus's suicide) are contained by the novel's reiterations of the finitude of clock time. Woolf's original title for *Mrs Dalloway* was "The Hours," which Cunningham claims as his title, and which Cusk employs as a motif. Juliet thinks about the "leaden hour" after school ends, recalling *Mrs Dalloway*'s refrain about "the leaden circles" of Big Ben's chimes "dissolv[ing] in the air." Griping inwardly about parenthood, Amanda thinks that Eddie is the "stultifying noon of her life's day" and that "he merely went through the hours ahead of her."[82] Cusk's novel, like Woolf's, repeatedly mentions the time of day, emphasizing the regimentation of mothers' schedules as they transport children to and from school, shop, and prepare to hostess.[83] Therefore, when Maisie feels, of an evening, that she has "lived a century" since she saw her husband that morning; when Maisie dreads that "she would always be walking up these stairs and that this moment would endure for ever"; or when Amanda envisions the "unrelieved expanses" of the unfortunate Liz Connelly's days, with "the prospect of time going on and on,"[84] the women's stretched-out experience of time entails no *transcendence* of the present, nor of sex and gender. Rather, as Cusk remarks in a 2009 *Guardian* article, "while women's lives have altered in some respects [over the last generation], in others they have remained much the same." Where biological sex is concerned, "if a woman's body signifies anything, it is that repetition is more powerful than change." Where gender roles are concerned, "Oppression, being a type of relationship, can never be resolved, only reconfigured." Hence, "'women's writing' might be another name for the book of repetition."[85] If the repetitive rhythms of farm life constrained the Brangwen sisters, then the repetitive rhythms of suburban marriage and parenthood— on top of the biological rhythms of pregnancy and its aftermath—prove scarcely less constraining to the women of Arlington Park.

If Cusk's characters are to achieve transcendence, therefore, they must find it *through* the dailiness of daily life, with all its gendered drudgery, not in a revelatory weather event, nor *in rejection* of suburban routine. The modernist one-day novel has a history of exploring transcendence through ordinariness. As one critic remarks, one-day novels rarely if ever "confine themselves strictly" to events taking place on that day.[86] Amanda's poetic lament about her "life's day" with its "stultifying noon" clues readers into the synecdochal quality of dailiness in *Arlington Park*. In *Mrs Dalloway*, Clarissa's trip to buy flowers, her hosting of a party that assembles intimates of decades ago, and her attunement to her doppelganger Septimus all suggest how dailiness can be a vehicle for going beyond a day. Just as Cusk learned from Woolf, Woolf learned from Joyce (most obviously from *Ulysses*, but perhaps also from "The Dead") how to derive, from the temporal constraints of a one-day story, a vast psychological landscape replete with memories that intrude unpredictably upon the present. And Cusk's precursors do not dispense with the logic of plot—of Cause X preceding Effect

Y. Rather, as Chapter 7 explains in detailing Clarissa's and Septimus's life stories, these authors condense backstories into fragmentary recollections or concise summaries of relevant events—so that the present can breathe more fully.

Joyce's and Woolf's genius as one-day taletellers also lay in their art of indirection. In "The Dead," as in *Mrs Dalloway*, readers learn about one character's traumatic loss from another character's point of view, and they are left groping for a sense of the event's ramifications, though it is clear that the present will never fully transcend the past: the one day being narrated is an unfolding of other days from long ago. In Joyce's story, Gretta Conroy is moved to tears by her chance hearing of a song that she associates with Michael Furey, a man who died in their youth ("for me," she believes[87]) and whom she loved more than she and her husband Gabriel have ever loved one another. Joyce's readers know little that they cannot glean from Gabriel's consciousness, and Gabriel can only imagine the depth of Gretta's long-unexpressed feelings for Michael. Yet readers intuit Gretta's interior world, and Joyce's narrative method evokes a strain of dissatisfaction and sadness in the Conroys' marriage more poignantly than could a linear tale that employed fewer omissions.

In *Mrs Dalloway*, to indulge a brief comparison, readers learn of the death of Clarissa's sister, Sylvia, in a brief portion of one of Peter Walsh's extended meditations on Clarissa[88]—a stray thought as easily forgotten as *To the Lighthouse*'s mentions of Prue and Andrew's deaths. How much should we imagine that this loss has affected Clarissa? Given the centrality of female-female intimacy to her nostalgia, the answer could be: quite a lot. Given the importance of Thoby Stephen's death to his sister Virginia—and given Thoby's thinly disguised appearance in *The Waves* as Percival, who dies and whom other characters think about—the answer could be: very much. For Clarissa as for Woolf, the loss of a sibling might never cease to be a burden. But *Mrs Dalloway*'s readers cannot know. Woolf's novel is stingier than Joyce's story with information about the impact of this long-ago tragedy.[89]

At first glance, Cusk's one-day short-story cycle might not seem to invoke its backstory with such ingenious indirection. Several women give up careers for marriage and motherhood; without needing details about those careers, readers get Cusk's point. But other elements of *Arlington Park*'s treatment of the past's lingering effects and of a life that *might have been*—including its use of *Mrs Dalloway* as a resource for these themes—are indeed sly. To claim that Solly Kerr-Leigh's first name sounds like Sally Seton's first name might be an interpretive stretch. But the lodger Paola plays a role in Solly's imagination similar to Sally's role in Clarissa's mind; Paola obliquely incorporates the theme of same-sex longing into a novel that one critic faults for being heteronormative.[90] Shaking Paola's hand upon their initial meeting "revealed a softer, more receptive surface" of Solly's, as if "Paola's hand had spoken to her." Part of Sally's fascination for Clarissa lies in her exoticism—she has French blood—just as Paola's Italian background intrigues Solly, who finds her "stylish." The young Sally also attracts Clarissa with her daring: she smokes cigars, reads Plato, and speaks of marriage as a "catastrophe."[91] Likewise, Paola intrigues and perhaps attracts Solly because she has given up her law practice and left her son behind in Italy with his father. Solly, as mentioned, is carrying her fourth child. Pregnancy causes her an "intense feeling of shame" and makes her think of litter and rubbish. When the fourth child turns out to be a girl, she thinks with relief that "another boy might have sunk her," even though—having birthed so many children already—she cares about this one less than the others.[92] (This connects her to a motif in *Arlington Park* of women's discomfort with their middle-aged, pregnant, or post-pregnancy bodies, complemented by another motif of their husbands' more pleasingly shaped middle-aged bodies.[93]) When Paola is out of the house, Solly opens her wardrobe and fingers the "fine cloth" of her "beautiful ruffled shirt," looks at Paola's bottles and jars in a mahogany chest, and removes lace garments from a drawer, compared to which her own threadbare jeans seem a "pitiful remnant of her femininity." Solly thinks of her husband Martin as a "hands-on father," but he's never home. By contrast, when Solly is in labor pain and Martin is stuck in traffic, Paola feeds her children, plays a game with them, puts them to bed, and gives Solly a wonderful herbal remedy.[94] Readers cannot know, and perhaps Solly herself cannot articulate, what she has "irretrievably lost" to marriage and motherhood—which is likely *not* a chance to love a woman, as Clarissa might have loved Sally. But Cusk pays *Mrs Dalloway* a tribute as rich as it is subtle in depicting a day in the life of one of her five protagonists, during which Solly enters a room not quite her own and contacts (at least in her own mind) a realm of feminine possibilities lost in the heteronormative, patriarchal world of the bourgeois family.

Beyond even its one-day format, however, *Arlington Park*'s most extensive tribute to Woolf, and most extensive engagement with a structuring device frequent in high modernism, is its dinner-party motif, which is as crucial to the novel's design as the symbolically ambiguous weather. The sub-subgenre of a *one-day dinner-party novel* might seem so narrow as to be of little critical value. But given that "The Dead," *Mrs Dalloway*, and *To the Lighthouse* all revolve around formal meals, the importance of such occasions in a novel as intertextual as *Arlington Park* might be illuminated by these precursor-texts. *Arlington Park*'s dinner parties, to Cusk's credit, do not merely recapitulate a Woofian device. Unlike Woolf (and Joyce), this twenty-first-century novelist thoroughly desacralizes such gatherings and largely refuses the consolation of nostalgia.

All three precursor-texts treat social gatherings with a combination of nostalgia, melancholy, and a keen receptiveness to beauty. Characters' biblical names (e.g., Michael, Gabriel, and Lily, a flower associated with the Archangel Gabriel) endow Joyce's story with gravitas, just as Homeric parallels do for *Ulysses*. The Misses Morkans' annual dance—the occasion on which "The Dead" is centered—has a long history; its attendees have complexly interlaced pasts, unlike the more itinerant attendees at Arlington Rise's gatherings. Likewise, there is dignity in Gabriel's nostalgia when he speaks of fading Irish hospitality, in contrast to Joe Lanham's polemical conversation starter—"The English race is dying out"—at his dinner party, in *Arlington Park*. (Cusk grants a dignified strain of nostalgia, instead, to Benedict, who recites a Philip Larkin poem that laments the destruction of the English countryside in a cynical tone reminiscent of Cusk herself.[95]) Gabriel's other speech topic—"sad memories"—and guests' recollections of "absent faces" (such as that of Gabriel's mother) link to their discussion of the lost greatness of the opera, combining personal and cultural nostalgia in a richly lyrical mood. Music and song grace their gathering, earning warm compliments for the singer, and the narrator further highlights the occasion's elegance with a loving description of the food and drink, as well as the dishes and bottles in which they're served.

Of course, there are causes for anxiety, both that evening and in general. When will latecomers (such as Gabriel) finally arrive? Will Freddy Malins be drunk? Will Gabriel's hyper-educated sensibility alienate him from others; will his speech go over their heads? When his wife leans on the banisters and he sees her in an aesthetic mode, "as if she were a symbol of something," does this indicate his alienation from *her*? When the spouses are alone and he feels diffident and speaks to her in a "false" voice, does this suggest that his sense of inadequacy—soon to be awakened when she tells him about Michael Furey—has other sources in their intimacy? Gabriel's feelings aside, how much pain does Gretta harbor at the thought of Michael's death?

And yet, in spite of all these sources of grief and anxiety—perhaps *because* of them— the Misses Morkans' dinner is a poignant, soul-making affair. "Generous" tears fill Garbiel's eyes when he recognizes the depth of Michael's feelings for Gretta, redeeming his "false" voice of moments ago.[96] All the depth of feeling in Gabriel's speech was made possible by the formality, ritual, and long history of the annual gathering. Even the sad, partially epiphanic revelation about Gretta's past is made possible by the party, because her appearance on the stairway and Bartell D'Arcy's chance singing of a song de-familiarize her from her husband, revealing a dimension of her mind that normal spousal proximity leaves hidden.

Mrs Dalloway and *To the Lighthouse* recapitulate some of these Joycean themes and motifs. They develop their own tonal complexity, or what Molly Hite calls "affective indeterminacy."[97] *Mrs Dalloway*'s mobile narrative consciousness, as Hite discusses, sometimes supplies contradictory tonal cues or withholds cues where they might be expected. Is Clarissa a sympathetic heroine, a sufferer who manages to cultivate mostly kind, solicitous feelings toward others? Or is she largely unkind; does Septimus's death—by serving a scapegoat function, sparing Clarissa the need to die—associate her with privilege and cruelty? If Clarissa *is* predominantly unkind, or complacent in her fortune, does the narrator critique her for this, or does the narrator (implicitly or explicitly) endorse her attitudes? If the novel is a "postwar elegy," as Froula argues, then does its dinner party provide the formal structure that enables mourning (for the war dead, for personal dreams of psychosexual fulfillment lost in the mists of time) to proceed toward healing? The language of *Mrs Dalloway* supports divergent answers to such questions, just as the language of *To the Lighthouse* supports readings that emphasize either the transcendent or counter-transcendent qualities of the Ramsay family meal.

My readings of these two Woolf novels emphasize suggestions of redemption, or at least community sustenance and possible regeneration, in their depictions of dinner gatherings, with their vestiges of sacred ritual. By contrast, Cusk's works including *Arlington Park*—though indeterminate within their own tonal range—offer much less to readers in search of hope. When Cusk's novels recall Woolf's texts in specific ways, they often do so by deflating whatever ambiguous suggestions of hope or acceptance Woolf supplies. Cusk thus represents one kind of modernist legatee—one who emphasizes the skepticism, even the cynicism or despair, that can be gleaned from modernism's archive of affects.

In *Mrs Dalloway*, in illustration of Woolf's tonal plasticity, there's a sense of excitement, maybe even aura, in Clarissa's party preparations, including her purchase of flowers, in a scene redolent with fecundity and beauty. The effort entailed in these preparations, and the ceremony of the event, is evident in doors being taken off their hinges, the cook whistling in the kitchen, and the typewriter clicking.[98] (In *Arlington Park*, by contrast, Christine doesn't like to cook any more than her mother Viv did, and she so resents this labor that she might have had little to serve her guests—given that her husband offers no help—if Maggie hadn't come to her rescue.[99]) Clarissa's role of matron-hostess has more than a touch of the Victorian about it, but nonetheless both the author and her character recognize its dignity.[100] In anticipation of the dinner, Clarissa has her extensive scene in front of the mirror, in which she metaphorically disassembles and reassembles herself before descending the stairs, resolving to mend her green dress.[101]

Socially constructed and constricted as this role—emblematized by the dress—may be, it helps her to achieve coherence and purpose. By defamiliarizing her from herself, the impending party and the mirror occasion a profound, soul-making exercise in contemplation. (By contrast, *Arlington Park* grants Maisie a scene before the bathroom mirror, prior to her departure to the Lanhams' party, but her introspection only goes deep enough for her to blame her parents—including for things beyond their control—to blame herself for her failure to "crystallize," and to think that her face is not "so bad."[102] Like Laura Brown of *The Hours*, Maisie lacks Clarissa's self-reflective range.) As if Clarissa's self-defamiliarization before the mirror were not heartening enough, Richard compliments their daughter Elizabeth, saying that he had stood looking at her in her pink frock and wondering who she was, before realizing that she was "his Elizabeth."[103] The Dalloways' party, in addition to assembling long-time friends and being graced by the prime minister, helps Peter to appreciate Richard's virtues[104] and rekindles a Dalloway father-daughter bond. Like the Misses Morkans' party, it has elements of grief (news of Septimus), antipathy (Richard's feeling for Dr. Bradshaw), and anxiety (Peter's bundle of neuroses). But to a greater degree than the Misses Morkans' party, it is an affirmative affair.

Similarly, the family dinner in the first part of *To the Lighthouse* occasions anxiety and self-doubt but ends up being—at least in Mr. Bankes's words—a "triumph."[105] Will Charles and Minta be late? Will the beef be spoiled? Will the mood be ruined by Charles Tansley's sexism and Lily's offense at it, or by Mr Ramsay's annoyance at Augustus Carmichael's request for a second serving of soup? Mrs Ramsay even wonders "What have I done with my life?" much as Clarissa Dalloway has profound temporary self-doubts.[106] Mr Bankes muses that family life isn't worth the trouble, a sentiment entertained by others as well. Lily behaves nicely to Charles only for the sake of Mrs Ramsay, then she regrets being insincere and thinks that all human relations are inauthentic, the worst being between men and women—a judgment that haunts the novel as it haunts many of Woolf's writings.[107]

But despite all these large and small threats to order, propriety, and decency—in *defiance* of them—Mrs Ramsay, the Woolfian artist-hostess *par excellence*, conjures an auratic evening into being. With candles lit, with faces around the table brought closer to one another and "composed" by the candlelight, and with the night "shut off by panes of glass," a change goes through everyone—according to the narrator (perhaps channeling Mrs Ramsay's feelings).[108] Paul and Minta return, tardy but engaged to be married, lending the first part of the novel the happy generic shape of a comedy. Family life is vindicated. Whatever new horizons for women are anticipated by Lily Briscoe's painterly talents, Mrs Ramsay proves her genius as a composer of intimate relations. The dark night beyond the window—in the form of war and the passage of time—will claim her and others' lives, but for now, her composition, like Clarissa Dalloway's party, is "an offering," perhaps "for the sake of offering."[109]

In contrast to these three shared meals, hosted by the Misses Morkan, Clarissa Dalloway, and Mrs Ramsay, the numerous gatherings in *Arlington Park*—for there is not one definitive occasion, though the Lanham's preparation and hosting occupy the final two chapters—are spiritually meager affairs. Unlike its precursors, and to the consternation of some of its critics,[110] Cusk's novel develops a motif of failed attempts at connection. It examines permutations of a social form drained of both aura and community-building efficacy. Detailed in its examination, *Arlington Park* depicts how guests prepare for dinners (Dom and Maisie bicker about their children and their impending social obligation, which she would rather avoid); how hosts prepare (Joe and Christine swap recriminations as her marginal hosting skills become comic fodder); how the social gatherings themselves unfold; how guests debrief afterward (Benedict criticizes Juliet for having been drunk, and she feels uncared for by him); and what hosts do afterward (Joe looks at his wife with "bottomless eyes" as he tells her "come here"[111]). The novel is framed by two such parties, one in the opening chapter hosted by the Milfords (Louisa abets her husband Matthew's chauvinism[112]), and one in the final chapter hosted by the Lanhams (Christine plays nice in front of guests but resents Joe in private). Between these events, Amanda invites people over for coffee in the second chapter, having previously hosted a failed dinner, and Christine organizes a trip to the mall for lunch with Maisie and Stephanie, in the third chapter. Arlington Rise's homes are tacky in *nouveau-riche* styles, lacking the elegance of the Ramsays' summer home and the conviviality of the Misses Morkans' comparatively modest dwelling. Cusk's mother-hostesses prepare no beef *en daube*, and when they lunch together at a crowded, tacky mall, immigrants of color are left to clean heedless consumers' mess.

Unlike Gabriel, Cusk expresses no nostalgia for a time when hospitality was warmer, and unlike either of Woolf's novels, *Arlington Park* pays no tribute to a domestic angel, however she might recall a civilization that Cusk would like to transvalue. Unmoored from admiration for a dignified past, faith in progress, hope for a more egalitarian and less crass future, or even doubtful hope that ritualized meals can build community and help mourners to heal, Cusk's satire is unsparing. Spousal relations in *Arlington Park* might be distant, or intimate, or alternate between these poles, but in any case they are rivalries more than partnerships. To recall the assertion of the critic Ashley Shelden, "Love has failed."[113] Nor do friendships in Cusk's novel ever click. (When Amanda thinks, of her lunch companions, that Christine is the only one she could consider a friend, her basis for this consideration is never explained.[114]) Even fellowship among neighbors never emerges. Cusk uses dinner parties to underscore these failures, as Joyce and Woolf use it to demonstrate how—with effort and attention to formality—meaningful relations can be fostered, whether at the familial or communal level.

Notwithstanding High Modernism's reputation for alienation and cultural despair, the three precursor-texts under discussion each affirm family, community, and a day's power to transcend its own constraints. To say the least, their successor-novel, *Arlington Park*, challenges readers who seek evidence of joy or the chance for renewal. (At novel's end, there is *some* Shelleyan promise in the "cold, fresh wind" blowsing into the Lanhams' home after guests leave. Joe's face appears "like a little stage with all sorts of things being acted on it." With their home to themselves, Christine dances, snapping her fingers, and Joe looks at her "with bottomless eyes," ending the novel with the words "Come here."[115] I read these words as menacing, though they arguably suggest that the party has restored their marriage's spark—that one thing "being acted" on Joe's face is passion, perhaps sadistic, but also affectionate. Cusk is an artful enough disciple of Woolf to retain this much indeterminacy.)

But *Arlington Park*, like Cusk's oeuvre, is parsimonious with hints of regeneration. Instead, Cusk sees Victorian oppression and conformism stretched out into the twenty-first century, sees in marriage and neighborliness mere empty forms, and sees no egress from daily drudgery—in particular for mothers of small children. "The future, of course, never comes," explains Cusk's 2009 *Guardian* article: "it is merely a projection from the present of the present's frustrations." *Arlington Park* lingers in these frustrations, offering no palliative suggestion of a better tomorrow. Although Shelden's *Unmaking Love* doesn't discuss Cusk, *Arlington Park* exemplifies Shelden's characterization of contemporary novels' "negative" attitudes—their association of love with "discontent," "inequity," and "divorce."[116]

Is this strategy a form of what Smith calls "miserabilism"[117]—of a conspicuously first-world sort? Virginia Woolf in particular and High Modernism in general have had detractors, from Queenie Leavis through Steven Pinker,[118] among other reasons because of their cultural despair, cult of difficulty, and alienation from how many people think, feel, and relate to one another. It would be ungenerous to see *Arlington Park* as merely indulging in an aesthetics of distance, not as *engaged* in current social and political thought. The same point applies to Cusk's oeuvre, much of which shares this novel's limited tonal palette and alienated vision of upper-middle-class mores.

Of course, Cusk cannot, by herself, work through the complex legacies of Woolf, Bloomsbury, or modernism. But in conjunction with her contemporaries, she can clarify which aspects of these legacies remain pertinent and provocative. The following two chapters on McEwan and Barker explore meta-Freudian terrain, to complement Cusk's meta-Woolfian preoccupations. These coming chapters depict challenges even more "stretched out," arguably, than those of Arlington Rise's housewives. McEwan's protagonist Briony spends over six decades and multiple drafts of *Atonement* trying vainly to atone for the harm she has inflicted on her sister and Robbie. Barker's protagonist, the therapist Rivers, spends three novels striving largely in vain to heal his patients and to heal and understand himself, under the shadow of a world war that will end only to sow seeds for another world war.

But just as the creation of *Atonement* can be a source of solace, recompense, or even triumph for Briony, likewise Rivers's many deep and loving relationships with his troubled patients, and the respect he earns from his colleagues, provide their own rewards. While neither McEwan nor Barker takes refuge in a simplistic notion that *things get better* for individuals or societies in dependable ways, each author paints on more temporally and psychically expansive canvases than *Arlington Park*, with its suburban ruts. Each confronts the menacing possibilities of cyclicality, compulsive repetition, and interminability. But each also allows that one person's or era's efforts, even if limited in their immediate success, can carry "seeds on the wind"[119] for subsequent seekers.

Notes

1. James and Seshagiri 93–7.
2. Smith, "Acknowledgements."
3. Cusk, "Introduction" to *The Rainbow* xii, vii, xiii.
4. *The Bradshaw Variations* 214.
5. Ibid. 111.
6. Ibid. 212.
7. *Arlington Park* 123.
8. Ibid. 221–3.
9. Lawrence, "Foreword" *Women in Love* 486.
10. Julavitz.
11. *Outline* 170.
12. Jameson, "The Cultural Logic of Late Capitalism" 16–19.
13. Fowler.
14. *Arlington Park* 24.
15. *A Room of One's Own* 82.
16. *Arlington Park* 9.
17. "In God We Trust" 388.
18. Berlant 2.
19. Ahmed, *The Promise of Happiness* 1–20.
20. Berlant 2, 5, 9, 10.
21. *Arlington Park* 34, 34, 31.
22. Giddens 185.
23. *Arlington Park* 24.
24. The statement about "all men" appears on page 20. The "murder" motif appears on 15, 23, 27, 160, and 170. The thought about Benedict is on page 25. Cusk's essay "Lions on Leashes" discusses her work for a London theater writing a version of Euripides' *Medea*, which depicts a woman killing her two young children—an event that Cusk sees as metaphorical. The essay speculates that, metaphorically speaking, children murder their mothers more than vice versa (94).
25. Neuman emphasizes the novel's theme of patriarchal domination.
26. *Mrs Dalloway* 36.
27. *Arlington Park* 172.
28. McCann x.
29. Smiley.
30. Berlant 2.
31. *Arlington Park* 213.
32. Ibid. 89.
33. Ibid. 108, *Mrs Dalloway* 3.

34 Ibid. 225, 236–7.
35 Ibid. 218.
36 Ibid. 213, 215.
37 *A Room of One's Own* 68–9.
38 Rave reviews of the trilogy have come from, e.g., Garner, Julavitz, and Blair.
39 *A Room of One's Own* 57, 98–9.
40 Ibid. 108, 189.
41 Ibid. 109, 101.
42 Ibid. 112, 115.
43 Ibid. 181, 189.
44 Ibid. 206.
45 Ibid. 178–9.
46 Ibid. 77.
47 Ibid. 49, 192–3, 38.
48 Ibid. 71, *Mrs Dalloway* 8.
49 Ibid. 74, Ibid. 183.
50 Ibid. 79.
51 *Mrs Dalloway* 11.
52 *Arlington Park* 67.
53 Ahmed, *The Promise of Happiness* 31.
54 *Arlington Park* 45.
55 I borrow this phrase from the title of Lynn Keller's 1988 *Re-making It New*, a study of the "legacies of modernism" before this became a catch phrase.
56 Briony Randall also mentions works by John Lanchester and Jon McGregor. My list, then, of responses to Woolf in the decade prior to *Arlington Park* incorporates Randall's novelists and still does not promise to be complete. Featuring but not limited to one-day novels, it includes Cunningham's *The Hours* (1998), Lippincott's *Mr Dalloway* (1999), Lanchester's *Mr Phillips* (2000), McEwan's *Atonement* (2001), McGregor's *If Nobody Speaks of Remarkable Things* (2002), Winterson's *Lighthousekeeping* (2004), and McEwan's *Saturday* (2005).
57 Monica Latham 196.
58 D'hoker 15.
59 "Modern Fiction" 150.
60 "Snow was general all over Ireland." "The Dead" 194.
61 In addition to the critics discussed below, Bonnie Kime Scott argues for a "greening" of modernism and offers a nature-oriented reading of Woolf to correct previous emphases on the "urban" and "technical" dimensions of her work (1–3). Christina Alt explores Woolf's interests in nineteenth-century life sciences, especially ethology (the study of animal behavior) and ecology. She discusses Woolf's importance to ecocriticism and feminism, including Scott's work.
62 *To the Lighthouse* 128–9, 132, 133.
63 This entire discussion of *The Waves* is indebted to Hite's "Introduction" to that novel.
64 Hite, "Introduction" xli.
65 D'hoker 14.
66 *The Years* 3.
67 Krouse 12. My discussion of *The Years* draws on Krouse's essay.
68 *The Years* 46–7.
69 D'hoker 14.
70 *Arlington Park* 147.

71	Ibid. 7, 141.
72	Ibid. 34.
73	Ibid. 125.
74	Ibid. 247–8.
75	Ibid. 244, 73, 241.
76	Ibid. 95.
77	Ibid. 70, 97, 243.
78	Ibid. 69–70, 111.
79	Ibid. 73, 101.
80	Ibid. 241.
81	Ibid. 101.
82	Ibid. 22, 78–9, *Mrs Dalloway* 4, 48.
83	Ibid. 43 ("It was nine-fifteen"), 62 ("It was ten to ten"), 64 ("It was one minute to ten"), 175 ("At six o'clock … Dom Carrington opened his front door" and "Maisie Carrington had returned to the house with her two children at half past three").
84	Ibid. 176, 188, 76.
85	Cusk, "Shakespeare's daughters."
86	Randall 596.
87	"The Dead" 191.
88	*Mrs Dalloway* 78.
89	See Abel, especially 166–7, for a discussion of what Woolf includes and excludes in depicting Clarissa's recollections and experience of childhood loss.
90	Schoene 162.
91	Ibid. 129, *Mrs Dalloway* 34.
92	The passages about Solly can be found on 141, 125, 136, 138, and 145.
93	Ibid. 87, 182, 216, etc.
94	Ibid. 135, 136, 144.
95	Ibid. 225, 244.
96	The foregoing *Arlington Park* citations are from pages 166, 176, 167, 170, 182, 188, and 193.
97	Hite, "Tonal Cues" 249.
98	*Mrs Dalloway* 3, 29.
99	*Arlington Park* 237.
100	David Dowling sees Clarissa, along with two of Forster's characters—*Howards End*'s Ruth Wilcox and *Passage*'s Mrs. Moore—as admirable matrons of civilization (136).
101	*Mrs Dalloway* 39.
102	*Arlington Park* 194–6.
103	*Mrs Dalloway* 194.
104	Ibid. 192.
105	*To the Lighthouse* 100. Mr. Bankes has the food in mind, but his approbation extends to the whole gathering, to Mrs. Ramsay's overall accomplishment.
106	Ibid. 82.
107	Ibid. 88–9, 91–2.
108	Ibid. 97.
109	*Mrs Dalloway* 122.
110	See Boileau and Schoene.
111	*Arlington Park* 248.
112	"I do think Matthew's got a point," Louisa repeats (17).
113	Shelden 57.

114 *Arlington Park* 67.
115 Ibid. 247–8.
116 Ibid. 3, 5, 5.
117 Zadie Smith, "F. Kafka, Everyman" 65.
118 See Leavis's review of *Three Guineas* 208. For Pinker, see *The Blank Slate* 170–1, 409–18.
119 *Regeneration* 249.

3

Post-Freudian Skepticism: *Atonement* in an Age of De-Conversion

Psychoanalysis shows us that history is neither a continuous nor a cumulative process, that it does not have a happy ending, that it does not evolve smoothly and that its course is marked by repression, repetition, and the return of the repressed.
—Jean Laplanche 2

This volume explores how Lyotard's idea about "incredulity" toward metanarratives remains suggestive, four decades after its formulation—but only if it is adapted in light of the complexities of intellectual and literary history. Were the incredulity meme to suggest merely that *moderns (or Victorians) were credulous and contemporaries are incredulous*, it would obscure as much as it illuminates, and indeed Lyotard himself does not posit a crude distinction between naïve and skeptical intellectual epochs.[1] In fact, a mixture of historical hope and anxious uncertainty has enriched literature since the modernist era, and writers have developed numerous non-programmatic forms in which to explore their feelings about the nature and likelihood of progress.

With these thematic and formal variables in mind, Chapters 2–7 employ the cultural-historical phenomenon of waning credulity as an interpretive tool in three ways. First, because intimacy is my guiding theme, I see novelists' depictions of the private sphere as opportunities for them to think, sometimes in subtle and indirect ways, about forms of progress often associated with public life. Family systems, parent-child relations, romantic couples, intimate friends (platonic or otherwise), and the analyst-analysand dyad all offer novelists contexts for examining how the present has improved (or not) on the past, and how the future likely will or won't improve on the present. Although the languages of intimacy and social justice differ—as D. H. Lawrence insisted—nonetheless, the dynamics of love and friendship in any historical milieu are never politically innocent. In depicting a spousal conflict or the emotional timbre of a father's relations with his children, writers can entertain (or reject) *grand* or *petit* hopes that interpersonal life *gets better* over time: that a generation can learn from its parents' blindness, middle-aged people can overcome their youthful ignorance or selfishness, and/or that social justice enriches domestic existence.

Second, I remain sensitive to authorial ambivalence. Rarely are the novelists under discussion wholly credulous or incredulous toward any conception of "progress," although some (such as Cunningham) give narrative forms to various kinds of social improvement that others (such as Cusk) do not. But however hopeful or despairing they are, in most cases their ability to respond to historical change in self-divided ways aids their artistry. Sometimes their ambivalence stems from an emotional attraction to the idea of progress, despite their intellectual wariness of their own yearning for guarantees.

Third—with this and other kinds of ambivalence in mind—I attend to novels' tones and forms in tracing the aesthetics of credulity and incredulity toward the idea of historical progress. On the one hand, *Arlington Park*, discussed in the previous chapter, evinces staunch incredulity toward progress in intimacy: it allows scant hope that violent weather can clear a toney suburb of its stultification and yield justice for women or intersexual happiness for anyone. Along similar lines, Salman Rushdie's non-linear conception of history, discussed in Chapter 5, contributes to *The Satanic Verses*' skeptical attitude toward transcontinental eros: i.e., toward a possible solution, in 1988, to the problems of the heart that *A Passage to India*'s Fielding and Aziz faced six decades earlier. But other novels are less skeptical. *On Beauty* (Chapter 6) depicts marital separation, the pain that precipitates it, and the suffering it puts families through, but it values the possibility for renewal inherent in this quintessentially post-1970s freedom in intimacy. It is also fitting for novels heir to modernist ambiguity to entertain optimistic and pessimistic intuitions about history simultaneously. Pat Barker's *Regeneration* trilogy (Chapter 4) allows for both a dark, anthropologically informed reading that stresses the human compulsion to violence, and a more historically sanguine reading according to which the intellectual and emotional development of its hero, Dr. Rivers, illustrates how society might grow wiser and more compassionate.

My claim that an *incredulity thesis*, if sufficiently complex and supple, can illuminate how writers think about progress and intimacy in history recalls other critics' accounts of god and intellectual history. Pericles Lewis's 2010 *Religious Experience and the Modernist Novel* contests the "secularization thesis," which risks simplification in contrasting "the knowing, sophisticated twentieth century with the naïve nineteenth century." Lewis sees a "continuity" between Victorians' and moderns' "central concerns" that can be obscured by moderns' formal originality. Citing Weber, he indicates that supernatural yearnings might persist in "disguised form" in "apparently secular contexts": capitalism's seemingly rationalized pursuit of profits might mask an irrational quest for salvation, for example.[2] Frank Kermode suggests additional ways in which sacred epistemology persists, not necessarily in disguised form, in Victorian and modernist literature. *The Sense of an Ending* (1967) contrasts a large intellectual-historical trend away from literal belief in apocalypse with writers' and readers' ongoing attachment to stories that offer surrogate comforts for a secular age. Victorian endings, on Kermode's account, tie up loose threads and offer synthetic moral judgments (and perhaps just desserts). Modernist prophecies, such as Yeats and Lawrence propound, belie accounts of their milieu as post-religious.

The object of the "incredulity" explored herein is not sacred, though progress has held enough allure for enough thinkers since the eighteenth century that in 1991 Christopher Lasch sardonically labeled it the "true and only heaven." Even in their optimistic moods—when they depict intimacy as subject to historical improvement—

the novelists under discussion do not view it as a "heaven." Nonetheless, *grand* and *petit* narratives of progress, disguised and undisguised forms of credulity derived from Enlightenment aspirations, counterbalance their skepticism and inform the narrative design of their novels.

The title of McEwan's 2001 *Atonement* suggests that it might pursue a theological grand narrative—one that predicates future perfection on restoration of past wholeness. But McEwan is a "new atheist" novelist, so it is not surprising that there is "an absence of [straightforward religious] atonement in *Atonement*," as Charles Pastoor, a religious-minded critic, laments.[3] Pastoor notes that Briony, the narrator, seeks atonement through various secular means, from caring for wounded soldiers to writing fiction, though she doubts the latter strategy's efficacy. Though beset by doubt, her quests may reveal metanarrative longing, a desire to subsume her personal crime and repentance into an archetypal pattern—one that in Pastoor's view is necessarily undergirded by Christian values.

Pastoor's reading is thoughtful, and it reinforces Lewis's claim that one function of modernists' formal experiments was to evoke and/or understand sacred experience, even when they didn't name it directly or express religious faith. But in distinction to Pastoor's religiously hermeneutical approach, I see *Atonement* engage in thinly disguised form with a secular twentieth-century *grand récit*: the Freudian myth of trauma, guided self-analysis, and healing at-one-ment with oneself. But *how* does McEwan employ Freudian epistemologies: does he empty them out, as Tom McCarthy's *Remainder* (discussed in Chapter 6) empties out the idea of "authenticity?" Does he admire them aesthetically, even intellectually, while withholding credulity from their prophylactic claims? Or does *Atonement*, precisely through its incredulity, pay tribute to Freud, specifically the elderly and skeptical Freud of "Analysis Terminable and Interminable" (1937), who had evidence of enough patients in therapy for long enough that he wondered whether therapy could cure?

These questions about Freud and *Atonement* belong to my overarching examination of the idea of progress and perfection in post-Bloomsburian fiction—and contemporary culture. Whether in hopes of being saved by Jesus, finding keys to wealth and happiness in New Age philosophies, finding the secret to healthy intimacy in pop psychology, being cured of substance addiction in twelve steps, or being cured of "neuroses" by Freudian analysts, Westerners of the last fifty and one hundred years have demonstrated robust appetites for narratives that promise improvement, meaning, and *telos*. That ours is an age of de-conversion is doubtful—even apart from resurgences of Islamic and Christian fundamentalism. Literature and the intelligentsia can play critical roles in the face of potential illusions—as Lyotard said that postmodern thought did, and as this chapter's epigraph from Jean Laplanche illustrates that psychoanalytic theory can play, in the face of its profession's utopian strains. But literature can also, as Kermode and Lewis detail, play complex roles vis-à-vis the dreams of its time, mediating between credulity and incredulity, seeking new forms for old myths from which it divests belief, and for new myths that it may not be conscious of believing in. Whether a novelist treats a religious or secular metanarrative, directly or obliquely, he faces numerous formal-epistemological choices. He might inhabit metanarrative forms playfully, exploding them from within. He might encourage his readers to see art—not just his own work, but artistic cogitation—as hostile to metanarrative world-making, rooted in the particular, contingent, and sensuous. Or he might fashion himself as an author-god, offering his tale as an entire world, a universally representative narrative if not strictly a metanarrative, a model of order in a chaotic world. Such options, though not necessarily worked through programmatically by novelists, can help critics draw together the strings of an epistemological and aesthetic milieu—an age of conversions, de-conversions, and re-evaluations, such as ours—to cast the philosophically savvy work of a McEwan or a Barker in a fuller rhetorical and ideological context.

Conversion, De-Conversion, and Re-Evaluation

Sigmund Freud once strode the intellectual landscape like a giant. With the help of Bloomsburians James and Alix Strachey, who edited and translated the twenty-four volumes of his *Collected Writings*, and of Leonard and Virginia Woolf, who published these translations, Freud invented a profession with international reach. Multiple schools of converts—English, French, American, South American, etc.—claimed him as their father. By the 1950s, psychoanalysis reached its apex, especially in intellectual centers like London and New York, where clinics and private offices overflowed with patients ranging from the mildly neurotic to the psychotic.[4] The Freudian metanarrative[5] promised to save them, after its fashion. From *Oedipal trauma* through the *repression and neurosis* of the unanalyzed adult to *catharsis and cure* via her free association and transference-love for her therapist, Freud's humanistic program would carry its aspirants. By engaging in the most artificial of intimacies—with a professional paid to listen non-judgmentally to everything she had to say—the patient hoped to heal her broken intimacy with herself and her internalized[6] parent figures, so that she could then heal her intimacies with her family or lover.

One of the metanarrative's selling points was its granular elegance. Of the following postulates, we might see the first four in generic forms and the following four as assuming shapes unique to individual analysands.

* All children pass through an *Oedipal phase* (roughly from age three-and-a-half to six), during which incestuous desire for a parent sows seeds for later neuroses.
* The shame surrounding *early childhood masturbation* likewise sows seeds of neurosis.[7]
* Oedipal fantasies and childhood masturbation are forgotten not passively but actively: a part of the mind *represses* what it does not want consciously known.
* *The engine of repression is The Unconscious.*

––––––––

* Through *hysterical symptoms, which differ with each analysand, the body evades repression to express psychic traumas* of Oedipal and masturbatory origins.
* *The talking cure, which follows different paths in each analytic encounter, works* because

* *Dreams, tics, etc. lead backward in a psychically determinant chain to the traumatic cause*, and
* *Once this cause is brought to light—i.e., when The Unconscious is made conscious—the symptom disappears.*

In formulating this account of sexual desire, guilt, self-alienation, and at-one-ment—this platform for a healthier pursuit of love-relations—Freud exploited the untapped literary potential of a new genre—the case history. His *grand récit* rested, or was intended to rest, upon the *petits récits* of patients such as Dora, the Wolf Man, and Anna O. His sexological precursors had written case histories as daring as his in challenging Victorian prudery and enlarging public awareness of human sexual variety. But their accounts differ from his in two important ways. First, they are less artful—perhaps because they are truer to the facts. Second, hopeful as their authors may have been about the possibilities for healing in an increasingly tolerant society, these case histories rest upon no medical *grand récit*, no archetypal account of how the sexually pathological (or perfectly healthy, but socially marginalized) individual can be reconciled to himself. By contrast, Freud's case histories, especially *Dora*, are extremely artful, including in their development of three-dimensional analysand characters. For better or worse, they exploit his novelistic skills to dramatize struggles between therapist and patient, and between the patient and her own Unconscious. And they do have a metanarrative hypothesis that their concrete particulars are meant to validate. But they founder, thanks to such messy contingencies as Dora's termination of treatment, before proving the grand hypothesis. At least they founder according to Freud's critics, for whom his urge to tell exciting stories compromises not just their scientific validity, but his probity in any sense.[8]

Regarding the first two items in the above psychotherapeutic metanarrative, anti-Freudians assert that neuroses have other sources than those adduced by Freud and that there's no such thing as the Oedipus complex. Regarding the next two, they say that other models better account for the mind's complexity than Freud's "psychodynamic" one and that there's no such thing as The Unconscious in the way Freud describes it.[9] (In fairness to Freud, while in some cases he capitalizes and nominalizes The Unconscious, in others he speaks adjectivally of "unconscious wishes," "unconscious motives," etc. This caveat aside, however, he is most influential, and his literary gifts are on best display, when he personifies the Unconscious, fashioning a figure more complex than Stevenson's "Mr Hyde," who employs multilingualism, punning talents, and vast knowledge of history to send coded messages around a censor.[10] Wittgenstein wryly names this elusive genius "Mr Nobody,"[11] while more sympathetic commentators, such as Richard Rorty, admire how Freud enables people to imagine themselves as inhabited by multiple selves with rich sets of attributes—which, Rorty believes, gives people more range in constructing narratives of their inner lives.[12])

Regarding the final four items, anti-Freudians assert that hysteria has physiological, not psychic, causes and thus that the "talking cure" cannot cure it. They claim either that dreams, slips of the tongue, etc. do not result in determinate ways from discernible causes—or that such symptoms do have determinate causes, but not the ones Freud named. Freudianism's detractors deny that patients can narrate themselves fully to themselves, back to their infancies. They see the idea of the patient's cathartic illumination—or "abreaction," as Freud called it early in his career, when he still believed in such a climax—as pure fiction.[13]

But for decades, for orthodox analysts, Freud's case histories offered empirical support for his psychodynamic narrative paradigm. Abreaction and full self-understanding did not seem like myths to them, but legitimate medical goals. Appropriately—as many hoped to effect conversion therapy on their patients—they had converted to Freud's doctrines about the mind and its prophylaxis.[14] And even for Freudianism's less orthodox admirers down to the present, its artfulness is its great virtue.[15] In the wake of the de-converts' assaults on its scientific pretensions and utopian hopes for cure, these admirers re-evaluate Freudianism's beauty, its power. Adam Phillips, an influential Freudian analyst, says that, for him, "there has always only been one category, *literature*, of which psychoanalysis became a part."[16] Phillips doesn't worry whether psychoanalysis "is true or even useful, but only whether it is haunting or moving or intriguing or amusing" or might persuade us to think and feel otherwise than as we do.[17] Literary fiction has been accused of lacking truth or use value, and few of its champions defend it as articulately as Phillips, when he has Freudian literature specifically in mind.

As this chapter's epigraph demonstrates, other admirers make concessions more extensive than Phillips's, concerning Freudianism's transformational ambitions. A tension has always enriched psychoanalytic thought, including Freud's, between fatalistic and optimistic or utopian intuitions. That people are doomed by the repetition compulsion; that the best analysis can do is to help them remember whence a compulsion arose, rather than blindly acting it out (though, once off the couch, they will continue to act it out); that insight bestows limited freedom at best; and that psychoanalysis should be free of advice and moralizing—such views are as common among analysts as their opposites. An old joke that asks "How many psychotherapists does it take to change a light bulb?" and answers "Only one, but it takes many years, and the bulb has to really *want* to change" expresses a fatalistic intuition that has enriched Freudianism through much of its history. "Analysis Terminable and Interminable" wonders whether, as the decades pass, standard analytic treatment will continue to lengthen. By this point in his career, Freud replaced his hope for abreaction with the more modest aim that patients could "work through" neuroses—an achievement that the severest revisionists see as equally elusive.[18] Freud's dream, in 1900,[19] of curing Dora within months morphed circa 1950 into many clients' decades'-long struggles to vanquish repression. "Interminable" analysis raises ethical quandaries in a profit-oriented field, but it belies a straw-man version of Freudian hermeneutics as inflexible, naïve, and hubristic.

Why value psychoanalysis, and psychoanalytic thought outside the clinic, if their practical utility—showing how our mind works; healing love-lives; curing sickness, whether in a flash of insight or a protracted "working-through"—is so doubtful? This is a species of questions faced by the humanities in general and literary studies in particular. Why value literature when the utilities once claimed on its behalf—that it conveys timeless truths about the human condition, improves society, and bolsters readers' morals—are doubted, and doubted most vociferously within the literary-studies academy? *Atonement* dramatizes these questions about Freudianism and literature, and it reminds us—in Phillips's spirit—that psychoanalysis is a kind of literature.

What Kind of Text Is *Atonement*?

Briony provides a limit case for the value of psychoanalytically inflected introspection in her six-decades'-long self-analysis, motivated by her guilt over having wrecked the lives of the two people—Robbie and Cecelia—with whom she was once most intimate. In Freudian rather than religious terms, her composition of *Atonement* might be seen as an attempted catharsis, or writing cure, to parallel the talking cure that Freud hoped for on Dora's behalf. But she shares Freud's tragic sense that quests for self-understanding necessarily commence *in medias res*, with damage partly if not wholly irremediable. By its very premise, the novel seems to undercut not only abreaction, but also working-through. Could Briony ever navigate "through" her past? Where would she work her way *to*?

It could be consoling to read *Atonement* in less solipsistic terms, as a lover's apology to her two most beloved intimates. But Briony's relations with Robbie and Cecelia cannot be healed—and they cannot forgive her—because they are dead, notwithstanding her temptation to write a happy ending for them.[20] So her introspection, her apology-with-no-recipient, needs another justification than this interpersonal one. She doesn't have the ear of a non-judgmental therapist on whose couch she can free associate, but can she find an alternative source of acceptance and comfort? It is asking a lot of any kind of writing, talking, or thinking to hope that it will offer illumination for the mind, or peace for the heart, in the context of such absences.

And Briony rejects of one kind of introspection, and opening-out of the self, long esteemed in Western culture: Christian contemplation, buoyed by faith in a metanarrative that promises reconciliation with God for believers whose intimacies with their fellow men and women are broken. "How can a novelist achieve atonement," she asks, given her own god-like powers over her narrative? "There is no one, no entity or higher form that she can appeal to or be reconciled with, or that can forgive her."[21] Whereas Pastoor reads such pronouncements against the grain, with an eye toward their religious implications, other critics, such as Arthur Bradley and Andrew Tate, see McEwan as "the New Atheist novelist *par excellence*," who gives fictional forms to the antireligious philosophies of Richard Dawkins and other polemicists.[22] In a middle ground between these religious and irreligious approaches, Elke D'hoker examines treatments of "confession" and "atonement" by secular novelists including McEwan. She distinguishes religious confession (which aims to gain *absolution*) from secular confession (which aims to present the *truth* of the confessant's *self*). She further distinguishes nonfictional secular confessions from two other forms of autobiography: memoirs (which present the *historicity* of the self) and apologies (which present the *integrity* of the self). These typologies enable her to compare and contrast fictional confessions like McEwan's/Briony's—which cannot be fact-checked—with nonfictional ones, concerning tellers' motives and strategies, readers' moral judgment, and the problem of when a confession is finished. Without endorsing the idea, D'hoker allows that "in a secular context the reader" of fictional confessions like Briony's may seem to assume "the priest's role as interlocutor and judge."[23] D'hoker does not argue that, in granting readers such priestly powers, McEwan fashions a metanarrative. But the "priest" she discusses has the authority to bring *closure* to a tale, and closure is among metanarratives' most treasured consolations.

As rich as these discussions are of *Atonement*'s Christian or post-Christian attributes, commentary on McEwan's novel has yet to investigate its Freudian, anti-Freudian, and post-Freudian characteristics. On my post-Freudian reading, *Atonement* issues from an author and a milieu that have de-sacralized both Freud the man and Freudianism the doctrine. Briony's confessional text cannot purge her guilt over or obsession with the past; it can reach the ear of neither a human nor a divine intended. It is an aesthetic object and nothing more—desperately though Briony and her readers might want it to be more. This predicament raises the questions "What value can literature hold, when other values are absent?" and "What kind of literature is *Atonement*?"

The Vicissitudes of Freudian Literature

The connections between Briony's atheistic introspection and Freudian literature may seem to apply only at a general level, especially given the criticism on *Atonement*'s resonances with texts by other authors, including Austen and Woolf.[24] But McEwan's novel recalls *Dora*—"uncannily," to use a Freudian term, or "hauntingly," to use one from Phillips—in many ways.

Freud's and McEwan's morality tales each feature a thirteen-year-old heroine who occupies an "ill-defined transitional zone" between childhood and maturity (McEwan's phrase, but it fits Dora) and whose "conflicts of affect" and poor self-understanding (Freud's phrase, but it fits Briony) precipitate harm to herself and those near her.[25] Each heroine can be the object either of pathos or judgmental irony: she can seem either to be the innocent victim of forces beyond her developmental capacities, or culpable in her own and others' suffering—depending on which way the narrator's attitude leans at a given moment.

Both narrators—whom I dub "old Briony" and "Freud"—are intellectually dazzling and unreliable, at once self-knowing and unself-knowing: peers of Conrad's and Ford's modernist narrators. Such an ironic understanding of "Freud" belongs to the reception history of *Dora* and other Freudian literature, and it can enrich a comparative reading of *Dora* and *Atonement*, regardless of whether McEwan reads *Dora* this way or whether he modeled *Atonement* on the case history. Such an ironic understanding of old Briony is central to *Atonement*'s reception history: readers know that any judgments old Briony renders on young Briony are suspect. How can we trust the judgments if we can't trust the accusing (or admiring) judge? And there are other reasons to doubt the judgments: McEwan's tale, like Freud's, employs complex temporal layering that makes it hard to discern whether its accounts of its heroine's adolescent deeds and motives are veridical or post-hoc, made-to-order evidence, fodder for the accusatory narrator's agenda.

Table 1 Comparison of Freud's to McEwan's techniques

FREUD THE AUTHOR	McEWAN THE AUTHOR
exposes, perhaps unwittingly, the unconscious ploys of	exposes, quite wittingly, the unconscious ploys of
"FREUD" THE FALLIBLE NARRATOR	OLD BRIONY THE FALLIBLE NARRATOR
who imagines that he has authorial command of	who imagines that she has authorial command of
DORA	YOUNG BRIONY

Developing this parallel between "Freud" and "old Briony" raises questions about authorial intent. Did Freud mean to ironize himself in *Dora*? Probably not—at least not consciously. In other words, one would have to read *Dora* (but not *Atonement*) against the grain to construct the preceding hierarchy.

The table's right column makes immediate sense to us, whereas its left column trips us up because we trust McEwan-the-author as we no longer trust Freud. We share McEwan's weltanschauung and accept his fabricated world, including its implicit and explicit moral judgments. On the other hand, if we imagine *ourselves* in place of Freud-the-author, then the left column clicks into place, with one editorial alteration: we very *wittingly* expose the Freudian narrator's fallibility.

This ironic perspective on *Dora* owes largely to Erik Erikson. In 1962, Erikson attacked Freud's abusive treatment of Ida Bauer ("Dora's" real name), who was a mere seventeen when analyzed by Freud and a mere thirteen when kissed by Herr K. In Erikson's view, there is no need to insist upon the adult sexual motives that Freud attributes to this patient (whose exclamation "No," Freud explains, reveals the severity of her repression, not the absence of desire).[26] Since Erikson's critique, it has been easier to see *Dora's* "Freud" character not as the author's neutral self-depiction but as his tendentious self-construction. Erikson has effectively invited readers to think not only critically but also creatively when interpreting the case history. For my part, in addition to seeing "Freud" as an unreliable narrator, I have also proposed seeing him as the antagonist, and "Dora" as the protagonist, of a drama that ends on a potentially happy note when she breaks off treatment.[27]

Pursuing a different interpretation, Janet Malcolm sees Freud transform defeat to victory by making Bauer's spurning of him the impetus for his foundational concept of "transference,"[28] which he blames as her reason—unconscious to her—for terminating treatment. But in my view, "transference" only partially illuminates their analytic encounter; "countertransference" is its necessary complement. *Dora's* failure to make "Freud's" countertransference an object of analysis—a more glaring omission given its author's admiration for his patient's physical attractiveness and mental adroitness—leaves the case history vulnerable to a standard Freudian critique (an opportunity that numerous readers have exploited). Freud says that self-betrayal "oozes out of every pore"[29] even when Dora does not verbalize her latent desires. Turning the tables on him, readers might discern a manifest and latent narrative arc to *Dora*, the former being a self-justification and the latter a confession by a man who admitted late in his career that he preferred theorizing to clinical work and that the latter often yielded disappointing results.[30] Manifest: Overwhelmed by her transference-love for me, Dora ended treatment before cure was achieved. Latent: Blinded by my countertransference-love for Dora, I relinquished analytic neutrality; my "evenly suspended attention"[31] became officious, and I drove her away before analysis reached fruition.[32]

Are There "Manifest" and "Latent" Levels to Briony's Kunstlerroman?

How could such a reading of Freud's case history bear on McEwan's novel? Since *Oedipus Rex*—and thanks to its interpreters from Aristotle to Freud—readers have admired the ironic chasm between manifest and latent content in psychological literature. The numerous ironies lurking beneath the surface of old Briony's narration (if it has a "surface" and a "depth") recall Freud's ideas about the "psychodynamic" mind. Because Briony is so sophisticated, and because she targets her young self for critique, readers might be dazzled into accepting her testimony at face value. As mentioned, in a metaphysical vein, and at the manifest level, old Briony insists that a novelist cannot "achieve atonement" given her god-like authorial position.[33] She admits being checkmated by Paul Marshall and his financial reserves, unable to expose his and Lola's treachery in the short time before dementia overtakes her. But in the same metaphysical vein at the latent level, old Briony leaves little doubt that the reader is her confessor, from whom she begs forgiveness and understanding, even as she flagellates herself. (Doesn't her self-flagellation elicit the sympathy from us that she apparently withholds from herself?)

In Briony's vein of self-evaluation, *Atonement*'s manifest/latent divisions multiply. Manifestly, old Briony indicates, "I repudiate young Briony, who was childish even for her thirteen years, and cruel." But without much disguise, she reveals that "I'm erotically drawn to the young Briony, who is me: the child is mother of the woman, who even now practices the child's craft. My confession is my Kunstlerroman, my artistic-epistemological coming-of-age tale." (Just as psychoanalysis is "interminable," aesthetic coming of age has no end point. Briony has many apparent epiphanies, but they are false,[34] and she never fully awakens from her callow fantasies into realism—whatever that would mean.) Perhaps it is less in her readers than in herself that she seeks the ideal auditor, who is at once compassionate and gently judgmental, who accepts her in all her imperfection and contradictoriness, although even this auditor cannot know her fully nor heal her.

Even when she muses on narrative technique, Briony's apparent (manifest) self-criticisms, with their suggestion of discontinuity between her youthful and mature aesthetic, belie a continuity—and perhaps a repetition compulsion. "I chickened out and was evasive," she charges (in so many words), "when my 'Two Figures by a Fountain' 'owed a little too much to the techniques of Mrs. Woolf,'" in the words of Cyril Connolly's ("CC's") rejection letter.[35]

It is important to note that this manifestly self-accusing letter might not be a genuine artifact from *Atonement*'s extra-textual world: Briony might have fabricated some or all of it. Regardless of its provenance, though, it conveys multiple editorial points of view.

One is McEwan's: he has carried on a long "conversation with modernism" concerning what he sees as its "dereliction of duty" regarding "the backbone of the plot," as he explained in a radio interview. The letter repeats this aesthetic judgment when it tells Briony "Simply put, you need the backbone of a story." And to ensure that readers understand the connection between aesthetic and moral cogitation, Briony thinks of herself, "Everything she did not wish to confront was also missing from her novella ... It was not the backbone of a story she lacked. It was backbone."[36]

As Seshagiri discusses,[37] McEwan is only one participant in the "conversation with modernism" that he invokes. Modernists themselves, including Woolf, conducted a "modernist autocritique" in which they questioned the "ethical implications" of their experimental styles. *Atonement* belongs to "contemporary fiction's modernist turn": its numerous "reactivations" of the movement's experiments ranging from those that admired their "auratic power" to those, like McEwan's, that judge harshly the movement's claims to epistemological privilege. McEwan's point of view trickles down, perhaps in distorted forms, into the opinions of both old Briony and (if he did write the rejection letter) CC. The letter might serve more importantly to represent part of old Briony's self-divided mind than to convey CC's aesthetic principles.

The accusatory letter worries that the young-adult Briony's attention was altered in several ways by her admiration for Woolf. First, her attention gravitated *toward* characters' mental processes, including her own. This is consistent with Woolf's complaint, in *Mr Bennet and Mrs Brown*, about Edwardian realism's focus on externalities. But the letter's use of the phrase "and so on" suggests that it finds Briony's obsessions tiresome. It discusses how a Woolfian focus on the present moment allows writers to "delve into mysteries of perception, present a stylized version of thought processes, permit the vagaries and unpredictability of the private self to be explored and so on." It sounds as though CC (if he is the author) has contemplated these themes and techniques before and needn't enumerate them all, given how familiar and stale modernistic experiments have grown.[38]

Second, the letter accuses young Briony's attention of gravitating *toward* "the quality of light and shade," "random impressions" to which she dedicates "scores of pages." Little wonder that Elizabeth Bowen finds young Briony's prose "too full, too cloying."[39] This brings me to a third feature of young Briony's aesthetic attentiveness: she seeks a prose style (lyrical? impressionistic?) appropriate to the dazzling mutability both of characters' minds and of the physical environment of a country house. In general, she pursues the modernist pearl of unknowability. "What is the self, or the perceived world," her early draft of "Two Figures" implicitly muses, suggesting that "they slip through our fingers when we try to grasp them."

These might not be such problematic themes and techniques, if Briony weren't agonizing over the need for a confession whose efficacy rests on the realist foundations of knowability and language's communicative powers. "Robbie did not assault Lola," the self-accusing old Briony longs to set down in black and white. "Paul Marshall did. Robbie is innocent, Paul is guilty. Lola too is guilty for abetting the lie against Robbie, and most importantly, I am guilty."

With this crime on her mind, what does young Briony's romance with Woolfian techniques bend her aesthetic attention *away from*? According to CC, two main things.

First, as discussed, he complains of "Two Figures'" lack of "forward movement."[40] Second, young Briony's attention angles *away from* moralizing. But CC exculpates her on this count, rather than proceeding in his largely critical vein. "We do not believe that artists have an obligation to strike up attitudes toward the war," he says, given that they are "politically impotent."[41] His phrasing is suspiciously tendentious—implying that some writers artificially "strike up" attitudes, rather than take principled stances—and many people would argue that writers are *not* politically impotent. Additionally, concerning the general theme of fiction writers moralizing, CC doesn't know about the unexpressed confession that wracks young-adult Briony. He doesn't know everything that *Atonement*'s readers know about the teenage Briony's ruminations on fiction and moral judgments. "She could write the scene three times over, from three points of view," the teenage Briony thought, in a precocious, perspectivalist frame of mind, after witnessing the scene by the fountain. Such a strategy, she then imagined, would deliver her

> from the cumbrous struggle between good and bad. ... She need not judge. There did not have to be a moral. She need only show separate minds ... struggling with the idea that other minds were equally alive .... only in a story could you enter these different minds and show how they had an equal value. That was the only moral a story need have.[42]

Because CC doesn't know about Briony's unexpressed confession, he can't know how irresponsible she might feel—for the most intimate reasons—for *failing* to judge characters against an objective standard of truth, for *failing* to depict "good and bad," for *failing* to show that different minds, in ethical opposition to one another, can have *un*equal values. He can't know that, as dazzled as Briony may be by Woolf's techniques, she is also burdened by a confession that she can't seem to make and that emulating Woolf might hinder her from making.

Because the final draft of *Atonement* is a palimpsest (if we can call it "final"—Briony's death or mental incapacity may be the only guarantees against interminable revisions), readers can infer that CC's advice has been crucial to its evolution. His letter expresses admiration for the phrase "the long grass stalked by the leonine yellow of high summer," and the final draft retains this passage.[43] In service of "forward movement," his letter suggests possible plot implications of the protagonist's misperception of the fountain scene. "How might it affect the lives of the two adults?" he asks. Might the girl "come between them in some disastrous fashion?" Might the girl "expose" the couple to her disapproving parents? "Might the young couple come to use her as a messenger?"[44] Given how much of *Atonement*'s plot follows these suggestions, CC might deserve credit for co-authorship!

But his advice is not sacrosanct to her: she *does* write about the war. Both the battlefield and the hospital ward get extensive treatment. (If this portion of the novel feels awkwardly incorporated into what is otherwise a family drama and Briony's Kunstlerroman, then McEwan has a built-in excuse: the shoddy workmanship is her fault, not his! It reveals her inability to integrate two ambitions for her writing: first, that it could tell the truth and pay penance, and second, that it could transcend good and evil, and dance with Woolf in the rarefied air of aesthetic experimentation.)

CC's letter is an ingenious synecdoche for *Atonement*'s problematization of manifest/latent categories. Old Briony uses some of CC's advice and rejects some; in some passages, his letter seems like a portion of her self-divided mind, while in others his ignorance of her love for Robbie and desire to atone for her sin leave him unable to supply the moral counsel she craves. If *Atonement*'s manifest content is a repudiation of young Briony's selfishness and evasiveness, and if its latent content is a defense or even exoneration of this blossoming artist, then we might imagine CC's letter as the meditation of a psychoanalyst to whom Briony is in the process of opening up. Does her depiction of this fragment of a therapy session afford old Briony one more opportunity to flagellate herself for failing to broadcast her and Paul Marshall's guilt, and Robbie's innocence, to the world? That is, do CC's justified critiques of her Woolfian techniques imply moral cowardice on her part, driving her self-exoneration further underground? Is the letter a futile but harmless exercise in autognosis, leaving Briony's self-knowledge and self-regard exactly where they had been? Or does the letter, with the "great interest" it expresses in Briony's work[45] and the respectful attention it pays both to "Two Figures"' technical experiments and its psychological content, underscore the difficulties of her aesthetic and moral predicament? Does the sensitivity with which she attempts to process CC's advice bring her self-exoneration closer to the surface, where it can facilitate her at-one-ment with herself?

To hope for the last and happiest of these possibilities might be to hope fondly, judging from the final draft of *Atonement*, which arguably one-ups Woolfian modernism with its postmodern text-as-construction model that calls attention to its artificiality and fallibility. When old Briony thinks back on her callow literary efforts, we can almost hear her chuckle at how she converted Robbie into a humble-woodcutter hero come to rescue a distressed maiden. But *Atonement*'s final draft, far from bending back toward Austenian realism, instead pictures Robbie as a war hero who protects a Flemish woman and her son despite "the pain in his side"—an allusion to the site of Christ's piercing by the holy lance and the last of his five holy wounds, whence the Gospel of John says that water and blood poured.[46] Whatever respect for Austen is suggested by *Atonement*'s lengthy epigraph from *Northanger Abbey*, in her old age Briony's inclination to idealize Robbie has metastasized. Her imagination has swung between extremes, from seeing Robbie (in her early teen years) as a sexual villain to depicting him (in her septuagenarian art) as a selfless martyr, as much symbol as man. If English realist fiction, like Freudian therapy, examines the tension between imagining beloved others through the distorting lens of fantasy and accepting them as they actually are (whatever that means), then Briony's treatment of the "Robbie" character illustrates how overpowering fantasy can be.

If readers are to pursue a classical Freudian interpretation even further, whence might they trace the "latent" or "repressed" sources of Briony's metaphysical ideas (her god complex), her self-evaluation (her narcissistic self-fascination), and her ideas about narrative technique (her repetitive-compulsive recourse to fantasy)? Seeking evidence of a psychodynamic mind in action, classical Freudians can always find what they're looking for. (So runs one of Frederick Crews's charges against Freudianism, though its logic could apply to many—perhaps to any—epistemological paradigm.[47]) A Freudian analysis might say that Robbie was like a brother to Briony as she grew up, that her love for him has an incestuous whiff,[48] a suggestion of "polymorphous perversity." Her parents are largely absent from her adolescent life, her mother bedridden by headaches, her father called from home by his work and mistress. This suggests that they were likewise absent during her formative years, opening the way for Cecelia and Robbie as substitute parent-figures. But these parents too are often so preoccupied that they cannot give the girl the attention she craves. Briony's jealous love for Robbie repetitively enacts her Electra complex. (How traumatic it must be to witness her substitute parents' primal scene in the library! No wonder she reacts so extravagantly to an event that McEwan seems to have imagined for the very purpose of invoking a Freudian concept.) Would such a reading enrich or reduce McEwan's artistry?

Briony's Writing as Hysteria

To speak of "manifest" and "latent" content is not necessarily to be Freudian. It's to be hermeneutical in the broadest sense, to posit a "surface" and a "depth" (the model that Susan Sontag inveighs against when she champions "erotic" reading[49]), to attribute *explicit* and *implicit* themes to a text. (Trying to distinguish "explicit" from "implicit" in *Atonement* could be a fool's game.) To find latent sexual motives throughout a text is not necessarily to be Freudian, either. Freud held no copyright on sexual hermeneutics any more than on hermeneutics in general. To apply the "Freudian" label to any story that turns on characters' sexual motives, including unconscious ones, would water down Freud's ideas.

Yet *Atonement* and Freud cannot be easily separated. If McEwan's novel is post-Freudian or even anti-Freudian—if it is as skeptical toward psychoanalytic concepts as religious ones—then it achieves this post-Freudianism only by working through a dense weave of Freudian concepts. In *Dora* as prominently as anywhere, Freud couples his sexually focused hermeneutics with an epistemology of comparable allure to ambitious exegetes. His *methods* for discovering sexual motives, indirectly expressed, have inspired admiration (and perhaps undue credulity) as much as the *content* he discovers. While Briony's self-depiction explodes whatever residual metanarrative optimism, whatever hope for cure, informs "Dora's" tale, it nonetheless uncannily recalls Freud's ideas about illness and its symptoms.

Young Briony presents no classical hysterical symptoms like Dora's aphonia, but old Briony likens her imaginative acts, written and verbal—her childish dramatic writings, her lie to the inspector, and her adolescent Woolfian efforts—to the manifest content of latent neuroses, the products of pathological tendencies. She reasons back not toward repressed Oedipal material, but toward her young self's compulsion toward fantasy and denial. Freud's analysis of Dora's "motives for being ill"[50] (i.e., hysterical) anticipates old Briony's analysis of young Briony's motives for being a compulsive fantasist.

A thin line separates compulsive fantasizing from compulsive lying, *Atonement* suggests, and thus Briony's writing enables her illness as much as it provides her tools for critically analyzing it. In and of themselves her plays—which simplify a confounding adult world into a clean fairytale with heroes and villains—are not harmful. But the epistemological orientation that they both reveal and strengthen can be perilous: by casting Robbie and Cecelia in such roles in her legal testimony, Briony initiates the novel's disaster. "Real life ... had sent her a villain in the form of an old family friend," she thinks.[51] Her act of perjury begins with a mistaken perception of a damningly *literary* type.

But are adult forms of literariness as culpable as such childish imaginings? *Atonement* indicates that Woolfian perspectivalism is, and suggests that all forms of storytelling, Austenian realism included, may also be. The novel's critical account of Woolfian narrative techniques and their distortive capacities recalls Freud's account of dreams and their distortions. *Dora* describes dreams as roads along which the conscious mind can be reached by mental material which, since repressed, is pathogenic: dreams are "*détours by which repression can be evaded*" (Freud's italics).[52] Let us replace "dreams" with perspectivalism, the medium of Briony's fuzzy thinking.[53] This narrative mode serves not as a detour by which repression is evaded, but as *the language in which evasion is achieved*, through which the pathogenic compulsion finds expression, muscling aside Briony's desire to confess her misdeed straightforwardly. The mode is not to blame for Briony's criminal act, of course, but if Briony's objective in composing "Two Figures" is to come to grips with this act, then Woolfian anti-realism is the wrong tool. It dilutes her confession in a sea (not just a stream) of sensitive consciousness. And with no confession, there can be no atonement, even of a written kind. (Arguably, confession only emerges as Briony's objective in later drafts of *Atonement*, and by the time of "Two Figures," she is still groping her way toward the novel's *raison d'etre*. If so, then the "symptom" of her textual production obeys a Freudian rule: Freud says that one symptom—e.g., a cough—can assume numerous meanings over time.[54])

In a world without theological evil, Briony's fantasy compulsion is a source of grave ill. It lands Robbie in prison in the first place (disguising her love for him in her lie to the inspector), and it latches onto Woolfian technique in the second instance (disguising her confession behind avant-garde showmanship). McEwan, in keeping with English realist precursors such as Austen, George Eliot, and Iris Murdoch, can be puritanical. Rather than condemning sexual desire or greed, as earlier Puritans might have done, *Atonement* condemns fantasy. It is endemic to Briony's mental life, and if she is a representative figure, then it is our common disease. But how are we to vanquish it? If only a Freudian shaman could cast this demon out of us! His hermeneutic and metanarrative endeavors would work in tandem. His hermeneutic investigation would reveal the deep truth of our neurosis, our fallen condition. And when our unconscious became conscious, at the climax of the metanarrative, we would emerge cleansed, reborn. We would journey inward so that we could move forward, upward. But if Briony represents our lost faith in this shamanism, then what is she to do? Can she draw on a lifetime's wisdom, serve as her own modified Freud, and control this demon, this compulsion to hysterical textual production that has possessed her for sixty-four years? Or, barring control over it, can she grasp its etiology?

Freud insists that, having seen an "abundance" of hysterical cases, he has not encountered a "single one" in which three determinants were not present: "a psychic trauma, a conflict of affects, and ... a disturbance in the sphere of sexuality."[55] In Dora's case, one "disturbance in the sphere of sexuality" is the sensation of Herr K's erection against her lower body. In Briony's case, first, the ambiguous fountain scene, wherein Robbie seems to be violent and bossy; second, the word "cunt" in Robbie's note; and third, the primal scene—or apparent sexual assault—in the library confront her with adult sexual realities that she is not equipped to handle. "Something brutal," and soon later, "something irreducibly human, or male, threatened the order of their household,"[56] writes the old Briony, evoking her younger self's fear and incomprehension—in language that could apply to Dora's encounter with Herr K. Without these interrelated sexual "disturbances," Briony's pathogenic tendency to fantasy would not have led to the hysterical acts that propel the novel's plot.

In Dora's case, her "conflict of affects" applies to various people—including her father and Frau K.—not just to Herr K., though without conflicted feelings for him, she would not have been "disturbed" ("traumatized?") by his embrace. In Briony's case, without conflicted feelings toward Robbie, would she fall into such grave misperception and crime? At age ten she confesses to Robbie that she loves him, and she even throws herself into the river, requiring him to dive in and save her like a hero in one of her tales—but she receives in return his rebuke "you stupid girl. You could have killed us both."[57] Robbie wonders whether she spent several years nursing her love, until the moment on the bridge when he made her the go-between for his note to Cecelia. When she read the note, he muses, she felt betrayed by his preferring her sister to her. If he is right, then where would Briony direct her jealous anger? At her sister, whom Robbie has apparently ordered to dive underwater (in an uncanny mirroring of Briony's dive)? Briony's fantasy compulsion can do better than that: she can recast the roles in the play she is always confabulating. Robbie, having banished himself from the part of willing savior, can become the villain. With Briony banished from the role of rescued maiden by Robbie's "stupid girl" remark, Cecelia can assume the part of besieged maiden. And with the role of savior now open, Briony can claim it for herself.

So conflicted are Dora's feelings for Herr K. that she experiences a "reversal of affect," a mechanism that Freud describes as both an "important" and a "difficult" problem in the "psychology of the neuroses"—one that he acknowledges he has not yet solved, though *Dora* maps in detail how its heroine's feelings reverse. This label fits Briony's feelings toward Robbie, between the river scene and the bridge scene three years later. In fact *Dora*'s categories fit Briony's case at a finer level. Freud describes as symptomatic "of a pathological condition" trains of thought that are "exaggerated," "reinforced," or "supervalent."[58] Could any label better evoke Briony's train of thought than "supervalent," when she imagines Robbie as a "villain," then a "maniac?" Freud says that "behind" a supervalent thought a contradictory one can "lay concealed,"[59] and by virtue of their exaggeration, Briony's epithets for Robbie effectively conceal her wounded but still active love for him, we might say.

How do we know when unacknowledged loves remain active? Freudian diagnostics offer myriad opportunities for such inferences. Regardless of whether we approve of such license, we may suspect that forgetting is not innocent. When Freud tells Dora that she must have been "completely in love" with her father as a young girl, she says "I don't remember that," but then tells a story about her cousin who pointed at her mother—whom the cousin said she hated—then said "when she's dead I shall marry Daddy."[60] (Naturally, Freud sees the story as a confession of what Dora doesn't "remember" about herself.) Later, Freud says that Dora masturbated, probably as a child, and she "denied flatly that she could remember any such thing." But then she plays with her reticule, which Freud sees as pantomimic of this behavior.[61] Minus the Oedipal and masturbatory elements, Briony's imagined encounter with Robbie when, at age eighteen, she confesses her crime to Cecelia and him, recalls Dora's dubious "forgettings." Robbie was "startlingly handsome," the eighteen-year-old Briony realizes, "and there came back to her from years ago, when she was ten or eleven, the memory of a passion she'd had for him, a real crush that had lasted days. Then she confessed it to him one morning in the garden and immediately forgot about it."[62]

In *Dora*, Freud explains why claims not to remember are untrustworthy; in *Atonement*, irony does the explaining. Of course Briony did not "immediately" forget the "crush," just because she "confessed" it. The ten-year-old Briony may have *denied* her love for Robbie after he rebuked her. And the eighteen-year-old Briony may enjoy a self-exculpating narrative that converts this denial to a forgetting—after all, this late adolescent has not yet come to terms with her crime, which a "reversal of affect" toward Robbie likely motivated. How much better *not* to believe that love, wounded pride, and jealousy simmered within her for three years, between the river scene and bridge scene, impelling a vengeful act against her beloved! The great irony of the eighteen-year-old's confessional scene, of course, is that it never happened:[63] Briony did not make the trip to Cecelia's flat, but counterfactually imagines what would have happened if she had. The seventy-seven-year-old author of *Atonement* ironizes her thirteen-year-old self, and the counterfactual scene enables her to ironize her eighteen-year-old self as well, for the way she clung to the idea that she had "forgotten" a feeling that supplied a strong motive force.

Destination: Textuality?

The mind of McEwan's septuagenarian narrator appears to be saturated with Freudian ideas. What else could explain her dexterous depiction of a reversal of affect—or, in broader terms, how the dramatic conflicts that she devises beg for psychodynamic analysis? Freud, her tale suggests, tells us much about intimacy and its discontents, and about the motives of its players, partly hidden from themselves and their lovers.

But surely, at this stage of literary-critical history, a classical Freudian exegesis would be retrograde. It would render us blind to the time-boundness of some of Freud's ideas, to their conspicuous absence from Briony's confessional tale. Formulaic hysterical symptoms, masturbation guilt, revelatory dreams that await unlocking by the master analyst, a minutely detailed psychic determinism—and most of all, a comforting metanarrative of cure—surely the lack of these materials in *Atonement* is as noteworthy as its many psychoanalytically inflected themes. At the risk of cherry-picking evidence of the novel's post-Freudian sensibility, we can cite Robbie's analysis of Briony's false accusation, delivered when the thirteen-year-old was still smarting from his rejection of her callow love. "At this stage of her life," Robbie thinks, Briony "inhabited an ill-defined transitional zone between the nursery and adult worlds which she crossed and uncrossed unpredictably."[64]

What an ingenious rejoinder to Freud's contention that the Unconscious never says "No!"—and perhaps to the whole model of manifest and latent material. Rather than insisting that adult motives lurk behind every childish display, Robbie's formulation enables the same flexible, non-reductive, "erotic" encounter with textual complexity that Sontag opposes to doctrinaire Freudianism, or to any –ism. But how much authority does Robbie's anti-hermeneutical idea have? All of *Atonement* is the product of old Briony's imagination (unless the text crisscrosses between her imaginings at various stages of life): she could have made Robbie's observation more expansive; she could have repeated it, like a musical motif; she could have put it in the mind (or dialog) of a different character. Is it an interpretive key to *Atonement*, meant to deflate the novel's apparent investments in "surface" and "depth," deviously disguised as a passing thought in the mind of a supporting character? Or does the novel have no interpretive key, not even the exhortation to *mistrust hermeneutics*?

Freud-bashing is an easy temptation now, as was the Freud worship of decades past. But if Briony is a "Freudian revisionist,"[65] then which Freud is she revising? The one who believed in abreaction, or the one who came to believe in "working through?" Isn't *Atonement* a tribute to the intricate beauty of "working through?" (Or ought we to read it as a parody of "interminable analysis?") When we think of Freud's ideas as evolving organisms; when—rather than using the idea of "manifest" and "latent" content to plumb McEwan's ironies—we instead use *Atonement* to tease out the uses and limitations of these concepts, the Freudian conversation may be "intriguing" enough, to use one of Phillips's terms, to justify its continuance. We have moved, in Roland Barthes' words, from "work" to "text." We no longer search for validating "origins"—where Freud got X or Y *right* about human nature. Instead we seek intellectual adventure in "destinations"[66]—places to which Freud, and his critical and admiring successors, leads us unpredictably.

How could a Freudian textual "destination" bear on our examination of intimacy and historical progress? It is easy, today, to despise or pity the past—or stereotyped versions of it—for its social inequities and pre-Freudian sexual innocence. The tale, rehearsed by McEwan, of the poor boy and rich girl denied love by a rigid class system plays well to an audience inclined to pride itself on its society's (supposed) egalitarianism and enlightenment. The country house, a ready-made symbol of antiquated wealth, allows twenty-first-century readers to sigh, "Thank goodness we don't live in *that* world," where a woman like Briony is beyond Robbie's station. The disaster resulting from Briony's sexual naivety invites the same readers to congratulate themselves on their post-Victorianism, the unlikelihood of their falling victim to their own innocence.

But in an atmosphere of thoroughgoing skepticism, such as "postmoderns" and their successors purportedly inhabit, neither the Freudian promise of full self-knowledge nor the melioristic liberal promise of socioeconomic equality is entirely plausible. In such an intellectual atmosphere, what value does McEwan ascribe to art such as Briony's? If we keep in mind Phillips's unconcern with whether psychoanalysis is "true or even useful"; and if we sympathize with his claim that, even in the absence of cure or transcendence, "it is worth speaking, and that some ways of speaking are better than others,"[67] then we can see the aesthetic grounds on which he values Freudian discourse. Briony and McEwan value literary expression on similar grounds. It doesn't take much digging into *Atonement* to get to this defense of art.

But the defense is beset by doubt. Has giving birth to *Atonement* been healthful for Briony? We have no extra-textual evidence by which to measure her psychological soundness by the time of its final draft.[68] Phillips admits that, while "the Freudian mind might be a poetry-making organ ... this in itself is not a cause for celebration .... Poets, after all, are not famous for their mental health."[69] This admission enables us to recast his claim that "it is worth speaking [and] some ways of speaking are better than others" by saying that, seven decades after Freud's death, readers and critics "*suspect* that it is worth speaking and writing, and that some ways of speaking and writing are *probably* better than others." Such is our muddle as we have come to doubt metanarratives—Christian, Freudian, Marxist, or liberal-progressive—and have come, in the wake of the canon wars and a global recession, to doubt the category of "literature." Perhaps our playful sense of disillusionment, our habit of recognizing our beliefs as constructs, enables Briony to speak to us post-Freudians so familiarly, as we struggle to comprehend our intimacies with our parents and their surrogates: our teachers, doctors, novelists, lovers, and ourselves.

Briony's intriguing predicament derives from an array of precursor-texts, some of them—like *Northanger Abbey*—explicitly acknowledged. But her tale resonates with Ida Bauer's so richly that the two heroines seem to espouse a common fable about the muddle of human intimacy, our dreams of resolving the muddle, and the value of literature—conceived broadly—in evoking our yearnings for clarity.

Notes

1 Nicholls (4–5) discusses Lyotard's appreciation of the radically skeptical possibilities inherent in modernism, including Lyotard's provocative claim that "A work can become modern only if it is first postmodern. Postmodernism thus understood is not modernism at its end but in the nascent state, and this state is constant" (*The Postmodern Condition* 79).
2 Lewis, *Religious Experience* 26–7.
3 Various critics have discussed McEwan in terms of this label, which followed upon the appearance of four antireligious polemics in three years, by Sam Harris, Daniel Dennet, Richard Dawkins, and Christopher Hitchens. (See articles by Pastoor, Wally, and Bradley, as well as Bradley and Tate's book.) Pastoor's quote comes from his title (203).
4 Nathan Hale 300–21 and Stepansky 11–14 discuss the post-Second World War decline of psychoanalysis in psychiatry.
5 Others have written about Freud in this vein, notably Peter Brooks, who casts Freud's 1920 treatise *Beyond the Pleasure Principle* as Freud's "masterplot," his "scheme of how life proceeds from beginning to end, and how each individual life ... repeats the masterplot and confronts the question of whether the closure of an individual life is contingent or necessary" (96–7). Freud finds the pleasure principle, which draws organisms out of themselves, insufficient to account for the repetition compulsion, which leads subjects constantly to work through painful experience. Thus, says

Brooks, Freud links the repetition compulsion to the death drive, an organism's desire to avoid external threats, so that it may master its environment and die according to its own organic processes. For Brooks, literature is imbued with the repetition compulsion. His discussion of Freud's "masterplot" and my analysis of the Freudian "metanarrative" have overlapping but different aims.

6   Though I have chosen a non-technical term, the nature and function of "internalization" have been sources of debate for Freud and his progeny. For a discussion of identification and the "introjection of the objects of the Oedipus complex," see Fenichel 103ff. For an influential early discussion of introjection, see Ferenczi.

7   *Dora* explains that an early history of a kind like its heroine's—her "premature sexual enjoyment" with its consequential bed-wetting, genital catarrh, and disgust—results in adulthood either in an abandonment to sexuality that "borders on perversity" or in repudiation of sexuality and neurotic illness. Apparently no happy medium is possible (87).

8   Frederic Crews is a leading Freudian revisionist thanks to both his own polemics and his compilations of work by Freud's other critics. Dating roughly from 1970, Freudian revisionism is a loosely affiliated set of critiques of Freud's theories, methodologies, and personal failings. The following discussion is indebted to Crews as both polemicist and editor (xxiv and elsewhere).

9   It is easy to oversimplify Freud's model, which evolved throughout his career. "Analysis Terminable and Interminable" worries that "dynamic" and "topographical" models of the mind de-emphasize the useful "economic line of approach," according to which, in the struggle between an instinct trying to express itself and the ego trying to suppress it, the quantitatively stronger force wins (226–7). Notwithstanding Freud's tendency to cast himself as a pioneer, he was not the first theorist to posit an unconscious mind, though his description is distinguished by its richness of detail, the degree to which he reformulated it, and the extent of its influence. For a history of the "unconscious" before Freud, see Whyte.

10 Timpanaro critiques the implausible virtuosities of this character (29–35, 39–40, 43–7, etc.).

11 Wittgenstein 69.

12 Rorty, "Freud and Moral Reflection," especially 146–8, where Rorty builds on Donald Davidson's sympathetic discussion of Freud.

13 For the first published appearance of the term "ab*reaction*," in the context of a discussion of various *reactions* to adverse circumstances (my emphasis), see Freud and Breuer, "On the Psychical Mechanism of Hysterical Phenomena" 9.

14 Classical Freudian theory has evolved in schools of ego psychology, object relations theory, self-psychology, and intersubjectivity, each offering refinements and alternatives to Freud's ideas about the Unconscious and other matters. How strong a connection classical Freudian theory retains with consensus thought in psychology and psychiatry today is a perplexing question. The chapter on "Defense Mechanisms" in the *Diagnostical Statistical Manual-IV's Sourcebook* begins by wondering "whether there is sufficient empirical evidence to support inclusion of an axis for defense mechanisms." It adds that "The DSM is designed for use by all mental health professionals. Concepts of defensive functioning have their origins in psychodynamic conflict theory," which is imbued with Freudian values and biases. "Will defense mechanisms," it asks, "be useful to clinicians of other theoretical and therapeutic persuasions?" (503)

15 For humanistic defenses of Freudianism that acknowledge its non-scientific status, see Adam Phillips, "Poetry and Psychoanalysis," especially 1–3, and "Promises, Promises," especially 364–5. Also see Ricoeur.
16 Phillips, "Promises, Promises" 364.
17 Ibid. "Promises, Promises" 364–5.
18 See "Remembering Repeating, and Working-Through," especially the remark that "working through … resistances may in practice turn out to be an arduous task for the subject of the analysis and a trial of patience for the analyst" (155).
19 Ida Bauer's (a.k.a, "Dora's") therapy took place in 1900, though Freud misremembered it as having occurred a year earlier (Rieff vii).
20 This claim depends on my credulous acceptance that "Robbie Turner died of septicemia … or that Cecelia was killed … by the bomb that destroyed Balham Underground Station" (350). But this suggestion of Briony's, like everything she says, could be unreliable. For a reading that doubts that Robbie and Celia are dead, see Jacobi.
21 *Atonement* 350.
22 Bradley and Tate 16.
23 D'hoker 38.
24 See Wells, Apstein, and Marcus ("Ian McEwan's Modernist Time"). For a discussion of L. P. Hartley's *The Go-Between* as an intertext, see Ingersoll.
25 *Atonement* 132, *Dora* 24.
26 "Fragment of an Analysis of a Case of Hysteria" 58–9.
27 Wolfe *Bloomsbury, Modernism, and the Reinvention of Intimacy* 51–78.
28 Malcolm 93–4.
29 "Fragment of an Analysis of a Case of Hysteria" 78.
30 See "Analysis Terminable and Interminable," e.g. 248, where Freud allows that psychoanalysis may be an "impossible profession"—the source of Janet Malcolm's book title.
31 "Recommendations to Physicians Practicing Psychoanalysis" 111.
32 Classical Freudian analysts today, as Malcolm explains (37), would never indulge the liberties that Freud and his acolyte Ferenczi took, shouting at, praising, arguing with, and accepting flowers from patients, and in Ferenczi's case, kissing them. The "latent" content I ascribe to *Dora* therefore depends upon an anachronism: associating the ethic of analytic neutrality—which was codified later in the history of psychoanalysis—with the Freud who wrote *Dora* at the beginning of the twentieth century.
33 *Atonement* 350.
34 For example, "Real life, her life now beginning, had sent her a villain in the form of an old family friend" (148), "Her childhood had ended, she decided now" (150), "If only she, Briony, had been less innocent, less stupid. Now she saw, the affair was too consistent, too symmetrical to be anything other than what she said it was" (158).
35 *Atonement* 294.
36 McEwan, interview with Michael Silverblatt, *Atonement* 296, 302.
37 Seshagiri. "Encounters with Modernism."
38 *Atonement* 294.
39 Ibid. 295–6.
40 Ibid. 296.
41 Ibid. 297.
42 Ibid. 38.

43 Ibid. 294, 36.
44 Ibid. 295–6.
45 Ibid. 294.
46 Ibid. 223, John 19:34.
47 See also the excerpt of Grünbaum's work in Crews's collection (76–84).
48 The novel's incest motif includes Briony's affection for Leon, with its faint sexual component: 4. More frequently, Briony's or Cecelia's feelings for Robbie, or his for Cecelia, occupy an ill-defined space between being innocently sisterly/brotherly and being sexual. See 74, 122, 193, etc.
49 Sontag 14.
50 "Fragment of an Analysis of a Case of Hysteria" 44.
51 *Atonement* 148.
52 "Fragment of an Analysis of a Case of Hysteria" 15.
53 Richard Robinson says that "*Atonement* seems to ventriloquize modernism and then to silence it" (474).
54 "Fragment of an Analysis of a Case of Hysteria" 83. Also see 54, where Freud says that a "new source of excitation" can pour into an old symptom "like new wine into an old bottle."
55 "Fragment of an Analysis of a Case of Hysteria" 24.
56 *Atonement* 107.
57 Ibid. 217–18.
58 "Fragment of an Analysis of a Case of Hysteria" 54 (including ftnt 1), 60, 62.
59 Ibid. 60.
60 Ibid. 57.
61 Ibid. 76–7.
62 *Atonement* 323.
63 See endnote 20 for a discussion of Briony's confession, on *Atonement*'s penultimate page (350), that her happy ending is an invention.
64 *Atonement* 132.
65 See endnote 8 for a discussion of Crews.
66 *A Theory of Adaptation* xiii, 106.
67 Phillips, "Poetry and Psychoanalysis" 15.
68 *Atonement* 3.
69 Phillips, "Poetry and Psychoanalysis" 11.

4

Post-Freudian Hope: *Regeneration* in an Incredulous Milieu

The Great War ... was a hideous embarrassment to the prevailing Meliorist myth ... the Idea of Progress.
—Paul Fussell, *The Great War and Modern Memory*

Simplifying to the extreme, I define postmodern as incredulity toward metanarratives .... The narrative function is losing its functors, its great hero ... its great goal. It is being dispersed in clouds of narrative language elements ... Each of us lives at the intersection of many of these. However, we do not necessarily establish stable language combinations, and the properties of the ones we do establish are not necessarily communicable.
—Jean François Lyotard, *The Postmodern Condition*

That the First World War killed the metanarrative has been proclaimed both before and since Paul Fussell's study of the naïve hopes with which Britain entered the conflict and the ironic reversals those hopes met on the battlefield. But just as Mark Twain noted that reports of his death were exaggerated, we might note that proclamations of the metanarrative's death have been overstated. (Why would Lyotard associate its demise with the failed revolutionary hopes of 1968 if it had been destroyed in trench combat by 1918?) The metanarrative impulse is adaptive and resilient—the desire not just to *record* history as a vast sprawl (or an ironic joke) but to *narrate* it, to find design and *telos* in it, to take inspiration from its apparent direction. The Marxist-inflected aspirations of the 1930s' radical left and the idealism of the 1960s' New Left testify that not one or even two world wars extinguished the age-old motivations to know what the flow of present events portends for the future, to tell a good story, and to inspire hope. Because these three motivations can work in tandem or tug against one another, their emergences throughout intellectual history—with its oscillations between metanarrative sanguinity and anti-metanarrative skepticism—are impossible to predict. Such proclamations as Fussell's have their own *grand-récit* quality, with their sketches of (1) a past when people innocently believed that history unfolds according to a predictable and benign logic, followed by (2) a present in which we have awakened from this consolatory fantasy.

The Great War, even from a secular perspective, was one of its century's great apocalypses: a disaster that uncovered meanings or unearthed buried energies. But the revelation depended upon who read the rubble. Henry James encapsulates the despair of many democratic-minded Anglo-Americans in a letter dated August 4, 1914—the day Britain declared war on the Central Powers. "The plunge of civilization into this abyss," says James, "so gives away the whole long age" when we thought the world was "gradually bettering" that to confront the gulf between reality and our naivety is "too tragic for any words."[1] But James's End-of-Belief-in-Progress interpretation says as much about him as about the war. Russian Marxists interpreted the war not as a betrayal of liberal ideals but as a revelation of capitalism's bloody imperial logic,[2] and they promulgated a metanarrative rooted in the dialectical-materialist belief that "the higher level of existence emerges from and has its roots in the lower [and] this process of evolutionary advance ... reflect[s] basic properties of 'matter in motion as a whole.'"[3] Feeling cheated of land by their Allied co-victors, Italian fascists developed a metanarrative infused with "vitalistic optimism": they would forge a "Third Way" in lieu of liberalism and communism, and build a "Third Rome" to revive the "First Rome" of antiquity and the "Second Rome" of the Renaissance. (The Nazis' "Third Reich" drew on a German variant of this mythology.) Italian fascists' "lay religion"[4] used narrative epistemology—stories stretching from the ancient past to the immanent future—to make sense of the present.

Therapeutic Intimacy and the Story of "Cure"

But global historical visions, either hopeful or disillusioned, are not the only ones inspired by apocalyptic warfare. As Marxism helped to shape twentieth-century secular metanarrative hopes for social history, so Freudianism helped to shape the century's hopes for personal histories. "In what ways," Freud and his many legatees asked in so many words, "might an individual's psychological, artistic, and moral careers—his entanglements in love, work, and family—be made to improve, not haphazardly, but according to codified therapeutic intervention? How rapidly and with what likelihood of success?" The First World War supplied psychiatrists in England and abroad with thousands of "shell-shocked" patients (as they were once called): apocalypses on a personal scale, men whose psychic destruction also held promise of revelation. Their hysterical symptoms, begging for etiological investigation, presented this growing class of physicians an opportunity to tell new stories about the psyche as they healed it. These labors helped to shape the Freudian legacy.

Physician-writers such as W. H. R. Rivers, the flawed hero of Pat Barker's *Regeneration* trilogy—as well as Barker—face questions about how to narrate post-traumatic experience. "Where was Freud right and wrong?" they ask, more and less explicitly. "Do his authorial skills give us models to emulate or temptations to avoid?" Freud fretted as early as 1895 that "the case histories I write ... read more like short stories and ... lack the serious stamp of science."[5] *Dora* (1905) showcases his techniques for characterizing an analyst and analysand locked in struggle, sometimes together against their common enemy of her suffering, and sometimes against one another, when (as Freud has it) she teams up with her suffering against his invasive eye. For many reasons, some articulated by *Dora*'s feminist critics,[6] subsequent writers are wary of employing Freudian tropes uncritically. But avoiding this pitfall is easier said than done.

The physicians in *Dora* and the *Regeneration* trilogy, along with Drs. Holmes and Bradshaw of *Mrs Dalloway*, struggle to reintegrate wayward subjects into societies malformed by oppression, homophobia, and sexual hypocrisy. As Elaine Showalter comments, Virginia Woolf connects "the shell-shocked veteran with the repressed woman of the man-governed world through their common enemy, the nerve specialist."[7] Thus, although Barker's style differs markedly from Woolf's, and although Barker helps to recover Rivers from historical obscurity, in the process de-centering Freud from her account of war-time psychotherapy, nonetheless Freud and Woolf remain important forebears for her trilogy. Freud's depictions of therapeutic sessions anticipate both its technique and its content. *Dora*, a precursor-text for many fictional and non-fictional case studies—from Alexander Luria's to Oliver Sacks's, from Virginia Axline's to Martha Emmett's, from *In Treatment* to *The Sopranos*[8]—demonstrates how tics, pregnant pauses, dream interpretations, and the labyrinth of transference and countertransference offer rich opportunities for literary treatment.

But Freud's oeuvre foreshadows Barker's trilogy in intellectual-historical ways as well as aesthetic ones. At a bird's-eye level, his decreasing faith in therapy's curative powers parallels the trilogy's anguished examination of how much good Rivers accomplishes, for all his noble intentions and "the combination of mental toughness and compassion" that Barker "reveres" in him as "the best that any human being can be."[9] These intertextual resonances suggest affinities between modernist-era and late twentieth-century literature: the common questions with which the two milieus wrestle and their ambivalent answers. They loosen up associations of contemporary skepticism with postmodern "incredulity" and modernism with (straw-man) credulity. Lyotard's "incredulity toward metanarratives" turn of phrase is a useful starting place for discussing works, like Barker's, with postmodern attributes.[10] But Lyotard's own accounts of *la condition postmoderne* and of postmodern aesthetics are more nuanced than any slogan.[11] Brian McHale's idea of a "change in the dominant" between the two milieus can apply to the degrees of metanarrative credulity that inform modernist-era and late twentieth-century treatments of intimacy, whether in the psychotherapeutic arena or elsewhere. Rarely are works from either era of one mind only concerning progress and *telos*, but incredulity may be a "dominant" note in contemporary fiction and an emergent one in modernism.[12]

Barker evinces incredulity in having neither of Rivers's main patients healed: the historical Siegfried Sassoon or the fictional Billy Prior. But the ending of her trilogy's first novel is hopeful—on a manifest level. It suggests lyrically that Rivers will heed the proverb "Physician, heal thyself,"[13] both in a political sense (he becomes more independent-minded, progressive, and anti-war—like Barker) and a personal sense (he becomes a more confident leader). Rivers's regeneration is catalyzed by his patients, including Sassoon, whose brave protest against the war the narrator calls "a completely honest action … such actions are seeds carried on the wind. Nobody can tell where … they will bear fruit."[14]

Thus, although Sassoon is not cured, Barker apparently extends therapy's metanarrative reach beyond the patient's life, into the analyst's, and into subsequent decades of history—as though individual psychotherapy might begin to heal society,[15] and as though the expiration date on this tonic is indefinite. But in addition to being hopeful, the "seeds on the wind" metaphor is also chilling, with its Darwinian evocation of a delicate organism's struggle for survival in a vast, harsh environment. Properly speaking, a metanarrative shouldn't rely on good luck ("the wind") for its happy ending: it should guarantee that "honest actions" will "bear fruit." An alteration of Barker's language, such as a Freudian might make, yields the observation "no one can tell *if* they will bear fruit" (my italics).

As I discuss below, a more programmatic alteration of Barker's language, according to the Freudian principle of projection, opens a broader vista onto *Regeneration*'s concluding paragraphs. When Rivers seems to transition from thinking about his own growth to thinking about Sassoon's grim predicament, he projects his dilemma onto his patient. At a latent level, *Regeneration* complicates—without cancelling—its metanarrative hope for its protagonist's healing. The whole trilogy blurs divisions between the minds of Rivers and his two main patients. All three men contribute to the war effort, though all three doubt its validity. In a sense they are all martyrs, sacrificing their health or life for the good of other soldiers. But in another sense they suffer from a *martyr complex*, to repurpose a piece of psychological jargon—as Rivers does when he diagnoses Sassoon's "anti-war neurosis."[16] What good, after all, do they do for these soldiers, if they abet the continuance of the war that claims so many of their lives?

In addition to being ambivalent toward their personal military labors, to the point where self-dissociation is a danger, each of these soldiers is also (possibly) gay—thus compelled in a second way to hide part of himself from part of society, and perhaps from himself. (*Mrs Dalloway* shadows this psychic constellation of Barker's, with its bipartite Clarissa-Septimus subject, who, like Barker's characters, is bisexual, traumatized by war, and vulnerable to therapeutic assault.) In Rivers, Sassoon, and Prior's entangled journey, Barker depicts a collective psyche struggling to cure itself, both inside and outside of psychotherapy, both in a psychosexual sense and as a citizen whose conscience cannot be ignored. Given that the psychic boundaries among these three characters are so fluid, what becomes of the hope that one man's "honest action" may "bear fruit" in another's life?

Metanarrative closure, if any is to be had, is deferred, or to use Lyotard's language from the epigraph, "dispersed." Should it be sought in Rivers's lived present (1918), as the war grinds to its end? Or in his, Sassoon's, and eventually Barker's future—beyond 1995, when *Ghost Road*, the trilogy's final installment, appeared? In this novel, Rivers continues to lurch toward self-integration, getting worse to get better, *deteriorating during treatment*, to borrow a Freudian formula.[17] Thanks to a prolonged hallucinatory fever, he regains his visual memory. Readers, schooled on Freud, who hope for a success story of abreacted hysteria may be partly satisfied. But as this *petit (personal) récit* gestures toward resolution, a larger historical *récit* delivers to the doctor a ward full of maimed and dying soldiers. Rivers cuts a poor Christ figure if his resurrection is narratively inseparable from the sacrifice of so many innocents.

Perhaps the ending of *Ghost Road*, the trilogy's final novel, supplies a larger truth than the ending of *Regeneration*, the trilogy's opening novel. In other words, perhaps a dark anthropological *grand récit*, focused on the universals of violence and death, contains the trilogy's overarching message. Perhaps it neutralizes several *petit récits*: a secular-Christian one that sees salvific power in Rivers's self-sacrifice, a Freudian one in which countertransference and fever-delirium effect the physician's healing, and a progressive-pacifist one in which the rubble of world war contains a lesson for future societies. Rivers was an accomplished anthropologist as well as psychologist; his fever restores his memory of fieldwork among Solomon Islanders whose culture was destroyed when Europeans, acting *in loco parentis*, banned headhunting. Without this outlet for violent energies, the native culture withered—reminiscent of Great-War soldiers reduced to hysteria by the enforced passivity of trench combat. At the ending of *Ghost Road*, as if in benediction, as if in forgiveness, the shaman Njiru appears in a hallucination, as the sun rises, to the sleep-deprived Rivers, and says ceremonially "There is an end of men, an end of chiefs, an end of chieftains' wives, an end of chiefs' children—then go down and depart."[18] The revenant chief seems to tell Rivers that death claims us all, but we can't hope for it to do so peacefully. Europe's war, in conjunction with native headhunting, tells Rivers (and the readers) that violence is endemic to the human psyche, organized violence endemic to human society, and that metanarratives that hope to sublate this grim truth in a grand synthesis are foolish. Partial regenerations of individuals like Rivers, lulls between wars for nations like England, are all we can hope for. *Ghost Road*'s ending intimates as much, encircling the trilogy's political critiques and therapeutic *petit récits* in a fatalistic vision.

Barker's trilogy recapitulates Freudian intellectual dramas in its critical depictions of therapy, its dissatisfaction with psychological science as the sole vehicle for metanarrative wisdom, and its retention of metanarrative hope—even if only residues thereof—in the teeth of fate, whether fate takes the form of war, trauma, cultural death, personal death, or ineradicable psychic forces such as the "death instinct." The parallels and divergences between Freud's and Barker's handling of teleological themes illustrate the important principle of similarity-within-difference in a comparative study of literary-historical periods.

The Rise and Fall of Freud's Metanarrative
Exhibit 1: Studies on Hysteria (1893–5)

At the outset of Freud's psychoanalytic career, he collaborated with Josef Breuer and boasted of the efficacy of hypnotic suggestion. The four case histories that Freud contributed to *Studies on Hysteria* are peppered with descriptions of patients' hysterical symptoms being relieved by warm baths, massages, hypnotic suggestions, and the "wiping out" of their memories under hypnosis.[19] Such anecdotes can allure, with their picture of a human subject plunged between conscious and unconscious realms, and a shaman-healer besting her sickness with expert skill. But Freud, whose oeuvre repeatedly expresses disenchantment with his own previous methods, came to doubt that hypnotic suggestion relieved more than symptoms. Perhaps it drove their root causes further from therapeutic access.

Thus it was superseded by talk therapy, which Freud credits Breuer with developing in his treatment of Anna O., the subject of the one case history that Breuer contributed to *Studies*. In conjunction with this new treatment, Freud formulated a range of metaphors. Patients "repress" traumas dating to their early years, he argues, and "resist" treatment that will reveal these shameful episodes with the help of psychic "defenses." But when they "transfer" emotions once felt toward their parents onto the analyst, their neuroses become visible—hence treatable—unless the analyst's "countertransference" blinds him.[20] As Freud's and Breuer's method of cure grew suppler and subtler, and as Freud's battalion of poetic concepts enlarged, his narratives of individual successes—and thus his metanarrative of what cure generically looks like—assumed the depth and richness that would continue to fascinate literary critics long after most practicing analysts ceased to espouse Freudian orthodoxies. Analyst and patient would no longer enjoy the short cut of hypnotic suggestion but would instead be locked in a fluctuating relationship of collaboration and conflict, begging for depiction by a master storyteller.

This relationship raised a host of ethical quandaries, as various psychoanalytic schools developed protocols, including boundaries between the confessing patient and what would become, on the classical Freudian model, her detached analyst. Early in his career, Freud argued with and shouted at patients, praised and accepted gifts from them, loaned them money, and traded gossip with them. His acolyte Sandor Ferenczi kissed patients, for which Freud rebuked him, asking why kissing shouldn't lead to pawing, peeping, and petting.[21] In Wilhelm Reich's "Orgone therapy," patients disrobed, lay face-down on a sheet-covered bed, and breathed deeply. The therapist palpated tense muscles to release pent-up emotions.

Studies explores the utility of therapist-patient boundaries, their inevitable violations, and both the dangers and potential therapeutic value of these violations. It describes Freud's use of the "pressure technique," wherein he presses his hand on the patient's forehead, bidding her memory to come loose. He acknowledges this as a gimmick,[22] but happily does whatever works (though he repeatedly changed his mind about what *does* work). *Studies* explains why the patient benefits from trusting and liking her analyst, admits that the analyst won't always like his patient,[23] notes the likelihood of "negative transference," and explains that "positive transference" can be harmful, as the patient longs to impress her physician at the expense of exploring her neurosis.

Rivers took no such physical liberties as Reich, but Barker shows his patients and him repeatedly violating boundaries. Prior and Rivers switch places, with Prior behind the doctor's desk asking questions.[24] Sassoon, convalescing from a head wound, tells Rivers that his advice to soldiers to "face up to their emotions" is misguided, because if soldiers "are going to have to kill … they need to be trained *not to care*." But even as the patient attempts to refute his doctor's theory, he cannot disguise his physical and psychic torment: "Siegfried gripped Rivers's hand so tightly," explains the narrator, "that his face clenched with the effort of concealing his pain."[25]

Although *Studies* talks as much about failed techniques and unrelieved symptoms as about successes, it nonetheless tells a story (or several stories) with hortatory aims. Its opening section, "Preliminary Communication," ends by reiterating how "psychotherapeutic procedure ... has a curative effect" by neutralizing the "idea which was not abreacted [expressed cathartically] by allowing its strangulated affect a way out through speech."[26] The exhortation to speak, the struggle to express the unspeakable, the climax (or anti-climax) of doing so—these remain fodder for compelling literature. "Dora" and Prior both suffer from aphonia: the loss of speech. Rivers's affliction, stammering, also recalls Freud's metaphor of "strangulated affect."

The struggle between strangulation and expression suits the purposes of two camps of writers, which Barker straddles. In one camp, therapies that culminate with discovery and psychic regeneration make for richly happy endings—more enjoyable if gratification is delayed by diagnostic challenges. Rivers has enough successes throughout the trilogy to make therapy look commendable, even if few are as perfect as his treatment of Herrington. This patient suffered from amnesia and nightmares of the face of the dead friend whom he saw "blown to pieces."[27] Treatment restores Herrington's memory, which is valuable since he demonstrated exemplary courage after his friend's death. Herrington's nightmares follow a "normal path to recovery,"[28] growing more symbolic, and both his self-esteem and his ability to grieve for his loss return within several weeks. Although Herrington endured major traumas, he enjoys the very sort of rapid cure that Freud came increasingly to doubt.

Other cases are less satisfying, either because the patient never gains insight or because his insight humiliates him. Rivers cures Moffet's hysterical paralysis by drawing "stocking tops" progressively lower down his leg and insisting that feeling will return as the stockings unroll. Convinced that the treatment's success exposes him as a malingerer, Moffet attempts suicide.[29] By contrast, Willard avoids such humiliation by remaining ignorant. When Rivers cures his hysterical spinal paralysis, restoring his ability to walk, nurses revere Rivers's "great medical feat." But Willard persists in believing that his spine was severed and that Rivers rejoined it, since acknowledging the contrary would be "tantamount to an admission of cowardice."[30] The patient's lack of insight into his condition leads Rivers—rightly or wrongly—to feel his "blaze of glory" to be "undeserved."[31] Prior represents a fuller success for Rivers, though he spends three novels working through a series of excruciating symptoms and never fully forgives himself for what he considered cowardly, nor fully accepts the dark, violent part of himself. When Rivers helps him discover the event that triggered his aphonia, Prior asks "*Is that all?*," beside himself with rage, as though the symptom were unjustified.[32]

But at least Rivers gets to the bottom of Prior's, Willard's, and Moffet's symptoms. By contrast, Rivers never learns in Barker's novels, as he never learned in life, the source of his own stammer. He assumes that it is congenital and not neurasthenic, which, thinks Prior, provides him too convenient an excuse for avoiding self-analysis.[33] In addition to stammering, Rivers, as mentioned, had "no visual memory." In Barker's depiction, Rivers suspects that he was not "raped or beaten"—contrary to Prior's diagnosis of this symptom[34]—but rather that his fearful childhood imagination exaggerated minor threats. Prior's assumptions about symptomatic etiology correspond roughly to those of the seduction-theory Freud (pre-1897), while Rivers's correspond to the post-1897 Freud.[35] The trilogy grants wisdom to each character—Rivers for recognizing that the traumatized mind thinks figuratively, and Prior for recognizing that his physician is as neurotic and prone to resistance as any of his patients. Despite being a victim of childhood sexual abuse, Prior comes to credit his doctor's idea that people project fears into memory gaps, according to the principle "Where unknown, there place monsters."[36] But the general value of this principle does not clarify whether Rivers correctly diagnoses his stammer or his visual amnesia. Barker leaves these puzzles unresolved. Such outcomes, at least as immanent in the Freudian encounter as their happier counterparts, suit the agendas of modernist-era and contemporary authors such as McEwan—and, on balance, Barker—who see perspicuous endings as fables to avoid.

But the hortatory Freud of 1895, loath as he is to make magical claims for therapy, refuses total irresolution. In *Studies'* concluding paragraph, a hypothetical patient complains, "my illness is probably connected with my circumstances [which] you cannot alter." Freud retorts, "much will be gained if we [transform] your hysterical misery into common unhappiness." With a restored mental life, he informs the patient, "you will be better armed against that unhappiness."[37] Even the early Freud—who is not yet disillusioned with hypnosis and catharsis—wants to be a realistic storyteller. Therefore the patient's life-troubles are not resolved. She is promised no transcendence of "common" woe. But happily, therapy "restores" her mental health, helping her confront woe more skillfully. A germinal metanarrative is discernible, as hysteria gives way to mere "unhappiness." But the story begs for a larger trajectory, with subtler descriptions of how pathogens can be diagnosed and obstacles to recovery overcome. Freud's later writings answer these narrative longings—in ambivalent ways.

The Rise and Fall
Exhibit 2: "Remembering, Repeating, and Working-Through" (1914)

Two decades after *Studies*, in the early months of the First World War,[38] in a mere nine pages, Freud complicated his curative template, introducing the terms "compulsion to repeat" and "working-through" in a paper that combines a renunciation of past credulities with what might be new ones. Freud wants the patient to "remember" what he has repressed so he can "work through" its symptoms. He does not want the patient to "repeat" symptoms in the motor sphere, but unfortunately, the patient is compelled to do so, compulsively re-enacting the past. Either the patient's "confused dreams and associations" repeat the "hopeless deadlock in his infantile sexual researches,"[39] or he defies his doctor as he once defied his parents. (This section of Freud's essay reads like a précis on Prior, with his polymorphous sexuality, disturbing dreams, father hatred, and compulsion to act out against Rivers.)

"Remembering" boasts about transvaluing Breuer's hypnotic method in "the far-reaching changes which psychoanalytic technique has undergone since its first beginnings."[40] Later, balancing criticism with praise, the essay thanks "the old hypnotic technique for having brought before us single psychical processes" in isolated form, which gave us the "courage ... to create more complicated situations in the analytic treatment."[41] But Freud expresses retrospective incredulity toward the hopes that he and Breuer once entertained for discharging hysterical symptoms. "Under the new technique," says Freud with ironic condescension, "very little, and often nothing, is left of this delightfully smooth course of events."[42]

In place of such "delightfully smooth" treatment, "Remembering" complexly evokes what—archetypally speaking—we could call the *descent into the (psychic) underworld*. Early in her treatment, the patient might deteriorate, which could lead the analyst to despair. But Freud's message, in so many words, is "hang in there!" Working-through can be "arduous" for the patient and a "trial of patience for the analyst," but this part of therapy "effects the greatest changes in the patient."[43] Freud explains that the road to recovery, which transforms the "compulsion to repeat" into a "motive for remembering," runs through transference. But before this transformation can occur, the patient must "overcome" his resistance to reliving childhood miseries. Beginning analysts, counsels Freud, might think their job is done when they point out the patient's resistance to him. But the recovery process is rough: analysts must push treatment forward until resistance is "at its height [and] repressed instinctual impulses" emerge.

Will liberated instinct effect cure? Likely not—that journey would be too smooth. Instead, many patients develop a "transference neurosis"—a fresh symptom caused by the treatment, as though the physician prolonged what he is paid to cure. But this new neurosis is therapeutic: transference "creates an intermediate region between illness and real life" which renders compulsive repetition "harmless, indeed useful," by laying it open for analysis.[44]

In one regard, Freud sheds his past credulities. He explains, in breathtaking theoretical detail, why analysis is more drawn-out than he once believed, and he scoffs at "abreaction" as a jaded playwright might mock a *deus ex machina*. But in another regard, the Freud of 1914 is more credulous than the Freud of 1895, and prepared to endow his metanarrative—at least its hopeful iteration—with its full dramatic shape. Whereas analysts learn little from hypnosis, Freud says that with his improved method "in some cases I have had an impression that the familiar childhood amnesia ... is completely counterbalanced by screen memories. Not only *some* but all of what is essential has been retained in these memories. It is simply a question of knowing how to extract it from them by analysis."[45] How much confidence do these sentences express? The first sentence alludes to "some cases" and an "impression," suggesting a tentative conclusion. But the following sentence asserts that everything "essential" is retained. Freud often slides from hypotheses in need of testing to declarations of faith in psychoanalytic principles. How tempting such credulity can be! If "all of what is essential" in a patient's past can be known, then he might achieve at-one-ment with all his selves, from childhood to adulthood.

Is "Remembering" as confident in cure as in the chance of a complete diagnosis? Freud's claim that "working-through" "effects the greatest changes" is usefully vague, since he doesn't explain *what* these changes are, nor how likely they are to succumb to the repetition compulsion (or other neurotic tendencies) years after analysis. Perhaps the formulation's vagueness marks it as a placeholder, with more research needed to determine the nature and extent of these "changes."

As discussed, storytellers working in Freud's wake—given this evolution between *Studies* and "Remembering"—might depict hysterics cured in a flash of illumination or expose every apparent epiphany as false. Prior bridges these possibilities. On the one hand, Rivers uses hypnosis—a method he considered a "last resort"[46]—to trace Prior's aphonia to a horrifying repressed memory. Prior was struck dumb when, in the wake of enemy shelling, he held a dead comrade's eyeball in his palm that reminded him of "gob-stopper" candies from his childhood.[47] His hysteria is displaced, so to speak, from one part of his comrade's body to a different part of his own body, just as Freud's "Dora" transfers upward, to her throat, the trauma of feeling Herr K's erection against her body.[48] When Prior recovers this memory, his symptom vanishes, much as Dora's symptom did in the 1905 case history, in her case thanks to free-association. This success would seem to be "delightfully smooth."

But Rivers's sleuthing comes nowhere near to relieving Prior—whose name indicates both temporal discontinuity and the need for secrets to be *pried* loose—of all his psychic fractures. Far from being at one after recovering his speech and memory in *Regeneration*, Prior suffers from a Jekyll-and-Hyde fugue state throughout the trilogy's second novel, *The Eye in the Door*. His Hyde-self claims to have been born "in a shell-hole in France,"[49] in repudiation of the pusillanimous self who lost his voice there. Arguably, his memory recovery does more harm than good, by more radically splitting his unconscious from his conscious—just as Rivers feared hypnosis might do.[50] Prior's aphonia—a passive and circumscribed anti-war protest—gives way to a more wide-ranging and self-destructive symptom: acting out. As Hyde, he betrays his pacifistic childhood friends by sharing their testimony with the Ministry of Munitions, which endangers his safety as well as theirs. Yet even as "Hyde" does the Ministry's bidding, Prior's opposition to the war and his attraction to socialism crystallize. His psychic conflict seems insurmountable: the only solution is to extinguish Hyde.

But so tangled are his symptoms and their sources that even extinguishing Hyde might not bring cure. Prior's habit of dissociating long predates the war: it stems from boyhood traumas inflicted by his father—or from his mistaken *impression* of what his father did to him.

Prior's diagnoses and treatments stand synecdochally for those of many Great-War trauma victims, for the public reception of the mental therapy they received, and for the evolution of psychoanalytic theories. Sections of the general public hostile to psychoanalysis—represented by Prior's father—doubted the genuineness of hysterical symptoms, seeing them as malingering. Freudian theory allows for slippage between cases of hysteria—wherein the conscious and unconscious minds are split—and "allied" "mental symptoms" such as phobias and obsessions. Ideally the analysts can distinguish any of these symptoms from a "clever *tour de force*" in which the patient feigns "somatic compliance."[51] But this distinction has a gray area: both the skillful malingerer and the hysteric depend upon somatic compliance—the body symbolically expressing emotional pain. Freud can attribute the same devious cunning to the unconscious that Prior's father believes is consciously produced, and even Freud sometimes read his patients as acting, rather than genuinely manifesting, their symptoms.

"Shell shock" was a popular diagnosis in the early war years, as Showalter details.[52] Freud and Breuer, by contrast, were astute enough as early as *Studies* to trace symptoms not to "a single, major trauma" but to "a *group* of provoking causes"[53]—an epistemology that may have its own dangers, judging from the far-fetched ways in which Freud decodes "overdetermined" symptoms.[54] In Barker's depiction, in addition to excelling at the "talking cure," Rivers takes the best of Freud's interpretive paradigm and discards the worst. For example, he demonstrates a Freudian wisdom in tracing infantry officers' breakdowns not to shell shock but to "prolonged strain,"[55] a diagnosis that requires the analyst to construct a lengthier and subtler narrative. Yet when Rivers has an opportunity lazily to attribute a different patient's symptoms to such "strain," he's wise enough not to. Anderson, a military doctor whose family expects him to pursue a medical career after the war, presents symptoms including haemophobia and complains of tiredness that he attributes to having performed up to ten amputations a day.[56] Eventually Rivers traces Anderson's neurosis to the conflict—which the patient does not wish to acknowledge—between his desire not to pursue medicine and his need to please his family. Rivers's theoretical paradigm enables this correct diagnosis. On the one hand, his belief that neurosis springs from present conflict—not, as Freud has it, from repressed infantile trauma—saves him from a wild etiological goose chase. On the other hand, his belief, indebted to Freud, that the psyche is self-divided and that these divisions are as likely as external shocks to precipitate neuroses precluded him from lazily diagnosing Anderson with "shell shock"—or even "tiredness," a label that would anticipate "PTSD."

The concept of PTSD developed from the work of Rivers and others. It gained legitimacy with its inclusion in *DSM-III* (1980)—an artifact of Vietnam, as Mark Rawlinson discusses in his study of Barker's trilogy.[57] Its increasing cachet is evidenced by the 1997 establishment of the Rivers Centre in the Royal Edinburgh Hospital, a psychiatric institution that preserves Rivers's spirit in its treatment of PTSD sufferers. Yet the term "shell shock" has retained popular appeal, vying with PTSD as a cultural meme. The coexistence of these different but not necessarily contradictory diagnoses testifies to the utility of different kinds of stories about trauma and recovery—stories of varying lengths that promise varying degrees of etiological certainty.

Shell shock corresponds to abreaction as PTSD corresponds to working-through. The former two terms describe a symptom with a single clear precipitant and a rapid, complete resolution. The latter two describe a symptom long in the making and perhaps as long as a lifetime in the unmaking. Extending the temporal reach of the latter concepts, theorists have argued that cataclysms such as war produce "collective trauma,"[58] meaning that "working through" is not limited to an individual client but that a culture, with the help of historians, critics, and novelists, might pursue it collectively. After the First World War, Sassoon largely retired from public life, but revisited the war in his three-volume fictionalized autobiography, *The Memoirs of George Sherston* (1928–36), and his three additional volumes of direct autobiography, written between 1938 and 1946. Whether these works helped him or his nation to process war trauma is debatable. Barker was born a quarter century after the 1918 armistice, but as Kennedy Fraser argues, she was "a survivor of the First World War as well," having been raised in the home of her grandmother and her grandmother's second husband, who was bayonetted in his side by a German soldier but never spoke of his "horrific wartime experience," making him a "forerunner" of all the traumatized "living specters" who haunt the *Regeneration* novels.[59] Even in the decades since this trilogy, Barker has continued to mine the conflict, in *Another World* (1998), *Life Class* (2007), and *Toby's Room* (2012).

Barker's effort to work through the war's traumas has hallmarks of interminability: a large and stirring undertaking that cannot assume *meta*narrative form because it has no logical end point. Likewise, within the trilogy, the persistence of Prior's and Sassoon's symptoms, even despite apparent therapeutic breakthroughs, indicates that processing trauma, inside or outside of formal analysis, is a process without an *end*, in a chronological or teleological sense. By moving back and forth among the French battlefield, the English hospital, and the melancholy of a dying Melanesian culture, Barker casts this interminable process in wide, even universal, terms. Likewise, with the 1920 publication of *Beyond the Pleasure Principle* in the shadow of the recently concluded war, Freud addresses, in the widest terms, the problem of people's seeming affinity for unpleasure despite their instinctual craving for pleasure. He too works against the philosophical and narrative craving for an *end*.

The Rise and Fall
Exhibit 3: *Beyond the Pleasure Principle* (1920)

On my revisionary account, *Beyond* is agnostic where metanarratives are concerned. By vigorously pursuing one line of thought and as vigorously pursuing an opposing one, the essay undercuts any *grand récit* it might develop. Just at the point in his career when Freud's *story containing other stories* might assume the "coherent organic shape" I mention above, the skeptic in him restrains the metaphysician, the eschatologist who would claim to discern an "aim," "beyond pleasure," toward which life is directed. The same skeptic, however, refuses to let the anti-metaphysician have the last word, to proclaim that science or philosophy has proven life to have *no* aim. If "postmoderns" doubt that *society improves over time*, then *Beyond* anticipates them by doubting that *life has a direction*, and in a sense surpasses them by being equally incredulous toward the idea that *life is directionless*.

This interpretation of *Beyond* sharply diverges from that of one of its prominent critics, Ernest Jones, and partly diverges from a prominent admirer, Peter Brooks. Jones laments what he sees as the essay's teleological certainties. In *Beyond*, says Jones, the idea of a "death instinct" went from being "purely tentative" to being "indispensable" to Freud, although, in Jones's eyes, "no biological observation can be found to support the idea … which contradicts all biological principles."[60] Whereas Jones mistrusts *Beyond* from a scientific point of view, Brooks values it from a narratological one. He fastens onto the essay's memorable phrase "the aim of all life is death"[61] as evidence of its implicit teleological themes. He says that this phrase gets us "near the heart of Freud's masterplot for organic life" and defines "masterplot" as "a total scheme of how life proceeds from beginning to end, and how each individual life in its own manner repeats the masterplot."[62] He follows Walter Benjamin in seeing death as the story's "sanction," even if not the conscious aim of its protagonist—a principle that holds whether death is literal or "some simulacrum, some end to a period, an arrest."[63] In Brooks's view, Freud ingeniously evokes the ways in which non-literal and especially literal death allow for "summing up." Death means fulfillment for the story it concludes, for the character who inhabits the story, and for the writer and reader whose imaginations shape it.

Brooks's reading of *Beyond* is rich and provocative, but I diverge from it by emphasizing the essay's provisionality. Admittedly, *Beyond* evinces some attachment to the concept of "natural death"—the idea that, at a cellular level, organisms are programmed to decay. (Hence Jones's quarrel with the essay.) Freud reviews scientific literature on whether germ plasms or "protista" are immortal, but multicellular organisms are mortal. Even if this is so, says Freud—even if death is a "late acquisition" of more complex life forms—then he still wants to see it as a latent "tendency" in their single-celled ancestors. "Biology" does not, he says, "flatly contradict the recognition of death instincts." But *Beyond* nowhere asserts "biology's" *clear support* for such a "recognition," either. It is a slippery essay: when Freud seems to put his thumb in the pan in favor of one answer, he withdraws it. Leaving the question unanswered suggests that it is unanswerable.

Is there even a preponderance of evidence—though not proof beyond reasonable doubt—in favor of "natural death?" I read *Beyond* as more tentative than this, concerning various postulated instincts—as illustrated by the supposed "instinct toward perfection," at which Freud scoffs. Emboldened, perhaps, by the Great War's carnage, Freud dismisses this pseudoscientific concept, anticipating, by a half century, Fussell's 1975 observation—in this chapter's epigraph—that the war rendered meliorism embarrassing.

Though Freud is repelled by the idea of an "instinct toward perfection" and attracted to the idea of a "death instinct," his handling of one illuminates his handling of the other. Each suggests that life has an aim, and each tempts therapists with the comfort of false certainty. If organisms were programmed to perfect themselves, then patients might want to get better, *for biological reasons*, and therapists might hope that properly designed treatment would guarantee "delightfully smooth" recovery. If, conversely, organisms were instinctually programmed to die, this might impede cure, but the analyst would know the nature of his nemesis, even when this nemesis took figurative shape, in the patient's flight from the unfamiliar, his desire for constancy.

Happily, instead of resting in either of these (or other) comforts, Freud is "not convinced" of the truth of his own hypotheses and does not "seek to persuade others to believe in them."[64] *Beyond* answers its own question, *Does life have an aim?* with the admission, *We don't know*. Perhaps this non-answer is a logical development from Freud's previous work. As we recall, "Remembering" pictured therapy as more protracted than *Studies* did, as a "working-through" rather than an abreaction, as an open-ended tale rather than one with a clean resolution. *Beyond* treats a broader subject—life, not therapy. It toggles between one storyline (*life has no aim*) sympathetic to Nietzschean and Sartrean existentialism and another (*its aim is death*) reminiscent of classical dramas about Destiny. If we read Freud's oeuvre chronologically, then we wonder in suspense what will happen in 1937, when the octogenarian revisits the topic of clinical treatment (never his favorite kind of labor).[65] Will he be confident in a pessimistic conclusion—that analysis is "interminable?" Will he be agnostic, convinced that there is no cause for certainty as to whether analysis has a terminus? Or will he be guardedly optimistic—buoyed by residues of his old metanarrative ambitions—that therapy can regenerate a traumatized mind?

The Rise and Fall
Exhibit 4: "Analysis Terminable and Interminable" (1937)

"Analysis" addresses Freud's worries that therapy drags on for decades, fails in its prophylactic aims (treating latent conflicts to prevent later neurotic outbreaks), and even fails to resolve present conflicts. If his oeuvre traced a simpler arc, then "Analysis" would unequivocally despair that treatment never "terminates" in cure— and it is possible to glean such resignation from this essay.[66] (The previous chapter reads *Atonement* as its narrator's interminable self-analysis—though McEwan arguably depicts this undertaking as *more* valuable for being a-telic.) But across its eight sections "Analysis" alternates between optimism and pessimism concerning psychodynamic cure. It reviews Freud's career as a series of trials and errors, and it embodies this experimental process with its unpredictable shifts between sections. Since not every trial fails, "Analysis" partly vindicates Freud's lifelong therapeutic project.

It is most self-vindicating in its penultimate section, which denies that analysts' inevitable errors and personality flaws are "impediments" to cure."[67] Freud explains that analysts can be trained and thereby acquainted with their own unconscious. He admits that trainees can use defense mechanisms, remaining unchanged, but offers another solution: they can be reanalyzed every five years. Finally, Freud dismisses the concern that repeated training makes analysis seem endless. He says that, while there may be no "natural end" for analysis, treatment can "go well." While patients will not attain "schematic normality," they wouldn't want to: individual eccentricities deserve respect. While they will not be "thoroughly analyzed" (which is only a hypothetical ideal), therapists can "secure the best possible conditions" for the functions of their egos. Freud is pointedly anti-utopian, suggesting that "schemes" suppress individuality and that only the "best possible conditions" should be sought, not the best imaginable.

This anti-utopian outlook informs the essay's slide from the comparative self-vindication of its opening sections to the self-doubt of most of its latter half. Sections one and two claim limited efficacy for talk therapy. Section one asks, *Can we hasten the end of treatment?*, reiterates that hypnosis does not work, and dismisses as quixotic Otto Rank's hope that a few months' analysis can cure a patient's "primal repression" stemming from his mother-attachment.[68] But Freud describes a tactic that can work— partially: the "blackmailing device" of "fixing a time-limit for the analysis." If the analyst's timing is right, says Freud, some repressed material will "become accessible under the pressure of the threat," but some will be "lost to our therapeutic efforts."[69] Such is the price of an *unnatural* end-date.

More explicitly teleological, section two asks whether there is a "natural end" to analysis—which could mean the patient is cured presently, or prophylactically, against future suffering. The answer is partly hopeful. If the "disturbance"[70] is traumatic, not constitutional, then analysis might succeed, says Freud. (Prior illustrates this distinction, with his aphonia and fugue state stemming from trauma, hence being curable, while his sadism, masochism, and death drive may stem from constitutional disturbances and hence be incurable.) Freud adds that trauma cannot be too strong if analysis hopes to succeed. Arguably, *Regeneration* is more optimistic than Freud on this front: Prior's aphonia stems from the cruelest trauma, yet it might meet its match in Rivers.

But Barker's optimism and Rivers's healing powers have limits, as evidenced by patients such as Burns, who is based on an historical case discussed in Rivers's December 1917 address, "The Repression of War Experience." Thrown in the air by an exploding shell, Burns landed on a German corpse whose gas-filled belly ruptured. Burns recalls that smell every time he attempts to eat, and he vomits regularly. Rivers sees his suffering as "without purpose or dignity."[71] Later in *Regeneration*, visiting Burns at his home, Rivers tries to imagine a future for him, but concludes that this patient "had missed his chance of being ordinary."[72]

Assuming a modest enough trauma—nothing like what Burns endured—analysis does "what it is superlatively able to do," says Freud, in a crescendo of enthusiasm. But he promptly admits that "kind fate" (i.e., positive changes in the patient's life-situation) may deserve credit where analysis appears responsible.[73] At this almost-terminal stage of his career, Freud's metanarrative teeters, propped up by caveats, but remains upright.

Section three expresses diminishing optimism, denying that analysis can *permanently dispose of instinctual demands*. A less utopian aim, he explains, "may roughly be described as a 'taming' of the instinct."[74] But sadly, therapy may lack the power even to do this, by correcting "the original process of repression,"[75] which would enable adults consciously to manage instincts that children unconsciously and neurotically express. More research is needed, but Freud fears that treatment does little good.

Freud sounds as if he's grasping at straws and should admit that the analyst faces an intractable dilemma. On the one hand, merely pointing out the patient's conflicts to her, or "insisting" that she recall repressed material, will not carry analysis "very far."[76] But artificially producing a transference-conflict damages her affection for the therapist, which is crucial to their pact against her illness.[77] Analysis seems doomed to fail. Physician and client inevitably miscommunicate, or *don't* communicate, about the elephant in the closet that brought her to his office. But Freud doesn't give up; he seeks "another angle" from which to explore "the variability in the effects of analysis."[78] He says that the "outcome of analysis depends on the quantitative factor," i.e., whether the analytic probe is stronger than the forces repressing pathogenic material. Although victory "as a rule" is "on the side of [repression's] big battalions,"[79] Freud hopes that this "rule" is not absolute.

Thus his metanarrative of cure moves from germinal possibilities (in 1895, in *Studies*) to diminished—but not extinguished—self-confidence (in 1939, in "Analysis"), as the therapeutic journey promises no clear end, narratively or therapeutically speaking. The 1939 essay is not *entirely* pessimistic: it touts psychotherapy's "superlative" abilities to treat certain symptoms and its protocols for maintaining therapists' professional competence. Coiled within this career-spanning metanarrative of cure lies *Beyond*'s tentative thought experiment, its masterplot of incurable morbidity. Each of these metanarratives has its own teleology, and the *aims* of getting better versus dying could be seen as contradictory: the latter could be seen as more fundamental and encompassing, with hysterical symptoms and their abreactions mere waystations on the road to mortality. But Freud's oeuvre refuses thematic closure. Not only does *Beyond* acknowledge itself to be a thought experiment, but across his career, every theoretical formulation that claims to correct his previous mistakes reveals its own vulnerability to being superceded.

Barker's trilogy, too, benefits from thematic irresolution, from the unsettling effect of raising questions that it can never answer and hopes that it cannot fulfill. Its morbid masterplot, its suggestion that the death instinct explains both European and Melanesian bloodlust, may seem to invalidate three metanarratives: the secular-Christian story of Rivers's healing touch; the counter-transferential story of the physician's self-healing; and the liberal-pacifist story of militarism yielding to pacifism, of Rivers the hawkish army doctor becoming Rivers the anti-war 1922 Labour candidate for Parliament. But instead, this masterplot allows these psychoanalytic and sociohistorical metanarratives to coexist in productive tension. Close readings of *Regeneration*'s and *Ghost Road*'s final pages reveal tonal ambiguities that also enable the coexistence of competing Riverses: one valorized, the other ironized.

Avatar # 1: Rivers as Postmodern Hero

Read unironically—and in conjunction with our knowledge of what Rivers does after the war—the ending of *Regeneration* justifies Dennis Brown in labeling him a "postmodern hero."[80] The doctor's integrity of mind, sensitivity, capacity for self-criticism, and eventual courage bring multiple metanarratives together. Intellectually, his anthropological studies lead him to an anti-foundational insight of Nietzschean scope, as he sees "the *Great White God* dethroned ... we [Westerners] quite unselfconsciously *assumed* we were the measure of all things [but] I saw not only that we weren't the measure of all things, but that *there was no measure*." This isn't his first de-conversion, to use a term associated with Victorian freethinkers like George Eliot. Instead, it extends the intellectual journey that bore Rivers beyond his father's religious orthodoxy, a journey explored in *Ghost Road* when, convalescing, he recalls one of his father's churches at Maidstone (where Henry Rivers was a vicar for fifteen years) with a window depicting Abraham's near-sacrifice of Isaac.[81] He contrasts Abraham's restraint to the ritual slaughter of bastard sons on Vao Island as symbolic of the difference between civilization and savagery. But the irony is unmistakable: as patriarchs of "civilized" Europe send millions of their sons to die on battlefields, this distinction collapses. Multiple versions of the Great White God—incarnated in Rivers's religiosity, his ethnocentrism, and his patriotic disinclination to question Britain's war policy—all succumb to his skepticism.

Barker roots these de-conversions in Rivers's acclaimed work in anthropology and psychology. (No other intellectual has attained such distinction in each field, though numerous psychologists, including Freud and Jung, incorporated anthropology into their work.) She goes a step further by rooting them in the *kind* of anthropologist and psychologist Rivers was. Each discipline has schools that value "detachment," anthropology out of concern for "the integrity of research" lest "anthropological inquiry" becomes "social work," and psychology out of concern that countertransference compromises analytic neutrality. But in each field Rivers plunges into intimacies with his subjects that gain him access to a depth of knowledge that "detachment" might preclude and that also humble him, opening him to potential transformation.

Yet Rivers's intimacies never grow too warm: he never takes sexual or emotional advantage of his patients, on an un-ironic reading of the trilogy, nor behaves exploitatively toward Solomon Islanders. Man of science that he is—not to mention being a bachelor who is divorced from his same-sex desires—he understands that without an ability to detach himself emotionally from his material, a neurologist or psychologist couldn't perform his research. But he also ruminates that the sociopath depends on this same capacity for detachment. Rivers is vigilantly self-aware, recognizing the potential for evil in his own skills. His heroism is multidimensional.

Yet these de-conversions, and his recognition of the thin line between the potential benevolence and malevolence of detachment, don't lead this incredulous, proto-postmodern thinker to Dostoyevskeyan despair or nihilism. As the first novel's final chapter commences, Rivers tells his research partner, Henry Head, about how his patients have changed him by way of an anthropological anecdote. "What would you do with a guinea," he had asked the Solomon Islanders years earlier; "who would you share it with?" Then they "turned the tables" on me, Rivers continues. "What would I do with a guinea? Who would I share it with?" Rivers's explanation that, as a bachelor, he wouldn't "feel obliged" to share it provokes the natives to "incredulous" laughter and Rivers to the epiphany that "their reactions to my society were [as valid as] mine to theirs," which entailed a feeling of "*amazing* freedom ... as if a ton of weight had been lifted." Their incredulity infects him: his ability to enter into their point of view helps him to see—in an existential, not merely academic, way—the contingency of his civilization's values. Many Western liberals espouse cultural relativism, but few have such empirical data, such rich firsthand experience, on which to base their conviction. Rivers functions as a surrogate for a class of European cosmopolitans and a bridge from anthropology's racist early decades into its more enlightened later work.[82] Barker's readers can congratulate themselves on having already arrived where Rivers journeys: a place beyond foundational illusions where philosophy is concerned and beyond bigotry where politics are concerned.

Yet these changes in Rivers, though profound, remain inward. What will ensue outwardly, readers might wonder at the conclusion of *Regeneration*, from lifting a "ton of weight" from his mind? British social conventions did not change as a result of his field work (though they were in flux before and during the war), nor was Rivers unleashed, upon his homecoming, into random acts of self-indulgence, sexual or otherwise. And yet some dam seemed bound to break when his patients reinforced the lesson of the islanders. Showalter and others have noted *Regeneration*'s "chiasmus" of Rivers catching Sassoon's anti-war complex in the process of healing it.[83] Rivers's discussion with the natives about spending a guinea left him feeling as though "you're walking around with a mask on, and you desperately want to take it off and you can't because everybody else thinks it's your face."[84] Now his adoption of Sassoon's attitude toward the war—however ambivalent—in conjunction with his awareness of Sassoon's (and by extension his own) repressed same-sex desires must make him feel all the more "masked." If we did not know that, fewer than four years after the Great War's conclusion, Rivers would seek the Labour nomination for the University of London constituency, we might wonder, *Will he pursue romance with a man? Will he act as a reformer from within the military-psychiatric complex? (It's hard to see how this would work: his job is to heal soldiers so that they can return to the front.) Will he follow the example of Sassoon's "Soldier's Declaration" and resign his position as an army physician, issuing his own "Psychologist's Declaration?" (It's hard to see what good this would do: Robert Graves's assessment of Sassoon's cause as "hopeless" would likely also apply to such a protest by the doctor.)*

But we do know what Rivers will do after the war, thanks to—among other sources—Richard Slobodin's 1978 biography, on which Barker draws heavily. The self-decentering spurred by Rivers's research in multiple disciplines does not paralyze him with doubt nor lead him to a quiescent relativism. De-throning a multi-faceted god makes Rivers more, not less, *engaged*: it clears ground for his opposition to the war and commitment to improve a world whose foundational philosophical convictions contribute to its political violence.

Avatar # 2: Rivers as Christ with a Small "c"

On this same un-ironic reading, Rivers's anti-foundational insights, and the emotional maturation that accompanies them, are not undercut by religious typology. In a landscape as de-sacralized as the trilogy's, a protagonist could hardly be—or strive to be—more Christlike; and even if his healing touch is not magical, its efficacy could vindicate small-c christian ministry. Even when his efforts fail—perhaps especially then—their nobility could be exemplary. The doctor visits Burns in Aldeburgh, at the literal and metaphorical "end of the line,"[85] and rescues Burns from a moat during a windstorm. Although he can imagine no future for this trauma victim, Rivers's willingness to listen when Burns is ready to speak, to extract Burns from whatever psychic basements allow extraction, add up to as much good as one man, in a non-magical universe, can do for someone in Burns's plight.

Exemplifying the same small-c christian charity, Rivers endures a barrage of flirtatious aggression and resentment from Prior, who even head-butts him;[86] yet when Prior emerges from his fugue, Rivers hires him as a secretary and invites Prior to live in his home while convalescing. No wonder Rivers succumbs to war neurosis and his colleague Bryce must order him to go on sick leave.[87] That Prior is fated to die at the

Sambre Canal does not lessen the significance of Rivers's kindness, as evidenced by the amount of time Prior spends thinking admiringly about Rivers, by the letters Prior directs to the doctor from the front, and by the progress Prior makes toward self-integration thanks to the autognosis of this writing. Total "cure" may be unattainable, according to late Freudian writings such as "Analysis Terminable and Interminable." But pragmatists can still see value—even small miracles—in partial healing.

That Rivers suffers from neuroses independent of the war—which Prior compels him to examine—better suits him to perform charitable services, above and beyond his analytic work. Prior recognizes this, musing that Rivers's "power to heal ... springs directly from some sort of wound or deformity."[88] Prior's analysis brings to mind the Jungian archetype of the wounded healer and its accompanying metanarrative template. In myths from multiple traditions, Jung says, this gentle and gifted teacher uses his pain to make himself a better healer, thereby healing himself.[89] Barker's texts blend aspects of this mythical storyline with extended illustrations of the transformative power of countertransference, in the Rivers-Sassoon and Rivers-Prior chiasmi.

Just as some anthropologists defend a "collaborative relationship" with their field subjects on epistemological grounds (you learn more from them if they trust you and work with you), likewise some therapists advocate utilizing countertransference—i.e., the analyst's impulses, feelings, and thoughts in response to the patient's transference— "for the understanding of the patient's psychological processes, since it is in these processes that the countertransference partly originates."[90] On this model, the analyst's deepening self-awareness and his ability to help his client go hand-in-hand. Barker's secular passion play might be titled "The Passion of Rivers." Its physician-hero—an archetypal healer before his work with Sassoon or Prior begins—welcomes the suffering that comes with treating them. They gain second sight by virtue of their dissociative disorders, marginal sexualities, and critical outlook on the war. Their insights become *his* second sight—a path out of his habits and assumptions.

Barker does not develop the wounded-healer storyline in as much detail as the small-c-christ storyline. But they each contribute to the first novel's and the trilogy's metanarrative momentum: their picture of a man moving in a heroic direction, and their intimation that if society could move with him, everyone would be ennobled.

Avatar # 3: Rivers's Christ Complex and Interminable Guilt

This metanarrative momentum, though, informs but one layer of Barker's tale. Like a stream with an undertow, the three novels also depict a man wracked by guilt that he cannot assuage, no matter how many people reassure, admire, and love him. On an ironic reading, Rivers suffers from a Christ complex: in his extraordinary devotion to his patients, he attempts penance for a sin so extensive, so amorphous, that it is unnamable and unpardonable. The encroachment of Christian typology into his therapy, unsurprisingly, carries a risk: Rivers can be diagnosed with countertransference neurosis:[91] i.e., a therapist's neurotic emotional reactions that interfere with his interpretation of the psychoanalytic relationship.

Guilty (or inefficacious) in many ways, and aware of some of them, Rivers fails to do right by Sassoon, cannot save Prior, and lacks the insight or courage to oppose the war while it is happening—i.e., while the trilogy unfolds. He is less an emblem of what society should aspire to than an ironized protagonist who attains too little wisdom too late to undo the harm he has done. This is a polemical reading, to be sure—one that sees Barker exploding any hopeful metanarrative from within—but the opportunity for such a reading lurks within the passage about the de-throning of the Great White God.

As *Regeneration*'s final chapter opens, Rivers consults unofficially with Head. He confesses his troubled conscience; his friend tries to exonerate him, but readers need not do so, and Rivers may not even exonerate himself (nor want to). First, Rivers blames himself for Sassoon's return to the front, and Head says "he was always going to go back," regardless of his therapist's wishes. Second, Rivers compares his methods to those of Lewis Yealland, a sadistic faradization enthusiast pilloried by Showalter—a comparison that one of his conscience-stricken nightmares has already made. Head tells him that this comparison is "the first sign of dementia … *self-laceration*." The latter portion of this half-joking diagnosis intuits Rivers's martyr complex. Though Head has less access to Rivers's inner life than *Regeneration*'s readers do, he senses his friend's despair. If Rivers strives to be christ—an impossible ideal even in small-c form—then he is bound to disappoint and end up punishing himself. In the context of these confessions—fishing expeditions on which Rivers seeks the reassurance that Head supplies—two details of Rivers's self-narration assume new meaning.

The first is the "*amazing* freedom" that Rivers says his anthropological studies yielded. Head asks, "*Sexual* freedom?" which is a key question. Rivers's psychological labors reinforce his anthropological ones by challenging him to confront the heteronormative Victorian inhibitions that he has internalized. But his answer to this question is evasive. He tells Head, "That too. But it was more than that. It was … the *Great White God* dethroned, I suppose." On a credulous reading, Rivers's answer re-frames Head's prurient question into something profounder, seeing sexuality as one piece of a larger puzzle. The ellipsis indicates the imaginative energy required to formulate the italicized term, just as the addendum "I suppose" suggests Rivers's uncertainty about the metaphor—an understandable uncertainty given the scope of what he attempts to articulate.

But if Rivers's self-narration is read skeptically, then Head's interrogation does not seem merely titillating. Instead Rivers's mention of "de-throning" is a defense mechanism, deflecting a personal inquiry. The ellipsis in Rivers's response—like a stammer—indicates the psychic energy required to suppress the thought of the sexual freedom that he still has not dared to explore. He's surrounded by brave gay soldiers; he's principled enough not to use knowledge of Sassoon's sexual orientation as leverage in attempting to persuade him to return to combat, but he's also pragmatic (or collusive) enough to counsel Sassoon not to make his homosexuality public. Sassoon tells him "I don't like holes in the ground," comparing closeted sexuality to trench combat,[92] and encapsulating how, in two ways at once, the doctor tells his patient, *Strangulate your affect*. Such advice couldn't run more counter to the Freudian theory, shared by Rivers, of the pathogenic effects of repression, and it suggests obliquely that Rivers—consciously or unconsciously—is counseling himself to strangle his own affect.

The second moment that exposes Rivers as an unreliable narrator of his own psychic development comes at the end of the men's exchange. Rivers explains that nothing changed in England after his return from the Solomons—when he felt like he wore a "mask"—prompting Head's follow-up question, "And now?" Rivers's response begins with three qualifiers and another punctuational equivalent of a stammer: "I don't know. I think perhaps," he says—these are the qualifiers—"the patients've ... have done for me what I couldn't do for myself." How credulous should we be toward something he has such trouble saying? The repetition of the word "have," once in contracted form, interrupted by the ellipsis, could suggest that complex psychological truths aren't easy to explain. Or it could indicate that *ad hoc* evasions aren't easy to contrive. The narrator then interjects a two-word sentence: "He smiled." This suggests that Rivers has gained his equipoise, and indeed he finishes his thought fluidly: "You see healing *does* go on, even if not in the expected direction."[93]

Table 2 Comparison of what Rivers thinks to what he may unconsciously mean

What Rivers thinks (rendered in free indirect style)	What Rivers may unconsciously mean
How on earth was Siegfried going to manage in France? His opposition to the war had not changed. If anything, it had hardened. And to go back to fight, believing as he did, would be to encounter internal divisions far deeper than anything he'd experienced before. Siegfried's 'solution' was to tell himself that he was going back only to look after some men, but that formula would not survive the realities of France	How on earth was Rivers going to manage his hospital work in England? His opposition to the war was crystallizing. And to go back to patching patients up so they could return to battle would be to encounter internal divisions far deeper than anything he'd experienced before. Rivers's 'solution' was to tell himself that he was looking after their welfare in the best way he could, but that formula would not survive the realities of the injuries and traumas he was sure to see ....
It was a dilemma with one very obvious way out. Rivers knew, though he had never voiced his knowledge, that Sassoon was going back with the intention of being killed. Partly, no doubt, this was youthful self-dramatization. *I'll show them. They'll be sorry.* But underneath that, Rivers felt there was a genuine and very deep desire for death.	It was a dilemma with one very obvious way out. Rivers knew, though he had never voiced his knowledge, that he was returning to his job—his new one, in London— with the intention of working himself into exhaustion. Partly, no doubt, this was middle-aged self-dramatization. *I've got the stamina, the skill, the compassion. I can assume the patients' war neuroses vicariously—and march forward.* But underneath that, there was a genuine and very deep desire for ... self-punishment? Martyrdom?
And if death were to be denied? Then he might well break down. A real breakdown this time.	And if death were to be denied? Then Rivers might well break down. A real breakdown this time.
Rivers saw that he had reached Sassoon's file ....There was nothing more that he wanted to say that he could say. He drew the final page towards him and wrote: *Nov. 26, 1917. Discharged to duty.*	Rivers saw that he had reached his own file ....There was nothing more that he wanted to say that he could say. He drew the final page towards him and wrote—referring to himself—*Nov. 26, 1917. Discharged to duty.*

Rivers's claim that *healing goes on* begs to be examined. By Rivers's own admission, Sassoon returns to a war in which neither man believes, likely to die—in part because he wants to die. ("You see, I think he's made up his mind to get killed," Rivers tells Head.)[94] Despite Head's confidence, we can't *know* whether Sassoon's death wishes would have been as strong, were it not for Rivers manipulating him to return to the front. Yet Rivers asks us—and Head—to believe that he is healing, that even as Sassoon courts death, his own mind is at ease; that even as the war grinds on and his doubts about it fester, his patients "have done" for him what needed doing.

The dubiousness of this proposition becomes apparent when Rivers contemplates Sassoon's physical and psychological peril—in ways that cut suspiciously close to the bone. The doctor, it seems, can only contemplate his own dilemma indirectly, by pondering his friend's analogous one. Table 2 (page 117) juxtaposes the manifest and latent content of Rivers's final thoughts in *Regeneration*.[95]

Rivers's Uncertain Conscience: "Shotvarfet" versus "Go Down and Depart"

In more than one way, the ending of *Ghost Road* revisits the questions raised so artfully, at the conclusion of *Regeneration*, about whether Rivers helps others to "heal" and about whether he can heal himself by projecting his desires onto others. First of all, *Ghost Road*'s final pages depict the garbled deathbed utterance—"shotvarfet"— of Hallet, a maimed soldier in Rivers's ward. Rivers decodes this verbal inkblot as "It's not worth it," i.e., the war hasn't been worth fighting—a sentiment that reflects Rivers's evolving political opinion. Hallet's father, a "retired professional army" man, insists that "it *is*," but other wounded soldiers in the ward voice a "wordless murmur" in support of Hallet's (apparently) anti-war "cry" from their "damaged brains and drooping mouths."[96] Perhaps Hallet didn't really mean "it's not worth it," but Rivers's guilty conscience constructs this idea from Hallet's meaningless syllables, both as a form of self-recrimination and as an articulation of his new stance on the war. But even if Rivers misconstrues Hallet's sentiment, he correctly intuits what Hallet's fellow patients feel.

While struggling to stay awake after Hallet's death, Rivers is visited by the ghost of Njiru, whose incantatory utterance—*Go down and depart*—offers relief to Rivers's conscience, as if Barker herself were exonerating the doctor.[97] Or perhaps this is only the exoneration that Rivers *wants*, and Njiru emanates not from Barker's god-like (and absolving) imagination, but from Rivers's mind. And perhaps Rivers is no less fallible when he exculpates himself with a visual hallucination than when he incriminates himself with an auditory hallucination. *Ghost Road*'s ending leaves open the meanings of both Hallet's articulation and the ghost's appearance, just as *Regeneration*'s conclusion is thematically inconclusive.

Barker complained that she couldn't craft a "genuine ending" for *Regeneration*, hence the novel became a trilogy.[98] But she may have been her own worst critic. If a "genuine" ending entails thematic resolution, then—to readers' benefit—"genuineness" seems to elude the entire trilogy. As Table 2 aims to demonstrate, in blending questions about Sassoon's and Rivers's futures, *Regeneration* leaves the questions open. Readers harboring metanarrative hopes—whether concerning the protagonist's psychological trajectory or society's capacity to heal itself—can choose their own meaning, if not their own adventure, finding Rivers valorized or ironized, and his "seeds on the wind" image either inspiring or Pollyannaish, depending on their reading of Barker's tone. Many modernist and contemporary writers, like Barker, make undecidability key to their aesthetic. As we saw in the previous chapter on *Atonement*, the narrator's recreation of her past can take radically different shapes, depending upon her current agenda. The Freudian principle of interminable analysis applies to McEwan's Briony and her guilt, as well as to Barker's Rivers and his guilt. These post-Christian protagonists cannot expiate their wrongs, but they can spend a lifetime (or a trilogy) working through their regrets.

On a sanguine reading of *Ghost Road*'s ending, Rivers's working-through has an end point. He sutures together his "internal divisions"[99] and achieves the self-integration that he attempts to help Sassoon, Prior, and other patients achieve. His extended fever restores his visual memory, the loss of which exacerbated his dissociation. Prior's aggressive interrogations compel him to recall the incident that *may* have caused his stammer (we never get a foolproof diagnosis), and when this pathogen ceases to be "unknown," it ceases to be a "monster." His anthropological studies pay off, as Njiru's ghost exorcises *Ave*, the "destroyer of peoples,"[100] in a rough parallel to how psychotherapists hope to abreact patients' strangulated feelings. Such a multi-layered resolution would make for an inspiring trilogy. But there are reasons to read *Ghost Road*'s ending more ironically.

Barker plays with readers' hopes in various ways. First, she has Prior, on a symbolic level, send Rivers an anti-war message via Hallet—but the message is contradicted by Prior's final, grateful thoughts about being back on the battlefield. Prior's extraordinary disregard for his own safety saves Hallet's life—although Prior wonders whether saving Hallet was worth it, given his mutilated condition.[101] Prior directs at least some of his compositions during the final weeks of war to "My dear Rivers"[102] (though they will never reach him), so the question of communication between these men—who have learned so much from one another as therapist and patient—hovers over the final chapter. *Does Prior have something left to demonstrate to Rivers,* readers can wonder, *whether about his own healing or about the war whose futility both men are coming to appreciate?*

Ghost Road alternates between Prior's and Rivers's experiences—Prior's being depicted in the odd-numbered chapters, Rivers's in the evens—prodding readers to wonder how dissociated these two portions of the novel's brain are, or whether a corpus callosum carries information between them. The final chapter quickens the pace of these crosscuts, alternating between Rivers and Prior every few pages. When Rivers looks at Hallet's file and notices that he was in the 2nd Manchesters, he wonders "if he knew Billy Prior."[103] When Rivers looks down into Hallet's "gargoyled face," he thinks, "why are you alive,"[104] recalling Prior's thought, as he nursed Hallet, "Die, can't you?

For God's sake, man, just *die*,"[105] but more importantly, telegraphing to the reader the question, *why is this character alive; what function does he serve?* Prior and Hallet die in one narrative moment, one on the French battlefield, the other in the hospital, telling readers, *this minor character links Prior to his doctor, so that the message "Shotvarfet" can cross the English Channel*. No cause invoked in the name of war can be worth this suffering, Rivers sees in (and hears from) Hallet, reinforcing the message he got from attempting to treat Burns in *Regeneration*.

But if this is the case, then why is Prior's final thought, "What an utter bloody fool I would have been not to come back?"[106] This thought rounds off a plotline that has carried through two novels. (Manning had offered Prior a job on the home front, and in declining it, Prior said that, if he were returned to France, he would think himself a fool for having refused safety when it was offered.) Why has his attitude reversed? Is he so selflessly devoted to his men that he can't bear to be safe while they are endangered? Is he addicted to the "sexiness" of combat? Or does military life—notwithstanding its class snobbery, which embitters him—give this man who is "neither fish nor fowl"[107] the only home he has known? As we cannot know what draws Sassoon back to combat, we cannot know what draws Prior. But whatever it is challenges Hallet's "it's not worth it" message.

For that matter, as mentioned, we can't know what Hallet's message really is, nor if he has any message to convey. If Rivers is the "blameless physician" that the poet H. D. saw in Freud, then his interpretation of Hallet's utterance must be accurate. Even more to Rivers's credit, he does not merely interpret Hallet, but gives voice to all the injured servicemen who redouble Hallet's cry. Rivers begins his political career before its official inauguration, in the most honorable way, as a voice of the people. From his privileged position, he makes sense of the inarticulate grievance of a dispossessed population; he facilitates their self-knowledge—on the road, hopefully, to justice.

But Barker may tease us with the *appearance* that Rivers channels Hallet's (and other men's) feelings, as she teased us with the suggestion that Hallet channeled something from Prior. An analyst's countertransference or guilt complex can lead him to hear a *cri de coeur* where none was intended.

* * *

These exercises—wondering about the significance of Prior's gratitude for being in combat and wondering whether Rivers correctly interprets Hallet—do not get us to the central puzzle of *Ghost Road*'s final pages. Whatever the trilogy's thematic ambiguities, its attitude toward the war is not among them. The three novels reiterate what Barker has expressed in multiple interviews: that the Great War was not worth it, with 8 million British dead and over 17 million total dead, and as *The Eye in the Door* depicts, its transformation of Britain into a paranoid surveillance state brimming with homophobia.

The ambiguity remains centered on Rivers and on how painfully "Shotvarfet" troubles him. Hallet's apparent indictment of his nation's war policy cannot rest easily on the protagonist's conscience: Barker suggests, to readers aware of Rivers's biography, that this moment helps propel him into political activism. Hallet has embodied Rivers's crippled and cowed conscience, helping to abreact his strangulated feeling about the conflict whose victims he has striven, often in vain, to heal. The physician has healed himself, with Hallet's unknowing help—*if* activating his conscience amounts to healing.

But if it does, then what is the need for Njiru's exorcism? *Do not yearn for us*, he says, *the fingerless, the crippled, the broken*. Were he talking of Hallet, he might have said "the faceless." His term "the crippled," if read psychologically, could apply to many of Rivers's patients, to Rivers himself, and to the Melanesians whose zest for life dies when they lose their sacrificial rituals. *Go down and depart*, Njiru concludes, *oh, oh, oh*.[108] This is not the voice of protest, of a conscience spurred to action, but the voice of acceptance, of self-forgiveness, perhaps of Rivers telling himself *let the dead be dead, lay down the burden of your guilt*.

On an incredulous reading, these final sentences of *Ghost Road* are antiheroic. Far from Njiru's ghost being real and rousing Rivers to political action, the subterfuge of a magical incantation leaves Rivers (at least for the moment) numb to mass slaughter.

But on a more sanguine interpretation, Rivers earns this exoneration, this rest, after so much extraordinary (and sometimes successful) effort. To quote a refrain from *The Satanic Verses*, what is a ghost except for unfinished business?[109] Rivers summons Njiru's spirit in an ingenious therapeutic maneuver, with himself as the patient, to give himself permission to move on. Maintaining metanarrative hope requires laying ghosts to rest: Rivers would be too emotionally crippled to grow into the social reformer we know he became, could he not coax the ghosts of the trenches to "depart"—at least for the moment. He will advocate on their behalf later.

Barker invites our metanarrative hope on behalf of Rivers and the exemplary—though imperfect—citizens he represents. He may be fated to wrestle interminably with the unanswerable question, *Was I fighting for years on the wrong side—for the war—and thus were my successful therapeutic efforts harmful?* Or he might take a page from the fatalism of *Beyond* and other texts where Freud attributes analytic failures to uncontrollable forces: a cellular drive toward death, an overpowering trauma, an implacable constitutional tendency. Rivers might ask, in a gentler mood than the above hypothetical question, *Were my failures really failures, or did I expect too much of myself?* If he does agonize over such questions, as *Ghost Road*'s conclusion suggests, then he is a finer Everyman, more lovable since all too human. And such questions do not preclude progress. As Barker said in a 2004 interview, "My major theme—of all my work—is recovery."[110] And as her 1992 interviewer Rob Nixon observed, "Few novelists are so unsentimentally animated by people's ability to chalk up small, shaky, but estimable victories over the most remorseless circumstances."[111] Nixon reformulates Freud's ambition to lift patients from "hysterical misery" to "common unhappiness."

In the Freudian metanarrative, physicians don't heal themselves. Such plot constructions became possible only after a revaluation of Freud and an extensive literature on countertransference. Barker revels in the ironies and opacities of post-Freudian countertransference. If circumstances for the patient are "remorseless," to use Nixon's language, then perhaps even "small victories" are beyond reach—as illustrated by Burns in *Regeneration*. So is Rivers only treating himself when he treats Burns (whether he knows it or not)? Perhaps the analyst and analysand cannot know who is being treated until well into the treatment (if ever), as they cannot anticipate when the analyst's loving generosity will reveal a Christ complex, nor when his empathic capacities will precipitate a countertransference neurosis. But they can still envision improvement, for the patient and maybe the physician—if they, like Prior, are perceptive enough patients, interested enough in the doctor's mental hygiene. If working-through is interminable, is it not still working-through? Barker's trilogy offers many opportunities to see Rivers as culpable, as ironized, and thus its metanarratives as emptied out. Her readers can also see Rivers as exemplary, a hero upon whose shoulders a metanarrative might be borne. Where metanarrative hope is concerned, perhaps the trilogy is like Hallet's utterance: empty until the reader—without realizing she does so—projects her expectations into it.

Notes

1. Lubbock 384.
2. Lenin's 1916 book, *Imperialism: The Highest Stage of Capitalism*, made this claim.
3. Jordan 167.
4. Ferraresi 35, 36.
5. "Case Histories: Fraulein Elisabeth von R." 160.
6. See Sprengnether, among many others.
7. Showalter 192.
8. Luria (1902–77), a Soviet neuropsychologist cited by Sacks as an inspiration, was a founder of cultural-historical psychology, which studies the interconnections of mind, brain, and culture in concrete social and historical contexts. Axline (1911–88), a clinical psychologist and play-therapy pioneer, authored *Dibs in Search of Self* (1964), which chronicles a year's worth of play-therapy sessions with an emotionally disturbed boy. Emmett authored *I Love the Person You Were Meant to Be* (1971), a fictional portrait of an acutely mentally ill woman that includes flashbacks to analytic sessions. Based on a well-regarded Israeli television series, HBO's *In Treatment* (2008–10), starring Gabriel Byrne as a psychologist, devotes individual episodes to individual patients, or to Byrne's character, in treatment with his analyst.
9. Stevenson 181.
10. Dennis Brown terms Rivers a "postmodern hero" (187) for reasons discussed below. In contrast, Whitehead reads Barker as a skeptical in a postmodern vein and Rivers as a naïve in a "modern" vein, with his hope that therapy provides patients unproblematic access to the emotion that generated their trauma.
11. Lyotard defines the "modern" subject as that which "sees itself as the narrator of history" and postmodern discourse as that which recognizes the instability of such a subject. Thus "a work can only become modern if it is first postmodern"—i.e., it can "forget" the subject's instability only after registering the shock of this condition (*The Postmodern Condition* 79). This effort to see postmodernism as "nascent" in modernism challenges such historiography as Jameson's with its nostalgia for a time before capitalism's hegemony. For an admiring discussion of this strategy of Lyotard's, see Nicholls, especially 4–5.
12. See especially Part 3 of McHale's essay (58–60). He describes ontological preoccupations dominating postmodern writing, whereas epistemological

preoccupations had dominated modernist writing—though neither era's interests were uniform. I ask epistemological questions about each era: whether incredulity dominates postmodern attitudes toward historical progress, whereas modernists were more attracted to the idea of progress—though neither era's attitudes were uniform.

13 *Regeneration* 106.
14 Ibid. 249.
15 Therapy's social ramifications have been explored from various angles. In his 1963 introduction to *Dora*, Philip Rieff, one of Freud's more admiring critics, notes that it is not Dora, but "the milieu in which she is constrained to live that is ill." Somewhat unreasonably, Rieff faults Freud and his "orthodox followers" for failing to examine "with ruthless honesty" the "limit" that psychoanalysis cannot treat a whole society. (x) As if in answer to this critique, institutions including the US Veterans' Administration have come to employ "milieu therapy," which involves not a whole society but therapeutic communities of roughly thirty, treated for nine to eighteen months. With a more radical agenda than the Veterans' Administration has in mind, the "Freudian Left," from Wilhelm Reich in the 1930s to Norman O. Brown and Herbert Marcuse during and after the 1950s, have linked therapy's battle against sexual repression to political struggles against social oppression. Likewise, Freudian feminists including Helene Cixous and Luce Irigaray have seen broad social ramifications in the therapeutic project of liberating a woman's unconscious from patriarchal thought structures.
16 *Regeneration* 15.
17 "Remembering, Repeating, and Working-Through" 152.
18 *Ghost Road* 276.
19 These details come from "Frau Emmy von N." 51, 59.
20 These concepts did not all appear in *Studies*. See "Remembering" 151 for an early use of "transference." See Strachey's Editor's Introduction (Vol. XII 85-8), including his footnote (87) on Freud's infrequent published discussions of "countertransference" in particular and psychoanalytic technique in general.
21 Malcolm 37-8.
22 "The Psychotherapy of Hysteria" 270-1.
23 Ibid. 265.
24 In *Regeneration* (97), Prior suggests that Rivers's stammer could be psychosomatic, prompting Rivers to ask sarcastically, "is that the end of my appointment?" In *The Eye in the Door* (136), when Prior queries Rivers about his lack of visual memory, Rivers indicates that they should switch seats, which Prior does "with considerable aplomb."
25 *The Eye in the Door* 231-2.
26 "Preliminary Communication" 17.
27 *Ghost Road* 227.
28 Ibid. 228.
29 *Ghost Road* 21, 57-8.
30 *Regeneration* 112.
31 Ibid. 220.
32 Ibid. 104.
33 Ibid. 97.
34 *The Eye in the Door* 137.
35 Freud's letter to Fleiss that year explains his loss of belief in the theory. Masson 264-6.

36 Rivers employs this phrase in *The Eye in the Door* (139). Later in that novel (247), Prior recovers a childhood memory of his father throwing him against a wall, which "bruised" him: a modest enough injury that his imagination may have projected something more "monstrous" where particulars were "unknown."
37 "The Psychotherapy of Hysteria" 305.
38 The paper appeared at the end of 1914, in the second issue of *The International Journal of Psychoanalysis*. Franz Ferdinand was assassinated on June 28 of that year, prompting Austria-Hungary to declare war against Serbia one month later (July 28). Germany declared war on France on August 3, and Britain declared war on Germany the following day.
39 "Remembering" 150.
40 Ibid. 147.
41 Ibid. 148.
42 Ibid. 149.
43 Ibid. 155–6.
44 Ibid. 154.
45 Ibid. 148.
46 *Regeneration* 52. Whitehead (211) discusses Barker's "notable" decision to depict Rivers using this technique.
47 Ibid. 103.
48 "Fragment of an Analysis of a Case of Hysteria" 30.
49 *The Eye in the Door* 240.
50 *Regeneration* 68.
51 "Fragment of an Analysis of a Case of Hysteria" 41.
52 Showalter 167–8.
53 "On the Psychical Mechanism of Hysterical Phenomena" 6.
54 *The Interpretation of Dreams* discusses overdetermined dream-content on 149, 283–4, and 306–8. *Dora* ("Fragment of an Analysis") discusses overdetermined hysterical symptoms: 47, 53, 60, 83.
55 *Regeneration* 222.
56 Ibid. 243, 30.
57 Rawlinson 92.
58 For recent work in trauma studies focused on collective experience, see Alexander, et al.
59 Fraser.
60 Jones 275–7.
61 *Beyond the Pleasure Principle* 38.
62 Peter Brooks 102, 96.
63 Ibid. 95.
64 *Beyond the Pleasure Principle* 9.
65 James Strachey mentions this disinclination of Freud's in several places, including his Editor's Note to "Analysis Terminable and Interminable" (212).
66 See the Editor's Note to this essay, 211.
67 "Analysis Terminable and Interminable" 242.
68 Ibid. 216.
69 Ibid. 217–18.
70 Ibid. 220.
71 *Regeneration* 19.
72 Ibid. 184.

73	"Analysis Terminable and Interminable" 220.
74	Ibid. 224–5.
75	Ibid. 227.
76	"The Psychotherapy of Hysteria" 270.
77	"Analysis Terminable and Interminable" 233.
78	Ibid. 228.
79	Ibid. 240.
80	Brown 187.
81	*Ghost Road* 103–4.
82	Slobodin (3–5) discusses the racism of Rivers's uncle, James Hunt, the founder in 1863 of the Anthropological Society. Slobodin speculates that, had Rivers lived into the 1940s, he would have been "the most leftward of leading British anthropologists."
83	Showalter 184–7.
84	*Regeneration* 242.
85	Ibid. 167.
86	Ibid. 104.
87	Ibid. 140.
88	*Ghost Road* 110.
89	Benziman, et al.
90	Racker 26.
91	For an overview of this neurosis and its array of manifestations and origins, see Racker's chapter "The Countertransference Neurosis" (105–26).
92	*Regeneration* 55.
93	Ibid. 242.
94	Ibid. 241.
95	Ibid. 249–50.
96	*Ghost Road* 263, 274.
97	Ibid. 276.
98	Stevenson 175.
99	*Regeneration* 249. (This language is also quoted in Table X.)
100	*Ghost Road* 268.
101	Ibid. 215.
102	Ibid. 254.
103	Ibid. 239.
104	Ibid. 264.
105	Ibid. 197.
106	Ibid. 258.
107	*Regeneration* 57.
108	*Ghost Road* 276.
109	*Satanic Verses* 133.
110	Barker, Interview with Carolyn T. Hughes 37.
111	Barker, Interview with Rob Nixon 3.

5

Forsterian Skepticism: Transcontinental Eros in *The Satanic Verses*

In 1924, E. M. Forster published a novel about multi-confessional India and its discontents, about British colonialism and racism, and about the possibility of interracial, same-sex "friendship"—with all of this word's ambiguous Bloomsburian extensions—under such menacing conditions. Its concluding verdict on this possibility—"not yet ... not there," in Mau, India, circa 1922—hints at a queer futurity, daring future novelists to ask the follow-up question *What about now and here*? After all, Aziz tells Fielding that Indians "shall drive every blasted Englishmen into the sea [and then] you and I shall be friends."[1] He doesn't phrase his dream in the language of probability, of how India *might* gain independence and how, *if* it does, then friendship *could* be possible. So after 1947's India Independence Act proved the first half of Aziz's assertion roughly true, and after many Indians and Pakistanis migrated freely to the UK (during the 1948–62 period of liberal immigration law),[2] shouldn't such friendships have found fresh soil in which to prove the second half of Aziz's claim equally true?

Since same-sex, and even sexual, intimacy (not merely interracial comity) is key to *Passage*'s dream, the punishing 1885 Labouchere Amendment[3] deferred that dream—as suggested by the indirect treatment of Wilde's love not just in *Passage* but in all five of Forster's novels published during his lifetime. But the 1967 repeal of Labouchere and 1969's Stonewall riots vindicated hopes of legislative and social progress, potentially opening space to recuperate Fielding's plangent question to Aziz—"Why can't we be friends now?"—from the narrator's grim "not yet ... not there" assessment. After independence and Stonewall, *Passage* dares novelists to answer their version of Fielding's question affirmatively—to have characters say, "Why *shouldn't* we be friends now? What's stopping us? What sort of intimacy do we want?"

By 1988—four decades after independence—no novelist would have seemed better poised to answer this challenge than Salman Rushdie. And no novel of his would have seemed a fitter vehicle for celebrating the benign ways in which newness can enter the world—in the thousand and one varieties of multicultural intimacy—than *The Satanic Verses*. Rushdie has voiced his disdain for the "absolutism of the Pure" and his preference, in human relations as in cooking, for "hotchpotch: a bit of this and a bit of that."[4] He proclaims, in defiance of the novel's critics, that *Verses* "celebrates hybridity, impurity, intermingling."[5] (He became so identified with this attitude that James Wood praised Zadie Smith for guarding against "a Rushdie-like orthodoxy about the worship of hybridity."⁶) As a child in Bombay, Rushdie attended the prestigious English-language Cathedral School, where he played happily with children from many religious backgrounds. This experience launched his departure from India at age thirteen, after which he remade himself, with astounding success, as an Englishman, a political lightning rod, and an experimental novelist worthy of modernism's most stringent precedents—later to open a new chapter of his life in the United States. He married and/or fathered sons with more than one woman of a different race. He fathered magical realism into Anglophone literature: *Midnight's Children* (1981) weds this genre's techniques to postcolonial themes even more quintessentially than *Passage* weds its (marginally avant-garde) techniques to its anti-colonial sentiments. Rushdie says that, since losing his faith at age fourteen, he has been a "modern, and modern*ist*, urban man," "drawn toward the great traditions of secular radicalism—in politics, socialism; in the arts, modernism and its offspring"—that have driven much twentieth-century history.⁷ And he has expressed mistrust of nostalgia: commissioned in 1992 by the British Film Institute to contribute to its "Film Classics" series, he chose to write on his boyhood favorite, *The Wizard of Oz*. Despite admiring the film, he disparages its "least convincing idea": that "there's no place like home." That Kansas is dirt-poor and inhabited by the dog-hating Miss Gulch makes it unworthy of Dorothy's "eulogizing," in his view. Readers might infer that Rushdie's attraction to new experiences *over the rainbow* inclines him to see any version of "home" in the bleak gray tones of the film's dustbowl landscape.⁸

But *Verses* eludes expectations: it pays tribute to the idea of "home" and doubts the promise of the wider Anglosphere. Readers familiar with Forster would have been disappointed, had they expected in *Verses*' passage *from* India the triumphalist verdict, *now and here, in the multicultural West, the barriers that frustrated Fielding and Aziz have been overcome*. Rushdie disappoints such hopes for three reasons. The first lies in his anti-teleological and anti-rational attitude toward history, informed both by the postmodern moment of *Verses*' conception and by Rushdie's training as an historian of the West and early Islam. The second and third reasons lie in the perdurability of racism and misogyny, even in the supposedly enlightened and feminist West, thirteen centuries after Islam's founding upon the rejection of female deities. These three reasons for holding the myth of progress at arm's length also motivate the novel's attraction to the conservative idea of home that Rushdie's *Wizard of Oz* book is too disillusioned to credit.

Critical discussion has been extensive both on Rushdie's 1988 novel and on The Rushdie Affair: the Ayatollah Khomeini's fatwa against the author's life, its implications for freedom of expression, and the author's time in hiding under secret-police protection. Scholars have discussed *Verses*' attitude toward Islam, with one arguing that—far from being an insult—it is a skeptic's "love letter" to the religion in which Rushdie was raised. (In a similar vein, Rushdie has claimed that *Verses* was intended to give voice to the very communities who reacted against it—that he was "rejected and reviled by [his] own characters.") Scholars have discussed *Verses*' depictions of women and its feminist dimensions. They have explored its formal politics—its difficult combination of styles and myriad cultural references enacting anti-absolutist and anti-puritanical values. Some scholars have put *Verses* into conversation with Forster's novel, asking whether it is "*A Passage to India* in reverse"—a strategy that Rushdie says he did not consciously intend. (As mentioned in the Introduction, Bart Moore-Gilbert describes a "discursive consistency" in literature written about Britain's long rule over India—a capacious formulation that enables discussion of intertextuality without reliance on "the troublesome category of influence.")[9]

I incorporate several of these traditional foci in *Verses*' criticism—including Islam, formal politics, and Forsterian resonances—while paying overdue attention to the topic of love, which *Verses* describes as necessary to human experience and Rushdie's criticism sees as a necessary ingredient in a successful novel.[10]

Saladin Chamcha's fraying relationship with his English wife and English civilization, troubled love for his father, and powerful attraction to his Indian lover are all key to *Verses*' formal epistemology and vision of postcolonial history. The novel is about intimacy in history.

Historical Skepticism, Narrative Anti-Realism

Very well then. Rushdie shares Lyotard's "incredulity" toward optimistic metanarratives, and he uses transcontinental loves—Saladin's for Pamela and Gibreel's for Allie—to dramatize, in a post-Forsterian vein, his skepticism toward the idea of "progress." (Rushdie's atheistic essay "In God We Trust" cites Roland Barthes's idea that myth is "statistically on the right,"[11] but perhaps *Verses* conveys the obverse point: that if "progress" is a contemporary myth, then the left has its own mythopoetry.) Such a philosophical commitment on *Verses*' part would logically entail—so it seems—a complementary aesthetic commitment. Narrative realism, along with historical rationalism, assumes a world that is "homogeneous, composed only of reconcilable elements." But in a Rushdian manifesto, *Verses*' Otto Cone tells his daughter Allie that anyone who sees the world this way belongs in a straitjacket.[12] Throughout the novel, schizophrenia and religious revelations (which are separated by a blurry boundary), along with movies, television shows, and product advertisements, all warp "homogeneous" reality. No wonder *Verses* opens with its protagonists surviving an airborne explosion—a stylistic calling card that promises a refusal of Victorian narrative comforts to complement a refusal of Enlightenment historical consolations.

But aesthetically as well as philosophically, *Verses* refuses simple categorization. As Sara Suleri observes, it "begins as Joyce [and] ends as Dickens": a slide toward realism distinguishes its latter from its earlier half.[13] Gibreel's seemingly magical powers yield to his schizophrenia and suicide, each of which suggests that objective reality exists and that losing contact with it is dangerous. Saladin regains—and retains—his human form. And the novel culminates happily, with Saladin's sentimental and (largely) realistic reunion with his father. Saladin simultaneously attains some combination of reason, psychic health, and national rootedness. By contrast, Fielding's and Aziz's passages *from* multicultural and multi-confessional India, back *to* their mono-cultural enclaves—Britishness and Islam—are not happy returns.

Such differences aside, *Verses* recalls Forster's last and profoundest novel both thematically and technically. It too examines multi-confessional India: both directly, in Gibreel's film exploits, beloved of numerous religious communities, and obliquely, in its depiction of multi-confessional seventh-century Arabia. It too explores the possibility of intimacy across lines of race, civilization, and geography: its pages abound with hotchpotch or geographically displaced couples, from the two central ones (Saladin/Pamela and Gibreel/Allie) to the Sufyans (transplanted from Bangladesh to London) and the politically motivated Abu Simbel/Hind pairing in phantasmagorical Arabia.

And *Verses*, like *Passage*, weaves homoeroticism—with all its ambiguous manifestations—into its picture of human intimacies. Admittedly, the novels treat homoeroticism differently, for different reasons: *Passage* evokes the phenomenon itself, though in coded ways; *Verses* depicts it openly and with comic brio, though for metaphorical purposes. Gibreel swims into Saladin's arms in the air, the men performing "germinate cartwheels" as they embrace "head-to-tail,"[14] not because of romantic attraction but because they're parts of a blended angelicdevilish self. Their corporal entanglement evokes psychic and metaphysical entanglement. Likewise, Gibreel wrestles Mahound on Mount Cone, Mahound's tongue in his ear and Mahound's fist around his balls, until Gibreel pins him down and Mahound falls into a "post-revelatory [read: post-coital] sleep." Sex is a figure for the psychic and physical intensity of the movie star's spiritual trial, as he attempts de-conversion.[15]

Notwithstanding the novels' different uses of homoeroticism, notwithstanding their authors' different sexual orientations, and notwithstanding the fact that Saladin and Gibreel (unlike Fielding and Aziz) are both Indian, *Verses*' treatment of male-male entanglement tightens its intertextual bonds with *Passage*. Forster's novel asks of its protagonist, *With whom and where might he form intimacies: members of his national tribe? His own sex? On his native soil? Abroad? How will his spiritual capacities (or lack thereof) influence his relationships? Can love be trusted?* Conversely, Forster's novel also asks, *What motivates Fielding's deepest antipathies? Might his fellow countrymen represent the things in himself that he most wishes to disown?* With the exception of homoeroticism, Rushdie's novel asks the same questions of Saladin.

Forster's Nascent Anti-Realism

Passage and *Verses* also have technical affiliations, despite Rushdie's complaint that Forster's "cool" prose is ill-suited for depicting India, which is "hot and overcrowded and vulgar and loud."[16] Rushdie's memoir recounts his epiphany that he is a "migrant" and that "migration tore up all the traditional roots of the self."[17] Blending his aesthetic agenda with his Cambridge training as an historian, Rushdie decided that "the great point of history" should become "the point of his fiction": to understand how people, individually and communally, are shaped by "great forces" yet retain "the ability to change the direction of those forces."[18] Needing a "language" for India's chaos and a form for the disruptive "point" of history, Rushdie suggests that Forster is a foil for his own experimentation. But Forster is a cagey stylist, as critics have noted in discussing his blend of Victorian and modernist qualities.[19] His use of *epistemological multiplicity* anticipates *Verses*' more flamboyant experiments.

I have discussed this technique in *Howards End* (1910),[20] wherein the narrator, Margaret, and Helen offer three different interpretations of the Schlegels' victory over the Wilcoxes. They reach different conclusions via different methods: one intuits supernatural influences where another does not, one emphasizes violence where another euphemizes it. *Howards End* does not manipulate point of view as subtly as *Mrs Dalloway*, nor relativize perspective as starkly as Browning's *The Ring and the Book* or Kurosawa's *Rashomon*. But it is heteroglossic, and one of its voices belongs to an "ambiguous"—i.e., mobile and indeterminate—narrator.[21] The novel shares modernism's post-realist, Einstein-inflected sense not merely that different observers have different perspectives on reality, but that "reality" is a function of perspective.

Passage refines this technique, and in so doing it anticipates Rushdie's more stridently anti-Victorian methods. In *Passage*, Godbole, the mystical Hindu; Fielding, the rationalistic Englishman; and Aziz, the irrational "Oriental," all think differently. Not only are their conclusions different, their methods are incompatible. Who was responsible for the alleged assault at the Marabar Caves? According to Godbole, many people, including himself, are implicated. "When evil occurs, it expresses the whole of the universe," he explains.[22] Fielding finds this mysticism useless; after all, some individual (or no one) must have attacked Adela. But Godbole is right, even in mundane ways: his lengthy prayers made Fielding miss the train, implicating himself in the Marabar fiasco; Fielding's absence from the expedition implicates Fielding, etc.

Passage brings the same technique to bear on the question of financial reparations for Aziz. Aziz feels "as if" Fielding stole money that was rightfully his, by dissuading him from seeking damages, then profiting by marrying Adela (as he wrongly believes Fielding to have done). On one level, this accusation is preposterous: Fielding's motives have always been honorable. But on another level, the accusation is perspicacious: Britain has plundered India of wealth; Fielding has come to support its colonial mission; and Adela has become one of his best friends, though not his spouse. Of neither his dispute with Godbole nor his dispute with Aziz can the reader say with certainty, "Fielding was right; the Indian was wrong" or vice versa. Instead *Passage* entertains multiple incompatible styles of understanding. The novel might not be stylistically multiple: its "narrative vision," as Barbara Rosecrance argues, might be predominantly Victorian,[23] leaving magical-realist successors like Rushdie room for radical self-differentiation. But nonetheless, *Passage*'s epistemological multiplicity anticipates the anti-realism of much postcolonial writing, *Verses* included.

Rushdie's Magical Realism

Even before *Verses*' 1988 appearance, Rushdie exploited magical-realist techniques, drawing on pre-modernist experimenters like Sterne and on post-Joycean figures. *Verses*' style recalls Mikhail Bulgakov's *Master and Margarita* (written 1937, published 1967), Alejo Carpentier's *Kingdom of This World* (1949), and Gabriel Garcia Marquez's *One Hundred Years of Solitude* (1967),[24] deploying the "ancient Arab story-tellers' formula" "it was and it was not so,"[25] building Heisenbergian mystery into the events it narrates, and signaling generic affinity with fairytales. The novel frames Gibreel's delirious dreams *as* dreams, hence Mahound as a figment of his fevered apostate mind. (Critics who accuse *Verses* of insulting Islam[26] miss the point that its Mahound sections tell us nothing—at least nothing directly—about Rushdie's feelings toward the religion, and everything about this character's "punishment of dreams."[27]) Or *are* Gibreel's dreams only dreams? The "it was and it was not" principle leaves open the possibility that he *is* an angel. (He falls from a plane and lives; people see and revere his halo; he might blow fire from his avenging trumpet.) That he is schizophrenic is certain; that he is therefore *not* an angel is far from certain, especially for readers who de-emphasize the distinction between the novel's more magical bulk and less magical concluding portions. Rushdie explains that Gibreel's loss of faith causes a "rift in the soul,"[28] and Gibreel's cognitive dissonance captures this rift dramatically. But Gibreel isn't *Verses*' only deconvert; modernity is also losing its faith. Gibreel's disbelief is a synecdoche for this phenomenon, and for the besieged and beleaguered place of Islam (especially the fundamentalist Islam of Hind, Ayesha, and the Imam) in a world dominated by the secular West. Gibreel isn't alone in his schizophrenia; the world is schizophrenic, which extends the range of the relativistic idea that whatever is "so" is also "not so."

When I said that Godbole's, Fielding's, and Aziz's epistemologies are "incompatible," I borrowed the label from Otto Cone.[29] The "it was and it was not" principle—i.e., Otto's "incompatibility" theory—is embodied in the magical realism of Carpentier, Marquez, and others who dramatize the Western domination of Latin America, the conflict between Western empiricism and native spirituality, and the propaganda emanating from Latin American governments. *Verses* one-ups them, embracing not just competing contemporaneous epistemologies, but the seventh and twentieth centuries (since modern Muslims such as the Imam, it suggests, cling to what they imagine about their religion's seventh-century roots). Nonetheless, as far as this technique might seem to carry *Verses* from Forster's more Victorian *Passage*, the novels' shared interest in multi-confessional India's encounter with Western power, and their shared epistemological multiplicity, draw them into conversation.

Moreover, as Suleri notes, magical realism is not *Verses*' only narrative mode. If Saladin's heart lies in his ancestral home, and if that's why his journey circles him there, then does the novel's ethical heart (if it has just one) lie in some modified form of realism? If magical realism is useful for evoking the fractured condition of the migrating self (which could be anyone, the migrant being a figure for all people[30]), then is realism better at evoking wholeness and enduring love?

Mythical Significance, Circular Design

The conservatism of Saladin's storyline lies in its circularity. Rather than beginning in one place and ending in another, his journey ends where it began, although we only learn this from backstory and although both Saladin and Bombay are transformed, by the time of his return, from what they were in his childhood. He leaves Bombay for understandable reasons. He is molested by an old man on Scandal Point, the psychic effects of which Rushdie leaves vague. Certainly, the assault fuels Saladin's symbolizing imagination: he associates Bombay with sordidness, Indian culture with tastelessness, and London, Vilayet—his Oz—with civilized refinement. Saladin also leaves because of his father's cruelty and his own bitterness. The Campbellian monomyth informs his departure from home, his instructive adventures abroad, his near-fatal encounters and supernatural aid (his heart attack, the Shaandaar fire from which the angel Gibreel saves him[31]), and his return home. When, near novel's end, Saladin "became aware that he was a rich man," his wealth applies on a literal level to the dead Changez's "vast fortune," but on a figurative level to his journey's spiritual *raison d'etre*.[32]

Saladin's alienation from and atonement with Changez recall other myths of reconciled fathers and sons, from Luke's Parable of the Prodigal Son to Luke Skywalker.[33] Changez Chamchawalla parallels the divine father in his son's alienated imagination, but theological figurations are not confined to Saladin's mind. The novel begins with an extensive allusion to *Paradise Lost* as the protagonists are expelled, á la Satan, from a heavenly height, and ensuing events reveal Saladin's Satanic capacities for disguise and cruelty. The narrator's identification with Satan—his "sympathy for the devil"[34]—suggests that Saladin's filial defiance is ennobling. The question of whether this (figuratively devilish) son will be reunited with his (somehow deified) father hovers over the entire novel.

Saladin's intimacy with Changez is the only one that achieves and maintains wholeness, in contrast to his marriage to Pamela, his friendship with Jumpy, and his intimate rivalry with his doppelganger, Gibreel. These three characters all die youthful deaths before their broken relationships can be healed, but Changez is too important to the novel's circular mythical conception for his life to be prematurely curtailed. The filial reconciliation places such demands on the novel's epistemology that magical realism burns away when Changez "teach[es]" his son "how to die"[35] without expectation of afterlife, and when Saladin—in a scene of Dickensian sentimentality—shaves Changez, "gently drawing the skin tight as the cordless shaver moved across it, and then stroking it to make sure it felt smooth."[36]

As with Odysseus's recognitions by his dog Argos and his wet-nurse Eurycleia, so Saladin and Chengez's love of many years is reaffirmed, or rekindled, or proven never to have died by a moment of tender physical knowing. It may have looked like Saladin's odyssey would return him to London, his self-chosen Ithaca; and Pamela may have seemed like his Penelope. After all, their domicile was invaded by a suitor (Jumpy) in the husband's absence. The adult Saladin's vessels—in his case, aircrafts—carry him from and to England, just as Odysseus's vessels carry him from and to Ithaca. But London turns out to be a false Ithaca; Saladin's more important journey of self-reparation carries him not away from and back to the English capitol, but from and to Bombay.

Verses' Surprising Neophobia

The circular, or conservative, design of Saladin's journeys radiates beyond the father-son plotline. Reflecting on Saladin's idealistic—or naïve—project of self-reinvention in England, the narrator says that "Love" was wreaking revenge upon the "foolish" lover, who had idealized four things: culture, city, wife, and a "dream" of a son.[37] In each of these areas England betrays him, but India has always been waiting—with open arms so to speak—for the prodigal son to return and claim his birthright. Moving through the list, the narrator says that Saladin had "loved the protean inexhaustible culture of English-speaking peoples."[38] This might sound like a good reason to emigrate to the language's mother country, especially given *Verses*' British literary antecedents, including Forster, Joyce, Sterne, Swift, and Milton. But it's also a reason to remain in India. After all, Anglophone culture is inexhaustible because it flourishes outside of England, as Rushdie celebrates in "The Empire Writes Back with a Vengeance." Saladin misses this point, fetishizing a nation over the borderless culture he thinks he "loved most." He lashes out against his native country—"Damn you, India … I escaped your clutches long ago"[39]—setting up readers to root for India, against him. When Saladin inadvertently addresses the stewardess in Indian English ("So, okay, bibi, give one whiskysoda only"), and when Zeeny tells him that his "Angrez accent … slips … like a false moustache,"[40] the joke is on Saladin. Readers sense that his act of *not* being Indian will yield to the identity he cannot escape. When Zeeny tells him "Change back!"[41]—as though, with a *Presto* and a snap of the fingers, he could—she articulates what the narrative encourages readers to want.

While India doesn't grant Saladin any of these four desiderata—culture, city, wife, or dreamed-of son—in pristine form, it gives him the possibility of each. Though he cannot "change back!" he can return. With Zeeny as his tour guide, he gets immersed in an Indian culture that is vibrantly democratic, self-critical as well as critical (in intellectually subtle ways) of American power, and friendly to radicals and artists. Zeeny, this feminist novel's moral and intellectual ballast, articulates Rushdie's disdain for the absolutism of the pure and celebrates India's hybrid culture, with its Aryan, Mughal, British, and other influences. She titles her book of art criticism *The Only Good Indian* and explains to Saladin, "Meaning, is a dead," with irreverent wit worthy of Rushdie's profanest characters. She demonstrates, by deed and word, that Saladin's homecoming requires neither conformism nor pursuit of chimerical "authenticity."[42] Given that English "civilization" has "broken" Saladin "upon its wheel," Zeeny's admonition "You keep your civilization, Toadji; I like this one plenty fine" seems wise.[43]

Just as Saladin's toady-ish love for British culture is unmasked, so too are the shaky foundations of his preferential love for London. Of course London's allure is powerful, and it's hard not to hear Rushdie's appreciation in the narrator's description of the City as a haven for immigrants from the world over, with architecture preferable to America's. Neither Pamela's ironic counter-voice, nor the fact that Saladin longs to "possess" London like a conqueror, cancels this encomium.[44] And of course, Bombay has problems, not limited to the Scandal Point pedophile nor the ever-shifting architecture and cinema in its "culture of re-makes."[45] But Saladin's contempt for his native city and idealization of his adopted one are irrational, as indicated by how the cities mirror one another. Just as Bombay is constantly torn down and rebuilt, so is London, not to Pamela's consternation but with her approval. Decrying what she calls the City's "museum values" that Saladin admires, she exclaims "Change everything! Rip it up,"[46] in a burst of naïve enthusiasm akin to Zeeny's "change back" directive. If this weren't an ominous enough hint of soullessness, Hal Valance—a "pure self-created image" of Thatcherite vulgarianism that would surely make Pamela shudder—extols the hyper-capitalist metropolis's creative-destructive energies and exults that Prime

Minister Thatcher aspires to "invent a whole goddamn new middle class."[47] London shares with Bombay not only a dizzyingly self-reinventive capacity (the very *will to change* of which Saladin and Gibreel are made), but also a cornucopia of criminality, from Granny Ripper to petnappers who steal rich people's dogs and sell them back to their "grieving" owners.[48]

Given London's pathologies, the British "culture" and "city" on which Saladin pegs his love seem like "foolish" choices, to repeat the narrator's judgment. But his latter two objects of love—his wife and dreamed-of son—are more poignant. India offers, and has always offered, the culture and city he spurned. But it does even better than that. Saladin's marriage with Pamela was troubled before his transmogrification and crumbling before she died—not surprisingly, given that she was fleeing the Britishness he fetishized. But Zeeny shares the cultural frames of reference, not to mention the comfort in her own skin, that could make for easy rapport and a fructifying partnership. Could she also supply the son he lacks—i.e., fulfill the "dream" that he mistakenly sought overseas?

Could she and Saladin achieve, in the context of India's hot, loud, and messy culture, their own version of what the sociologist Anthony Giddens terms "intimacy as democracy?" In Giddens's telling, such intimacies enable individuals to determine "the conditions of their association" and to "develop their potentialities and express their diverse qualities."[49] *Verses'* interracial loves fall short of this ideal. Gibreel's abjection leads him to manipulate and exploit Allie. Saladin and Pamela, though they associate on more equal terms than Gibreel and Allie, nonetheless miscommunicate, fail to produce offspring, and are unhappy together.

Hypothetically, if Saladin and Zeeny's budding romance is *to be continued* after *Verses'* final pages, then it might—in contrast with the novel's interracial loves—more nearly approximate what Forster termed "Love, the Beloved Republic."[50] In their unique version of "intimacy as democracy," Saladin and Zeeny might dispute questions about love and politics, with their mutual respect, attraction, and solidarity sharpened by their differences. Arguably, *Verses* opens out into a happy (implied) ending because its protagonist jettisons his dreams of foreign loves in favor of the domestic ones that were always his birthright.

Regardless of how Saladin's and Zeeny's romance might hypothetically unfold, Rushdie's novel completes—or gestures toward completing—a more virtuous circle than we see in *Passage*. By contrast, when Forster's novel begins, Aziz is eager to meet Fielding, and readers learn that Fielding had been "caught by India late."[51] Each man aspires to expand, or even defy, his cultural horizons, and the latter's late arrival in bigoted Anglo India suggests that his mind will not be circumscribed by its prejudices. But sadly, as mentioned, each retreats into a national or sectarian enclave, never to trace a virtuous circle and regain the cosmopolitan sympathies he once had.

Saladin's virtuous circle reveals that *Verses* is not as cynical toward love, in all its varieties, as it might seem to be. Instead, which is perhaps sadder, its disillusionment centers on *new* loves. Saladin suffers from his love for England and for every object in which he seeks it symbolically (Pamela, the Queen, the culture that grants him work only as a *voice* actor).[52] Hence, wholeness and plentitude flower more in his reconstituted love for his dying father and mother country—plus his potential love for Zeeny, i.e., India in one womanly package. The orphaned Gibreel's failed loves reinforce the point that wholeness is to be found in family and that family is given, not chosen. His biological parents may be poor, and by naming him "Gibreel" his mother may afflict him with an angelic identity that proves his undoing,[53] but her love is the prototype that he can never recapture. Not film stardom, not an "avalanche of sex" with female fans who forgive his infidelities, not Rekha's attachment to him, not even his gift for "fulfill[ing] people's most secret desires without having any idea of how he did it"[54] can fill the emptiness of lost mother-love. Can faith do so? For a time, in combination with film stardom, it may satisfy Gibreel in some ways (though without curing his mother-ache). But God's failure, as he experiences it, to answer him in his physical sickness combines with Rekha's suicide to precipitate his calamitous mental sickness. His love for Allie, the "blonde yahudan,"[55] also represents something over the rainbow for this darker-skinned Muslim Indian, and it develops the novel's neophobic sentiments by ending with a recapitulation of the Rekha tragedy: another multiple fatality at Everest Vilas.

Of course, Allie Cone represents not only the new but also the old. Her first name echoes Al-Lat, the goddess-rival of Allah, and her last name recalls Mount Cone, where Mahound receives god's word. If Allie symbolized either *one* of these principles—the impossible blondness of a post-Islamic future or the inaccessible summit of a religious past that Gibreel cannot escape—then Gibreel's love for her would doom him to neurosis, and whatever love she offers in return would doom her to disappointment. That she symbolizes *both* principles—how Gibreel would move forward (away from India and Islam) by moving back (to the beginnings of Islam)—indicates how schizophrenic his desire for her is. Loving her is a path not out of sickness but deeper into delirium. Gibreel's quest for transcendence in the form of Alleluia Cone, rather than on the summit of Mahound's Mount Cone, has the structure of a repetition compulsion. In Freudian terms, Gibreel does not "remember" and "work through" his neuroses the way Saladin—his non-orphaned counterpart—can do, by reuniting with his biological father, whom he ceases to see as a vengeful god-figure and learns to love as a dying man. No such virtuous circle is in store for the film star, deprived by age twenty of both biological parents.

The sentimentalism of Saladin's reunion with Changez (and possibly with Zeeny and India), and its place in the novel's moral vision, might get buried beneath its avalanche of anti-sentimental rhetoric. But Rushdie's oeuvre reiterates the importance he sees in interpersonal intimacy. His essay "In Good Faith" suggests that human beings "become whole" "through the love of their fellow men and women" rather than "through the love of God."[56] His 1987 review laments V. S. Naipaul's diminished "affection for the human race" and criticizes Naipual's *Enigma of Arrival* as "bloodless" due to the absence of the word "love" from its pages. "A life without love," Rushdie concludes, "or one in which love has been buried so deep that it can't come out," is *Enigma*'s topic and the reason that it's so sad.[57]

I have discussed Ashley Shelden's 2017 *Unmaking Love*, which argues that contemporary novelists carry modernist skepticism toward love to its logical extension, recognizing that "love has failed"—that it is a bankrupt and harmful fantasy. Rushdie is not included among Shelden's contemporary subjects, and his review of Naipaul suggests why. He is temperamentally and philosophically unwilling to give up on love: however many individual loves fail, he does not see love itself as an ideological mystification, a trick played on duped victims.

Presumably, then, Rushdie's fiction—including *Verses*, which appeared the year after his review of Naipaul—strives *not* to be "sad" in Naipual's way, but rather to value love. When *Verses*' Mimi Mamoulian lists "some notions I do not require: patriotism, God, and love," her cynicism requires parsing. Rushdie is a hardline atheist, but his fiction is committed to exploring "the sacred and the profane ... without pre-judgement";[58] this is a major motivation behind his magic realism. Since the Rushdie Affair, his political comments have grown less dissident, more pro-Western, and even more patriotic. But he remains a scourge of jingoism—hence *Verses*' merciless satire of Hal Valance, skewering of American foppery in the figure of Eugene Dumsday, and lament over American malfeasance in the Union Carbide disaster. Mimi's rejections of "patriotism" and "God" chime with values that Rushdie has espoused throughout his career, but "love" is a different matter. Mimi's author does not follow her down this path of rejection—though he seems to do so as long as Saladin remains in the UK.

Verses strikes this note of seeming unattachment and disillusion very early, when cataloging the exploded *Bostan* plane's wreckage: the "debris of the soul" includes "extinguished futures, lost loves, the forgotten meaning of hollow, booming words, *land, belonging, home*."[59] But the dead and their loved ones are not *Verses*' only figures whose link to "home"—and the unique love it provides—is severed. The *Bostan*'s victims stand metaphorically for migrants who survive voyages to England but whose lives there effectively explode the loves and homes they leave behind. *Passage* begins with the question "Whether or no it is possible to be friends with an Englishman,"[60] and *Verses* wonders whether or no it is possible for someone like Gibreel or Saladin, after surviving the explosion, to find loves and homes in England. *Passage*'s Hamidullah believes that friendship with an Englishman is possible, but only in England, where he was a visitor. Saladin, his literary descendant sixty-four years later, bids to become a permanent resident there, with mixed results at best in his intimate life.

Saladin and Gibreel are particular characters, and I have said that *Verses* pretends, á la Mimi, to be cynical about love in universal terms. Hence its narrator opines "Love, a zone in which nobody desirous of compiling a human (as opposed to a robotic, Skinnerian-android) body of experience could afford to shut down operations, did you down, no question about it, and very probably did you in as well."[61] For both travelers and homebodies, to be human is to love, and to love is to suffer, to be done down. (I mentioned Rushdie's multiple marriages, which of course entail multiple break-ups.) Readers might trace Saladin's and Gibreel's failed intimacies to their migratory pasts, focusing on Saladin's and Pamela's opposed—and equally irrational—attitudes toward Englishness. But, following the narrator's invocation of *"human* experience" (my italics), readers might instead de-emphasize race or social inequity in explaining why loves in *Verses* are never easy. The novel's three storylines abound with troubled couples: I have not mentioned, for example, Mirza Saeed and Mishal, whose marriage begins on a pinnacle of (apparent) bliss, before Rushdie dashes it. Love after love in *Verses* is unsettled by the very things that motivate it: the selfish longing to fill a gap in oneself, and illusions about oneself and especially about one's beloved. "If I was

God," laments Gibreel in the pit of sleeplessness, "I'd cut the imagination right out of people and then maybe poor bastards like me could get a good night's rest."[62] But without imagination, people wouldn't have love—or religion, for that matter—and thus, according to the novel's philosophy, they wouldn't be human.

This universal point about love—which might seem to de-politicize the emotion—is adumbrated repeatedly by the narrator as well as being illustrated by character behavior. "Not only the need to be believed in, but to believe in another," the narrator ruminates. "You've got it: Love. Saladin Chamcha met Pamela Lovelace five and a half days before the end of the 1960s, when women still wore bandannas in their hair."[63] But because these characters are particular, their marital disappointments illuminate them as much as they illustrate universals. Pamela's last name hints at her incapacity for intimacy. Is she a *love-lace* because she binds her partner as a love-chain might do? She doesn't seem to be a merely ornamental lace, although she represents the treasures of England in Saladin's colonized imagination, and although the abovementioned "bandannas" might be knotted in women's hair with ornamental late-1960s' flourish. Alternatively, if her last name is pronounced "loveless," as in the case of the cavalier poet Richard Lovelace, then Saladin's crush on her is doomed from the start. His "need" to "believe in another," if she is loveless, compels him to see her for what she is not.

This "need" explains not only Saladin's orientation toward Pamela, but also his love for England and his hatred for his father, in whom he "believes"—emotionally speaking—as a tyrannical deity. In each case, his "belief" distorts *reality* (if the latter term can be used without scare quotes). Changez is neither omnipotent nor irredeemably cruel, as his son avers, and neither England nor Pamela is the postcard that he (despite copious counterevidence) believes them to be. The empty vocabulary in which Pamela complains about Saladin's idealizations illustrates how difficult they are to counter. "You couldn't get [Saladin] to look at what was really real," she tells Jumpy. "But I'm really real, too, J. J.; I really really am."[64] Because no one can—in Gibreel's words—"cut the imagination right out of people," especially when they're in love, it might be impossible for Saladin to recognize what's "really real" in Pamela, or for her to recognize this in herself. If Zeeny symbolizes India for Saladin (albeit a progressive, de-essentialized India), just as Pamela had symbolized England, then his latter romance might also dissolve, as his "belief" in Zeeny suffers for lack of a "really real" object.

Saladin's need to "be believed in" stems from his migratory misadventures (as well as antecedent familial causes) and motivates his thespian efforts. His lack of an essential self occasions both playful and serious commentary. As she cups his chin in her hands, Pamela calls his face "round and cherubic," the latter adjective signaling his affinity with the angel Gibreel. Offended, Saladin insists that he has "bone structure," to which she replies sardonically, "somewhere in there."[65] But Saladin's sensation of de-realization is dramatized more seriously when he unintentionally addresses the stewardess in Indian argot and fears, "I'm not myself," then catches himself and wonders, "what does that mean anyway ... after all, 'les acteurs ne sont pas des gens' ... masks beneath masks."[66] Lest readers think this self-perception mistaken, the narrator and Jumpy each recognize Saladin's desperate and selfish "need for love." "The actor's life," says the narrator, "offers, on a daily basis, the simulacrum of love." Jumpy says that Saladin would "change into any shape, if it earned him a loving word."[67]

But the many theatrical and televisual occasions on which "Saladin Chamcha, actor, self-made man"[68] transforms into characters are mere shadows of the larger drama in which Saladin Chamcha, inter-civilizational migrant, transforms into a person he's not. Zeeny's comparison of his accent to a false moustache emphasizes the parallel between the (potentially soulless) self-reinvention of the emigrant and the stage-actor. (*Verses* extends this motif of existential emptiness in the Imam, a political exile to parallel self-exiled emigrants like Saladin. "Exile," explains the narrator, "is a soulless country."[69])

So perhaps love itself is not indicted, despite the narrator's sometimes universalizing gestures. After all, if a couple is formed of people like *these*—Pamela, whose very name signals lovelessness; and Saladin, who, being an actor, is not a person, and who is a migrant to boot, severed from the family and community that endowed him with whatever self he once had—then their broken marriage indicts *their version* of love, not the feeling itself.

Rushdie's Historiography and the Question of Progress

But if *Verses* does not look askance at love, universally speaking—if it shares with Rushdie's criticism a belief in its efficacy, as illustrated by the Saladin-Changez relationship—then its disillusionment with migratory interracial love is more glaring. Earlier I mentioned three reasons why—despite potentially propitious circumstances—Rushdie was not ideally poised to revise Forster's "not yet ... not there" verdict. First comes Rushdie's skeptical attitude toward progress throughout the 1980s—the decade after Lyotard diagnosed incredulity as endemic to postmodernism. "In God We Trust" argues that the idea of progress—"heaven on earth"—is a surrogate for the West's lost nineteenth-century certainties. But, with its focus on "things" instead of the "soul," progress wouldn't be emotionally satisfying, even if economic expansion continued indefinitely. As it happens, says this 1985 essay, progress is chimerical, as communist and democratic-capitalist countries alike confront economic contractions. As any good advertising person knows, says Rushdie—who shares Leopold Bloom's advertising background—overselling a product leads to consumers' "cognitive dissonance." Hence the 1980s is a "disillusioned age."[70]

Rushdie's essay adds that, when "progress" fails, people "fall from the dream of politics into the dream of god" and patriotism, in both the United States and the Ayatollah's Iran. This "fall" lands them in paradoxes. Religious revivals, Christian or Islamic, hope to reclaim a lost "Messianic time" of static purity. But history proceeds; nations are defined by movement through "clock time" or "calendric time." Hence nationalism inevitably moves forward even while claiming to look back. And hence a vanguard Iranian intellectual pronounces that Khomeini's revolution is a "revolt against history," language that Rushdie quotes in his essay and imports into *Verses* three years later, when the Imam relishes "smashing clocks."[71]

Rushdie's complex attitude toward progress enriches his fiction. *Verses*' motif of characters moving forward by looking backward—or claiming to *move* backward—illuminates their psychic travails. Perhaps Saladin, with his circular return to India, succeeds somewhat in what "In God We Trust" calls "progress-by-retrogression," although India has not stood still during his British sojourn and he cannot return to what he left. Nor can Hind Sufyan reclaim her past. She laments her husband's diminished status, relative to his position as a teacher in Bangladesh, but in London they cannot revive the patriarchal order that she misses, and she is compelled to run the family business. Gibreel has a more tragic experience, moving forward through his new-found atheism by looking back schizophrenically at Islam's early days. To borrow the language of "In God We Trust," the apostate Gibreel suffers "cognitive dissonance," and Saladin endures his version of this affliction, milder than Gibreel's but severe nonetheless, when Britain—vulgar, racist, and crime-ridden—defies its promise. It has been "oversold," though Britain never sold itself to Saladin as vigorously as he sold it to himself.

Rushdie's ideas about progress explain why, as a successor to *Passage*, he is *not* the right man to say, *now and here, multicultural 1980s London has worked through the pathologies that plagued Fielding and Aziz*. Rushdie does not see calendric time move "forward" in a linear way, and, as mentioned, *Verses* depicts racism and misogyny as powerful contemporary forces, even though Enlightenment rationalism, tolerance, and progress should be tailor-made to combat them.

Saladin's embittered attitude toward his own country and his fawning admiration for its former colonizer are among *Verses'* early hints that late twentieth-century racism is systemic and international, drawing energy from pre-Independence times. Admittedly, following partition, South Asians had compelling reasons to emigrate, given continued internecine violence on the subcontinent, and educational and employment opportunities in the UK. Saladin attends Cambridge, as Rushdie, Rushdie's father, and Forster all had. (Syed Masood, Forster's love object and the inspiration for Aziz, attended Oxford.) In *Passage*, Hamidullah's "cordial welcome" at Cambridge[72] led him to believe "friendship" possible in England. Prior to Forster's and Rushdie's eras, Britain had a long history of amorous hotchpotch, of natives coupling with both Europeans and non-Europeans. Interracial marriage increased in the seventeenth century, when the East India Company brought scholars, laborers, and seamen to Britain.[73] (Several centuries later, during the First World War, the Royal Navy employed many such seamen.) By the Victorian era, businessmen, tourists, and students, whose ranks Masood would later join, increased the volume and variety of South Asians in Britain. The UK did not outlaw mixed marriage—unlike numerous states in America, where only in 1967 did the Supreme Court's "Loving v. Virginia" ruling invalidate such legislation. Indian seamen, British women, and their offspring developed dock-area communities with their own subcultures. Such mixed-race offspring, however, were often excluded from polite society. The better part of a century after Queen Victoria's 1901 death, Saladin and Pamela were either not lucky enough to parent their own intercultural offspring, or—considering their rocky marriage—lucky enough not to.

Sociological and psychological research attest that intercultural families across the world face external challenges such as exclusion from mainstream society, racism, and language barriers—challenges common for minorities generally—and that mixed-race children sometimes cannot fit in. Generational gaps in such families can alienate children from parents, a phenomenon common enough in single-race families. Unfortunately, intercultural families might reproduce the racial and cultural tensions of their society, rather than being a haven from them.[74] In a sociological vein reminiscent of Forster, Smith's *On Beauty* examines how religious, political, racial, and national affiliations act as wedges, separating Howard Belsey, a secular, liberal, white English father, from his African-American spouse and children.

For several decades, though, research has deemphasized the burdens faced by such families and disputed the assumption that "in-betweenness" is a marginalizing, psychologically tormenting experience. Instead, some studies argue, heterogeneous family systems effectively prepare adults and children for a heterogeneous world, conferring well-being advantages on children, especially in the wake of America's "biracial baby boom" following upon "Loving v. Virginia."[75] In 1987—not long before the publication of *Verses*—Anne Wilson reported largely "hopeful and positive results" of a study, carried out in the late '70s, according to which many children "found a happy and secure identity for themselves as 'black mixed race,'" especially if they were able to draw support from other mixed-race children.[76] Americans of mixed heritage "express pride in being different or unique [and] in being able to ... appreciate multiple viewpoints."[77] Such research emphasizes the value of seeing racial and ethnic identity as fluid, and it vindicates dreams of progress, of bigotry waning with time, once-taboo loves flowering proportionally, and new kinds of families finding comfortable niches—even in the absence of full integration—in multiracial societies. Such research suggests how Giddens's "intimacy as democracy" model can extend from analysis of one (biracial) couple to their children, and even to other biracial couples and their children, all of whom determine the conditions of their association, develop their potentialities, and express their diverse qualities.

But *Verses* is not Pollyannaish. Rather, in response to 1970s and '80s "Paki-bashing," it takes a "strong anti-racist line," according to Rushdie's defense against critics who decry its portrayal of Islam. Repeating this self-justifying rhetoric, Rushdie recounts his "anti-racist broadcast" for Channel 4 television, the polemical "rhetoric" of which he cites as one (albeit minor) cause of the tension in his first marriage, to Clarissa Luard, which effectively dissolved in 1984.[78] The novel hardly requires this defense, given that its fifth (and by far longest) section, titled "A City Visible but Unseen," details the struggles of London's South Asian population, including their mistreatment by the police, the bigoted customers who menace the Shaandaar Café, and the community's attempt to organize resistance.

Saladin may be reluctant to join the resistance, having carried his internalized racism to his new country, but *Verses* skewers his naivety and culpability. After he falls from the plane with Gibreel, the latter transforms upward (so to speak), into some version of the angel that his name suggests he was meant to be. By contrast, Saladin transforms downward into the devilish goat that racists see in dark-skinned people. And racists aren't just the urban flotsam that pass through a café; they're also the police. The leading bully among Saladin's arresters—Officer Stein—has a Scottish accent, suggesting that, in an effort to prove his English *bona fides*, he abuses a suspect who is, after all, not white.[79] Saladin's racial profiling lands him in the detention center where the manticore, baldly explicating one of the novel's themes, says of the white power structure, "They have the power of description, and we succumb to the pictures they construct."[80] No wonder the arresting officers treated Saladin's metamorphosis as "banal and familiar."[81]

Rushdie's dramatization of how racial stereotypes get woven into patterns of perception is consistent with his general ideas about the power of imagination. "In Good Faith" argues that people's "response to the world is essentially *imaginative*: that is, picture-making .... We first construct pictures of the world and then we step inside the frames .... in certain circumstances, we will even go to war because we find someone else's picture less pleasing than our own."[82] Systemic racism perpetuates a vicious circle: "pictures of the world" that demean dark-skinned immigrants condition immigrants to embody them, and the police (due more to their selective vision than to suspects' behavior) see immigrants confirm their bigoted expectations. Therefore, the immigrants—even if, like Saladin, proven by the Police National Computer to be a "British citizen first class"[83]—must run for safety. How a victim of racial profiling should resist such systemic bias is unclear, but Saladin's toady-ish attitudes implicate him in the problem. Godbole's analysis from *Passage*—"When evil occurs, it expresses the whole of the universe"[84]—could apply to intercultural strife in *Verses*.

Even before Saladin's demoniasis and arrest, his experience in England supports the manticore's idea that minorities "succumb" to constructed pictures. Saladin's thespian skills land him work only as a voice actor or a television star in an alien costume—a metaphor, like his demoniasis, for his racial outsider's status. But the costume offers too thin a disguise to last—at least according to Hal Valance, who announces Saladin's ouster from *The Aliens Show* by saying that "audience surveys show that ethnics don't watch ethnic shows .... They want fucking *Dynasty*, like everyone else."[85]

All these Rushdian ideas—about people's response to the world being imaginative, about racist pictures conditioning both white England's expectations of South Asians and South Asians' self-presentations and self-perceptions—contextualize *Verses*' use of Saladin's marriage as a barometer of social progress. When Jumpy moves into the home and bed of his presumed-dead friend, he recalls his own failed attempt, years ago, to pick up a girl at a college party. On his heels, Saladin appeared, "ready to be anything [white women] wanted to buy," "reeking of patchouli, wearing a white kurta, everybody's goddamn cartoon of the mysteries of the East," and the girl left with him in five minutes.[86] Even allowing for the distortions of Jumpy's resentment, his memory completes a picture of Saladin as conforming—"succumbing," in the manticore's words—acting, in many contexts. He acts the part of an Englishman, cultivating a haughty mien and an accent to accompany it, to integrate himself into his chosen country. He acts, with the help of his protean voice, a thousand and one silly parts; then he acts in an alien costume; and along the way he acts like an exotic ethnic to get laid. What about when he falls in love with Pamela: is he able to discard these masks and become—whatever this would mean—himself? Judging from the vulnerability and capacity for love that Zeeny elicits from him, the answer seems to be *No*: in England, all of Saladin's actorly masks are tailored to his subordinate position. The only idioms he can draw on as a lover and spouse are conditioned by a racial hierarchy, including his desire, in Jumpy's words, to "conquer" England, of which Pamela is a "part."[87]

Does Saladin's experience explode Hamidullah's belief in "friendship"—genuine interracial intimacy (sexual or platonic)—in England? *Verses* is not so categorical: Saladin can both love and be loved across a racial line. But an aching homelessness, lodged more deeply than he is conscious of, migrates with him into his intimacy. Macro-level myths of social progress elide such stubborn, individualized, barriers to happiness in intimacy.

Nor are internal-external circulations of racism the only barriers to healthy intimacy. Misogyny too has migrated—however transmuted its forms—from medieval Arabia to modern London. In making this claim—in conjunction with labeling *Verses* a "feminist" novel—I plunge into a critical debate about Rushdie's gender politics, in *Verses* and elsewhere.[88] My sympathetic reading of *Verses*—as a novel with a strong anti-misogynist line to complement Rushdie's "strong anti-racist line"—is premised on three contentions. First, *Verses* depicts how misogyny works in men's minds; and second, its complex, sympathetically drawn female characters rebuke these prejudices, even if (as in the case of Hind Sufyan) women reproduce patriarchal attitudes. But female interiority in *Verses* is fraught, which leads to my third premise: all the men and women depicted in Parts 2, 4, 6, and 8 should be read as projections of Gibreel's psyche, not as full-fledged characters. Whatever attitudes toward femininity or religiosity are embodied by, for example, the Jahilian Hind or the Titlipurian Ayesha do not reflect the novel's textual unconscious. Instead, they reveal disturbances in Gibreel's mind. He might be misogynistic, but the *more* he is, the *less* the novel is, as it critiques this schizophrenic, suicidal, and pitiable protagonist. (Just as Islamic critics can misconstrue Mahound by forgetting that he is Gibreel's dream-figment, feminist critics can misconstrue the functions of characters from *Verses'* even-numbered sections, seeing them as embodiments of authorial misogyny rather than as Rushdie's canny evocations of how Gibreel thinks.)

Theories of misogyny claim that men simultaneously need women and resent them for this sign of weakness in themselves. Broadly, this paradox takes the form of exaltation/debasement; when sexualized, it takes the form of desire/repulsion.[89] These complex and contested ideas about men illuminate how Gibreel thinks about Rekha, Ayesha, and Allie, and how Saladin thinks about Pamela and Allie. (In keeping with my third premise, I will distinguish between Gibreel's non-hallucinatory and hallucinatory states.) Rekha's ghost, who appears early in *Verses*, serves as an entry point for its handling of what one theorist of misogyny terms the "male malady."[90] Gibreel sees this ghost as a *femme fatale*: he thinks that she deceives him to pull him away from god. Given the novel's critical attitude toward faith and the absolute demands faith makes on some believers, Gibreel's perception seems pathological. It recalls Mahound's feelings toward Hind—a combination of attachment and hatred likely too deep in Mahound for him to understand. It also recalls Mahound's attitude toward the Jahilian goddesses—extensions of the feminine principle that Hind represents—who pull him away from his one (male) deity, until he dismisses the verses exalting them as Satanic. When Gibreel dismisses Rekha's ghost as a "caterwauling mist," on the one hand this is a sign of temporary sanity: he distinguishes his hallucination from reality. But on the other hand it suggests his self-identification with Muhammad (or Mahound): Gibreel renounces one invisible being because he's in thrall to another. He even tells Rekha's ghost "There is no God but God."[91] He reverts to this enthrallment when, deliriously, he blames Allie for not believing in his hallucinations. "Having reassumed the role of archangel" with all its "archangelic memory," explains the narrator, Gibreel decides that he was "saved" from "danger" when he left Allie's "vicinity," and he compares Allie unfavorably to the Prophet's wife Khadija, who convinced him "that he was not some raving crazy but the Messenger of God.—Whereas what had Alleluia done for him?"[92] With Allie as with Rekha's ghost, Gibreel shores up his religious certainty by scapegoating the feminine.

Mirza Saeed's feelings for Ayesha—laced with secular certainty—reinforce the novel's anti-misogynist line. Saeed's lust for this *femme fatale*, this avatar of Khomeini, humiliates him, given his love for his wife. In tandem, Saeed's attitude toward Ayesha and Gibreel's attitude toward the "mist" develop the same feminist point. Each man reacts against a feminine force, whether he believes her to pull him toward or away from God. Saeed, who is Gibreel's avatar, learns his lesson—he learns humility—as his storyline concludes and he opens his heart to Ayesha's oceanic path. But Gibreel experiences no such redemptive humility: he never faces up to the wrong he has done to Rekha/her ghost. Consciously and unconsciously, Gibreel is unsure whether God is good or bad: God seems good when he opposes Rekha and tyrannical when he allies with Ayesha. But in both cases Gibreel sees a temptress as his enemy. This is the face of misogyny, whether it is religiously inspired or it betrays the residue of Islam's woman-problem that a progressive world should outgrow.

Although Gibreel, in delirious and megalomaniacal moments, sees Allie as another temptress, alluring "from the roots of her hair to the soft triangle of 'the loveplace, the goddamn yoni,'"[93] *Verses* does not construct her this way. Allie, though a secondary character, is the center of her own drama. She is damaged and imperfect, to be sure. Gibreel's complement, she suffers the same affliction: a grand passion. He yearns for revelation atop a mountain, whereas she yearns for the mountain itself, the physical manifestation of the spiritual height that he seeks. Her passion dooms her as ineluctably as Gibreel's dooms him, regardless of whether the lovers' paths cross. She and her suicidal sister inherit the propensity for this affliction from their suicidal father. Allie's passion enables her transcendent splendor as well as her doom. It is entangled in her family's Jewish history and in the will to self-reinvention that leads them to migrate to England and change their name from Cohen to Cone. But the trait is not universal in their family: Allie's mother Alicja is *Verses*' great critic of this Schopenhauerian force. Her flourishing after Otto's death, when she loves a new man in yet another new land (the United States), broadens the novel's portrait of women, including their ways of loving. This varied portraiture does not, however, imply historical triumphalism: while Western women in the 1980s might enjoy more freedom in intimacy than their forebears (like the Jahilian Hind) did, or than their contemporary Asian counterparts (like Hind Sufyan) do, happiness in intimacy remains elusive for them.

As Gibreel's passion transfers (partially or temporarily) from Islam to Allie, hers transfers (partially) from mountains to Gibreel. But this is not a happy trade-off. She is subject to his Othello-like anger, jealousy, and paranoia. She becomes his caretaker, but she can never count on her peripatetic partner's whereabouts—until desperation returns him to her doorstep. Not that she is blameless. The narrator lists the "flaws in [their] grand passion" and begins with Allie's "secret fear of her secret desire, that is, love." Men can simultaneously feel desire and repulsion for the other sex, and Allie is no different: her fear leads her to "hit violently out at the very person whose devotion she sought most."[94] Her unhappiness in love is largely of her own making, both because of the neuroses she brings to the relationship and because of her willingness to succumb to the role of abused caretaker. Just as the promiscuous Gibreel's previous lovers played a part in his mistreatment of them, so does Allie.

Allie's multiple flaws enhance her dimensionality—even within the magical-realist context that makes her a reincarnated mountain—and thus enhance the novel's feminism. Readers can see all the symbolism that Gibreel sees in her, but they can also see more. Similar analyses can draw out the dimensionality in other of *Verses'* women, including Hind Sufyan—flawed and capable of nastiness, but dynamic and sympathetically imagined. The women in the framed/hallucinatory narratives present trickier cases, since they function not as full-fledged characters but as Gibreel's projections. The thematic richness of his visions, taken *in toto*, testifies to the complexity of his de-conversion. Moreover, the variety of women that he envisions suggests, to his credit, that he does not view all women through a narrow lens, even unconsciously. Admittedly, the devouring-woman figure recurs in his visions, from the Titlipurian Ayesha to the Al-Lat who bursts from Ayesha's shell, ready to do the Imam's bloody bidding. But other women, young and old, with other motives and attractions, also populate his visions.

Thus, it is difficult to say how much Gibreel—with his unquenchable mother-love; his history of promiscuity, typical enough for a megastar; and his overdetermined visions—should be seen as a misogynist. Whether or not *Verses* holds out monogamy as an ideal, as Gibreel's partners die in eerie succession at Everst Vilas, a key motif running through his sexual intimacies is his self-absorption. After Allie's death, newspapers quote his former co-star Pimple Billimoria as saying that he "hates women."[95] The novel provides no *overwhelming* support for this accusation, but in granting Pimple this obituary platform, it gives readers the heuristic option of understanding Gibreel's motivations this way.

Saladin is more self-aware than Gibreel, and mentally healthier in general, but he's also the megastar's doppelganger. His goatish transformation fulfills racist attitudes, but it also befits a cuckold. When Jumpy usurps his marital bed, though Saladin is not yet aware of the fact, this Renaissance trope indicates that he is sexually possessive. When Pamela, his marital property, is trespassed upon, his physique registers the violation—a suggestion that the male psyche (at least his) has not progressed much since Shakespeare's time. If monogamy is an ethical priority in *Verses*, then Pamela might be forgiven for jumping to Jumpy for comfort, given that she thought Saladin dead. But Saladin knowingly cheats on his wife. This behavior, in conjunction with his cuckold's features, doesn't exactly make him a hypocrite, in the way that Margaret Schlegel recognizes Henry Wilcox as a hypocrite, since Saladin doesn't espouse a sexual double standard. But the cuckold symbolism suggests the deep-rootedness of the double standard: Saladin avails himself of an extra-marital privilege with no apparent effect on Pamela, but her (unwitting) commission of the same infraction so disturbs his universe that he grows horns.

Despite his penchant for anger and cruelty, Saladin is introspective, which makes his vulnerability to a dehumanizing transformation more symptomatic of a general male malady. His self-awareness does him little good in the face of his misogynistic bitterness. When Saladin returns home, the narrator explains that his "discomfiture" stems from his realization "on seeing Pamela, with her too-bright brightness, her face like a saintly mask behind which who knows what worms feasted on rotting meat (he was alarmed by the hostile violence of the images arising from his unconscious) ... that he had quite simply fallen out of love."[96] That he recognizes his unconscious hostility holds promise, just as it holds promise that Gibreel recognizes Rekha's ghost as a "mist." But what hostility! In his marital jealousy and alienation, as in his filial rage—notwithstanding his self-awareness—Saladin is subject to his own grand passion. His intimacy with his father is rescued just in time from this passion, but his marriage is not, and it is unclear whether his intimacy with Zeeny will be damaged by it.

Saladin's ambivalent feelings for Zeeny illustrate familiar misogynistic dynamics, albeit in milder form. When she tells him to "change back," he thinks of her as a "siren, tempting him back to his old self."[97] Culturally, spiritually, and physically, she is alluring—and threatening for that reason. When the lovers reach common ground in their argument about Indian identity, she "knif[es] him with a kiss."[98] Of course this image is playful, as the lovers are (for the moment) frolicsome. But nonetheless it is ominous. Earlier the narrator explains that "by the time of his illness [Gibreel] had all but forgotten the anguish he used to experience owing to his longing for love, which had twisted and turned in him like a sorcerer's knife."[99] For each male doppelganger, love brings pain, whether (like Gibreel) they long for it or whether (as in Saladin's case) it germinates in them. So it is not difficult for them to blame women they see as "tempting" them toward this pain, no matter how powerful their longing.

Saladin's romance with Zeeny might betray only traces of his misogynistic capacities, but across *Verses*, especially where Allie is concerned, Rushdie doesn't bury the theme very deeply. Saladin is so enraged (and perhaps aroused) by Gibreel's divulgences concerning his sex life with Allie that, when Saladin gets close to Allie, he feels "his reborn animosity towards Gibreel extending itself to her ... Why, before she'd even opened her mouth, had he characterized her as part of the enemy?" The answer, admittedly, concerns more than sexual identity. National and ethnic identity, the latter emblematized in Allie's blonde hair, also elicit Saladin's contradictory feelings, as the narrator explains in answering, "Perhaps because he desired her." In particular, Saladin desired the "inner certainty" that he mistakenly believed Allie to possess, and he "sought to damage what he envied ... Chamcha invented an Allie, and became his fiction's antagonist." The Saladin-Allie relationship develops Rushdie's theme of people's "essentially imaginative" response to the world, and it recalls Ian McEwan's treatment, discussed in Chapter 3, of how wrongly imagining another person can wreak havoc on multiple relationships. Perhaps readers should be especially troubled that interracial and inter-civilizational romances in *Verses* trigger the protagonists' misogyny: as if, when these men strive most to transcend their given selves, to be made new by loving a woman who represents an ideal, they fall prey to their basest capacities. So much for associating progress and freedom, in an Indian man's love life, with Allie, the "blonde yahudan," or with Pamela, Saladin's would-be incarnation of English "warm beer, mince pies [and] common sense."[100]

In tracing *Verses'* anti-misogynistic line, I intend a with-the-grain reading, an alternative to critiques that see the novel reinscribe gender codes.[101] But just because *Verses* critiques misogyny (as it critiques racism) does not mean that it points the way confidently out of these maladies. It views history too equivocally—it is too doubtful of progress—for such an ideologically happy resolution. The causal role of racism or misogyny in Saladin's and Gibreel's love-sicknesses is impossible to determine, just as the promise of Saladin's and Zeeny's romance is impossible to gauge. There seems, however, to be cause for hope in the ending paragraphs, when Saladin seems to turn away from "fairy tales" and accept Zeeny's invitation to "get the hell out of here."[102] But what counts as a fairy tale? Was England nothing more than one, and was Zeeny always Saladin's Penelope, despite her protestations against essentialism? If history's "great point," as Rushdie claims in *Joseph Anton*, is that people are shaped by "great forces" yet retain "the ability to change [their] direction," then readers might have hoped that Saladin, as a migrant-lover, would command more freedom and happiness in intimacy than he did. Sadly, his bid for self-reinvention in the love of an Englishwoman who "believes" in the self he invents carries *Verses* a rather short distance from *Passage's* "not yet ... not there" verdict on post-First World War inter-civilizational "friendship."

In an age of ethnonationalism, Forster's 1924 novel speaks to assorted cosmopolitan readers of a longstanding dream—one that does not see political justice as a solution for interpersonal challenges, nor hotchpotch intimacies as a blanket cure for social ills, but that nonetheless envisions progress in one sphere supplying momentum for the other. As discussed in the Introduction, *The Satanic Verses* is not the only novel of the last three decades that reanimates Forsterian questions. The literary afterlife of Britain's colonization of the subcontinent is far from over.

But *Passage* does not supply the only template for Forsterian questions about how intimacies can challenge—or be rent by—demographic divides. As the coming chapter discusses, Zadie Smith's 2005 *On Beauty* takes inspiration from Forster's 1910 *Howards End* not in spite but because of their different temporal, geographical, and demographic settings. Forster's narrative strategies prove pliant and resilient. His mobile narrative voice, by turns ironic, earnest, and even lyrical; his humanistic values, threatened by the self-doubts that are their lifeblood; even the "cool" qualities of his prose that Rushdie found unfit for the heated subcontinent—*On Beauty* demonstrates the pertinence of all these strategies to a twenty-first-century examination of intimacy, progress, and the legacies of Bloomsburian modernism.

Notes

1   *A Passage to India* 312.
2   See Appendix B, Table 2.
3   Section 11 of the Criminal Law Amendment Act 1885—also known as the Labouchere Amendment—after its author, Henry Labouchere—criminalized "gross indecency" in the UK. The law was invoked broadly where male-male sodomy could not be proven. In 1895, Oscar Wilde was prosecuted under the amendment and sentenced to two years in prison with hard labor. In 1952, Alan Turing was

prosecuted under it and sentenced to chemical castration (estrogen injections) as an alternative to incarceration. The ordeal may have precipitated his suicide two years later.
4   "In Good Faith" 394, "In God We Trust" 377.
5   Ibid. 394.
6   Wood.
7   "In Good Faith" 405.
8   *The Wizard of Oz* 14, 17.
9   For a discussion of the Rushdie Affair, see Rushdie's memoir *Joseph Anton* as well as Pipes, Mufti, and Ranasinha. Regarding *Verses*' skeptical love for Islam, see Jussawalla. Regarding its depiction of largely invisible minority communities, see "In Good Faith" 395. Regarding women and feminism in *Verses*, see Salih, Wang, Kathy J. Phillips, and Parashkevova. For a discussion of the anti-absolutism and modernism of *Verses*' form, see Begam. The comment about "the troublesome category of influence" is from Abravanel (181). The discussion of *Verses* as "*A Passage to India* in reverse" occurs in Neumeier 173 (ftnt 26). Moore-Gilbert discusses both the "consistency" of themes and tropes in literature related to Britain's Indian empire, and the need for criticism—in the wake of Edward Said's emphasis on such consistency—to recognize the varied "regimes of power and knowledge" involved in imperial management and the "varied literature" representing empire (25).
10 *Verses* 411–12, "V. S. Naipaul." Yaqin is one exception to my generalization about critics' lack of interest in *Verses*' depictions of love, friendship, and family life.
11 "In God We Trust" 391.
12 *Satanic Verses* 305, 325. Also see "In God We Trust," where Rushdie says that the "rationalism" of literary realism can "seem like a judgement" upon faith (376).
13 Suleri 222. Rushdie details his reasons for admiring Dickens in "Influence" 64.
14 *Satanic Verses* 7.
15 Ibid. 125.
16 *Joseph Anton* 56.
17 Ibid. 53.
18 Ibid. 55–6.
19 See Gasiorek.
20 Wolfe, *Bloomsbury, Modernism, and the Reinvention of Intimacy* 96–7.
21 Paul Armstrong develops this idea about Forster's narrator in ways including, but not limited to, his sexuality.
22 *A Passage to India* 169.
23 Rosecrance 11. Despite its "omniscient" and "intrusive" qualities, Rosecrance also finds Forster's narrator "elusive."
24 Hart and Ouyang 1–5. Also see "In Good Faith" 403.
25 "In Good Faith" 409, *Satanic Verses* 35, 38, 147, 283.
26 Brians (3) cites Simawe, who discusses Islamic skepticism toward *Verses*, and Jussawalla, who discusses Islamic revisionism in Muslim India. Pipes surveys reactions to *Verses* from around the world, including by protestors who read snippets out of context, as well as the international politics of the "Rushdie Affair."
27 *Satanic Verses* 32.
28 "In Good Faith" 397.
29 *Satanic Verses* 305, 325.
30 "In Good Faith" 394. "[From] the migrant condition … I believe, can be derived a metaphor for all humanity."

31 *The Satanic Verses* 482–3.
32 Ibid. 549.
33 Luke 15:11–32.
34 *The Satanic Verses* 295.
35 Ibid. 545.
36 Ibid. 538.
37 Ibid. 414.
38 Ibid. 412.
39 Ibid. 35.
40 Ibid. 34, 53.
41 Ibid. 59.
42 Ibid. 52.
43 Ibid. 415, 58.
44 Ibid. 412–13.
45 Ibid. 64.
46 Ibid. 413.
47 Ibid. 274, 278.
48 Ibid. 59.
49 Giddens 185.
50 Forster, "What I Believe" 67.
51 *A Passage to India* 55.
52 Wang.
53 For a discussion of *Verses* in light of Freud's ideas about religion and dreams, see Coppola and Coppola.
54 *The Satanic Verses* 26, 19.
55 Ibid. 31.
56 "In Good Faith" 395.
57 "V. S. Naipaul" 148, 150, 151.
58 "Is Nothing Sacred?" 417. Also see the poet Bhupen Gandhi's desire not to "prejudge" religious belief (*Verses* 551), which Rushdie quotes in his essay "In Good Faith" (396). Finally, see Rushdie's aforementioned comment about the "rationalism" of literary realism (endnote 12).
59 *The Satanic Verses* 4–5.
60 *A Passage to India* 5.
61 *The Satanic Verses* 411–12.
62 Ibid. 124.
63 Ibid. 50.
64 Ibid. 181.
65 Ibid. 139.
66 Ibid. 34–5. The line from *Les Enfants du Paradis* translates as "Actors are not people."
67 Ibid. 180–1.
68 Ibid. 49.
69 Ibid. 214.
70 "In God We Trust" 388, 379.
71 Ibid. 383, *Verses* 220.
72 *A Passage to India* 6.
73 Fisher 106–81.
74 Ibid. 10–12, 119–22, 180–2, etc.

75 Brunsma 1131.
76 Wilson vi. Her complex study is sensitive to the racial challenges faced by such children, and to the many influences—familial and extra-familial—affecting their developing sense of self. But she adds that their mothers' "overt encouragement" to see themselves in terms other than "'only just' non-white" contributes to their "positive black/mixed-race identity" (193). Also see 140–2, 166–9, etc.
77 Lopez 25.
78 "In Good Faith" 411, *Joseph Anton* 65.
79 *The Satanic Verses* 165.
80 Ibid. 174.
81 Ibid. 163.
82 "In God We Trust" 377–8.
83 *The Satanic Verses* 169.
84 Quoted above on page 131. See *A Passage to India* 169.
85 *The Satanic Verses* 273.
86 Ibid. 180.
87 Ibid. 181.
88 Hai gives an overview of this debate in the context of discussing Rushdie's "ambivalent feminism."
89 Gilmore xi.
90 As Gilmore's title (*Misogyny: The Male Malady*) suggests, he sees this "malady" as pervasive in male-dominated culture the world over.
91 *The Satanic Verses* 346.
92 Ibid. 331–2.
93 Ibid. 454.
94 Ibid. 325.
95 Ibid. 554.
96 Ibid. 416–17.
97 Ibid. 59.
98 Ibid. 55.
99 Ibid. 26.
100 Ibid. 181.
101 See Hai, as well as Mann.
102 *The Satanic Verses* 561.

6

Forsterian Optimism: Zadie Smith's Post(?)-Realist Homage

Like D. H. Lawrence, the novelist-essayist discussed in Chapter 2 as a precursor to Rachel Cusk's meditations on sex, femininity, and sexism; like Virginia Woolf, whom Zadie Smith describes as "my favorite writer-critic";[1] and like E. M. Forster, her intellectual companion and *On Beauty*'s raison d'être, Smith herself uses narrative and expository forms to think through interrelated questions. The themes that animate this volume—intimacy in history, craft, and the legacies of modernism—also animate Smith's oeuvre. Her life tests the possibilities for intimacy in a changing transnational world, and the roles that literature plays in both creating and comprehending these possibilities. The daughter of a white British father and a Jamaican mother, Smith attended Forster's alma mater—King's College, Cambridge—where she won early literary stardom. There she met her future husband Nick Laird, a poet from provincial Northern Ireland who remarked that at Cambridge he met a Black person and a Jewish person, both for the first time.[2] The story of their love and literary successes is at once one of cultural and socioeconomic mobility—of the blending and de-essentializing of racial and national categories—and of the concentration of privilege in elite educational-literary establishments. Smith and Laird previously lived in Rome and currently split time between New York and Queen's Park, London, recalling the transatlantic peregrinations of another King's College alumnus—Salman Rushdie—who relocated to the Union Square area of New York in 2000, and of Cusk, who spent parts of her childhood in Canada and California.

Not surprisingly, given Smith's personal history and regard for Forster, *On Beauty* extends *Howards End*'s sociologically schematic premise, with lovers and spouses hailing from different classes and espousing different feelings about national and international identity. Critics have described *On Beauty* as a "retelling of Forster's story for the new millennium's globalizing world" and as making "transformative use of *Howards End* through formal and thematic surplus," while achieving "autonomy" from *Howards End* through "connections with academic satires other than Forster's."[3]

On Beauty updates *Howards End*'s treatment of "personal relations," those endlessly challenging endeavors that Helen Schlegel calls "the important thing for ever and ever."[4] Among the Forsterian materials transformed by Smith are the questions "What can help spousal and parent-child intimacies to evolve and flourish in fluid, twenty-first-century conditions? What if such relations are threatened—and constituted—by such differences as male/female, Black/white, religious/secular, and old/young? How do problems of sex and sexuality impact these relations, e.g., a young adult's awkward exploration of his sexuality, two spouses' different sexual desires and needs (both *Howards End* and *On Beauty* endorse the monogamy code), and a middle-aged man's 'second adolescence,'[5] with its erotic impulses? What room does family life leave for extra-familial friendships, and how do they affect family life? How should a narrative account for the sexual spectrum and the possibility that heteronormative values curtail intimate possibilities for characters who are not visibly queer?" (Kiki's talk with Carlene about her youthful lesbian experiments, and Carlene's thought that "it must be easier to know the other person" in a same-sex intimacy because "they are as you are," inject this question into a novel about the difficulties of loving across difference.[6])

For all of *On Beauty*'s arguably stodgy realism, it finds playful Derridean ways to investigate the permutations and intersections of sex, sexuality, race, and literary and social history. To recall the title of Robyn Wiegman and Elizabeth Wilson's 2015 essay, *On Beauty* develops a kind of "queer theory without antinormativity." It contests various prejudices in non-reductive ways, without assuming that all social norms (e.g., those pertaining to academic discourse, racial identity, and sexual self-expression) are alike, self-consistent, narrowly prescriptive, or necessarily oppressive.

On Beauty's questions about intimacy directly recall *Howards End* and more obliquely recall *A Passage to India*, given that novel's interracial-coupledom theme. Their intertextual dimensions make *On Beauty*'s questions about intimacy circa 2005 also about intimacy in history. Smith's joke that "this isn't 1910"[7] encourages readers to ask how early twenty-first-century love and friendship are like and unlike their Edwardian counterparts. Just as Cusk's and Cunningham's Woolfian intertexts—as we saw in Chapters 2 and will see in Chapter 7—evoke both continuity and change in the history of love and friendship, so too does *On Beauty*.

Perhaps more tender-minded than *The Hours*, and certainly more so than *Arlington Park*, Smith's novel—notwithstanding its liberal self-critiques—seems to impart happy news: that things are getting better.[8] In broad terms, to recall the language of the sociologist Anthony Giddens, "intimacy" is coming to look more like "democracy," by protecting people from "coercive power," expanding their economic opportunities, and enabling them to "express their diverse qualities."[9] Interracial love is now both legal and socially feasible, though it entails thorny challenges. (See Appendix B, Tables 3–5.) Heterogeneous family systems—encompassing people from multiple backgrounds and involving separation or divorce—can be flexible, durable, and healthy for their members. (The freedom both to love whom we choose and to leave when we choose has more benefits than drawbacks.) Parents and children needn't have the formal, standoffish relations of Henry Wilcox and his sons in *Howards End*. They can be playful and physically affectionate: *On Beauty*'s Howard Belsey teases his son Levi about his clothing, squeezes his shoulders and "pulls him close"; Levi's lips "buzz Howard's skin through his shirt."[10] Twenty-first-century parents and children can be emotionally connected: whatever dangers arise when a mother like Kiki seeks a friend or confidante in her adult son Jerome, benefits outweigh drawbacks as "disciplinarian" parents give way to "bonders"—either in a pendulum swing or in a sustained movement away from authoritarian values.[11] Plus, the Belsey siblings love and find shelter in each other, in spite of divergent interests and values (such as Zora's ironic attitudes toward Levi's embrace of the "street" and toward Jerome's Christianity). "People talk about the happy quiet that can exist between two lovers," says the narrator, sliding into Jerome's mind, in an unreservedly romantic passage.

> But this too was great; sitting between his sister and brother, saying nothing.... Jerome found himself in their finger joints and neat conch ears, in their long legs and wild curls .... He did not consider if or how or why he loved them. They were just love: they were the first evidence he ever had of love, and they would be the last confirmation of love when everything else fell away.[12]

Admittedly, *Howards End* indicates that close sibling love was not exotic in 1910 (judging from the Schlegel sisters), just as Lawrence's *Sons and Lovers* illustrates that intense mother-son love, with all its dangers and Freudian overtones, belonged to the same modernist-era culture.[13] But a bond such as Margaret's and Helen's is conspicuously absent between either Schlegel sister and Tibby. For whatever this small sample is worth—and notwithstanding the question of Tibby's sexuality—the Belsey siblings, a century later, seem better able to love and appreciate one another across gender than their Forsterian forebears. This may be one of *On Beauty*'s ways of suggesting that things are getting better. But before pursuing this historically sanguine reading, and before exploring it as an extension of Bloomsburian themes (especially Forster's), I will inquire into the methods through which Smith depicts this apparent cultural and intra-familial conviviality and expresses guarded faith in progress—in the Enlightenment's promises of freedom, equality, and flourishing being realized in the personal sphere. Bloomsburians, after all, understood formal innovation as a way of thinking afresh about the problems of the heart.

Smith as Theorist and Critic: The Prestige of the Avant Garde

Beyond the confines of *On Beauty* and beyond the theme of intimacy, Smith's fiction and essays wonder, "Which modernist legacies—among other literary inheritances—are most valuable?" *On Beauty*, her third (and most Bloomsburian) novel, was published in 2005, when she was thirty—old enough to contemplate her youthful foibles, yet young enough that many narrative modes remained for her to experiment with. This same period between the release of her second novel (*The Autograph Man*, 2002) and her fourth novel (*NW*, 2012) also saw her essay collection, *Changing My Mind* (2009), which explores the same tensions and ambivalences that enrich her fiction. Smith appreciates the realist tradition, from George Eliot's fiction to Iris Murdoch's theory, but also finds it stifling and admires avant-garde alternatives. She is leery of identity politics and sees Blackness as a "cultural residue," not a valid standard of authenticity, but she admires Zora Neale Hurston for drawing inspiration from Black idiom in lieu of an elusive "neutral universal."[14] She notes when white avant-garde writers, even those she admires, associate Black characters with dubious "authenticity." Questions about modernist legacies in her fiction and essays concern not merely literary craft, but also ethics, identity, and social justice.

The following chapter's title, "Cunningham's Modernist Homage," highlights *The Hours*' unabashedly Woolfian thematic and technical ambitions. But Smith in general and *On Beauty* in particular are tricky—hence the question mark in this chapter's title, "Smith's Post(?)-Realist Homage." Was Forster a "lyrical realist," to borrow a term that Smith's essay "Two Directions for the Novel" generally connotes negatively?[15] Or— though some critics question his modernist bona fides—was he epistemologically skeptical, formally varied, suggestive to novelists who are committed to technical innovation? Does he, to borrow a phrase from the same essay, "push on his subject," in a formal sense, as "hard" as Smith credits him with doing?[16] And if so, then does *On Beauty* channel Forster's feistiness and "push" back against lazy lyric-realist habits? Or does it lapse into sentimentality fitting for nineteenth-century fiction and the sure-fire humor of the sitcom?

A critic's answers to these questions regarding *On Beauty* might not anticipate his answers to similar questions regarding *NW*, a polyphonic one-day novel that shifts among narrative methods á la *Ulysses*, or regarding Smith's fifth novel. The unnamed first-person narrator of *Swing Time* (2016) shares Smith's mixed-race heritage and housing-estate background, and experiences herself as a "kind of shadow," having been personal assistant to a pop star but never having developed her own identity. Her description of her own life recalls the narrative method of Cusk's *Outline* and one of its precursor-texts, Woolf's *Jacob's Room*, as discussed in Chapter 2. *Swing Time*'s stories about four other women—the narrator's mother, two of her friends, and her former pop-star employer—provide outlines for the narrator's identity, which emerges in a negative space. With such stylistic variety among her novels—honoring the marginally avant-garde Forster, channeling the uber-avant-gardist Joyce, experimenting with Woolfian indirection—Smith borrows from and pushes back against different realist precedents, with different aims and varying degrees of success.

Before testing *On Beauty* against Smith's theoretical-critical postulates, therefore, I will examine her multidimensional ideas about realistic epistemologies and their relation both to the craft of fiction and to ethics (hence also to intimacy). On the one hand, Smith's "aesthetics of alterity"[17] derives from a philosophical tradition, shared by many Anglo-American novelists including Murdoch, which holds that the capacity to appreciate the reality of other minds, and to love them, is a cardinal virtue, but that people's natural tendencies toward egocentric fantasies cloud their ability to do so. Combined with the deadening effects of habit—which may be intensified in a late-capitalist, TV-saturated culture—people's egocentrism can make them "sleepwalkers," Smith worries.[18] Minus the critique of late capitalism, this attitude is thoroughly Victorian. Jane Austen demonstrates how pride and prejudice impede characters from appreciating other people's uniqueness, and George Eliot teaches comparable lessons with greater scope. And Murdoch is perhaps the twentieth century's most eloquent proponent of this moral attitude, so dear to Victorian realism—as critics including Andrzej Gasiorek have discussed.[19] (*On Beauty* honors Murdoch by naming the Belsey family dog after her.)

Smith blends her valuation of the uniqueness of individuals with the Austenian and Eliotic principles that underpin Murdoch's aesthetic philosophy. Smith argues that novelists should express their way of being in the world, free of literary-critical or political cant. Self-expression is necessarily a matter of style, because styles enact epistemologies; various styles serve various ends; and readers and critics should not narrow-mindedly mistake one style's virtues for those of literature in general. Nor should T. S. Eliot's "High Church" manner intimidate them into believing that, in perfecting a style, an author "escapes" from her personality. On the contrary, Smith insists, if "personality" is understood in its proper, wide sense (not a narrow autobiographical one), then a literary style is one of its most complete expressions— including Eliot's austere intellectualism. "When we account for our failings as writers," Smith says, the strongest feeling is "a betrayal of one's deepest, authentic self."[20]

But a novelist's duty, in Smith's view, is *not* merely to express her own viewpoint. Instead, by being heteroglossic—fashioning characters radically alterior to one another and to herself—she can manifest the reality of other minds: her aesthetic vision is also an ethical one. In depicting egocentrism, novels offer cautionary examples: characters such as Howard Belsey, who fail to recognize the reality of others, exemplify what literature helps good writers and readers *not* to do. Such characters make poor spouses, parents, and friends; thus a study of intimacy in literary history dovetails with a study of the evolution of Murdochian realism.

How can a novelist-essayist with such traditional ideas about genius and such Victorian ideas about literature's moral function also champion the avant garde? And where does Forster fit in Smith's map of narrative epistemologies: how can she claim that he is less like Austen than like the post-realists she admires? Smith endorses avant-garde values in multiple pieces—but in service of pluralism. "In healthy times, we cut multiple roads," she says. "These aren't particularly healthy times. A breed of lyrical realism" dominates the literary scene.[21] Writers split into camps, with realists defending realism and experimentalists defending experimentalism—unlike Forster, who "didn't need everyone else to be like him" and who defended writers with styles and values unlike his own, including Woolf, Joyce, and T. S. Eliot.[22] Popular tastes consign experimentalists to a margin: yearly polls rate *Middlemarch* as English readers' favorite novel, followed by *Pride and Prejudice* and *Jane Eyre*. Smith laments these "conservative" tastes not because she dislikes these canonical works but because "forms, styles, structures ... should change like skirt lengths."[23]

Smith critiques aesthetic conservatism in the essay "Two Directions," which contrasts two novels, the austerely experimental *Remainder* (2005) by Tom McCarthy, who has said that "the task for contemporary literature is to deal with the legacy of modernism,"[24] and the lyrically realistic *Netherland* (2008) by Joseph O'Neill. One novel "is the strong refusal of the other," she says,[25] and all her critical comments about *Netherland* offer readers chances to ask of *On Beauty*, "is it guilty of the same sins?" O'Neill's novel, she says, "is perfectly done—in a sense, that's the problem."[26] It's the post-9/11 work we've been waiting for, though it's less about 9/11 than about anxiety. It's anxious about whether the "Anglo-American liberal middle class" is cocooned in privilege, cut off from authentic experience, and unworthy of sympathy. And it's anxious about whether the "realism of Balzac and Flaubert," which assumes "the transcendent importance of form, the incantatory power of language to reveal truth, the essential fullness and continuity of the self," still commands credulity.[27] It's narrated by Hans van den Broek, a Dutch stock analyst who lives in New York with his wife and son. After 9/11, the family relocates to the Chelsea Hotel; soon later, Hans's wife and son separate from him and move to London. On alternating weekends, Hans either visits them there or plays cricket on Staten Island, the sole white man in a group including Chuck Ramkissoon, a witty Trinidadian with dodgy and violent business schemes. When Chuck tells Hans that cricket is a "lesson in civility" (i.e., when O'Neill signals to readers that cricket is an important metaphor), Smith complains that Chuck—the most important person of color in a novel about white guilt—functions as an "authenticity fetish."[28]

Smith sees in *Netherland*'s parable of interracial athletics as good citizenship, and in its protagonist's nostalgic introspections, both some trademark signs of decadent realism and the potential to challenge them. First, *Netherland* indulges realism's "consoling myth," as Smith calls it: that "the self is a bottomless pool."[29] (Readers might detect this "myth" in *On Beauty*.) Second, in spite of gestures of skepticism, *Netherland* never disowns its thirst for "authenticity." Smith says that random details aim to confer "authenticity" on many realist texts—formulaic proof that they are not mere formula. On a train ride, Hans catalogs sights from his window, including clouds and clifftops (predictable details of landscape portraiture) and a near-naked white man walking by the tracks, whose appearance is unexplained and who is never mentioned again.[30] Smith sees technical "perfection" achieved via artfully random detail and fetishized minority "authenticity" as shopworn.

That Hans and by extension O'Neill's novel are anxious both about white privilege and about realist metaphysics—that they "retain the wound" that Joyce inflicted on realism—is to their credit, Smith allows. But this is a back-handed compliment: Smith quotes a retrospective passage that begins with Hans critiquing a "cheap longing" for authentic experience but ends with Hans sentimentally defending this longing. "Two Directions" criticizes *Netherland*'s Flaubertian quest for "the Real" more than it praises the novel's self-awareness of this quality.

By contrast to O'Neill's *Netherland*, McCarthy's *Remainder* empties out the idea of authenticity in the spirit of a philosophical game. Its unnamed narrator was traumatized by something that fell from the sky. (The modernist trademark—or formula—of a traumatic event precipitating formal "difficulty" is unmistakable.) The man is compensated eight and a half million pounds—recalling the title of a non-realistic Fellini film—which he spends paying actors to re-create vaguely remembered scenes from his past, in hopes of recovering an authentic experience of the world, rather than the fractured one bequeathed by his trauma. But from the beginning, the joke is on him: he will never satisfy his thirst for authenticity, no matter how elaborate, violent, and pricey his re-enactments grow. By extension, the joke is on anyone—trauma victim or not—who quests for authenticity. *Remainder* pursues a negative project, rejecting both a concept ("authenticity") and a corollary novelistic mode (realism, anchored in the full and continuous self). Smith values negative projects, having described her own writing as a "process of elimination," a removal of dead language, other people's truths, contemporary myths, etc.[31]

In contrasting these two contemporary novels, each close to perfect in its way, Smith reprises themes from Murdoch's 1961 essay "Against Dryness," which sees twentieth-century prose fiction divided between two degenerate descendants of nineteenth-century novels about "real various individuals struggling in society." In place of this fulsome model, Murdoch complains, the twentieth century sometimes offers "crystalline" works: "small quasi-allegorical objects portraying the human condition." (Murdoch means for the phrase "the human condition" to sound unwieldy.) Other times the twentieth century offers "journalistic" fiction: "large shapeless quasi-documentary" objects.[32] McCarthy's *Remainder* certainly seems "crystalline" in Murdoch's sense, though O'Neill's *Netherland* is not exactly "journalistic." (*Howards End*, with its loose ends, is more nearly "journalistic," though it's not as long as the baggy novels of which Murdoch complains. *A Passage to India*, with its elegantly counterposed "Mosque," "Cave," and "Temple" sections, approaches the "crystalline.")

Among Smith's remarkable—and Forsterian—qualities is her humility. The unfinished manuscript of "White Teeth" was so anticipated that, while still an undergraduate, Smith signed a two-book contract. But this did not lead her to be defensive. Instead, when James Wood critiqued this debut novel, she called his observation "painfully accurate." Wood coined the term "hysterical realism" to describe "big contemporary novels" like *White Teeth*, in which "stories and sub-stories sprout on every page." He blamed such writing for documentary over-inclusiveness and (along with Rushdian magical realism) for overabundant coincidences and obscure cultural references. Recalling Murdoch's distaste for novels about "the human condition," Wood says that hysterical realism pretends to explain "how the world works" rather than dramatizing "how somebody felt about something."[33] Wood's villains include David Foster Wallace (about whom Smith has written an admiring essay) and Thomas Pynchon (Smith had a quotation from *Gravity's Rainbow* pinned to her dorm wall as she wrote *White Teeth*). Nonetheless, Smith not only assented to Wood's critique of "overblown, manic prose,"[34] but her essays reprise Wood's (and Murdoch's) distaste for empty abstraction. Smith complains that readers "wish to be 'represented,' as at the ballot box, and to do this, fiction needs to be general, not particular."[35]

Smith's essay on Hurston's *Their Eyes Were Watching God* extends her defense of novelistic particulars in ways specific to her position as a Black woman writing largely within a largely white male canon extending across realistic and avant-garde works.[36] Smith pokes fun at her young self, who resisted her mother's endorsement of this novel's "soulfulness," preferring to talk generically of "great writing." Then, however, Smith makes a "double turn," crediting her young self and claiming that Black women writers replace negative falsifications with fetishizations. It is not the Black Female Literary Tradition that makes Hurston great, but Hurston herself—says Smith, in recoil from the notion of "soulfulness." But Smith's essay isn't done: she makes *another* turn, back toward her mother's point of view, recognizing her response to *Their Eyes* as personal. "Cultural residue" or not, her "Blackness" can't help but respond to Hurston, Smith admits. "Soulfulness" sounds like *Black authenticity*, which threatens to efface Black people as "real various individuals." But this quality is crucial to Hurston's aesthetic, so Smith makes peace with it.

Other essays by Smith also execute "double turns," to quote Lionel Trilling's admiring term for Forster's liberal style of thought.[37] Smith titled her collection *Changing My Mind*, and the strategy of doubling back or changing—at once aesthetic and ideological—recurs in her essays as frequently as in Forster's corpus. As Dayna Tortorici observes, the strategy lends consistency to Smith's non-fiction. By contrast, Tortorici says, Smith's fiction is inconsistent, "and the change is a matter of style,"[38] e.g. from realism to avant-gardism. Perhaps Smith is a deft enough critic-practitioner to remain *consistently liberal* across her essays and *stylistically inconsistent* across her novels, all while staying more or less true to her authentic self (even though she doesn't entirely believe in one).

Smith brings, to her lifelong engagement with Forster, her appreciation for both avant-gardism and realism, her skepticism toward various kinds of authenticity, and her understanding of this idea's allure. She admires Forster as cannily skeptical and Freudian, though not a gamesman like McCarthy. She thinks that Forster enlarged "the comic novel's ethical space" by superceding a raft of Austenian strategies, although Austen "heavily influenced" him.[39] First, Austen's protagonists are "good readers": their skills as interpreters of themselves, their situations, and others help them to live well. Further, the exposure of secrets in Austen yields happy results—for example the revelation of Lydia's affair with Wickham in *Pride and Prejudice*. Characters' muddles get resolved; stories end happily. Austen's one-dimensional, or "flat," characters—to import a term of Forster's[40]—serve circumscribed purposes. Neither Mr. nor Mrs. Bennet changes, nor elicits complex sympathy or antipathy. Austen asks readers to tolerate someone like Mrs. Bennet, but never to love her.

This all changes in Forster's tales. Even his most admirable characters misread their situations. The exposure of secrets does not yield beneficent outcomes, but Leonard Bast's death, for example. Characters' muddles are terminal, in keeping with a post-Freudian worldview that sees psychic "cure" and moral perfection as elusive. Not only are the minds of Forster's characters muddled, so are his plots. By contrast, Anna Karenina and Emma Bovary may be as "irrational as any Forster protagonist," but they are "held still for our examination within a … rational narrative."[41] Formally speaking, Tolstoy and Flaubert are not committed to depicting an irrational universe. Comparing Forster favorably to these realist masters is high praise indeed.

Forster's ethical method, says Smith, recalls Keatsian "negative capability":[42] he thinks there's little good in human nature, that at root our minds are "faulty and fearful." But they are also "mysterious," hence Forster's readers can remain in uncertainty about his characters. He asks readers not merely to tolerate, but also to love, characters who aren't very good and won't get much better: his ethical rigor informs the seeming inelegance of his plots. He also evinces a curiosity absent in Austen. She, says Smith, is interested not in *why* Mr. Bennet (for example) is as he is, merely *that* he is so. But *Howards End*'s readers might well wonder why Tibby, like Mr. Bennet, is a "conscientious abstainer" who views life aesthetically and ironically rather than participating in it. Does this stem from his sexual orientation and/or independent income—traits he shares with his author? In Forster's post-Freudian world, the question of *why* pertains, even if it admits of no easy answer.[43]

Moreover, Forster is no "literary miserabilist."[44] Many of his characters have "undeveloped hearts"[45] stunted by unconscious distrustfulness. But Forster "nudges" them toward consciousness of this weakness, against which they "do battle … and win."[46] In a broadly Freudian sense, Smith indicates, Forster's characters make their unconscious conscious and overcome themselves. To what degree *On Beauty*'s characters "battle" their weaknesses and "win" pertains, therefore, to Smith's responses to modernism, Forster, and Freud.

On Beauty's Cautious Optimism

Arguably, Smith's essays, with their critiques of Austen and other realists, endorse a degree of formal austerity that this "hommage" lacks. Readers of Smith's essays might wonder whether *On Beauty*'s "round" characters will have "bottomless pool" selves, akin to the "soul" of Christian metaphysics. Will Smith's novel eschew authenticity fetishes, regarding race or other matters? (Merely poking fun at Black characters for having such fetishes might not get it off the hook.) Will it employ "double turns," undercutting its own apparent attitudes—toward race or anything else—as dextrously as Forster does? For example, complementary to beliefs in the continuous self and in people's capacity for improvement, lies faith in the power of nature and art (fiction by Forster, music from Mozart to rap, paintings from Europe to the Caribbean) to call forth our best selves and even to repair personal relations. Forster was a humanist who could doubt the value of humanism; will *On Beauty* do likewise?

Readers of Smith's essays might wonder whether *On Beauty*'s characters will be good readers of people and situations. Will exposing secrets produce happy outcomes? Or will *On Beauty* follow Forster's and Freud's ideas about the psychological roots of human unfreedom and end on a "diminuendo" (as she admires Forster's fiction for doing),[47] like an extended psychotherapy treatment that concludes without cure?

Whatever the answers to these questions, how much historical hope will *On Beauty* express? Trilling sees disenchantment with "culture itself" as a modernist trademark.[48] But as my first monograph discusses, Bloomsbury retains some Victorian traits, such as (ambivalent) hope for the future—its sense that intimacies will grow freer and healthier as society progresses. *On Beauty* could channel both Forster and Bloomsbury by modeling a "cautious optimistic creed"[49]—a feeling that *things are getting better* for spousal love, parent-child love, and freedom in intimacy. If it does so, then—despite Smith's avant-garde rumblings elsewhere—it might be her liberal fable.

However disenchanted or cautiously optimistic *On Beauty* might be, will its nods to Forster reinvigorate his legacy? Or will Smith's response to O'Neill's lyrical realism apply to her own homage: it's "perfectly done—in a sense, that's the problem?"

Reclaiming Howard's Soul

Smith has said that Kiki is "my kind of hero," a "free female consciousness" whose middle age releases her from the beauty industry and the "marital fantasy industry."[50] In conjunction with these functions of Kiki's, her husband Howard is an "antihero"[51] on many fronts. He grows only after being humbled, by having the hard walls of his ego broken down, in his intellectual life generally, in his professional life particularly, and most importantly, in his intimate life. Intellectually, he's an antihero because of his sterile anti-humanism: in his perpetually unfinished Rembrandt book, his argument "against the human" is "boring even to itself."[52] In and out of class, Howard trots out stale Marxist and post-structural arguments. He denies the reality and beneficence of beauty, which is ironic for several reasons. His name is Bel-sey ("see beauty"), he is something of a disengaged aesthete (like *Howards End*'s Tibby),[53] and when he lets his guard down, he can be moved to tears by Mozart's *Ave Verum Corpus* or captivated by Rembrandt's painting of his love Hendricjke, which reminds Howard of Kiki. In this haughty theorist who "relishes" students' fear and uses his "carefully preserved English accent" to maintain it,[54] Smith distills a hollowly fashionable set of academic tastes and ideological attitudes (or postures). Howard's fondness for the electronic band Kraftwerk, and Victoria's joking compliment that she loves his class for being so "properly intellectual" that he would never say "I like" an art work,[55] round out Smith's satirical portrait of a faux avant-garde scholar. Whatever intellectual integrity may once have bolstered Howard's skepticism, he squandered over decades of rehearsing anti-humanist mantras. (I spoke earlier of the Derridean playfulness with which *On Beauty* permutes questions about intimacy. By contrast, Howard's reflexive and predictable oppositionalism exemplifies the kind of "antinormativity" that Wiegman and Wilson see as the bane of queer theory.) Even professionally, Howard is unheroic: few students take his classes (albeit for the reason that Victoria admires them—their astringent intellectualism), he can't finish his book, and he begins the talk on which his job might hang only to realize that he's left his folder of necessary materials in his car.

The Forsterian provenance of Howard's anti-humanism suggests why it is not merely an intellectual deficiency. In *Howards End*, Helen lectures Leonard Bast about the dangers of Nietzsche's thought. "There's a nightmare of a theory that says a special race is being born which will rule the rest of us ... because it lacks the little thing that says 'I,'" she explains. "No Superman ever said 'I want,' because 'I want' must lead to the question, 'Who am I?' and so to Pity and to Justice." She concludes that "if you could pierce through" the Superman, "you'd find panic and emptiness" in place of an "I." (Helen also suspects that Wilcoxes fear "the personal note in life" and that one would see "panic and emptiness, could one glance behind" their façade of self-possession.[56])

Admittedly, the younger Schlegel sister is fallible. Prior to her speech about Nietzsche, she wonders why she spent eight pounds "making some people ill and others angry. Now that the wave of excitement was ebbing ... she asked herself what forces had made the wave flow."[57] Reminiscent of the Superman, Helen's aggression originates from no discernible "I," but from an impersonal "wave of excitement." Unflattering to *her* as this picture of her rashness may be, though, it supports *her theory* about the dangers of coming unmoored from the "I."

Howard Belsey is far from a Nietzschean Superman, but he has flaws more consequential than his limitations as a thinker. He appears to resent his family for his own disappointments, judging from Kiki's question "I want to understand what it is you think we've done to you.... Have we deprived you of something?"[58] His parenting skills are wanting (not that hers are perfect), judging from Kiki's warning—which later events roughly bear out—against rushing to England, in a mood of anger and disrespect toward Jerome, to dissuade him from marriage. "If you go about it this way,"

Kiki predicts, then "the exact opposite of what you want to happen will happen."[59] But the coup de grâce is his infidelity—a shadow that hangs over the novel's opening scene and motivates Kiki's frustration with him even before she knows the other woman's identity. These flaws and mistakes all expose his moral *character* in an old-fashioned humanist sense. Howard's self-importance, lack of empathic imagination (the very capacity that the study of art is meant to enlarge), impulsiveness, and lack of self-discipline all indicate an unstable "I"—and they all contribute to his estrangement from his environment and the people near him. Switching to a Christian register, one might say that his soul needs reclaiming.

This is a strange claim to make of an author who disparages the "myth" of the self as a "bottomless pool." But prior to *On Beauty*'s publication, Smith had already plumbed the character—or soul—of a troubled middle-aged man. *White Teeth* opens with the suicide attempt of Archie Jones, a forty-seven-year-old whose unremarkable life has included a loveless (recently concluded) thirty-year marriage, who will soon impulsively marry a nineteen-year-old girl, and whose default thought patterns can be both misogynistic and racist.[60] Yet Smith's debut novel pulls readers into rooting for this hapless protagonist. Wood complains that *White Teeth*'s "hysterical realism"—its mass of subplots, eagerness to teach a moral lesson about "multiracial multiplicity," and display of Smith's sociological erudition—veers into caricature, away from the humanizing characterizations of Archie and others that are among the novel's strengths. Nonetheless, Wood holds out hope for Smith, who is "much more interested in" and "naturally gifted at" making characters "human" than Rushdie is.

On Beauty can be read as a response to this critique. Although it, like *White Teeth*, is long and features a large cast of characters whose plots intersect, it eschews the wild Dickensian (or Rushdian) coincidences of her debut novel, in favor of more modest Forsterian ones. It invests less energy than *White Teeth* in imparting what Wood calls "information" about contemporary society, and more energy, for example, in exploring how Howard—married for thirty years, like Archie—might or might not change his mind. (Wood complained that *White Teeth*'s narrator announces characters' mind changes but does not depict them in psychologically plausible ways.)

If Wood's admonitions are among *On Beauty*'s incitements, then it might maintain a steadier focus on Howard, less diluted by frenetically paced events, than *White Teeth* maintains on Archie. *On Beauty* might place a larger wager on lyric-realist values, appealing to readers' concern for an unlikeable protagonist whose "self" should be more or less "continuous" (hence legible). *On Beauty*, in this case, might invite readers to share Smith's vision of human connection (as *White Teeth* also does) and to trust that literary language can communicate it, not merely produce ideological obfuscation or "fail better" to convey a writer's concerns.

Of course, though, the instability of the self—any self, not just one like Howard's— nags humanists. "Psychology has split and shattered the idea of a 'Person,'" laments Forster's essay "What I Believe." "We don't know what we are like. We can't know what other people are like. How, then, can we put any trust in personal relationships ... in theory we cannot." But Forster pushed back against these doubts, and against the cultural forces—including Nietzschean and Freudian conceptions of the unconscious—that inspired them. Although "in theory we cannot" trust personal relations, Forster asserts that "in practice we can and do .... For the purpose of living, one has to assume that the personality is solid, and the 'self' is an entity, and to ignore all contrary evidence."[61] For Forster, interpersonal relations entail a secular version of Pascal's wager. They require a leap of faith, but without the leap, where would we be?

Because Howard has a self, he might be redeemable. But his path to wholeness will require him to recognize the reality of other selves, in keeping with Murdoch's ethos. Kiki, serving as Smith's mouthpiece, drives home this point when she says she was ashamed of Howard's response to 9/11 (with a canned theoretical point about simulated wars), then tells him "this is *real*. This life. We're really here—this is really happening. Suffering is *real*. When you hurt people, it's *real*. when you fuck one of our best friends, that's a *real* thing and it *hurts* me" (italics in the original).[62] As sexy as McCarthy's *Remainder* seems for denying "authenticity," and as compromised as O'Neill's *Netherland* seems for failing to transvalue it, Howard is equally hollow for repudiating it.

Chapter 5 discusses similar moments in Rushdie's *Satanic Verses*, when plot fulcrums are also formal, i.e., epistemological, fulcrums. First, Pamela complains that she couldn't get her husband Saladin, addicted as he was to idealizations, to "look at what was really real." She tells her lover, "I'm really real, too ... I really really am."[63] Pamela's complaint about her (presumed-dead) spouse is valid, but her language strains. The noun "real" is vague enough; preceded by the adjective "really," it becomes comical. Up until this moment, *Verses*' magical-realist techniques and skepticism toward common sense have eroded the foundations of Pamela's would-be realism. Magical realism serves Rushdie brilliantly in evoking the perils (and wonders) of human imagination: how lovers pour their illusions into a woman, god, or civilization they adore. But this technique serves Rushdie less well in depicting an intimacy that works. Hence, when Saladin reconciles with his dying father, a more realistic style (even a sentimental Dickensian one) conveys the physical tenderness that rekindles filial love. Saladin shaves his frail old father, "gently drawing the skin tight as the cordless shaver moved across it, and then stroking it to make sure it felt smooth."[64] Rushdie is a modernist legatee if there ever was one,[65] but even his anti-realism is not pure.

Of course, *On Beauty* is more invested in a realist ethos than *Verses*. Hence Kiki's repetition of the word "real" doesn't beg for the same ironic reading as Pamela's. To refer to Smith's essay "Two Directions," *Verses* "pushes" hard on its subject (the nature of love, the possibility of a lover accurately perceiving the "real" beloved, the ability of literature to depict such a meeting of souls) when Pamela complains about her husband. But *Verses* eases the pressure when Saladin shaves his father. Readers might wonder how hard *On Beauty* ever applies such pressure. How much pressure should it apply, if its main concerns include the redeemability of Howard's character, and of his and Kiki's love?

Just as O'Neill's *Netherland*, according to Smith's essay, is anxious about white liberal privilege and its estrangement from authentic experience, so too is *On Beauty*. But Howard has a time-tested humanist route out of egocentrism, back to what's "really real": loving attention toward other people, art, and nature. These cardinal values of secular-liberal Bloomsbury infuse the group's "sacred book,"[66] G. E. Moore's 1903 philosophical treatise *Principia Ethica*, which remarks that "Personal affection and the appreciation of what is beautiful in Art or Nature, are good in themselves."[67] Moore ranks his preferred goods in their order of mention. Human fellowship comes first. Art appreciation comes second, given that it often has the virtue of promoting humanist values, but the limitation of doing so indirectly, via fictional representations of people rather than intimacy with real ones. Appreciation of nature comes third, because natural objects lie at a further remove from human creativity than artworks. Metaphysical postulates, such as god, earn no place on Moore's list. His Platonically inflected analogy of "the good" to "the beautiful," and his belief in "the good" as a metaphysical entity worth retaining, so deeply impressed Murdoch that, in reviewing twentieth-century philosophers' attempts to "correct" this Platonism, she remarked, "on almost every point I agree with Moore and not with his critics."[68] Like Murdoch, Smith's homage leans into these Moorean values, both topically and stylistically.

Howard is jolted into appreciating nature in a Moorean (i.e., Forsterian) way when Kiki separates from him. His backyard smells of "tree sap and swollen brown apples, of which maybe a hundred" lay scattered on the lawn, but only after ten years, and only in the absence of his homemaker-wife, does he "realize" the culinary opportunities presented by this bounty. More broadly, his time alone bequeaths him "a new knowledge of the life cycles of his house. He now noticed which flowers closed themselves when the sun set; he knew the corner of the garden that attracted ladybugs."[69] Smith waxes lyrical when she has an important ethical point to make. With the help of Howard's *attention* to it, nature becomes his Wordsworthian nurse.

Smith is crafty enough, though, to suggest mystic dissociation in Howard's revery: he has just grumblingly signed separation documents, before stepping barefoot onto a hot patio. This combination of distraction from human affairs and absorption in natural processes recalls two moments in *Howards End* when Margaret discusses Helen's pregnancy, with her attention wandering each time to natural scenery. On the latter occasion, Margaret counts pigs' teeth embedded in a wych elm.[70] Is she a wise mystic or a silly dreamer—or, speaking charitably, a burdened individual seeking deserved refuge from troubles of others' making? *Howards End* doesn't cleanly separate one possibility from the other, just as *On Beauty* doesn't depict Howard's attunement to his backyard as unproblematically redemptive.

These ambiguities stem from Smith's ambivalence toward Forster's treatments of nature in general. At one moment she praises him for never, like some middle-aged writers do, believing "the hills alive," but at another she acknowledges that "there is a lot in Forster that fails, is both cloying and banal," such as his Pantheism. "The mystic will occasionally look the fool."[71] If Margaret of *Howards End* and Howard of *On Beauty* are mystics and fools at once, then they share company with Forster, whom Smith praises for taking risks, which occasionally result in "small patches of purple prose." Smith's 2003 apology for Forster sounds like an advance apology for *On Beauty* (2005): an acknowledgment that her own prose can grow "purple" but that this stems from commendable "risks" through which she forges "connections"[72]—as Forster did— between prose and passion, author and reader, etc. As Margaret can be distracted by pigs' teeth, so Howard (and Smith, who has a story to tell) can be distracted by apples falling and flowers closing themselves. This is predominantly to their credit, according to *On Beauty*'s liberal-humanist ethos.

The humbling attention to natural beauty evident in Howard's awareness of "life cycles" also informs the more important dimensions of his redemption. Personal affection and the appreciation of art—Moore's first two intrinsic goods—depend on the same turn *away from* the self. In mirroring scenes, *On Beauty*'s concluding chapters develop the idea that the appreciation of an art object can illuminate and facilitate the appreciation of an intimate other. (In Elaine Scarry's words, "beauty leads us to justice."[73]) One scene triangulates Howard, Rembrandt, and Levi, and the other triangulates Howard, Rembrandt, and Kiki.

The first scene opens with Howard snidely recalling art history's "traditional"—and, in his mind, "fatuous"—interpretation of Rembrandt's *The Sampling Officials of the Drapers' Guild*: that it depicts "rational benign judgement." (See Image 3.) Howard has "shticks" about this and other paintings, which he has "seen so many times that he can no longer" see them at all. But in spite of his self-protective ideology, he remains vulnerable to the painting. He enlarges the image until it fills his computer screen. One paragraph mentions multiple times that Howard "regards" or "looks at" Rembrandt's men and even that he "feels some affection" for one. When Howard was fourteen and first saw the painting, he "had been alarmed and amazed by the way the Staalmeesters seemed to look directly at him." He even, as an adolescent, felt judged by the Staalmeesters (whose job is to judge fabrics), and he wonders "but what was their judgement now?"[74] Howard doesn't have a therapist with whom he can work through insecurity or guilt, a priest to whom he can confess sins, nor a friend to act as his conscience. (His best friend Erskine, a "veteran of marital infidelity," advises him to "deny everything."[75]) But he does have art. Although Rembrandt's painting has nothing to do with sexual mores, it serves Howard (perhaps implausibly) as a surrogate conscience. The lengthy paragraph on Howard's encounter with the Staalmeesters concludes with the repetition of two sentences: "Howard looked at the men. The men looked at Howard. Howard looked at the men. The men looked at Howard." An interchange is occurring; Howard is again growing intimate—so to speak—with the art work, and the visually oriented verb, "look," indicates the moral work underway.

Murdoch's essay "The Idea of Perfection" argues that metaphors of movement impoverish our conception of moral life, associating moral choices with the will, not unlike a shopper selecting items from a store. But metaphors of seeing can enrich our idea of introspection and illustrate how some important exertions require no physical effort. For Murdoch, "the meaning of freedom" depends largely on "what goes on inwardly" between moments of "overt movement."[76] (Bloomsbury—with its emphasis on freedom, friendship, and contemplation—could hardly have put it better.) Howard, with Rembrandt's help, may be growing into a reader of the kind that Murdoch values. If he can read a painting well—being vulnerable to its moral themes—and if he can read his backyard attentively, then perhaps he can read himself and his loved ones more accurately than his self-absorption has allowed him to do.

Howard perspires, perhaps out of fear of the Staalmeesters' judgment, then Levi enters the room, feels his father's sweaty brow, and expresses mock offense at Howard's (accurate) inference that he has come to ask for money. Father and son tease one another—one of their primary means of expressing love. In light of the painting, the ensuing passage—including its use of the words "looked" and "real"—indicates the

Murdochian dimensions of Howard's midlife awakening: "he laughed and looked at his son with fond wonder…. His children were … real people who entertained and argued and existed entirely independent of him … They had different thoughts and beliefs. They weren't even the same colour as him. They were a kind of miracle."[77] By "looking" at a painting and a person, Howard contacts the "real"—precisely the metaphysical postulate that Smith's essay "Two Directions" mistrusts in O'Neill's *Netherland*. If that's not enough of a concession, then Howard's apprehension of his children as a "kind of miracle" (as the narrator's point of view blends with his) affirms *On Beauty*'s heteroglossia, its blending of disparate voices and values, from secular to sacred.

Nonetheless, certain values predominate. *On Beauty* is so committed to the humanistic dream of Rembrandt's art being morally instructive that its concluding scene dangles the possibility of a different painting repairing the Belsey marriage. As Howard's talk begins, he wonders "what did he look like" to the audience,[78] reprising the theme that he does not merely judge others but *is judged* by them. Unexpectedly, he sees Kiki, with a "scarlet ribbon threaded through her plait … her shoulders bare and gleaming," "looking" at *Hendrickje Bathing* behind him. (See Image 4.) Kiki is real, particular, and fleshly, not in a narrowly sexual sense—though her gleaming shoulders do evoke her beauty—but in a broader sense, as a complex and partly inaccessible other, like Rembrandt's subject. Hendrickje is a "pretty, blousy Dutch woman in a simple white smock" who "looked away, coyly" from the audience. The adverb "coyly" has erotic overtones, consistent with Hendrickje's nearly visible bosom and pubis, but Smith reads the painting more broadly. She explains that the "surface of the water was dark, reflective," with the adjective "reflective" suggesting introspection, but "dark" suggesting opacity—conjoined themes consistent with Murdoch's ideas about the difficulty of accessing reality, e.g., the reality of another's mind or one's own. Cementing the link between Kiki and Hendrickje, the narration continues, "Howard looked at Kiki. In her life, his life. Kiki looked up suddenly at Howard—not, he thought, unkindly." Decoding her visage is difficult and important, like decoding the painting, hence "looking" is essential, and the fact that each looks at the other is promising. A few sentences later, Howard "smiled at her. She smiled. She looked away, but she smiled." Kiki does not look away "coyly," like Hendrickje, but the parallel is strong nonetheless. Whether her smile gives only Howard cause for hope, or should give the reader hope as well, is unclear—fittingly for a novel with modernist echoes, by an author who admires Forsterian diminuendos.

How open is *On Beauty*'s ending? How hopeful is the novel that—to the degree that its characters bear allegorical weight—things are *getting better* for twenty-first-century lovers and families like them? There is much that readers don't know: what will become of the Erzulie painting, which Monty arguably stole from Kiki before Levi stole it from him; what will become of the Belsey separation, of Howard's career, or of Carl Thomas (Leonard Bast's counterpart), who disappears unceremoniously from the narrative—to one critic's chagrin.[79] A different critic, Lourdes Lopez-Ropero, approvingly cites these loose threads, and credits *On Beauty* for being both darker and more open-ended than its precursor.[80] I disagree with her comparison, seeing *On Beauty* as the more optimistic text. *Howards End* fears that modernity will homogenize distinctive rural traditions. Its conclusion's repeated allusions to the spread of "grey cosmopolitanism" undercut Helen's idyllic exclamation about a "crop of hay."[81] *On Beauty*, by contrast, largely welcomes an urban future with its promise of heterogeneous intimacies. One of its crucial revisions of *Howards End* lies in its more hopeful attitude toward history, which it rarely spells out and which it evinces in comic joie de vivre and a largely forgiving attitude toward human weakness.

Intimacy in History, Historical Hope, and Black Women Keeping the World Together

Of course, the question of how hopeful *On Beauty* is, specifically regarding intimacy in history, begs the question of what ending a reader craves. Would a happy ending reunite Smith's "hero" Kiki with Howard, or grant a strong Black woman independence in middle age? The question, *should she stay with him?* underpins both Forster's and Smith's tales of entangled families. *Howards End* asks, *once Helen is free of Paul, should Margaret marry Henry: what would a woman of 1910 gain and lose by alliance with such an insensitive man?* Smith's novel reformulates this premise as, *once Jerome is free of Victoria, should Kiki permanently leave Howard: what would a Black woman of 2005 gain and lose by separating from a man more cultivated than Henry Wilcox?*

For readers craving a marital reunion, it would be comforting to supplement the adage that "opposites attract" with the faith that "opposites endure together, strengthened by their differences." But *On Beauty*—published three decades into the "era of mass divorce"[82]—isn't readily comforted. In discussing their many friends with troubled marriages, Kiki tells Howard, "It's not just us" breaking up. "It's *everyone*. That's the fourth [Carlos and Theresa] since the summer …. It's pathetic … [worse] it's *predictable*."[83] Kiki doesn't specify what she thinks "predictable"—she may mean divorce in general—but the names "Carlos" and "Theresa" suggest another intercultural couple. If Kiki sees something predictable in the struggles of this form of intimacy, she might be right.

The social implications of people's increasing *legal* freedom to marry whom they choose are still up for grabs. "Assortative mating," or "homogamy," has been correlated with variables including physical traits, age, ethnic origin, religion, socioeconomic status, and intellectual variables.[84] In recent decades, marriage has been studied as a vehicle for social sorting—i.e., class stratification.[85] But some recent research on disassortative mating, which is slowly becoming more common, suggests that it is not a predictor of separation or divorce, but that "the rise in divorce" among demographically similar *or* dissimilar couples "is probably caused by increased social acceptance of divorce."[86] Kiki and Howard test this hypothesis along lines of race, class, and nationality. Anglo-American differences are a comparatively minor concern, but Smith does not neglect to highlight the foreignness of American culture to Howard.[87]

Class differences pose more serious challenges than national differences to the Belseys' interfamilial understanding, conviviality, and longevity. Kiki is alienated from the social milieu into which Howard's book smarts have lifted him, as indicated both by her dismay at his talk of "simulated wars" (she can't remember Baudrillard's name, which Howard supplies for her) and by her relief at not being an intellectual.[88] She has this latter thought when she sees Jerome—despondent over his break-up with Victoria—plunged in introspection. When she tells Howard, "everywhere we go, I'm alone in this ... this *sea* of white,"[89] race is not her sole reason for feeling like an outsider. Levi's alienation from universities illustrates that class division persists through an additional Belsey generation, following on the educational and cultural divide that poisons Howard's relationship with his father.

Race might be an even more sensitive subject than class in Belsey relations (and the two categories intersect in more ways than Levi's love of the "street" and his discomfort with universities and toney suburbia). It is a sign of Howard's growth that he recognizes his children as a "kind of miracle" despite—or partly *because of*—their being "not even the same colour" as he is. But the color line underscores differences between Howard and his spouse, and Howard and his offspring, that time does not efface. Hence, Howard "dislikes and fears conversations with his children that concern race."[90] Admittedly, he dislikes and fears numerous things, but nonetheless, this sentence divulges volumes about the emotional undertones of Belsey family relations. Interracial families can bridge or soften racial barriers, but they can also reproduce them, as *On Beauty* (like *The Satanic Verses*) is tough-minded enough to depict.

When race intersects with gender, the implications for Belsey family politics are more explosive than when it intersects with class. *On Beauty* develops numerous feminist themes, including how popular images of "extreme femininity"—"princesses and pink"—shape females' self-conceptions. "I am really grateful that I am not eight years old in 2010 and a girl," Smith told an interviewer, "because it is a nightmare ... compared to the landscape when I was ten [in 1985], in which extreme femininity was an option but you could easily ignore it."[91] *On Beauty*'s heroine is a wronged wife whose intellectual growth as a young adult was spurred by feminist counterculture and who claims agency by separating from her spouse. Feminist values inform Kiki's parenting even if they give her no clear roadmap. Zora's diet reminds Kiki of her dread at "having girls: she knew she wouldn't be able to protect them from self-disgust ... she had tried banning television," lipstick, and women's magazines, but "it was in the *air* ... hatred of women and their bodies."[92] Nor do female objectification and the cult of thinness only harm women: Smith also dramatizes how they corrupt men. Victoria, as psychologically brittle as Zora, bolsters her self-esteem with sex appeal—so skillfully that looking at her is a "strange bondage" for Howard.[93] During an argument, Howard admits that men's "concern with beauty is imprisoning" and infantilizing. Kiki, jealous and enraged, has said of his affair with Claire "You married a big black bitch and you run off with a fucking leprechaun?" and he has replied, "Well, I married a slim black woman, actually."[94] Even for him, this utterance is shockingly insensitive, but it supports both his theory that beauty imprisons men and Kiki's theory that hatred of women's bodies is "in the air." (Her "big black bitch" comment suggests that this hatred can focus on *heavy* female bodies, specifically on *heavy Black* female bodies,[95] even when it issues from such women's husbands.)

Beginning with the publication of *White Teeth*, Smith has won praise for depicting sociologically varied characters, from their dialects to their manners and beyond.[96] But the acclaim has not been universal. Tracey Walters ultimately praises Smith's handling of Kiki because she is the character in *On Beauty* who "makes the most change," ceasing to cater to Howard and trading familial loyalty for self-empowerment. But Walters—writing in 2008, after *On Beauty*'s publication but before *NW*—blames Smith, across multiple writings, for featuring white male protagonists and one-dimensional Black women. She sees in Kiki many marks of the stereotyped matriarchal mammy: dark skin, a Southern accent, a no-nonsense attitude, shapeless dresses, a flame-colored headwrap, and a large body. Only by virtue of her late-won self-reliance, in Walters's view, is Kiki distinguished from Smith's other disappointingly imagined Black women, including *White Teeth*'s Hortense Bowden, an "emasculating" black matriarch.[97]

Whatever its reliance on some forms of shorthand to mark characters demographically, *On Beauty* takes pains to depict Black diversity. Black people can be Christian and/or conservative (permanently, temporarily, or only apparently), as with Jerome and the Kipps children. They can be secular and liberal (Zora). They can be born from a line of poor Southerners, including a great-great grandmother who was a house slave (Kiki), or accustomed to northeastern privilege (Zora). They might or might not be enamored of the "street." They can be Haitians, in which case they might be political refugees, domestics, and/or cleaning staff workers at the university. Displaced Haitians might hustle stolen merchandise, like Levi's friend Choo, or they might sell jewelry legitimately, like the man with the stall at the town-square festival who completes Kiki's sentence "I'm from *here*, but of course ..." with the perfunctory "we are all from Africa."[98] This tired slogan expresses a desire for racial affinity born of essential Africanness, but it cannot conjure such an essence into being.

But notwithstanding the pains *On Beauty* takes to portray Black diversity in place of a Black essence, and notwithstanding Smith's wariness of a Black Female Literary Tradition that makes aesthetic sacrifices for the sake of positive images, Kiki and Carlene are virtuous Black mothers and wives who heroically hold their families together. Each has a philandering and egocentric husband, each has young adult children struggling with their identities, sexuality, and/or moral integrity. The two women, each in danger of being excessively influenced by their opinionated spouses, meet across an ideological divide. Their friendship might never gel, due to their families' claims upon their attention, Carlene's illness, and their different ideas about whether women find meaning based on "what" or "whom" they live for.[99] But thanks to their good will, gentleness, and tolerance (qualities their husbands lack), they overcome their differences and form perhaps the most meaningful connection that blossoms in *On Beauty*'s narrative present. *Howards End*'s women—the two Mrs. Wilcoxes—understand one another deeply enough (so Ruth appears to think) that Ruth bequeaths Margaret a portion of earth. In *On Beauty*, Carlene is moved enough by Kiki's kindness and appreciation of the Erzulie painting (and is perhaps alienated enough from her family) that she bequeaths Kiki this art work—the novel's equivalent of the Howards End property. I have mentioned *Principia*'s valuation of friendship, as well as the humanistic faith—shared by Moore, Murdoch, Forster (perhaps), and Smith—in the moral utility of contemplating art and nature. It takes a novel to weave Moorean goods together in narrative fashion: Forster depicts nature stimulating friendship between two white women of different generational milieus, and Smith depicts an art work stimulating friendship between two correspondingly dissimilar Black women.

Only Margaret, of these four characters, is self-consciously intellectual, yet in *On Beauty* two ostensibly non-intellectual women derive incalculable value—aesthetic and interpersonal—from a cultural object. Thus Smith conveys an aspiration and hope, dating (at least) to the Enlightenment, that culture fuels progress—even when said culture is not housed in a university or museum. Murdoch sees "goodness" as "rare," "hard to find," and "perhaps most convincingly met with in simple people—inarticulate, unselfish mothers of large families." She admits that these hypothetical cases are not very "illuminating,"[100] but the idea of the self-sacrificing mother appeals enough to her that she evinces no qualms about its political implications. Perhaps Murdoch's intuition about such mothers—along with the precedent of Ruth Wilcox—motivates Smith's admiring conception of Kiki. Ruth befuddles Margaret's friends by being "thankful not to have a vote,"[101] but she also resides like a *genius locus* over the Howards End property, and by extension over Forster's novel. Smith revises this precedent by denying Carlene (who, like Ruth, dies) Ruth's broad symbolic importance, and by combining in Kiki qualities of intellectual prowess with the goodness of Murdoch's "simple" mother. Despite Kiki's claims not to be intellectual, multiple occasions, including her exchange with Carlene, illustrate her thoughtful opinions about society and politics, and her eagerness to share them in respectful exchange.

Arguably, there is something Victorian, even medieval, in the premise of a womanizing man loving a woman with a heart of gold, unspoiled by excessive learning, whose goodness can nurture him—if only he lets it. This premise might frustrate readers who seek in *On Beauty* a thoroughly progressive vision of gender and intimacy. But Smith's novel—which is not parsimonious toward liberal wishes—might be stronger because of Kiki's links to the mammy tradition and to the Angels of the House who provoked Woolf's criticism. After all, in *Howards End* and elsewhere, Forster exploited ideological tensions to his aesthetic advantage, although some readers were disappointed by his refusal to resolve these tensions.[102] Kiki's angelic qualities and mammy traits might be *designed* to frustrate some of Smith's readers. Her readers might suspect that Kiki and Howard are bound to reunite—and either dread the thought or enjoy its moral ambiguity. Or they might imagine that Kiki couldn't possibly reunite with Howard, that in tearing away from a retrograde spouse, she tears away from multiple retrograde roles, that Howard's soul (tamed by art, nature, personal failure, and self-reflection) matters less than Kiki's soul (liberated by singlehood).

In Giddens's "intimacy as democracy" model, individuals are free to develop their potentialities and pursue economic opportunities. Arguably, Kiki fully enjoys these fruits of "democracy" only when she severs her intimacy with Howard and finds her own lodgings. Alternatively, a more sentimental reader—one who infers a likely spousal reunion after the novel's closing pages—might see each spouse developing their separate, atrophied potentialities (Kiki's masculine self-sufficiency, Howard's feminine sensitivity) while their cohabitation is on temporary hold and their intimacy in a process of regeneration.

Before her fiftieth year, Smith has donned multiple narrative personae and may have many ahead of her. Though she calls Woolf her favorite critic-practitioner, Forsterian values and techniques (and their ambiguous relation to the avant garde) seem to preoccupy her more than Woolf's many suggestive examples. As we saw in Chapter 2, texts including *Mrs Dalloway* draw rigorous experimentalists like Cusk into territory both Woolfian and perpetually transforming, unsettled into reified techniques. Smith argues compellingly for Forster's feisty plotting and characterization. But *On Beauty* suggests that he does not primarily stimulate her avant-garde instincts, that his liberal humanism and humane narrative voice draw her into territory more Murdochian, more lyric-realist, than her subsequent novels care to remain in.

But our examination of intimacy in history and literary form isn't done with Woolf, however tangential she is to *On Beauty*'s artistry. Woolf profoundly affects Cunningham, who said that reading *Mrs Dalloway* felt like "something that happened to me."[103] The following chapter on *The Hours* will bring our journey through Bloomsburian legatee-texts full circle, back to an examination of Woolf's stylistic inspiration. Our two most recent chapters—on legatees of *A Passage to India* and *Howards End*—illustrate the range of Forster's suggestiveness despite his numerically modest six-novel corpus. The chapter on Cunningham will further illustrate the suggestiveness of *one* of Woolf's nine novels, with its Joycean handling of a day in the lives of two doppelgangers in a capitol city and its penetrating insights into love, sexuality, and selfhood. Just as *Mrs Dalloway* provoked Cusk to ruminate on paralysis, it also provoked Cunningham to ruminae on intimacy in *history*—on the forces of change and progress that have shaped women's emotional lives since Woolf's time.

Notes

1 "Fail Better."
2 He mentioned this in a 2006 public radio interview. http://www.thefullwiki.org/Nick_Laird. Accessed November 20, 2019.
3 Moraru 133, Lopez-Ropero 7, 13, 14.
4 *Howards End* 170.
5 *On Beauty* 398.
6 Ibid. 177.
7 Ibid. 15.
8 Lexi Stuckey argues that Smith's optimism darkens after her debut novel, *White Teeth*.
9 Giddens 185.
10 *On Beauty* 22.
11 Gottleib discusses a possible pendulum shift between these two attitudes toward parenting, in the context of which she cites Watson (mentioned in endnote 13). Also see Arnett.
12 *On Beauty* 235-6.
13 Behavioral psychologist John Watson devoted a chapter to what he saw as "The Dangers of Too Much Mother Love" in his popular 1928 child-rearing guide (69-87).
14 "What Does Soulful Mean?" 12, 11.
15 "Two Directions for the Novel" 73.
16 See "Two Directions" 81, where she discusses realists "pushing" on their subject, though she doesn't discuss Forster.
17 Dorothy J. Hale 816.
18 "Fail Better." Also see Smith's essay on David Foster Wallace, "Brief Interviews with Hideous Men," including the quotation from Wallace with which she opens the essay.

19 Gasiorek.
20 "Fail Better."
21 "Two Directions for the Novel" 73.
22 "E. M. Forster: Middle Manager" 23.
23 "*Middlemarch* and Everybody" 40, "Two Directions for the Novel" 74.
24 Purdon. Quoted in David James, "Mapping Modernist Continuities" 6.
25 "Two Directions" 72.
26 Ibid. 73.
27 Ibid. 73–4.
28 Ibid. 76.
29 Ibid. 75.
30 *Netherland* 60.
31 "Fail Better."
32 "Against Dryness" 291.
33 Wood.
34 Smith, "This Is How It Feels to Me."
35 "Fail Better."
36 Lopez-Ropero points out that *On Beauty* fits neither the "writing back" model of postcolonial intertextuality nor the Bloomian model of influence anxiety (8).
37 Trilling, *E. M. Forster* 17. For a discussion of *On Beauty*'s "liberal aesthetic," see Dick and Lupton. Numerous critics of Forster discuss his liberalism, including Stone and May.
38 Tortorici 32. By contrast to Tortorici, Glab takes at face value Smith's claim to "ideological inconsistency," crediting her with eluding "the categories that dominate contemporary theories of literature" (492).
39 "Love, actually."
40 *Aspects of the Novel* 67–73.
41 "Love, actually."
42 Ibid. For another defense of "negative capability," see Lionel Trilling's introduction to *The Selected Letters of John Keats*, especially 28–30.
43 Ibid.
44 Smith applies this term to Franz Kafka and Philip Larkin. "F. Kafka, Everyman" 65.
45 Forster employs this term in his 1926 essay "Notes on the English Character" 5.
46 "E. M. Forster, Middle Manager" 20.
47 "Love actually."
48 Trilling, "On the Teaching of Modern Literature" 3.
49 Foreword xiv. In this context Smith is cautiously optimistic not about historical progress but about her capacity to capture "truths on the side of life" rather than the side of abstraction. But the same "creed" applies to her, and *On Beauty*'s, sense of history.
50 Penguin.
51 Dick and Lupton use this label and apply it in particular to Howard's anti-humanism (115).
52 *On Beauty* 117.
53 Glab 498.
54 *On Beauty* 155.
55 Ibid. 312.
56 *Howards End* 231–2, 23.
57 Ibid. 231.

58. *On Beauty* 15.
59. Ibid. 15.
60. *White Teeth* 7, 19, 46.
61. "What I Believe" 65–6.
62. *On Beauty* 394.
63. *The Satanic Verses* 181.
64. Ibid. 538.
65. See Begam, "Rushdie and the Art of Modernism."
66. Regan 3–28.
67. *Principia Ethica* 237.
68. Murdoch, "The Idea of Perfection" 301.
69. *On Beauty* 434–5.
70. *Howards End* 310–11. The previous scene comes on page 300.
71. "E. M. Forster, Middle Manager" 14, "Love, actually."
72. "Connection, as everyone knows, was Forster's great theme," writes Smith in "E. M. Forster, Middle Manager" 17.
73. Scarry, *On Beauty and Being Just* 63.
74. *On Beauty* 384–5, 144.
75. Ibid. 109.
76. Murdoch, "The Idea of Perfection" 305, 301, 306.
77. *On Beauty* 386.
78. This and the following quotations in this and the following paragraph come from *On Beauty* 442–3.
79. Driscoll 68.
80. Lopez-Ropero 16. Lopez-Ropero alludes to previous critiques of *Howards End*'s so-called "fairy tale" resolution, including that by Alfred Kazin (42).
81. *Howards End* 320, 340.
82. This era commences around 1970. See Roderick Phillips 185–223.
83. *On Beauty* 350.
84. Buss 47.
85. Pinker, *Blank Slate* 106–7.
86. Frimmel et al., 907.
87. *On Beauty* 7, 63–4, etc.
88. Ibid. 43.
89. Ibid. 206.
90. Ibid. 85.
91. Wachtel 131–2.
92. *On Beauty* 197.
93. Ibid. 255.
94. Ibid. 206–7.
95. See Shaw (9) on the "fat black female body" as an "inverse signifier" of feminine beauty. Walters cites Shaw in discussing Kiki's symbolic resonances (130).
96. For a recent discussion of *White Teeth* and religion, see Mirze. For an argument that *White Teeth* handles multiracial themes in a distinctively Caribbean—not a generically British—way, see Dalleo. For a defense of *On Beauty*'s depiction of Kiki in light of writings by Zora Neale Hurston—and a rejoinder to critics who see this character as freighted with too much racial symbolism—see Fischer.
97. Walters 126, 129–33.
98. *On Beauty* 49.

99   Ibid. 176.
100 Murdoch, "On 'God' and 'Good'" 342.
101 *Howards End* 75.
102 At once admiring and critical of *Howards End*, Daniel Born discusses how "critics on both left and right" have "gleefully" noted its "unresolved tensions" (366). Born wrestles with Margaret Schlegel's desire to "see life whole," which he links to liberal intellectuals' "attempt to fuse public and private virtue" (368). He argues that "limitations" in her character result when she abandons the "attempt to articulate" a "vision" that accommodates such fusion (369).
103 PBS.

7

Woolfian Optimism: Michael Cunningham's Modernist Homage

Michael Cunningham described *Mrs Dalloway* as the "first great book" he read. It "feels," he said, "like ... something that happened to me."[1] And he is not alone: *Mrs Dalloway* continues to impact literature and literary scholarship. But neither the individual legatee, Cunningham, nor the collective one—contemporary Bloomsburian fiction—passively absorbs a Woolfian force that they leave unchanged. Instead, to invoke a term of Forster's, each legatee highlights *aspects* of Woolf's artistry, whether for purposes of celebration and continuation (Cunningham and Cusk) or critique and transvaluation (McEwan). Cunningham's 1998 *The Hours* extends Woolfian themes, including psychosexual queerness and women's sadness, and emulates Woolfian narrative strategies in light of three quarters of a century of psychiatric and sociocultural history since *Mrs Dalloway*'s 1925 appearance, including the canonization and commercialization of Bloomsbury and Woolf.[2] Throughout this volume, the theme of sadness is not wholly private, but informs intimacy in history, including questions about whether increased freedoms in intimacy since Bloomsbury's time have yielded greater happiness, now that intersexual fraternization, same-sex love, interracial love, and divorce have grown more common.

    Mrs Dalloway responded to its own thematic and technical antecedents before inspiring its legatees. First, it followed *Ulysses*'s example of narrating a single day in a metropolitan capitol—a modernist variation on the classical unities that, as Laura Marcus explains, has seen many iterations in high modernism's afterlife.[3] Thus *Mrs Dalloway* depicted "ordinary" experience—a word repeated throughout Cunningham's homage[4]—in ways that both draw on and fly by Victorian realism. Second, the challenges imposed by *Mrs Dalloway*'s confinement to one day of Clarissa's life push it to seek temporal elasticity in other dimensions. When characters' past and present experiences blend, the June 1923 day expands vertically. When the point of view shifts among characters, unguided by a stable omniscient narrator—spurred by a backfiring car, airplane ad, or Big Ben's chime—a moment in the June day expands horizontally: what happens objectively becomes less important than how it is perceived and responded to. Finally, *Mrs Dalloway* bequeathed to experimental novels new ways of imagining character. Its free indirect style blends omniscient and limited perspectives, softening boundaries around individual minds. Furthermore, its characters bleed into one another, thanks primarily *not* to point-of-view shifts, but to Woolf's handling of doppelgangers (Clarissa and Septimus) and life-memories that link Clarissa, Peter, and Sally in a common narrative.

The quality of Cunningham's response to these aesthetic happenings is a barometer of modernism's continued vitality. On the one hand, if Cunningham merely copies Woolf's achievements, then *The Hours* lapses into pastiche,[5] sacrificing historical depth and epistemological radicalism. But on the other hand, to adopt David James and Urmila Seshagiri's language, perhaps Cunningham "inventively, self-consciously" engages with modernist precedent by "inhabiting [Woolf's] consciousness," in one version of "metamodernism."[6] Jesse Matz argues that *The Hours* carries forward impressionism's "legacies," though not at the moments when it is most recognizably "impressionistic," such as in the Prologue's prosaic depiction of Woolf's suicide. Matz prefers it when Cunningham depicts Mrs. Woolf's mind—in the spirit of modernist stream of consciousness—moving erratically from perceptions to ideas, base sensations to existential longings.[7] Prior to the work of James, Seshagiri, and Matz, Cunningham's methods had rationales in theories of postmodernism, including Linda Hutcheon's "historiographic metafiction" (a "reworking" of past aesthetic forms motivated by "an awareness of history and fiction as human constructs"[8]) and Brian McHale's distinction between modernism's epistemological preoccupations and postmodernism's ontological ones (what is a world, what kinds of worlds are there? what happens when boundaries between them are violated? what is the mode of existence of a world projected by a text?).[9] By shifting among the "worlds" of Virginia Woolf (in 1923 and 1941), Laura Brown (1949), and Clarissa Vaughan (late 1990s), *The Hours* signals that each world is constructed. To adapt McHale's language, *The Hours* blurs "boundaries" between historical constructs (Woolf's suicide) and fictional ones (Laura Brown reading *Mrs Dalloway* or Richard Brown nicknaming his friend "Mrs Dalloway"). This encourages readers to question boundaries between their experiences of reading *Mrs Dalloway* and *The Hours*, and the "constructs" of their extra-literary lives.

Cunningham builds these textual worlds, with their ambiguous borders, in pursuit of questions about freedom and happiness in intimacy. He told a radio caller that *The Hours* began with the "relatively simple idea" of placing Clarissa Dalloway "in the world today, where women have more freedom," to "see what her life would be like," although this plan grew more complex, resulting in three storylines.[10] The resulting novel explores freedom and its consequences in different contexts. How much freer is Mrs. Brown than Mrs. Woolf to forge satisfying intimacies or escape from imprisoning ones? How much freer is Clarissa Vaughan than Mrs. Brown? If the answer to at least one of these questions is "much freer," then how much happiness does this social progress promise? *Mrs Dalloway* cannot ask exactly these questions because it doesn't extend into the 1990s. But it does reach from the 1890s through the 1920s—including the "five years" of 1918 to 1923 that Peter Walsh deems "very important"[11]: it too historicizes intimacy and gender, much as *To the Lighthouse* does by contrasting Lily Briscoe and Mrs. Ramsay.

In exploring freedom and its limits in different contexts, Cunningham's homage develops a kind of "queer theory without antinormativity," to invoke Robyn Wiegman and Elizabeth Wilson. Without sacrificing its critique of heteronormativity in any of its three storylines, *The Hours* does not depict sexual norms as unitary oppressors.

Because of social progress, norms evolve. Even if Cusk is correct to observe that "oppression, being a type of relationship, can never be resolved, only reconfigured,"[12] its reconfigurations—including its ameliorations—deserve the attention of historical-minded novelists.

Although *The Hours* asks questions that *Mrs Dalloway* cannot, its debt is immense to this precursor whose methods it adapts and, in many cases, simplifies. *Mrs Dalloway* narrates one day in two people's lives: Clarissa's and Septimus's. It uses no chapter breaks to lighten readers' labors. The role of pivots (e.g., Big Ben) in effecting point-of-view shifts often becomes clear only upon rereading. Even as *Mrs Dalloway* stresses the relentless succession of hours, its psychological timescape disrupts linear temporality. It does so in spite of abundant plot material: the heroine had three love objects; she married and had a child with one, with mixed emotional results. His career prospered, though not brilliantly. She suffered physical and mental sickness and recovered. Her doppelganger, Septimus, fell in love with Isabel Pole and went to war partly for her sake, where he suffered shell shock *and* fell in love with a man who died in battle, all before he married a solicitous foreign woman who could not prevent his suicide. This partial summary of the protagonists' careers doesn't even touch on their links to Peter, Sally, and Dr. Bradshaw. Woolf's de-emphasis on plot in the traditional sense does not mean that nothing happens in *Mrs Dalloway*, but rather that the significances of events—many of which revolve around intimacy and sexuality and transpired decades ago—merit more attention than events themselves.

The Hours presents a comparable wealth of life-events somewhat more accessibly. Its chapter headings—"Mrs. Woolf," "Mrs. Dalloway," "Mrs. Brown"—maintain readers' bearings. If, within a chapter, the point of view shifts, for example from Mrs. Brown to her son and back, then the transitions are usually signaled clearly. But Cunningham pays subtle tribute to Woolf in his use of pivots between points of view and motifs linking his three storylines. The linking function played in *Mrs Dalloway* by Big Ben or a singing woman[13] is played in *The Hours*, for example, by yellow roses, which show up on Dan's birthday-cake icing, in Angelica's grave for the thrush, and in the vase Clarissa prepares for Richard's party.[14] Stephen Daldry and David Hare's film adaptation of Cunningham's novel employs more finesse,[15] weaving its floral motif into characters' clothing, interior spaces, and the outdoors. (Images 5–10 show two stills of each of the three heroines—Virginia, Clarissa, and Laura, respectively—in different flower-saturated settings. Image 11 reproduces a montage that links flowers as household decorations in three times and places. From top to bottom, Clarissa, Dan, and Virginia's maid move bouquets from one spot to another.) In these two adaptations—from Woolf's novel to Cunningham's novel to the film—one modernist legacy unspools.

Despite its tapestry of motifs and its use of three one-day storylines—whose endings vary from being morbidly closed to being somewhat open—Cunningham's novel has more linear momentum than Woolf's. Though its stories are chopped up in order to be interspersed, this punctuates their forward orientation more than restraining it. To adapt the language of Stanislavskian theater, each of Cunningham's heroines is propelled by an objective and each confronts obstacles, external and/or internal. Each woman hostesses under duress: Mrs. Woolf's sister shows up frustratingly early;

Mrs. Brown would rather not have to throw a birthday party for her husband, replete at the day's close with birthday sex; and Mrs. Dalloway prepares an elaborate party for Richard, which he would rather not attend. The gatherings are less important in themselves than as occasions for existential questions.

Cunningham interrogates intimacy in history and the progress of women's freedom via his heroines' mental illnesses, their gendered roles and obligations, and the love of their intimates (which can stifle as well as support them). Mrs. Woolf is eventually forced into suicide; Mrs. Brown flees her family and considers suicide (which she does not commit, though her son later does); and Mrs. Dalloway endures, remaining loyal to friends and lovers, despite "mortal sickness ... queasiness of soul."[16]

Because his heroines ponder mortality less pathologically with the passage of history, Cunningham hints that *things get better*. Linear momentum powers not only the novel's storylines but also its metatextual tale about gender roles, female homoeroticism, mental illness, and happiness—or at least resilience. Psychiatric literature details a spectrum of suicidal ideations.[17] On the benign extreme, people entertain fleeting thoughts, a category that applies to Clarissa Vaughan. In an ambiguous middle ground, people make incomplete attempts on their lives, which may be constructed to fail or be discovered. (This category might fit Virginia Woolf's unsuccessful suicide attempts in 1904 and 1913. It might also fit her character, Clarissa Dalloway—whom the following remarks will treat as a *silent* figure in Cunningham's novel—though Woolf only alludes obliquely to Clarissa's past illnesses. The diagnosis might also fit Laura Brown, though Cunningham supplies limited and ambiguous information about her "thwarted"[18] attempt, through Clarissa Vaughan's reportage.) Finally, on the sad end of the ideational spectrum lie suicidal attempts that are meant to succeed, a label that fits Mrs. Woolf, if one assumes, as I do, that her hesitation ("She imagines turning around, taking the stone out of her pocket, going back to the house"[19]) does not indicate an overriding ambivalence nor an intent to fail. This bleak label also fits Mrs. Woolf's character, Septimus, and Cunningham's character, Richard Brown—an exception to my claim that *The Hours*' characters grow less pathological across history.

Cunningham uses historical traumas as framing devices in his suggestions of historical progress. He depicts Mrs. Woolf writing in the wake of one world war, then taking her life in the midst of another, as she hallucinates "bombers dron[ing] in the sky."[20] Outside the pages of Cunningham's novel, in 1939 Woolf and her Jewish husband planned a joint suicide in the event of a German invasion of England. Before her body was found, Woolf's brother-in-law Clive Bell wrote that she was "in for another of those long and agonizing breakdowns ... the prospect of two years' insanity, then to wake up to the sort of world which another two years of war will have made, was such that I can't feel sure that [her suicide] was unwise."[21]

Clarissa Dalloway, the explicit character in Woolf's novel and the silent one in Cunningham's story, is, like her author at the time of *Mrs Dalloway*'s composition, a post-war figure. Each woman was born into late-Victorian society (Clarissa being about a decade older than her author), when gender spheres were more strictly defined. Each was well into adulthood when a global war erupted, by which point at least Mrs. Woolf, and perhaps Clarissa too, had long wrestled with mental illness. But unlike Mrs. Woolf, Clarissa does not kill herself.

Mrs. Brown, who is one to two generations younger than Mrs. Woolf, struggles to be cheerful in the wake of the latter world war, as America strives to consolidate gender roles and economic prosperity, much as Britain strove to do after the First World War. Stultifying peacefulness engulfs Mrs. Brown's Pasadena as it had engulfed Mrs. Woolf's Richmond. Mrs. Brown attempts suicide (seemingly) but fails.

Mrs. Dalloway, the most contemporary of Cunningham's three heroines, recurrently feels lost in her life and thinks about insanity, hopelessness, and dying.[22] She loses a dear friend to another war (of sorts) that besieged gay communities in New York and other major cities beginning in 1981.[23] Just as *The Hours* has a high-modernist lineage, it also belongs to a family of art about AIDS. But unlike Mrs. Woolf, this 1990s-era heroine doesn't kill herself, and unlike Mrs. Brown, she doesn't try to. Does this mean that things get better?

Telling a *simple* inspirational tale, a smooth melioristic myth, cannot be the aim of a novel that employs two world wars and the AIDS epidemic as reference points, and that weaves storylines around multiple successful or "thwarted" suicides. *The Hours* might be read as a lament that things *don't* get better, or that social progress cannot cure a woman like Clarissa Vaughan of mortal sickness, despite her wealth, stimulating career, socially poised and thoughtful daughter,[24] considerate partner, and friends going back three decades. But Cunningham has said that "Kodak moments" are fine on their own and that "what we need art for is a little bit of solace, a little bit of company in trying to deal with the darker stuff."[25] Perhaps *The Hours*' focus on "darker" matter is the *basis* for its historical optimism, or at least its testing ground for such sanguinity, as the novel "places" its version of Clarissa Dalloway in today's world, with psychic difficulties like those of her prototype, but with professional, social, and romantic opportunities that Woolf's heroine lacked. After all, curing mortal sickness or getting completely better—on the individual or social level—is one thing. Making meaningful progress is another. Cunningham hopes that fiction can offer *help* with "darker stuff," not freedom from darkness. *The Hours* leaves unclear whether "Kodak moments" grow more frequent as society grows freer, and whether happiness remains elusive even for wealthy and beloved people. Nonetheless, an expanded look at the four heroines' struggles can clarify how Cunningham uses Woolf's ideas and techniques to question the idea of progress.

* * *

Mrs. Woolf: A suicide. Were it not for the grisly Prologue, Mrs. Woolf's storyline would offer happy resolutions. She achieves her two main objectives: she writes her novel and convinces Leonard to move from Richmond to London. In achieving the first objective, she triumphs over internal obstacles—her headaches and her tenuous mental and physical health—as she skips breakfast over Leonard's objections. True to Virginia Woolf's fondness for psychological plot points, *The Hours*' first "Mrs. Woolf" chapter shows the novelist land on her opening sentence, "Mrs. Dalloway said she would buy the flowers herself." The chapter opens with her groping toward the sentence and ends with her articulating it, and the next chapter begins with Mrs. Brown reading it in the published novel, *Mrs Dalloway*. Mrs. Woolf's final chapter culminates with the novelist deciding that Clarissa will not die but that a "deranged poet" will.[26] With these two creative breakthroughs *and* the success of Virginia's campaign to move to London, we have the makings of an inspirational "Mrs. Woolf" tale. The sequence of Mrs. Woolf writing *Mrs Dalloway* and Mrs. Brown reading it dramatizes the direct efficacy of Woolf's creative labors. Woolf's novel outlives her, communicating something (about the mysteries of sex and selfhood? about the disappointments of love and the risk that marriage could hinder a woman's self-discovery? about the sustaining powers of everyday beauties, including beautiful prose, to one beset by depression and confusion?) to an audience desperate for whatever consolations—or questions—it offers.

Not only does *The Hours* emphasize Woolf's creative achievements, it also eschews numerous explanations for her suicide: that she is a tortured artist, stifled lesbian, trapped wife, or woman grieving over her childlessness. The myth of the tortured artist is tenacious, though borne out marginally at best by empirical studies.[27] It belongs, of course, to the Woolf cult, and Cunningham has ample opportunity to invoke it, given the attention he pays to creative isolation, with Virginia upstairs and Leonard downstairs, engaged in separate tasks. But just as he satirizes Laura Brown for imagining herself to possess a "touch of brilliance,"[28] likewise he demurs from associating Mrs. Woolf's psychic anguish with visionary powers. Instead he depicts the novelist's mental illness and creative energies paratactically: readers can couple or decouple them as they see fit. Leonard may or may not be an ideal caretaker for someone with Virginia's illness, but, convinced as he is of her genius, he does everything he can to facilitate her artistry.

But if Mrs. Woolf is not dying for her art, then—to repeat Laura Brown's question—"how could someone" able to write such beautiful sentences "come to kill herself?"[29] When a reader asked Cunningham, "Why did Laura Brown leave her family? Was she depressed or was she a lesbian?" he responded, "Neither one! ... her sexuality was complicated, and had lesbianism in it," but she shouldn't "be dismissed as merely depressed or a lesbian, who leaves her children."[30] The same distaste for reductionism informs Cunningham's conception of Mrs. Woolf, including his depiction of how Mrs. Woolf imagines Clarissa Dalloway. As Cunningham knows, the historical Woolf could be classified as bisexual, and she had a passionate erotic friendship with Vita Sackville-West. *The Hours* shows her kiss her sister on the mouth, which thrills her with its daring and supplies the inspiration needed for her to finish mentally outlining *Mrs Dalloway*. She decides that her heroine Clarissa will "have loved a woman" when young. So far, in Cunningham's recreation of Woolf's invention of Clarissa, all the elements are in place for her—unlike Laura Brown—to be a lesbian and a straightforward indictment of heteronormativity. But Cunningham complicates this potential piety. Mrs. Woolf decides that Clarissa and her beloved will have had "one kiss, like the singular enchanted kisses in fairy tales, and Clarissa ... will never find a love like that which the lone kiss seemed to offer."[31] If the mention of fairytales isn't enough to make Mrs. Woolf's Clarissa appear starry-eyed, then the verb "seemed" signals that the kiss doesn't really "offer" what Clarissa imagines it does. Mrs. Woolf's outline does not treat the kiss as a key to Clarissa's authentic sexuality, but instead treats Clarissa's *memory* of the kiss as a sign of her girlish sentimentality. The "trapped lesbian" label, in other words, is inapplicable to Woolf's heroine (at this stage of her conception), just as it would be too simple to fit Mrs. Brown. In tandem, these two examples suggest that the label is also inapplicable to Mrs. Woolf: Cunningham does not indicate that, in conceptualizing a protagonist with an indeterminate sexuality, Mrs. Woolf denies her own inmost nature.

So if the authoress isn't a tortured genius like Van Gogh, nor a trapped lesbian, could she at least be a trapped wife? Another way of asking this question is: how will Leonard be depicted? And the answer is: Cunningham couldn't appear, on a first glance, to be much kinder to him.[32] Admittedly, he peppers Leonard with humanizing flaws. An overworked manager of Hogarth Press, Cunningham's Leonard "scowls" at manuscript proofs, at his watch if Virginia stays up late, and at Virginia if she goes missing. He is "autocratic" and "unfair" to his assistants.[33] But virtually none of his menacing energy is directed at his wife. She has ample time to write, to order her maid about (not in the kindest way), and even to take walks during which her imagination roams, despite Richmond's limited stimuli. Leonard asks solicitously about how she slept and gently admonishes her to eat according to the medical recommendations of the time. (The 1920s' conventional medical wisdom has been rebuked by critics who sympathize with Woolf, as it is in *Mrs Dalloway*.) He flexibly agrees to move back to London, though Mrs. Woolf wishes she were "happy with the quiet life."[34] An October 1937 entry in Woolf's diary speaks of being "overcome with happiness." After twenty-five years of marriage, it says, "can't bear to be separate ... you see it is enormous pleasure being wanted: a wife. And our marriage so complete."[35] Cunningham doesn't include this material in his novel, but he conveys its sentiments by incorporating Woolf's suicide note in full. Unless it is read severely against the grain, this document indicates a marriage of substantial love, not one whose unfreedoms precipitated her death. "You have given me the greatest possible happiness," it tells Leonard. "You have been entirely patient with me & incredibly good."[36]

Laura Brown's question, then, continues to nag: why did Mrs. Woolf do it? Might she regret her childlessness? Mrs. Woolf envies Vanessa's "art," her "effortless gestures"[37] in talking to children, servants, and Virginia herself—a skill set that motherhood has likely honed. (Woolf's fiction abounds with admiration for women who are proficient in such mundane arts of life.) Watching Vanessa's children while contemplating her own writing and Victorian culture, Mrs. Woolf thinks that raising a child "is the true accomplishment; this will live after the tinselly experiments in narrative have been packed off along with ... the china plates on which Grandmother painted."[38] Her derogatory reference to her own writing style is provocative. But—rather like our glimpse of her hauteur toward her servant—it's a thread that *The Hours* doesn't follow very far. The hint of Woolf's unfulfillment as a childless woman is only a hint. We do not see her—as we see the heroine in *Mrs Dalloway* and Clarissa Vaughan in *The Hours*—mull a life unlived or wonder why she chose the life (and partner) she did, suggesting that this choice burdens her.

As a feature of Virginia Woolf's biography, her suicide is what a Freudian diagnostician might call "overdetermined": numerous plausible causes present themselves. But in *The Hours*, Mrs. Woolf's suicide is underdeveloped rather than overdetermined: between the scenes of her writing in 1923 and the Prologue depicting her drowning in 1941, readers confront a void. While Cunningham was prudent to eschew pat theories about why she did it, the spareness of Mrs. Woolf's storyline and the limited exploration of her suicidal motives (returning headaches and auditory hallucinations, a sense that she and other women she loves have "failed"[39]) are conspicuous. While even a *Mrs Dalloway* devotee cannot be expected to match Woolf's skill in digging "caves" behind his characters, a more detailed exploration of why Mrs. Woolf feels beset by failure could have enriched Cunningham's treatment of intimacy in history and female sadness.

The limited exploration of *why* Mrs. Woolf killed herself, coupled with the lyrical depiction of this act,[40] moderates the psychic demands that *The Hours* makes on readers, despite its submersion in "darker stuff." (Even readers of *The Hours* who were previously unacquainted with Woolf learn in the Prologue where her affliction leads, and its shadow darkens her creative breakthroughs and pending move to London.) *The Hours* preserves its inspirational, or historically optimistic, qualities—such as they are—with its linear narrative momentum. Slowed but not stopped by Woolf's successful suicide and Laura's "thwarted" one, this momentum propels Woolf's art into the reader's present. Cunningham's "Mrs. Woolf" achieves something more definite, closer to satisfying the demands of a traditional plot, than Woolf's Clarissa Dalloway achieves by throwing her party. Admittedly, *Mrs Dalloway* ends with the partial satisfaction of a tender moment between the Dalloway father and daughter, and with Clarissa's radiant apparition before Peter's eyes ("For there she was"[41]). But nonetheless, it lacks a resolution—other than, perhaps, its heroine's continuance, buoyed to some ambiguous degree by Septimus's sacrificial death. By contrast, Cunningham's "Mrs. Woolf"—though her death may lack symbolic grandeur—leaves behind something more substantial than a fine party: a novel that enables Laura's continuance.

Does Richard's suicide nullify this (potentially) inspirational vision of a reader's relationship with an admired writer? After all, while his dementia offers sufficient motive for his plunge from the window, his grief over maternal abandonment colors his life, and his sense of failure as a writer colors his final days. Art's powers to console and sustain are, to say the least, limited: what they do for the mother they cannot do for the son, though he is a writer. Nonetheless, even though "Mrs. Woolf's" masterly novel cannot save Richard, its effects on the lives of the survivors (Laura Brown and Clarissa Vaughan) remain unknown.

Clarissa Dalloway: Woolf's fictional *alter ego* (or half of it) inhabits *Mrs Dalloway*'s pages, and by osmosis she also inhabits the imaginations of Laura and Richard Brown and Clarissa Vaughan. Cunningham recovers this character, from her finished appearance in *Mrs Dalloway*, as an idea in progress. He depicts her evolution, in Mrs. Woolf's mind, in two ways. First, he presents her as originally a suicidal figure who only later becomes non-suicidal. Mrs. Woolf spends much time thinking that Clarissa will kill herself, and Cunningham evokes the motives for this plan in Woolf's condition. The experience of burying the thrush with Vanessa's children moves her, even after the Bells return home. She "would like to lie down in [the bird's] place," she thinks, as she lingers by its grave, arguably in a suicidal ideation. But then, sliding without a clear transition from thoughts about herself to thoughts about her heroine, she imagines "Clarissa ... is not the bride of death after all. Clarissa is the bed in which the bride is laid." In the kitchen, drinking tea with her sister, she muses "there is so much in the world .... How could [Clarissa] bear to leave all this?"—invoking the beauties of nature, the tenderness of the young (Quentin handles the thrush "immeasurably gently"), and the consolations of family.[42]

What does *The Hours* gain by imagining this moment early in Woolf's creative process? Thematically, it reiterates the idea—already clear in its pages—that suicide is a ubiquitous possibility. Laura could have died in the hotel, and Clarissa Dalloway would have died had her author retained her original plan. (On one critic's reading, *Mrs Dalloway* is palimpsestuous, and even in its final form, in one layer of meaning Clarissa *does* take her own life in the final pages.[43]) Where Woolf's biography is concerned, Cunningham's depiction of this moment of creative revision collapses the distance between personal experience and aesthetic creation, making *Mrs Dalloway* seem like a *roman a clef*. Clarissa Dalloway's fate seems dependent on her creator's changeable—but, for the moment, resilient—state of mind.

But in deciding that Clarissa will live, Woolf does not banish death from her authorial plan: her novel, like her life, retains its suicidal destination. She decides that "sane Clarissa—exultant, ordinary Clarissa" will love "her life of ordinary pleasures," and "a deranged poet, a visionary," will die.[44] Thus, the second half of Woolf's *alter ego* is born: Septimus, who throws himself from a window, as Woolf did during her 1904 confinement to a nursing home. Just as *Mrs Dalloway*'s Clarissa and Septimus are psychically joined, so too are *The Hours*' Laura and Richard Brown. In each novel, the younger male figure is sacrificed so that the older female figure can stagger forward.[45] The elaborateness of this parallel may further explain Cunningham's decision to highlight Clarissa Dalloway's originally suicidal conception. If Septimus and/or Richard really are sacrificed—the way societies sacrifice scapegoats for the good of the body politic, or surgeons excise infections for the good of the body—then the moment imagined in *Mrs Dalloway*'s planning stages dramatizes why the sacrifice was necessary. Someone had to die: Mrs. Woolf couldn't spare Clarissa without exacting a blood price somewhere. *Mrs Dalloway* was (before Septimus's conception) and remained (after his conception) *about* self-inflicted death. The novel's question always was: what can the meaning of this act be: can it be an "embrace," an "attempt at communication," or a noble "defiance?"[46] Can it be an artwork, more beautiful and affecting than a party attended by a prime minister? Cunningham's novel, largely through the vessel of Laura, shifts this question from *what* to *why*, from *what is the meaning of a suicide?* and *how beautiful might one be?* to *why does someone like Mrs. Woolf or Richard commit one, or someone like Laura not do so?*

The second evolution that Cunningham depicts, in Mrs. Woolf's planning of Clarissa Dalloway's character, regards her sexuality. In addition to considering, then deciding against, making Clarissa a suicide, Mrs. Woolf also considers, then revises, the idea of making her a "tourist lesbian," to employ contemporary lingo. Early in her planning process, Woolf thinks that Clarissa "in her first youth, will love another girl" and anticipate "a rich, riotous future," but eventually "come to her senses, as young women do, and marry a suitable man." The words "come to her senses" and "suitable" beg for an ironic reading, as though they convey stultifying bourgeois values, and as though Clarissa's turn toward heteronormativity will be a forfeit. But Cunningham does not supply the necessary nudge to justify such an ironic interpretation. Instead, at this early stage of Woolf's drafting process, she plans a conservative tale. Clarissa "will kill herself," Woolf's line of thought proceeds, "over some trifle (how can it be made convincing, tragic instead of comic?)."[47] Woolf scholars know that the short story "Mrs Dalloway in Bond Street" handles the title character more satirically than does the novel for which it supplied germinal material. In *The Hours* this creative process is streamlined. In lieu of showing Woolf working through a more ironic short story toward a more emotionally resonant novel, Cunningham reconstructs the development of the novel alone, with "tragic" resonances developing from "comic" beginnings, as Woolf's attitude toward her heroine evolves.

I said above that the verb "seemed" ironizes the "love like that which [Sally's] lone kiss seemed [to Clarissa Dalloway] to offer." But Cunningham depicts Woolf's ironic attitude toward Clarissa subsiding with time. Clarissa becomes less of a tourist lesbian swept up in transient Sapphic feelings, such as some readers see in Laura Brown. She blossoms, in Cunningham's words, into a woman "bereaved, deeply lonely"[48] and possessed of melancholic grandeur. In *Mrs Dalloway*'s final draft, Clarissa's memory of Sally's kiss is no trifle, but the impetus for a profound and lengthy rumination in the novel's celebrated attic scene. In Cunningham's novel, whatever girlish delight Woolf derives from kissing Vanessa "not quite innocently"[49] behind the maid's back is transmuted, in her heroine's case, into a more womanly combination of longing, loss, and the consolations of memory. Thus Cunningham preserves a degree of aesthetic autonomy for *Mrs Dalloway*, which no longer seems like a rehearsal of an impending authorial suicide, nor a straightforward transcription of a sudden plunge into depression. Cunningham siphons the suggestions of girlishness, associated with Woolf's earlier conception of Clarissa, partly into the sister-kissing Woolf character and more substantially into a 1949 Los Angeles housewife, where they provide occasion for both satire and pathos.

Laura Brown: Having previously decided to "place Clarissa Dalloway in the world today" and to juxtapose this character's experiences with those of her author, Cunningham added a third story evoking "a day in my mother's life."[50] This storyline, and Mrs. Brown's many parallels with Mrs. Woolf, help *The Hours* to multiply a range of themes present in the other storylines, including the limited efficacy of diagnosis, the limited value of intimacy for some sufferers, and the potential value of reading and writing. Additionally, Cunningham's generally compassionate handling of this character, laced with irony though it is, encourages readers to extend their empathy to a figure—the family-abandoning mother—who is an easy target for shunning.

How might Laura's condition be labeled? Before her suicide attempt, her mood and behavior might be taken for signs of dysthymia, or persistent depressive disorder, a condition lasting two years or more, which has fewer symptoms and is milder than major depression, although it can plummet into periods of major, or "double" depression. Given that she is pregnant during the June 1949 day depicted, she might be diagnosed with antepartum depression. But given her suicide attempt, a diagnosis of *merely* low-grade (dysthymic) depression would seem inaccurate, and given her subsequent (postpartum) abandonment of her family, a diagnosis of antepartum depression would seem half-accurate at best. A more politically inflected account of domestic depression—what Betty Friedan called "the problem with no name"—fits Laura well; *The Feminine Mystique* is an intertext in the "Mrs. Brown" chapters.

But as we have seen, Cunningham advises against summing up Laura as "depressed" or "lesbian"—a warning worth also applying to Mrs. Woolf and Mrs. Dalloway. Who's to say that one's "mortal sickness," another's compulsion to flee her family, and another's drowning stem from frustrated same-sex longings or the pain of social marginalization? The novel's tales of three sad women (four if we count Clarissa Dalloway), most of whom forgo love not just with an individual but with a whole sex, encourage readers to speculative diagnoses. But they can only be speculative.

The Hours follows *Mrs Dalloway*'s diagnostic humility, with the source-novel's rich, individualized pictures of Clarissa's and Septimus's anguish, lacerating critiques of poor medical care in the figures of Holmes and Bradshaw, and question marks where medically clear pathologies might be. *The Hours* also follows Virginia Woolf's biographical legacy in this humility: in the decades since Woolf's death, numerous theories, emphasizing congenital and environmental factors, have attempted to explain her condition, none conclusively.[51] Medical science is one place that thinkers often look for evidence of historical progress; sufferers and/or their loved ones often crave diagnoses and cures; in *not* depicting cures, *The Hours* refuses one kind of sanguinity.

But if Cunningham does not play the diagnostician, his "Mrs. Brown" chapters nonetheless have an agenda. Feminism, from high literature to popular culture, has aimed to humanize and dignify ordinary women's struggles. But even after literary examples like Anna Karenina and biographical examples like Doris Lessing, powerful biases remain against "the woman who [flees] her family," as Clarissa Vaughan describes Laura.[52] (The man who flees his family, it need not be said, is so common that he inspires less revulsion.) Cunningham confronts this bias. "Anything we do can be forgiven," he said, "if it's seen in its context."[53]

To a large degree, *The Hours* makes Mrs. Brown (and by extension women like her) sympathetic. But Cunningham balances pathos with irony. The two Clarissas, Dalloway and Vaughan, have male suitors—Peter Walsh and the mature Richard Brown—whose passions give texture and meaning, if not always joy, to their lives. But Laura's suitors are the uncomplicated Dan (whose courtship of her is correspondingly untextured) and her three-year-old boy, "devoted, entirely to the observation and deciphering of her"[54]—which might be unsettling because she would rather not "decipher" herself. The Clarissas each experience love of some depth with a woman named Sally. Though Clarissa Dalloway's erotic encounter with Sally Seton is brief, it provides material for decades of introspection. Though Clarissa Vaughan frequently judges her partner Sally, and though their intimacy lacks fire, it provides her not only stability but also fuel for introspective soul-making.

But when Laura introspects, she—like Maisie of *Arlington Park*—achieves only modest depth and range. Despite Laura's fantasy of her own "brilliance," we see her do nothing more dazzling than read in bed. Later, when Kitty damns her cake with the faint praise of "cute," Laura melodramatically thinks that she "had hoped (it's embarrassing, but true) to produce something of beauty."[55] Her fatuous flights of fancy are mitigated by their ordinariness (who has not shared such feelings?) and by her self-awareness, evinced by her "embarrassment." But the mitigation is limited. Laura has no philosophically rich self-examination, such as *Mrs Dalloway* grants its heroine. (It's as if Laura remains the protagonist of "Mrs Brown on Bond Street" and never blossoms into the heroine of *Mrs Brown*.) Laura, for example, never ruminates on the meaning of Kitty's kiss. Clarissa Dalloway wanders through vast interior spaces where she recalls her love (still present) for Peter, represses knowledge of his presence in London and thus his imminent appearance at her party, and tells herself that "she had been right … not to marry him."[56] Clarissa Vaughan also covers vast interior spaces: though her arguments with herself achieve no resolution, they endow her with what Forster would call "roundness."[57] By contrast, Laura's arguments with herself—if they can be called that—are so incomplete as to seem immature. After the Second World War, Laura recalls, Dan was received as "more than an ordinary hero" who could have had "any pageant girl," yet he proposed to her, "who had never been sought after … What could she say but yes?"[58] Her introspection ends almost as soon as it begins. She neither accuses herself (for being foolish or cowardly in deciding to marry), nor does she appreciate Dan's good qualities and feel grateful for her marriage. She voices no bitterness toward society for proscribing the sentence "Laura liked Kitty." In terms of self-articulation, she lies at an opposite pole to her idol Virginia Woolf, who left behind nine novels, numerous short stories, letters, and volumes of diaries. Laura's character might be said to make a feminist point in leaving her family. But she serves a more rigorous feminist purpose by illustrating how a woman's angelic housewifely role not only chokes off her public life, but also mires her interior life in clichés and half-baked fantasies.

How, other than by fleeing familial duties, is a woman like Mrs. Brown to blossom? If diagnoses are elusive (even harmful when inaccurate), then can literature provide succor that science cannot, by giving readers opportunities to identify with troubled characters and, through them, with their author? Cunningham uses Laura to pose these questions. He told PBS that he "would never write a pessimistic book. I think writing is, by definition, an optimistic act,"[59] and the solace—perhaps life-saving—that *Mrs Dalloway* provides for Laura seems to vindicate this endorsement. Laura can be seen as an ideal reader of Mrs. Woolf's masterpiece, who comes to the novel with profound needs and emerges profoundly altered. The beauty of Woolf's sentences contrasts with the trite "ordinary hero" and "pageant girl" of Laura's ruminations, and Laura's appreciation of their beauty indicates her intellectual capacity. If things do *get better*—even some of the time—then great writing, it would seem, aids this meliorism. All the labels that Clarissa Dalloway provisionally applies to Septimus's suicide—an "embrace," an "attempt to communicate," a "defiance"[60]—might better apply to the acts of writing and reading, which effect an "embrace" between Mrs. Woolf and Mrs. Brown and encourage the latter to "defy" her matronly and wifely roles.

But Cunningham's novel is not unreservedly "optimistic" about writing. Perhaps Mrs. Woolf's writing, Mrs. Brown's reading, and/or her son's writing (specifically about her) deepen the solitude of one or more of these alienated people. In a study of the relations between creative (scientific and artistic) professions and psychiatric disorders, including those with psychotic features, Kyaga and colleagues found that creative professionals were not more likely than controls to suffer from a lengthy list of psychiatric disorders.[61] But being an author was associated with increased likelihood of schizophrenia, bipolar disorder, and suicide. Correlations, of course, do not prove causation, and while diagnosing real-life figures is dicey, diagnosing fictional characters can be dicier. Nonetheless, just as *The Hours*' satirical strains complicate its sympathetic portrayal of Mrs. Brown, likewise its inclusion of two suicidal authors and one nearly suicidal reader complicate its "affirmation" of the value of writing and reading works like *Mrs Dalloway*.

If neither scientific medicine nor high literature provides a magic pill, then where is the sufferer to turn: can intimacy provide the succor that they cannot? *The Hours* is, if anything, more tough-minded than *Mrs Dalloway* in refusing optimism on this front. Mrs. Brown and Mrs. Woolf each have kind husbands bent on keeping them safe. Since long before 1998, storytellers have shown how outwardly ideal marriages (and even emotionally enriching ones) leave some spouses unsatisfied—or suffocated. Unlike Emma Bovary or Anna Karenina, Mrs. Brown does not have an affair, though she could be said to be unfaithful to her family. Her infidelity lies not in kissing Kitty (which leads nowhere, save perhaps in her young son's confused imagination), and not in spending an afternoon in a hotel, but in her permanent leave-taking—although the only person for whom she abandons her family is herself. Cunningham portrays the oppressiveness of intimacy in Laura's disgust: a "spasm of fury" rises in her throat when Dan "sprays spit" on the birthday cake; his erection reminds her of a paper snake popping out of a novelty-shop peanut can.[62]

Parallels between Mrs. Brown's and Mrs. Woolf's cases underscore how even the best-intentioned kinds of love, or those that conform most to social convention, can be harmful. A novel can straightforwardly *take the side* of a suicide victim, as does Septimus's portion of *Mrs Dalloway*. Septimus's insensitive, self-important, buffoonish doctors precipitate his suicide rather than healing him. Septimus's storyline expresses Woolf's rage at the mental-health profession, which has not endeared the novel to all readers.[63] Its depictions of Holmes and Bradshaw might have opened *Mrs Dalloway* to charges of caricature, had Septimus been the main character. But Woolf managed her art deftly, in part by casting Septimus in a supporting role and in part through her handling of his spouse. While Holmes is sharply drawn, Rezia's character is more ambiguous. A foreigner who may lack a niche in English society, she has her own suffering to manage. Yet she focuses her attention on her troubled spouse, toward whom she could not be more loving. Her efforts to get Septimus out of his head, paying attention to the world around him ("Look, look Septimus!"[64]) seem sensible. While the doctors she hires offend him, what choice does she have but to turn to experts? While Septimus may have married her for unwise reasons—in a panic that he could not feel, after the loss of Evans (as Laura Brown likely marries Dan for unwise reasons)—is she culpable in this case? After all, she was young, as was Septimus.

Yet *Mrs Dalloway* leaves room for readers to see even Rezia as part of a battalion of people who, for all their loving intentions or professional experience, don't know how to listen to the suicidal sufferer. Taking the sufferer's side, readers might acknowledge that Septimus's hallucinations and monologues are opaque in some ways, but insist that their key message is clear: *I don't trust these doctors; keep them away from me.* Having taken Septimus's side, readers can ask how skillfully Rezia listens. If they have also taken Clarissa Dalloway's side, they can ask how skillfully Richard listens to her, whether he provides what she wants and needs, or imposes what he (or a health professional) thinks she needs.

These questions about how to interpret *Mrs Dalloway* belong to *The Hours*' deep background. Mrs. Woolf meets the same grim outcome, in 1941, as she planned in 1923 for her fictional "deranged poet." Like Septimus, she has a spouse who loves and cares for her, the best he knows how. As I said above, Cunningham couldn't be much kinder to Leonard—on a first reading. But does a second reading reveal Leonard to be a poor listener? Virginia awakens alone at the start of the first "Mrs. Woolf" chapter; each spouse spends hours immersed in his or her work. Leonard asks if she has breakfasted; she lies and says yes; he detects the lie and says he'll have Nelly bring her food; she rebuffs this plan; he presses on while giving ground, saying playfully that she'll have lunch "by force" if necessary; she acquiesces "impatiently but without true anger."[65] This scene could depict two spouses deeply in love, who respect one another's privacy and work, and who avoid arguing despite venturing into sensitive terrain, reaching a compromise in the heroine's best interests, just as their subsequent agreement to move to London serves her interests. Or, in the eyes of a reader who *takes the suicide's side*, it could depict a husband who assumes that doctors know better than his wife what is best for her and who cedes ground—concerning dietary freedom or urban stimuli—only after emotionally draining negotiations. Virginia, on such a reading, shouldn't have to stage a near-escape from Richmond by train to communicate her needs. On such a reading, her suicide note's assurance that "you have been entirely patient with me & incredibly good"[66] is true—but not the whole truth. Without portraying any of its three heroines as ideal partners, *The Hours* leaves room to wonder—as *Mrs Dalloway* does— whether people who love the suicidal sufferer, and whom she loves, can be distant, obtuse, even oppressive. Is Mrs. Woolf driven to despair not wholly *in spite of* her loving partner, but in part *because of* how he exercises care? Is Dan Brown terminally unable to detect his wife's misery? Is Richard Brown's self-inflicted death hastened by the party that Clarissa Vaughan plans in his honor? If intimacies with extreme sufferers can play the same cruel jokes on their caretakers and lovers in the 1940s and 1990s as in the 1920s, then we have another reason to doubt whether things get better.

Clarissa Vaughan: That some things get better, nonetheless, is the premise of the storyline about a Clarissa "in the world today, where women have more freedom." These freedoms include how to advertise one's sexuality to society, whom to partner with, and (for couples who live where same-sex marriage has been legalized) whether to do so inside or outside of matrimony. "Mrs. Dalloway's" story, bearing *The Hours* up to the end of the twentieth century, rounds out the novel's big question: do increased freedoms yield greater happiness within and beyond intimate relationships? The meaning of this question, though, depends on the ontological status of happiness. The novel suggests that happiness is a passing, not abiding, state, though it can recur often and intensely.

Clarissa Vaughan's state of mind—both her differences from and similarities to *The Hours*' other heroines—invites both psychological and historical diagnoses. She never considers suicide, but "nameless fear" accompanies her.[67] If she suffers from dysthymia, then historically sanguine readers might wonder whether her freedoms and privileges, relative to those of Mrs. Brown, have palliated her condition, and whether in another fifty years, even fewer women will suffer from a "problem" that now has a "name." But fatalistic readers might suspect that, for someone like Clarissa Vaughan, dysthymia is the best to hope for, in keeping with Freud's scaled-down ambition to lift patients from "hysterical misery" into "common unhappiness."[68]

Clarissa Vaughan's moods, like those of her namesake from *Mrs Dalloway*, often lead to self-accusations. After she embraces Louis in greeting, she notices that he has been crying, and the narrator—in a free indirect rendering of her consciousness—observes that "Clarissa, the more sentimental one ... never seems to cry at all, though she often wants to."[69] (This self-accusation recalls the heroine's worry in *Mrs Dalloway* that, as Peter Walsh alleges, she is "cold."[70]) Nor is this her mind's sole occasion of recoil against itself. Enthralled by the beauties of New York, she sees her friend Walter Hardy, who "aims his lips" for hers, but she "instinctively" offers her cheek instead, and her ecstasy at the city's beauty dissolves. "I swoon over the beauties of the world, but am reluctant," she despairs, "to kiss a friend on the mouth."[71] Later, when she turns sideways to receive Richard's kiss on her cheek and tells herself "It's not a good idea to kiss him on the lips—a common cold would be a disaster for him,"[72] it is unnecessary for Cunningham to supply any self-accusatory thoughts she might have. The question of her "coldness"—regardless of her medical reasons for sparing Richard exposure to her germs—raises the specter of Clarissa's guilt.

Guilt haunts her in other forms as well. Julia's mentor Mary Krull, the parallel to Doris Kilman from *Mrs Dalloway*, "mocks you," Clarissa thinks, "for your comforts and your quaint (she must consider them quaint) notions about lesbian identity."[73] How far society has come (at least certain parts of society) since Clarissa Dalloway's day! In *Mrs Dalloway*, the heroine may fear society's disapproval of Sapphism, and her daughter is exhorted by a conventional-minded Christian who rivals Clarissa for her daughter's respect. In *The Hours*, the heroine fears the disapproval of a queer theorist whose command of the radical zeitgeist positions her as a rival mother-figure. Mary finds Clarissa insufficiently dissident in challenging homophobia, and she objects to Clarissa's essentialistic thinking, being convinced that the "lesbian" category is an imprisoning fiction. Recalling Wiegman and Wilson's language, Mary might be accused of dogmatic "antinormativity": no matter how flexible or expansive a new norm appears to be, she stakes out a position of principled opposition, purportedly still *outside of* the norm's spreading embrace. Cunningham handles Mary with much the same ironic judgment with which Woolf handles Doris. But regardless of whether Mary's judgments are just, they magnify Clarissa's self-doubts, as do Richard's fallible judgments of Clarissa's cowardice and conventionality.

Clarissa Vaughan's dissatisfaction also leads her into more explicit counterfactual exercises than Clarissa Dalloway entertains, as she wonders, *What if I'd partnered with Richard?* and *Should I be with Sally?* "That summer when she was eighteen," explains Cunningham's free-indirect narration, "it seemed anything could happen." Clarissa, Louis, and Richard "could sleep together in a strange combination of lust and innocence" and not worry about what it meant. But in retrospect, Clarissa thinks "it was the house" that led to her lifelong romantic entanglement with Richard, and that without it, a different "chain of events" might have led to different adult lives.[74] But as her ruminations continue, she allows that her own choices, rather than a chain of events, may have been decisive. She wonders "what might have happened if ... she'd returned Richard's kiss on the corner of Bleecker and MacDougal, gone off somewhere (where?) with him."[75] The structure of Cunningham's sentence reinforces Clarissa's uncertainty. The word "somewhere" evokes the vagueness of Clarissa's fantasy, and the parenthetical question "(where?)" reemphasizes this quality. The parentheses also beg the question *Who asks "where?"* Does Clarissa interrupt her own train of thought with another thought? Or does the author's voice intrude on the narrative? (*The Hours* lovingly replicates *Mrs Dalloway*'s description of how Clarissa "would still find herself arguing ... that she had been right—and she had too—not to marry" Peter.[76] Cunningham's sentence interrupts itself in the same way as Woolf's does, begging the same question about who does the interrupting.)

The answer to Clarissa's *what if* question might not be happy. Richard, though more her soulmate than Sally, is also her tormentor. When he welcomes her with the words "Oh, Mrs. D. Oh, come in," she wonders if it isn't time "to dispense with the old nickname,"[77] and readers wonder, *after thirty-four years, and only now that he is on his deathbed, will you broach the topic*? And she does not: her moniker remains unchallenged. Prior to this scene of his teasing, allusive greeting, Clarissa recalls that "before Richard's decline, [they] always fought," and that for twenty years he saw a "weakness" in her decision to live with Sally "that indicts ... women in general." Not content with indicting Clarissa's morals (because, jealously, he begrudges her love for Sally?), Richard gratuitously insults her whole sex! Mary Krull never expresses such an extravagant prejudice as this. Surely Clarissa Vaughan was wise not to partner with such an "infuriating companion," just as Clarissa Dalloway is wise not to have partnered with Peter Walsh. And yet Clarissa Vaughan "wants the argument she and Richard would have had about Walter."[78] Her evaluations of him are destined to alternate: "She loves Richard, she thinks of him constantly, but she perhaps loves the day slightly more," the narrator explains, obliquely entering her mind and recalling the heroine's rumination in the attic scene of *Mrs Dalloway*. Her uncertainty—her terminal muddle—endows her with a kind of heroism, or at least representativeness, for readers of a skeptical sensibility.

Clarissa's muddle extends through her feelings for her trustworthy partner of eighteen years. On one occasion, for "less than a moment," Clarissa views Sally "as if they were strangers." Sally appears "pale, gray-haired, harsh-faced, impatient, ten pounds lighter than she ought to be," and dressed in the wrong color. In addition to tenderness, Clarissa feels "a vague, clinical disapproval." On another occasion, as they survey the remains of Clarissa's party preparations, Sally kisses her forehead. Clarissa, in addition to withholding the words "I love you," can only see her lover's gesture as firm and competent, "in a way that reminds Clarissa of putting a stamp on a letter."[79] Her habit of judging Sally seems never to abate—a canker at the heart of their intimacy.

Clarissa has no answers to her *what if* questions, any more than Cunningham's readers have definitive answers to questions about where the point of view resides in his most Woolfian uses of free indirect style. Instead, Cunningham's heroine carries forward her namesake, Clarissa Dalloway's, ennobling psychological burdens to the end of the twentieth century. She also carries forward Clarissa Dalloway's joy in a *flâneuse*'s banal pleasures: the stimuli of a great city, the scent of fresh flowers, and unpredictable exchanges with friends and acquaintances on the street, with home as the errand's terminus. In a novel like *The Hours* that celebrates beautiful prose, Clarissa Vaughan's ability to respond to beauty in many forms is exemplary.

But Cunningham reminds his readers how tenuous this capacity is. His heroines labor to retain positive frames of mind. How much of a boon can Clarissa Vaughan bear forward, into 1998 and beyond, by snatching ordinary pleasures from a context of dissatisfaction and psychic dislocation? When Woolf's Clarissa Dalloway exclaims mentally "What a lark! What a plunge!"[80] this is part of her ongoing pep talk, as the Rezia portion of her mind labors to convince the Septimus portion that the day's treasures deserve appreciation. When Cunningham's Clarissa Vaughan thinks "What a thrill, what a shock, to be alive on a morning in June,"[81] she struggles for similar self-motivation, though her demons are less ferocious. While the successes of these Clarissas' campaigns are uncertain, the success of Laura Brown's pep talk is more doubtful, when she tells herself (in the narrator's third-person rendering) "She will not lose hope. She will not mourn her lost possibilities ... She will remain devoted to her son, her husband, her home and her duties, all her gifts. She will want this second child."[82]

Cunningham's novel is narrated in the present tense, a risky choice that he pulls off skillfully. Neither a distraction nor, for the most part, a modernistic alienation effect, this device helps readers to identify with the heroines' moment-by-moment experiences. Ingeniously, however, they often experience a lack of unity with themselves—hence Laura's future tense ("she will not ... ") and Clarissa's slightly forced present tense ("What a thrill ... "). Clarissa's temporal dislocation is more acute after Richard's death, when she thinks in the subjunctive tense about what she would tell him "if she could speak": "she would talk to him about how she ... loved him in return .... She would confess to her desire for a relatively ordinary life ... She would ask his forgiveness" for not kissing him on the lips.[83]

Temporal dislocation is an oft-noted feature of modernist alienation and despair,[84] but it is also associated with intellectual and creative freedom. The subject can project herself into the future, rupturing herself in order to imagine a transformed version of herself. She can plunge into the past, interweaving it with the present, reordering its contents in linear or nonlinear ways, in quests for insight or self-transformation. Sometimes the feelings of alienation and despair that attend "falling out of time"—to use Richard Brown's words[85]—are separated by a razor's edge from the ecstasy of flying, in imagination, beyond clock time.

Both *Mrs Dalloway* and *The Hours* can be described in part as "inspirational." But the ways in which inspirational messages will be used, and even which messages will be taken as inspirational, are not always easy to predict. Laura takes inspiration from the ravishing beauty of Woolf's prose, which promises a world less dreary than her kitchen and bedroom. But at the same time, the novel may be a beacon luring her away from life and familial obligations. After wondering how Woolf could have killed herself, Laura summons "resolve" and "closes the book" to "rise and be cheerful."[86]

Many of Woolf's devotees have drawn inspiration—not a summons toward oblivion—from her work and life. Suzette Henke says that the "extraordinary" thing about Woolf's biography is that, during her final twenty-six years, "she suffered from persistent migraine headaches, flu, pulmonary distress, and recurrent toothaches" without breakdowns "while continuing a prolific reading program, travel and social engagements, grueling labor alongside Leonard at the Hogarth Press, and most importantly, literary creation."[87]

This study that opened with a discussion of Woolf's historically pessimistic admirer, Cusk, has journeyed into the work of her more historically sanguine disciple. *The Hours* offers no promises that freedom or perseverance will bring happiness in intimacy; that producing or consuming art will reduce suffering; or that struggles for social justice, personal fulfillment, and love will fit hand-in-glove. But the "solace" and "comfort" of which Cunningham spoke to PBS may nonetheless lie in its pages. Cunningham derives from *Mrs Dalloway* messages of an un-Cuskian temperament, from the hope that the future promises on both social and personal levels to the solaces that sufferers need—and can find—in an imperfect present. As Cunningham's character Laura finds comfort in the manner (more than the matter) of Woolf's writing, likewise Cunningham's readers may find suggestions of freedom and happiness—however provisional and intermittent—in the Woolfian manner of his writing.

Like *Mrs Dalloway*, *The Hours* is a carefully plotted tale of love, marriage, break-up, and death—the extraordinary events that punctuate a life and make it possible for a novel to plunge into the ordinary without sacrificing high drama. Like *Mrs Dalloway*, it values psychological significance over brute fact, and it shares Woolf's determination to depict time and causality as *experienced* non-chronologically. Like Smith's homage to Forster, Cunningham's homage to Woolf evinces a tenacious hope that art—in particular, Bloomsburian-modernist art—is useful, soul-making, palliative. And it evinces hope, however qualified, that social progress can pay dividends in the deepest recesses of our emotional lives: that as societies grow more tolerant, individuals can figure out how best, and when, to be intimate with others, or intimate only with themselves.

Notes

1 PBS.
2 For an interesting exchange over whether *The Hours* trades on the "cult" of Woolf and her suicide, see Justin Spring's interview of Cunningham.
3 Marcus, "The Legacies of Modernism" 85–8.
4 *The Hours* 10, 11, 211, 221, 225.
5 Jameson, *The Cultural Turn* 4–5.
6 James and Seshagiri 88, 93.
7 Matz, "Pseudo-Impressionism?" 129, 125.
8 Hutcheon, *A Poetics of Postmodernism* 5.
9 McHale, "Change of Dominant" 58, 60.
10 Fowler.
11 *Mrs Dalloway* 71.
12 Cusk, "Shakespeare's daughters."
13 *Mrs Dalloway* 48, 80–1.
14 *The Hours* 99, 119, 123.

15 Alley prefers the film adaptation of *The Hours* to Cunningham's novel, claiming that Cunningham's use of the present tense and narrative framing techniques lessen the audience's "sympathetic experience" by pointing out linkages among characters rather than allowing the audience to "undergo" them (402–3).
16 *The Hours* 23.
17 Gliatto and Rai.
18 Clarissa describes Laura's attempt this way (221). Shortly later, Clarissa thinks of Laura as "the woman who tried to die and failed at it" (222).
19 *The Hours* 5.
20 Ibid. 3.
21 Flood.
22 *The Hours* 48, 220.
23 In an interview, Cunningham compares AIDS (those who have it and those, like himself, who don't) to Clarissa Dalloway, who survives the First World War, and Septimus Smith, who doesn't, "really." See Canning 95.
24 *The Hours* 218.
25 Cunningham, Michael. Interview with PBS. April 20, 1999.
26 *The Hours* 211.
27 See Kyaga, et al.
28 *The Hours* 42.
29 Ibid. 41.
30 Fowler.
31 *The Hours* 210.
32 By contrast, for a biographer who blames Leonard for controlling Virginia (as well as blaming doctors for prescribing the wrong medicine), see Poole.
33 *The Hours* 32, 210, 171, 73.
34 Ibid. 209, 172.
35 *The Diaries of Virginia Woolf*, V: 115, October 22, 1937.
36 *The Hours* 6.
37 *Mrs Dalloway* 115.
38 Ibid. 118.
39 *The Hours* 4–5.
40 For two highly critical appraisals of this lyrical depiction of Woolf's suicide, see Matz (115–16) and Henke (10–11).
41 *Mrs Dalloway* 194.
42 *The Hours* 121, 153, 120.
43 Mendelson.
44 *The Hours* 211.
45 See Driscoll for a discussion of how many modernist and contemporary British novels, including those discussed in this book, marginalize working-class characters. Driscoll discusses *Mrs Dalloway* on 34–5.
46 *Mrs Dalloway* 184.
47 *The Hours* 81–2.
48 Ibid. 211.
49 Ibid. 210.
50 Canning 93, Young 11.
51 See Detloff.
52 *The Hours* 222.
53 Fowler.

54 *The Hours* 192.
55 Ibid. 42, 104.
56 *Mrs Dalloway* 7.
57 Forster, *Aspects of the Novel* 73–8.
58 *The Hours* 42.
59 PBS.
60 *Mrs Dalloway* 184.
61 Kyaga et al.
62 *The Hours* 205, 213.
63 Schlack 55. "Holmes and Bradshaw are … the object of an authorial hatred so stubbornly relentless as to become gratuitous."
64 *Mrs Dalloway* 21.
65 *The Hours* 32–3.
66 Ibid. 6.
67 Ibid. 23.
68 Freud, *The Psychotherapy of Hysteria* 305.
69 *The Hours* 125.
70 *Mrs Dalloway* 8.
71 *The Hours* 15–16.
72 Ibid. 68.
73 Ibid. 23.
74 Ibid. 95.
75 Ibid. 97.
76 *Mrs Dalloway* 7.
77 *The Hours* 55.
78 Ibid. 19.
79 Ibid. 89, 224.
80 *Mrs Dalloway* 3.
81 *The Hours* 10.
82 Ibid. 79.
83 Ibid. 203.
84 James and Seshagiri 89, 93.
85 Ibid. 62.
86 Ibid. 41.
87 Henke 10.

8

Bloomsburian Horizons: Intimacy in a Polyamorous Light

The Introduction describes this volume as "meta-Bloomsburian," with a nod to David James and Urmila Seshagiri's discussion of metamodernism. The previous six chapters have offered two meta-Woolfian intertextual exegeses in light of twentieth-century demographic and moral progress, two meta-Freudian exegeses, and two meta-Forsterian ones: a mosaic of modernist literary and philosophical contributions and how contemporary novelists extend and complicate them. With its focus on polyamory, this concluding chapter moves in a different direction—into the present and future of intimacy in history.

T. S. Eliot described the past as "altered by the present as much as the present is directed by the past,"[1] and in this spirit Chapter 8 will review the Bloomsburian past in light of the poly present, to see if this light "alters" Bloomsbury. I will characterize the poly present mostly with the help of contemporary apologists, but partly with Bloomsbury's help. Thus, on the one hand, the coming pages will magnify Bloomsbury's importance moving forward, suggesting that to appreciate polyamorous intimacies over the last century is to see the group writ large. On the other hand, these pages will magnify polyamory's importance looking backward, arguing that, because the movement has become so self-conscious, it sheds light on the past that Bloomsbury was unable to shed on itself.

Scholarship on current poly practices credits Bloomsbury as a forerunner, but rarely and briefly[2]—an oversight that begs for correction. In the early twentieth century, Bloomsbury began to (re)invent what some twenty-first-century polyamorists practice with greater deliberateness. Bloomsburians defied Victorian gender segregation with loving intersexual fraternization; they defied Victorian homophobia by joining erotically with fellow group members of each sex; they remained friends and collaborated for decades after their university years—and yet ...

And yet how their erotic and emotional lives turned out, and even the visionary scope of their thought, disappoint utopian wishes. In their twenties, many Bloomsburians shared the disdain for bourgeois coupledom captured in *Women in Love*'s label "egoïsme à deux."[3] But would they resist the institution's lure and pressure? What would they want instead, and if they knew what they wanted, would they find it? Would sex be a lasting source of pleasure and intimacy for them, not merely a topic of liberated discussion? Would having children call forth their best selves? The answers to these questions evolved and were never clear. Throughout their quests, with the benefit of hindsight, we might think of polyamory as the Bloomsburian love that dared not speak its name, or that lacked the clarity of vision to speak its name, even among these daring and clear-thinking artists.

E. M. Forster graduated from a celibate young adulthood in Bloomsbury's proto-poly culture, to a promiscuous middle age in which he embraced his homosexuality, to a satisfying polyamorous triangle beginning in his fifties, to sedate autumnal years at King's College, the site of his transformative undergraduate years. His travels to India and Egypt exposed him to non-Christian sexual regimes marred by their own patriarchy, homophobia, and hypocrisy. With admirable success but also much failure, he sought homoerotic outlets in fictional compositions, diaries, and letters. More broadly, throughout his adulthood he sought alternatives to mixed-sex egoïsme à deux that would yield psychosexual authenticity and satisfaction. At age twenty-three, he had a "very unsatisfying love affair" with his friend H. O. Meredith marked by "fully clothed embraces, chaste kisses, and florid talk of … friendship."[4] To Forster's disappointment, Meredith would marry—and he was not the only gay or bisexual Bloomsbury associate to do so. Forster would remain a virgin until he was nearly thirty-eight, a source of tension, dissatisfaction, and self-doubt. Even as a rich and famous novelist, he felt himself to be less than a grown man; he lived with his mother, by whom he felt stifled, and ached for a male partner. Perhaps this "queasiness of soul,"[5] to quote from the previous chapter's discussion of *The Hours*, stemmed from Forster's sense that homosexuality was "the core of his identity"[6] under the shadow of the Labouchere Amendment (1885–1967) that criminalized "gross indecency."

Not only did these circumstances deprive Forster of experience; they also curtailed his articulateness. He struggled to find a language fitting to his experience as a sexual minority, and he mistrusted numerous things about sexology (its modish terms including "intersexual" and "homosexual" and its theories about the causes of homosexuality), as he would come to regard Freudian theories suspiciously. Forster recognized this struggle to craft a satisfactory language, and the aesthetic toll of its failure, as a predicament common to gay writers. He faulted Henry James's fiction for sacrificing the "common stuff" of human life to an aesthetic "pattern" and privately diagnosed James's "repressed homosexuality" as the source of this evasion.[7] Lawrence leveled a criticism—in person and by letter—against Forster's writing that echoes Forster's criticism of James. Your books are "intentional and perverse and not vitally interesting," Lawrence ranted. "One must live through the source, through all the racings & heats of Pan."[8]

Forster's oeuvre of public and private writings indicates how close Lawrence's criticism cut to the bone. His post-*Howards End* lament has often been cited: his "weariness of the subject that I both can and may treat—the love of men for women and vice versa."[9] Readers have mused on the loss to literature resulting from *A Passage to India*—published forty-seven years before his 1971 death—being his final novel. When he showed homosexual stories to his mentor Goldsworthy Lowes Dickinson, the latter's shock led Forster to burn them.[10] He was then working on *Maurice*, his only explicitly gay novel, which remained unpublished until his death and the writing of which filled him with "loneliness."[11] In the context of these decades-long frustrations, moments in Forster's fiction that don't explicitly invoke homosexual loss can gain poignancy. In *Howards End*, when Margaret tells her sister that she expects to end her life "caring most for a place"[12]—although "personal relations" is their sororal slogan—readers might infer an authorial confession of loneliness.

Two years prior to completing *Passage*, shortly after Forster had seen his Egyptian lover Mohammed el Adl for the last time, when he was depressed and struggling to complete the manuscript, Woolf encountered him in London and mused in her diary about his creative and sexual frustration. "The middle age of buggers is not to be contemplated without horror," she wrote.[13] Perspicacious as she was to intuit that his novelistic energies—as a gay man—were withering, she had no idea of the variations of sexual pleasure that his middle age would bring. After completing *Passage*, Forster was ushered by the younger writer J. R. Ackerley into a "gay and all embracing" subculture where he no longer felt "disembodied."[14] In his forties, living the "double life" of a closeted gay man, he commenced flings, sex in various forms, and assorted intimacies with men married and single, middle-aged and often young. He proudly reported to Ackerley that his eighteen partners hailed from varied backgrounds—a modest tally compared to Ackerley's "two hundred or so."[15]

Thrumming beneath Forster's appetite for sexual self-exploration and pleasure was his yearning—"bourgeois," it might be called—to love and be loved by one partner. In this as in many ways, he was far from a radical. He felt emotionally disconnected from his largely working-class lovers (and suspicious of his own sexual motives), missing "imaginative passion," wondering "lust + goodwill: is anything more wanted?" and feeling "not happiness, but proud to be alive."[16]

Until Forster was over fifty, his sex life and love life—or the latter's absence, given his limited satisfaction with superficial intimacies—offered as much disproof as proof of Carpenterian ideals. As discussed, Carpenter and his younger working-class lover George Merrill symbolized the Millthorpe sage's hope that "homogenic" love could bridge class divisions. Extending this Whitmanesque aspiration across racial and civilizational lines, Forster fell in love (albeit chastely) with Syed Masood, whom he met in 1906 when he was twenty-seven. The seventeen-year-old Masood, with his "matinée-idol" looks, lived with the Forsters' neighbors while preparing for Oxford's entrance exams and hired Forster as a Latin tutor. Prefiguring the celebrated passage from his 1938 essay "What I Believe" ("if I had to choose between betraying my country and betraying my friend I hope I should have the guts to betray my country"), Forster wrote in his diary that "Masood gives up duties for friends—which is civilisation." Prefiguring the Schlegel sisters' slogan in *Howards End*, Forster added that, in Oriental states, "personal relations come first." The men's affections deepened over time—they traveled together in Paris for a week and in Italy for a month—and Forster struggled to gauge Masood's feelings for him and the wisdom of expressing his love to Masood. At the end of 1910, when Forster mustered the courage to do so, Masood listened calmly and said "I know," leaving Forster wondering whether he had ruined their friendship—which he had not. But in 1911, when he visited Masood in India and discovered that his friend planned to marry the following year, Forster felt their bond loosening and developed an association of India with longing and loss that would enrich his last novel, which he dedicated to Masood.[17] *Passage*'s concluding question—"Why can't we be friends now? It's what I want. It's what you want"—divulges Forster's dissatisfaction with the seeming outcome of what was, at its time, the strongest love he had ever felt. Thankfully, though, on Forster's next trip to India a decade later, he was happy to see Masood married, and they renewed their friendship. Throughout their passionate Platonic time together, their love both did and did not surmount barriers of geography, culture, and heteronormativity.[18]

Less chastely, 1917, the thirty-eight-year-old Forster fell in love with the (perhaps) seventeen-year-old Egyptian tram conductor el Adl while working at the Red Cross hospital in Alexandria. This provided him a second chance to test Carpenterian ideals. (Forster wrote in a letter that "to be trusted across the barriers of income race and class, is the greatest reward a man can receive.") Shortly prior to this relationship, in a self-imposed rite of passage, Forster had "parted with Respectability," as he described his loss of virginity—his stilted language indicating his difficulty in articulating his desire. He had brief anonymous sex on the beach with a recuperating soldier. This experience seems both to have prepared him for a tenderer bond with another man and emboldened him to press el Adl for sex. The younger man allowed Forster to masturbate him, an act of intimacy that contributed, four decades later, to Forster seeing their relationship as "one of the two greatest things in his life."[19] Like Meredith and Masood before him, el Adl disappointed Forster by announcing plans to marry. The union—to el Adl's widowed sister-in-law's unmarried sister—was motivated not by love but familial needs, including the desire for children. Forster feared for its effects on his friend's health but was eventually pleased to see that matrimony seemed to make el Adl happy.

Sadly, after the war ended, when Forster left Masood in India to return to Egypt and see el Adl again, he discovered that his lover was mortally ill with tuberculosis. He arrived soon enough to consult a leading specialist (who confirmed el Adl's imminent death), spend money making el Adl and his family comfortable, and feel "a mixture of awe, gratitude, and love" at his fortune in seeing his beloved one last time.[20] Nonetheless, this relationship, like the one with Masood, left a version of Fielding's question in Forster's heart: *Why not? It's what I want.*

But what *did* Forster want? He didn't know: identitarian gay language had not yet crystallized, the prospects of a durable romance seemed dim, and youthful Bloomsbury's proto-polyamorous network was fading into a glossy memory (not that Forster had been sexually active or polyamory named as such in those years).

Thankfully, in 1930, five years after Ackerley had ushered him into gay social circles, Forster met the policeman Bob Buckingham, who would become the "greatest love" of his life.[21] Forster, Bob, and Bob's wife May—whom Bob met shortly later and whose relationship with Forster initially faltered—eventually settled into what polys call a V, with Bob at the tip. But this arrangement did not present itself to them clearly. The fifty-one-year-old novelist had taken the twenty-eight-year-old working-class man under his tutelage, shaping his reading list and initiating him into highbrow culture. In 1932, when Bob announced that May was pregnant and that they would marry, Forster was disconsolate and even thought of suicide. He mistrusted May and was not always kind to her. But he was determined that he would not break up a marriage—a possibility that confronted many gay men like him who had intimate relations with "special friends" who were married. And Bob—calm and sensible while Forster panicked—managed Forster's feelings, deferring their time together.

It worked. Not long later, Forster became a regular visitor at the Buckinghams' flat; Bob spent half days off and other weekday hours with him; and Forster was financially generous with their family. Bob visited West Hackhurst, where Forster lived with his mother Lily, who viewed the men's friendship suspiciously. Forster treasured his private time with Bob at his Brunswick Square residence, which was "a little like being married": Bob had a key, and in a letter Forster told a friend about meeting Bob on the street after Bob had "already got breakfast ready at the flat." Forster wrote in his Commonplace Book that he was "happy" and "would like to remind others that their turn can come too." May would later write of a "debt of gratitude" she owed the novelist for "widening of horizons, by meeting his friends, but mostly by his talk." The couple named their one child, Robin Morgan, after E[dward] M[organ] Forster and made him godfather.

But suffering and compassion were most responsible for tightening Forster and May's bond. In 1935, May contracted tuberculosis and spent a year recovering in a sanatorium. Meanwhile, Forster spent time with Bob and their son (which served his own needs) and sent May small gifts, frequently writing to her and insisting that the family should be alone together upon her discharge. May was so gracious that she even became friends with Forster's mother.

In the late 1960s it was Forster's turn to suffer physically: a series of strokes weakened him, and May often nursed him. She confided her grief to him over her son's 1962 death from Hodgkin's. Although he was an annoying patient—over-talkative and in her way—the Buckinghams' care was so great that, after Forster's final stroke, they removed him from King's College to their home. For most of the morning of his death, he held May's hand. She wrote that "over the years [Forster] changed us both and he and I came to love one another."

Their polyamorous arrangement, in other words, seemed to have resolved elegantly. Except ... Forster's strokes had loosened his tongue, and he spoke frankly to Bob about his physical passion for him. This shocked Bob, making him irritable and distant; May played peacemaker. But how could this have been shocking? They had slept together, according to Forster' biographer Wendy Moffat.[22] During their decades together—their travels abroad with Robin during May's sickness, the morning when Bob had breakfast ready at Brunswick Square—had Forster hidden the intensity of his passion from his "greatest love?" Had Bob been lying to himself about the nature of Forster's affection? Or was Bob terrified of having something mentioned in *or near* May's presence that she had probably long inferred? The Buckingham-Forster V fell short of the poly ideal of multiple partners all being transparent with one another and themselves about their needs and feelings. (Admittedly, this ideal is hard for any threesome to satisfy, even in an explicitly polyamorous, twenty-first-century context.)

Whatever its limitations, Forster's relationships with the Buckinghams largely vindicate Carpenterian and polyamorous aspirations. In 1910, when Forster was thirty-one, *Howards End* imagined two sisters raising a child in a vanishing rural paradise, with a once peremptory but now chastened older man relegated to the periphery. By the time Forster was in his fifties, real life had supplied, in many ways, a happier arrangement. Erotic opportunities and multiple residences were available to Forster and the Buckinghams: Bob and May maintained an amorous marriage, Forster occasionally had other lovers, and Robin was raised by two loving parents plus a godfather who cared for all three Buckinghams. (The Schlegel sisters might have envied such an ample network of love and support.)

Despite his erotic and emotional disappointments and the terror of living under Labouchere, Forster came closer than many sexually non-marginalized people to finding lasting romance and joyful erotic variety. But queer and polyamorous angles of analysis illuminate the laws and prejudices against which he struggled. They allow us to ask *What if?* What if young men like Meredith hadn't felt burdened by marriage expectations, especially if they didn't want children? What if, by the early twentieth century, same-sex romances had emerged from the shadows? What if Forster's mother had understood and accepted her son's sexuality? And more broadly, what if poly theorists—whether from within or outside Bloomsbury—had been explaining, since Queen Victoria's death, how the group's pursuit of intimacy could serve as a model to be emulated, critiqued, and refined?

Had Woolf lived longer and written her 1922 memoir "Old Bloomsbury" decades later with the benefit of poly hindsight, its account of post-1903 Bloomsbury might have differed. A polyamorous theory, systematically articulated, could have further elucidated her father's prejudices, plain though they were to her. It could have helped her explore options between the mixed-sex (largely gay) collective of youthful Bloomsbury and the more conventional (often matrimonial) arrangements of middle-aged Bloomsburians. Even though middle-aged group members never *achieved* an intimate utopia between the 1920s and 40s, nonetheless a poly theory in a 1990s version of "Old Bloomsbury" might have envisioned what they missed.

With two decades of hindsight, Woolf charitably reviewed her naivety at age twenty-one. She failed then to notice that she was so comfortable on Thursday night gatherings with many young men because they were gay! But this comfort dulled because it did not compel her to "show off" as she would for heterosexual men, which is one of life's "great delights" and "chief necessities."[23] Conversely, though, moving out of Bloomsbury's comforting proto-poly culture into more heteronormative and patriarchal settings provoked her discomfort and trenchant critiques. Neither kind of male company satisfied her: gay men were nonthreatening and elicited her intellectual honesty but were enervating; heterosexual company was exciting but reinforced the limitations and falsities of Victorian femininity. Woolf made aesthetic use of negative spaces: *Jacob's Room* evokes Jacob by his absence, and *The Waves* does so with the character Percival, a stand-in for her brother Thoby. With twenty-first-century hindsight, readers can see that "Old Bloomsbury" evokes poly possibilities—in their sexually egalitarian, uninhibited ideal form, which this chapter will discuss below—partly through their absence.

Notwithstanding the limitations of Bloomsbury and of marriage, each paradigm contrasted sharply, in Virginia's twenty-one-year-old mind, with her father Leslie Stephen's cloistered moralism. In remarking that there was "nothing that one could not say [or] do" at 46 Gordon Square, and in praising Bloomsbury's tolerance of sexual "variations," she sardonically recalls "the one word" that her father "thought fit to apply to a bugger or an adulterer; which was Blackguard!" Such "sentimental views of marriage" led to Virginia's secret feeling that it "was a very low down affair." When Vanessa remarked "I can see that we shall all marry. It's bound to happen," Virginia felt a "horrible necessity" threaten their "freedom and happiness."[24] Her father and his generation's sentimentality burned away in the cauldron of Bloomsbury's discussions, when Woolf realized that "there is nothing shocking in a man's having a mistress, or in a woman's being one."[25]

Constructing her father as an intellectual and moral foil, however, didn't resolve all of Woolf's quandaries. Reading Freud helped her to realize that her "violently disturbing conflict of love and hate" for her father was "a common feeling; and is called ambivalence."[26] Stephen's capacious library was instrumental in her intellectual blossoming. His earnest intellectual energy, the respect he earned from his peers, his progressive political ideas, his atheism, and the courage it took for him to embrace the latter, all earned her respect—and yet as a husband and father he was a more negative than positive example. Moving from his home into a room of her own—from dark, heavily upholstered Victorian residences into brightly painted interiors with siblings and friends—symbolized moving from one paradigm of intimacy into another.

But what did she and her cohort move *to*? Her sexless marriage indicates the limited erotic fulfillment she was able to find after "old Bloomsbury" largely disbanded. Did her erotic frustrations stem from her mental illness and/or her nervous personality in addition to the heteronormative order that she and Bloomsbury so incisively critiqued? Woolf has defenders and detractors; poignantly, the latter include her loved ones and, arguably, herself. Echoing his father Clive's attitude, Quentin Bell told Woolf's biographer Viviane Forrester that "From the perspective of sexual life, one cannot call her a complete woman. She was cold."[27] Leonard called his wife both "frigid" and "excitable," and Vita Sackville-West reinforced this diagnosis, telling her husband that she was "scared" of arousing Woolf's erotic passion because of her madness. Forrester reads against the grain of these cruel assessments, seeing Woolf as unfairly maligned and the positive reputations of her father, sister, and husband as dubious. She describes Woolf as "forever permeable to the world, which was a living organism for her, entirely erotic," and she accuses Leonard of starting the "legend"—believed by Virginia—according to which she was not only frigid but "would be mad" save for his "vigilance." Forrester explains that Leonard consulted doctors, sometimes without Virginia, and concluded that having children would be dangerous for her mental health, although she wanted them and although her psychiatrist thought motherhood would benefit her.

Against this biographical background, moments in *Mrs Dalloway* that allude to the protagonist's ostensible sexual failures assume new dimensions. Clarissa remembers, "through some contraction of this cold spirit, [having] failed [Richard] … again and again," and Peter Walsh calls her "cold, heartless, a prude."[28] At the risk of a biographical fallacy, it is tempting to infer self-criticisms—sadder the more unjust they are—in these characters' judgments of Clarissa's capacity for erotic joy.

However closely one thinks that *Mrs Dalloway* hews to its author's psychosexual travails, in tandem Woolf's life and art testify to the complex challenges of transvaluing Victorian habits of mind. The liberated sex *talk* documented in her memoirs did not guarantee a liberated and happy sex *life*. What paradigms of intimacy did Bloomsbury craft—or grope toward? Something, perhaps, that peered beyond the years of *l'entre deux guerres*, toward the sexual revolutions of the '60s and '70s, and into the polyamorous experiments of the 90s and later? Disappointments were inevitable as their partly inchoate aspirations confronted intransigent laws and customs, just as joys were theirs to craft on new terms. A century after Woolf read "Old Bloomsbury" to the group's Memoir Club, Bloomsbury has left to its cultural descendants, operating in a freer sexual climate, the task of clarifying what can be learned from its balance of transgressions and accommodations.

* * *

In addition to the rare acknowledgments of Bloomsbury as a precursor in poly historiography, there is surprisingly little invocation of the group in poly-themed creative writing. This diverse literary field is proliferating: poly novels in realistic, sci-fi,[29] and other genres explore interracial poly families, the relation between poly subcultures and the larger (nominally) monogamous culture, and other topics that combine the excitement of being up to the moment with insights into the historical dimensions of intimacy. Bloomsbury's afterlives and poly culture's coming lives seem likely to intersect, in both theoretical and creative work. So what *is* polyamory—at least for the time being, pending possible evolutionary shifts?

Modernism in Relationship Forms

A multivalent social formation, polyamory is at once a lifestyle (both countercultural and not,[30] like Bloomsbury) and an inspiration for critiques of several enduring systems—heteronormativity, mononormativity, and amatonormativity—discussed below. The *Oxford English Dictionary* dates the first usage of the term "polyamory," from the Latin roots for "loving many," to 1992. Elisabeth Sheff defines it as "consensual and emotionally intimate nonmonogamous relationships in which both women and men can negotiate to have multiple partners."[31] Literary historians might think of it as a form of relationship modernism, given its anti-essentialism (it doubts the naturalness of traditional sex roles) and its formal explorations (its intimate configurations may or may not find analogues in aesthetic styles). Inspired by free-love, feminist, and LGBTQ movements,[32] it encourages men and women to combat stigmas and go "off script," having disengaged from "auto-pilot" by recognizing the constrictive norms of intimacy and sexuality that they have internalized.[33] Sheff says that, once someone has seriously considered polyamory, she cannot unthink it. Everyone has the capacity to be polyamorous, whereas not everyone has the capacity to be gay. Polyamory celebrates sex positivity in an egalitarian atmosphere and seeks utopian possibilities for erotic intimacy and love. Women disproportionally occupy leadership roles within poly communities and among scholars who study them.[34]

The pervasiveness of polyamory is difficult to measure.[35] Self-conscious practitioners date to the 1970s, two decades before the term was invented. Initially it emerged in urban centers in North America, Western Europe, and Australia. Its mostly white, middle- and upper-class champions were emboldened by social privilege to love as they want to and come out of the closet whenever possible. Many of these demographic markers recall Bloomsbury. (Gay men, it can be added, had long been doing something like polyamory—and continue to. Gay and poly circles don't always overlap; gay men are rare in poly communities, while straight men and bisexual women are common.[36]) More recently, poly life has emerged in non-urban centers, thanks largely to the internet, and grown more diverse, with polyamorists of color both reaching out to white poly communities and developing separate groups.[37]

As understood by its apologists, polyamory has a long history,[38] though articulate celebrity practitioners like Bloomsbury supply only a fragmentary record of people who have sought non-scripted forms of love. Advocates make strong claims for polyamory's popularity, and, in a nod toward sexual essentialism, its naturalness. People are "horny creatures," assert Janet Hardy and Dossie Easton, who see the nuclear family as a relic of the twentieth-century middle class and perhaps merely a temporary obstacle to a reconfiguration of erotic life.[39]

Since the mid-nineteenth century, European and North American subcultures have organized sexual life in numerous iconoclastic ways. There have been religiously inspired polygamous settlements, free-love communities predicated on racial equality, many poly collectives that seek alternatives to market capitalism (in keeping with Carpenter's values), and others with capitalistic priorities, for whom free love and free markets dovetail. Numerous as such precedents are, however, they have been short-lived and attracted limited memberships.[40]

Lovers in urban poly hubs of the last half century have assumed various "poly geometries." *Poly singles* and *open couples* are self-explanatory categories in the wake of the swinging '70s. *Vees*, as the metaphor suggests, include one member—like Bob Buckingham—who is sexually intimate with the other two, who don't have sex with one another. (This label doesn't perfectly fit Virginia, Leonard, and Vita, given the Woolfs' sexless marriage. Likewise, it doesn't quite fit Vanessa, Clive, and Duncan. Because Vanessa's erotic intimacies with these men probably did not overlap—her sex life with Clive ended around 1911[41]—Vanessa could be seen as a serial monogamist, not the point of a V.) In poly *triads*, all three members share sexual pleasure. Poly *quads* are often less stable than vees: when two couples blend sexual affections (and perhaps households or finances), they often lose one member to "poly-style divorce." *Moresomes* expand poly geometries further, involving sex among various non-cohabiting group members who usually don't consider themselves "families." *Intimate networks* are longer and more loosely connected than moresomes. Alfred Kinsey and his research team not only earned polyamorists' gratitude for their studies of human sexuality, but had sex with one another, and can be termed an "intimate network," "polycule," or "constellation," which are all roughly synonymous.[42]

In all their geometric arrangements, polys believe that no one should "own" another's sexual or emotional affection. Some polys strive to avoid all hierarchies of attachment, while others clarify different levels of commitment, from *primary* attachments (marked by long-term togetherness, blended households and finances, and perhaps children), to *secondary* ones (in which families make major decisions separately, in consultation), to *tertiary* ones (the definitions of which vary case by case).[43]

Durability and Polyaffectivity

On the one hand, like Lytton Strachey and other Bloomsburians, polys of the last half century have irreverent, hedonistic, and anti-establishment streaks. "Sex is nice and pleasure is good for you," counsel Hardy and Easton. Rather than adopting a "starvation economy" mindset, they think of love on a loaves-and-fishes model, where one partner's gain does not imply another's loss. Skeptical of stigmas across sexual and emotional spectra, Hardy and Easton proudly label themselves "ethical sluts" and suggest that so-called "sex addiction" and "intimacy avoidance" are "exploratory behaviors" that get unjustly pathologized.[44] The concept of "polysexuality" incorporates a range of proclivities and practices, including "outercourse," which—in keeping with polyamory's anti-essentialist strains—does not involve penile penetration. Notwithstanding such anti-essentialism, for some marginalized people, the term "polyamory" has had a revelatory, identity-forming effect.[45]

On the other hand, also like their Bloomsburian forebears, recent polyamorists are conscientious ethicists. Although they disdain *some* social rules and sex roles, they police themselves according to their own guidelines, and they prize honesty: if a member of an outside couple expresses interest in polyamory, no subterfuge is allowed toward his or her partner. With their children, poly parents share truths about human sexuality as they see it, and about social prejudice, when the children's maturity level allows. Given their commitment to sexual equality, poly men retain childrearing duties even after sexual attachment to the mother ends; in shouldering "women's work," they make it more visible and redefine masculinity.

In service of honesty and equality, polys (far from being free-wheeling lovers) constantly rearticulate their needs and renegotiate boundaries. Ever aware of the danger of jealousy and sexual possessiveness, they have developed terms for one's lover's lover (a "metamour") and for the pleasure one can take in a lover's pleasure with a third party ("compersion").[46]

Finally, amid these reconceptualizations of loyalty, poly families retain a cardinal virtue of what Freud called the "middle-class social order": they put kids first.[47] They redraw adult boundaries with children's needs foremost in mind—an ethic not explicitly articulated by Bloomsburians, many of whom, admittedly, were childless. Poly children—whose households often have more than two parents—complain of crowding and surveillance but not neglect.[48]

Many researchers see the poly ethos, forged amid the challenge of social marginalization, as a source of durability for poly groups and an example for others.[49] Poly families' logistical and emotional challenges and their habit of self-examination help them to cultivate interpersonal skills that can be instructive for serial monogamists (whose attachments with former lovers might persist), monogamous families who divorce, and families with multiple parents.⁵⁰ Poly experimentalists, in other words, see the social acceptance of their loves—limited though it is—as a sign that *things are getting better*, and that progress is unfolding in the intimate sphere.

In keeping with this sense of enlightenment about sex and love, polys redefine what count as "successful" relationships (that question of such interest to Sally and Peter, concerning the Dalloways⁵¹) and do not value staying together for its own sake. Instead, they value amicable group relations, co-parenting, and meeting people's sexual and emotional needs for specific periods of time. Thus, even as geometries shift, many poly networks maintain bonds over decades—the very durability that Bloomsbury's admirers often remark upon.

The concept of "polyaffectivity" both embraces and exceeds those of "poly identity" (with its focus on the individual subject) and "polysexuality," even in the form of outercourse. Sheff defines polyaffectivity as "emotionally intimate poly relationships that are nonsexual." It can apply both to polys who see one another as family members but were never sexually attached, and to people who remain strongly attached, in nonsexual ways, to former lovers. As past lovers learn *not* to see sex as a hallmark of attachment, they become more grateful for their bonds with their chosen family.⁵² As mentioned, conversation was at least as important for Bloomsburians as sex—and polys repeatedly relearn this lesson, for example in friendships with past lovers. In an epoch marked by rising loneliness, such bonds can provide the life satisfaction and psychological resilience that many adults lack.

Poly experiments of the last fifty years reprise many Bloomsburian themes. Sometimes they do so with variations: in a more open social atmosphere, poly families strive to be more transparent with their children than Vanessa, Clive, and Duncan were with Angelica about her parentage.⁵³ Other times, polyamorists reprise Bloomsburian themes obliquely: some confess to "poly fatigue." Weary of "drama"—always morphing interpersonal boundaries and the mandate to communicate feelings—some people exit poly life for the comforts of monogamy.⁵⁴ *Women in Love*'s Ursula expresses fatigue with Birkin's ongoing rejection of the idea of "love" and his desire for another intimate partner. Clarissa Dalloway's choice of a spouse suggests that she may have felt fatigued by loving Sally *or* Peter (let alone both of them), especially given her tenuous mental health. Speaking biographically, Virginia's long and (as I see it) satisfying marriage to Leonard—which the sex-advice columnist Dan Savage might call "monogamish,"⁵⁵ given its open borders—indicates that she found at least as much value in a dependable partner as in the excitement of an additional amour.

Requeering Bloomsbury

The editors of the 2016 volume *Queer Bloomsbury* remark that the two words in their title are redundant, that there could not be an "unqueer" Bloomsbury.⁵⁶ But this might not be entirely true. Given the durability of the monogamy code and the threat that polyamory poses to it, poly concepts provide chances to requeer the group. Regina Marler, one of *Queer Bloomsbury*'s contributors, discusses how the group's life practices anticipated, even if they did not directly influence, subsequent sexual counterscultures. Her essay "The Bloomsbury Love Triangle" describes the group's unconventional loves as part of its "modernist project" and its triangles as the "adaptations" of a "family of choice" that accommodated both "attachment and new desire."[57] Admittedly, the group's relationships could be stormy and Bloomsburians could be jealous on the corporate level, as illustrated by Vanessa's judgmental attitude toward Lydia Lopokova, whom Keynes married, although Vanessa encouraged him merely to keep her as a mistress, denying her full group membership.[58] Bloomsburians were also jealous in individual cases: Virginia's flirtation with Clive, shortly into Clive's marriage to her sister, likely both stemmed from Virginia's jealousy and provoked Vanessa's.

While acknowledging such tensions and rivalries, however, Marler admires Bloomsburians' ability to maintain bonds. Echoing polyamory's defenders, she says that, while Bloomsbury's triangles sometimes caused "exquisite pain," other times they improved, rather than threatening, existing two-person intimacies.[59] Also in keeping with poly scholarship, Marler catalogs the models of intimacy forged by Bloomsburians and their associates. Open marriages, such as Vita and Harold's, Ottoline and Philip Morrell's, and James and Alix Strachey's, are easy enough to recognize. Serial monogamists such as Roger Fry are also familiar types, even to those unfamiliar with polyamory.[60] Marler says that her titular "triangles" are harder to define, and she suggests a wide range of possible examples. In a unisexual rivalry that never quite formed a triangle, Keynes and Lytton Strachey competed at Cambridge for the affection of Arthur Hobhouse. Ralph Partridge shared a household with Dora Carrington and Lytton Strachey, but then fell in love with Frances Marshall, who came to live part-time at Ham Spray.[61] Marler marshals these and other examples to defend Bloomsbury's preference for honesty above fidelity (as traditionally conceived) and for friendship and intimacy over "forms and tradition."[62]

Theoretical Implications: Heteronormativity, Mononormativity, Amatonormativity

Bloomsburians and other modernists challenged norms, taboos, and stigmas against sexual nonconformists for several related reasons. Stigmas against consensual adult love punish victimless behaviors. Restrictive norms block sources of pleasure and happiness not only for people who would like to pursue them, but also for people who have so thoroughly internalized the norms that they never consider alternatives. Finally, norms—even those as pervasive as monogamy and romantic love—are rooted in particular social and cultural traditions, meaning that alternatives exist. Being intellectually deprogrammed from the assumption that heteronormativity, mononormativity, or even amatonormativity is inevitable, "natural," or god-given can be intoxicating, regardless of where it leads one's sex life. Bloomsbury's novels, essays, and life-experiments supplied momentum for the abovementioned critiques of norms, taboos, and stigmas, and polyamory has carried these critiques in new directions.

Bloomsbury's Ambivalent Challenges to Compulsory Coupledom

Often, Bloomsbury's critiques of Victorian ideas about gender and marriage were richer because they were self-divided. *A Room of One's Own*, for example, sounds liberated and modern when it extols androgyny, speculating that neither a "purely masculine" nor a "purely feminine" mind is creative. But as Brenda Helt notes, prior to this passage, Woolf watches a couple enter a taxi and contemplates "a profound, if irrational, instinct in favor of the theory that the union of man and woman makes for the greatest satisfaction."[63] Given its heteronormative cast, readers might infer scare quotes around the word "instinct," as though it were a shibboleth to which Woolf succumbed only momentarily. But in totality, the taxi-cab passage pushes back against the notion of an androgynous mind, honoring Woolf's "instinct" with the adjective "profound."

On a theoretical level, *A Room of One's Own* does not reject sexual dimorphism as a fact of nature or a basis for intimacy. On a more practical level, it does not reject what Adrienne Rich termed "compulsory heterosexuality," nor the related dynamic of "compulsory monogamy,"[64] although it critiques each of these things. In 1983, Rich argued that compulsory heterosexuality assures men physical, economic, and emotional access to women. In 2016, Mimi Schippers noted the de jure and de facto existence of compulsory monogamy. In juridical terms, laws against polygamy can make coupling virtually mandatory when singlehood is uncommon, and they impact such things as child custody, insurance, and hospital visitation rights. In social terms, Schippers argues, the common association of monogamy with "serious" relationships, psychological health, and maturity stigmatizes other forms of love and sexual attachment. Prejudices that associate polyamorous people with promiscuity lead to their rejections by monogamous friends and even their own families.[65] Schippers de-emphasizes the themes of male dominance and female subjection that Rich stresses. But she reiterates that the "discursive conflation" of the *pure relationship* with monogamy is legally and socially harmful.[66]

Like *A Room of One's Own*, *Women in Love* also—in ambivalent ways—anticipates Schippers's perspective on monogamous coupledom. Despite its searching examination of Birkin and Gerald's bisexual affection, and although the men's erotic interest in one another lends some trappings of a poly *quad* to the intimacy among the four main characters, the novel does not speak the name of a polyamorous intimacy for which its concluding pages almost call. When Ursula tells Birkin that the "other" (man-man) kind of love that he wants is "false, impossible," she reinforces the "discursive conflation" that Schippers decries between a "pure" relationship and two-person mixed-sex eros. Admittedly, Ursula's perspective at the end of *Women in Love* represents only one moment in Lawrence's explorations of nonstandard forms of love. From *The Rainbow*, a sort of prequel to *Women in Love*, to the latter novel's canceled Prologue, which defends bisexual desire, to its final draft, which concludes with Birkin and Ursula's argument unresolved, Lawrence dramatizes how many questions about human sexuality remain intractable. But even he tends to think within the paradigm of the couple. Neither *Women in Love* nor Ursula entertains the idea that she, Birkin, and Gerald might have formed a V, had Gerald lived.

Woolf and Lawrence are not the only members, critics, and/or legatees of Bloomsbury whose ambivalent critiques of compulsory mixed-sex coupledom illuminate the challenges of transvaluing this multifaceted norm. Like *Women in Love*, *Howards End* and its homage, *On Beauty*, also illustrate how ingrained the monogamy norm is, even as they critique heteronormativity. *Howards End* excoriates sexual double standards, male privilege and hypocrisy, and even slut shaming. Little if any authorial distance separates Forster from his protagonist, Margaret, when she condemns Henry for canting with his deceased wife's memory in refusing Helen one night's stay at his unoccupied Howards End property.[67] Helen has had an affair with a married man (Leonard), who impregnated her; Henry had an affair while married to Ruth. His mistress, Jacky, is in tow with Helen, denying Henry the luxury of running—literally or metaphorically—from his infidelity. Forster puts his thumb in the pan, illustrating that it would be wrong for society to banish Helen (and her faultless child) for her sexual transgression, if it should even be seen as a transgression. Henry's affair with Jacky was unseemly; their class difference and her indigence give it a whiff of exploitation. His denial of any parallels between his case and Helen's—more than merely indicting him—indicts an entire class of Victorian and Edwardian husbands who thoughtlessly exploited a double standard. Henry's rhetorical invocation of Ruth illustrates the fatuousness of the Victorian sexual regime, populated by supposed virgins and whores, in which a housewife should be angelically pure but her spouse will be understood to enjoy dalliances.

Forster is a formidable ethicist. Margaret's exposure of Henry's hypocrisy helps to convey a multifaceted moral vision in narrative form that "Old Bloomsbury" articulates in germinal form. Whereas Woolf's memoir scoffs at her father for thinking of adulterers as "blackguards," *Howards End* punishes the Wilcox men more severely, after Charles inadvertently kills Leonard over a "sentimental" idea—as Woolf's memoir terms it—of sexual honor. The conclusion of the novel, wherein Henry is enfeebled, his son is imprisoned, the Schlegel sisters inherit Howards End, and Helen's son stands heir to its idyllic expanse, rounds out Forster's vision with just desserts. Leonard, who impregnated a woman out of wedlock, becomes something of a martyr in death, and his killer proves himself a blackguard.

But what's missing from the vision; what are the philosophical limits of Margaret's indignation and the plot's mechanics? From a polyamorous and sex-positive perspective, it would be wrong for Henry to deny acceptance and support to Helen and her child—Forster is forward-thinking in this regard. But how thoroughly should Ruth, to the degree that she is valorized, be associated with angelic domesticity and intellectual incuriosity? And is it shameful that a husband of many years, with several grown children, once had a brief extramarital affair? That the affair was secretive—i.e., dishonest—*is* shameful. But the shame is collective. It belongs to a society convinced that spouses are one another's lifelong sexual property (or perhaps that the wife *is* her husband's possession, whereas he must merely *appear* to be hers). This idea establishes society as a sexual policeman—not that polys oppose policing any sexual norms, but they see the ideal of lifelong monogamy as cruel to both sexes.

Had a sex-positive polyamorist written *Howards End*, it could have differed in multiple ways. Henry's affair with Jacky might have been coded as natural and pleasurable to each lover, perhaps even offering Ruth an opportunity for "compersion." A polyamorous *Howards End* might peep into Ruth's extramarital love life or explore whether she desires one. In service of *putting kids first*, it could give more attention to Helen's son—and the obligations owed him by Helen, Margaret, and even Henry. But Bloomsbury was not a twenty-first-century collective. Its most celebrated writings are not always as radical as their authors' most daring thoughts, or possible thoughts. Hence their successor texts have opportunities to extend and revise their insights.

On Beauty follows *Howards End* in critiquing male sexual privilege, both in its protagonist's traits and in the cultural dynamics that form him. Also like *Howards End*, it assumes that infidelity and dishonesty are immoral, but not that a cultural norm enjoining lifelong sexual exclusivity is problematic. Married for three decades, Howard Belsey is hiding a recent affair with his colleague, Claire, when the novel opens. His wife, Kiki, knows he has strayed, and the knowledge poisons their marriage. But she doesn't yet know the mistress's identity; when she discovers this, the marriage effectively ends. The message that Howard is morally wanting (but not irredeemable) is reinforced in numerous ways, most forcefully by his additional affair with the much younger Victoria Kipps. Readers also learn that Howard was so jealous of Kiki's male friends or lovers *before* they met—thirty years ago—that he had "bullied, threatened, and frozen" them out of their lives.[68] If *Howards End*'s Henry Wilcox is guilty of a sexual double standard, then *On Beauty*'s Howard Belsey is a more glaring hypocrite: a paranoid and controlling husband who compulsively succumbs to sexual temptation. He doesn't even get much enjoyment from his furtive affair with Claire, nor from sex with Victoria (he climaxes too quickly).

Smith, like Forster, is a compelling moralist. With its complex depiction of Howard's interrelated moral shortcomings, *On Beauty* offers a rich study in *character*, as that term applies to realist and modernist masters from Austen to Forster. But from a poly point of view, *On Beauty* doesn't probe social norms as deeply as it might. Should readers fault Kiki for being as jealous of Howard's extramarital sex life as he is of her premarital sex life? Smith doesn't explore her chance to examine—and perhaps critique—the spouses' jealousies in tandem. Neither the narrator nor Kiki questions the necessity of monogamy. Why not? In a heart-to-heart talk with Carlene, Kiki confesses to having been intrigued with lesbianism as a young woman. Rich's 1983 essay on "compulsory heterosexuality" pursues a critical inquiry that Kiki might have entertained, and poly philosophy indicates how it could be extended. Wondering, first, what became of her same-sex erotic curiosity, Kiki might next question the general value of monogamy and wonder whether she and Howard have both made—or in his case tried and failed to make—unnecessary sacrifices for their marriage. But neither she nor *On Beauty* muses that the Belseys' long-standing union—with its three lovely offspring—might have allowed Kiki to explore her lesbian curiosities and Howard to enjoy sex with a friendly colleague, without moral opprobrium or emotional collapse. Mononormativity is a baseline assumption of Smith's novel, as it is of Forster's, despite each work's wide-ranging skepticism.

The aforementioned works by Woolf, Lawrence, Forster, and Smith do not exhaust the writings by Bloomsbury and its legatees that both critique and reproduce received wisdom about sex, gender, and intimacy. As stressed previously, these texts frequently draw philosophical and aesthetic strength from a combination of self-awareness (an ability to recognize their prejudices and assumptions *as* assumptions) and moral ambivalence (a sense that hypocrisies should be exposed and inherited values transvalued—carefully and selectively).

In their ambivalence, these Bloomsburian texts dramatize the theoretical challenges and dilemmas that Wiegman and Wilson outline so ably. Decrying "antinormativity's queer conventions," Wiegman and Wilson warn against the temptation to see norms as immutable and narrowly defined—and thus to imagine "antinormativity" as something pure and self-evident. These twenty-first-century theorists remind readers not reflexively to praise Bloomsburian fiction every time it transgresses a norm, nor castigate it every time it reproduces one. They remind readers (though Bloomsbury is not their topic) that this group of insider/outsider modernists sometimes *inhabited* norms—marriage in Virginia Woolf and Clarissa Dalloway's cases, friendship in Forsterian texts including *Passage* and "What I Believe," love in Birkin's case, with some coaching from Ursula—for the best reasons. By straddling a norm, Bloomsburians could imagine new boundaries. Admittedly, though, their vision only leapt so far.

A century after the 1920 ratification of the 19th Amendment guaranteed American women suffrage, and a half century after the 1969 Stonewall riots, it is easy for readers of Bloomsbury and its legatees to celebrate their critiques of sexism and heterosexism. But polyamory presents more complex moral challenges. How many of Bloomsbury's readers would *want* to celebrate its poly ethos rather than its feminism, queer politics, and pacifism? Heteronormativity strikes many today as unfair, but mononormativity does not.[69] Yet in some ways, even mononormativity might not provide the best benchmark for measuring Bloomsbury's efforts to rethink intimacy in history. It is one thing for a Bloomsburian (or other) text to ask what forms love can take: same-sex or mixed-sex, monogamous or open, sexual or platonic, etc. It is another thing to ask—as *Women in Love* arguably does—whether *any form* of the love ideal promotes happiness, or whether all of its forms constrain affection and freedom.

Amatonormativity, or Compulsory Love: Bloomsburian Ambivalence and the Polyamorous Challenge

In 2012 the philosopher Elizabeth Brake coined the term "amatonormative" from the Latin *amare* (to love) and *norma* (a standard). She defines it as "the assumption that a central, exclusive, amorous relationship is normal for humans … a universally shared good [that] *should* be aimed at in preference to other relationship types."[70] In Brake's view, while marriage and mixed-sex love might no longer be compulsory, pair-bonded love—in its broadest sense—still is. "Singlism" stigmatizes unpartnered people such as quirkyalones and asexuals.[71] The unpartnered male is seen as an unkempt man-child; the unpartnered woman calls to mind the eccentric cat lady, a redux of the Victorian spinster. Amatonormativity also, says Brake, stigmatizes nontraditional relationships such as urban tribes, polyamory, and care networks. Given the breadth of amatonormative discrimination, people are pressured into presenting themselves as romantic partners, whether or not they prefer this label—for the sake of social acceptance and legal rights such as partner benefits.

Brake has two criteria for relationships that society should value. First, they should be *just*, an abstract concept drawn from the liberal tradition, which is often not satisfied in pairings (such as abusive ones) that outwardly conform to amatonormative conventions. Second, relationships should be *caring*, a concrete criterion the shape of which changes case by case. Our amatonormative system puts the cart before the horse, sanctioning many harmful or unsatisfying relationships, and either failing to recognize nonstandard ones that flourish, or preventing their flourishing in the first place. Both sexes are burdened by this system, women especially.

Perhaps it is not surprising, though, that mononormativity, and by extension amatonormativity, is being questioned. As Brake mentions, by 2005 over half of US and Canadian women were living without a spouse, and by 2010 married couples were no longer a majority in the United States.[72] (The same was true by then for married couples in England and Wales. See Appendix A, Table 2.) Of course, some commentators decry these trends, associating them with the loneliness epidemic.[73] They lament the *fraying* of amatonormativity, not the social constraints it entails. Proponents of marriage and long-term mixed-sex pair bonding seek support from biologically inflected arguments that people, especially women, are "naturally" suited to monogamy.[74]

But other thinkers echo Brake's criticisms of the romantic ideal for numerous reasons, including the association of femininity with low sex drive. Savage warns against the myth of "the one": the dream, still precious to many men and women, of a lifelong sexual partner and friend who will satisfy all of one's needs, and for whom one will do the same. Polys contend that this expectation sets up couples for disappointment: each partner resents the other for failing to be "the one" and blames themself for failing to live up to this untenable standard.

Amatonormative values, according to their critics, harm both sexes in some ways that are not gender-specific. But they also prolong an ideal of female sexuality that should by now be defunct. Questioning the association of women with monogamous virtue, Savage cites decades-old and more recent data on men's and women's self-reported infidelities. Older data had men reporting higher rates of infidelity, while recent data on subjects under the age of forty has the sexes in parity.[75] This suggests, says Savage, that the earlier discrepancy stemmed not from innate sexual difference but from power. As women have become more financially independent and freer to own their sexuality, they have reported higher rates to questioners, dispelling the myth that they are sexually "virtuous."

Jenkins draws similar conclusions from the discrepant data of other older and newer studies into women's sexual desires. In debunking the idea of asexual femininity, she and Savage cite the large number of sexless marriages and the fact that men's desire for their longtime female partner often tapers (or remains robust) while women's complementary desire often plummets. Rather than inferring that aging women lack libido, Jenkins and Savage suspect that women are not naturally monogamous. Cases of middle-aged women's sex drive rejuvenating after a break-up with their longtime partner bolster this inference about female sexuality and reinforce Savage's mistrust of the idea of "the one."[76]

Like Savage and Jenkins, polys including Hardy and Easton remain alert to vestigial expressions of philogyny[77]—the patronizing association of women with virtue. Even as redoubtable a scholar as Giddens might perpetuate philogyny. As discussed in Chapter 1, Giddens claims that women, from within Victorian domestic cages, articulated non-competitive values that improve men morally. Hardy and Easton laugh at the notion that "men are gas pedals and women are brakes," and Jenkins argues that romantic love, not women, stifles men's *and* women's sexual and emotional experience.[78]

What retrospective light is shed on Bloomsbury by contemporary critiques of amatonormativity, mononormativity, and the idea of women as "brakes?" Woolf could be a radical critic of Victorian sentimentality and gender roles: witness her discussion of the "Angel of the House." She could also take measured diagnoses of how gender roles impact individual women, such as Clarissa Dalloway and *To the Lighthouse*'s Mrs. Ramsay, each of whom recalls admirable aspects of Woolf's very Victorian mother. But coiled within these diagnoses lies Woolf's indignation at the limitations of heteronormative womanhood into which her mother's generation—not to mention her own—was born. Chapter 2 limns this indignation in *Arlington Park*, which amplifies *Mrs Dalloway*'s protest, not just against the gender hierarchy, but against the kind of "love" this hierarchy molds.

Rereading *Mrs Dalloway* with Cusk's novel in mind clarifies anger's role in the novel, along with feelings from joy to grief, fatigue, and suicidal ideation. Love itself—not men or chauvinism—occasions Clarissa's anger when she thinks "Love and religion, how detestable they are!"[79] Her diction notwithstanding, Clarissa is not hostile to love per se. Her passionate youthful feelings for Sally were a kind of love that she still treasures three decades later and that neurochemistry sometimes associates with dopamine. Her mellower but equally profound attachment to Richard is also a form of love—associated with oxytocin.[80] The bulk of *Mrs Dalloway* does not suggest that she finds either emotional state "detestable." But what about a social order that bars her from enjoying long-term intimacy with Sally, that subsumes her in a corporate "Dalloway" identity, and that sharply distinguishes Richard's public from her domestic achievements? A woman, like Clarissa, born circa 1871 would be born into this idea of "love," and she might, by 1923, come to find it detestable, even if she lacks her author's theoretical acumen. Across Woolf's oeuvre, her critique of femininity—a historically specific version—broadens into a critique of amatonormativity. Her awareness of gender roles as constructed—and constricting—led her to critique love as well, as much as she appreciated her loving marriage.

An entire book could explore where Bloomsburian texts do or do not challenge love norms. Might a literary critic employing Brake's concepts see *Passage*'s Fielding as a "quirkyalone" or "asexual" whose happiness and integrity are threatened by the amatonormative system, including the marriage industry? Far from being a man-child, the Fielding who "traveled light"[81] was courageously independent, impervious to his countrymen's bullying, an exemplar of Forster's liberal-internationalist and humanist values. But what about Peter Walsh? Is he a man-child, unable, in middle age, to settle down with an unmarried woman? In other words, does *Mrs Dalloway* employ Peter as a negative model, to reinforce an amatonormative idea of virtue, according to which

Richard Dalloway exemplifies what a mature man—even one with his intellectual limitations—should be?

Bloomsburians, their associates, and their legatees have asked productive questions about intimacy in history and expanded the possibilities for what love *could be*, to invoke Jenkins's title (*What Love Is: And What It Could Be*). But amatonormativity illuminates how boundary-pushers can also be boundary-enforcers. As Jenkins catalogs, writers from antiquity (Ovid) through the Renaissance (Shakespeare, Burton) and beyond have associated love with sickness or insanity and advised lovers on how to cure themselves of this condition.[82] Yet the allure of love remains. Bertrand Russell, one of Jenkins's lodestars, claims—to her dismay—that people who have not shared sexual love "cannot attain their full stature" nor feel "generous warmth," and are inclined to "envy, oppression, and cruelty."[83] (Clive and Quentin Bell harbored similar suspicions concerning Virginia's "coldness.") As discussed in Chapter 5, *The Satanic Verses* combines the *love as sickness* trope with the idea that love is essential to a full human experience. Rushdie's novel reiterates that one cannot grow into an adult man or woman without being—and suffering as—a lover.

Jenkins, Hardy and Easton, and other poly thinkers survey these pervasive ideas— the amatonormative equation of full humanity with sexual love; the romantic love ideal, with its male and female prototypes; and the mononormative mandate—and wonder how many people they harm, as well as how many successful intimacies they fail to embrace. The problem, it seems, with the critical and exploratory attitude toward love developed by Bloomsburians and other modernists, and extended by polys, is that it has no stopping point. What's left of love if people view *any* version of it (not just today's) as a kind of cage? In fact, this problem predates modernism. Social conservatives of Wollstonecraft's time were right to fear the combination of love and freedom, to sense that it threatened social and familial cohesion. Perhaps their fears are vindicated by the critic Ashley Shelden's claims in 2017 that "love has failed" and that contemporary novelists are laudable for saying so.[84] Could Wollstonecraft's peers have foreseen that twenty-first-century freedom-seekers would coin the term "amatonormative," declaring love *not liberating enough*? Could Giddens have foreseen in 1992 that the "pure relationship," with its democratic valuation of individual dignity, would bend away from coupledom in *two* directions—both toward singlehood and toward romantic groupings of three or more?

Jenkins sees the polyamorous challenge to mononormativity as one in a series of generational paradigm shifts that have dismantled hierarchies. The US Supreme Court's 1967 "Loving v. Virginia" decision helped destigmatize interracial love, and its 2015 "Obergefell v. Hodges" decision helped destigmatize same-sex love. On the one hand, Jenkins is an optimist: she says that, as racial and sexual hierarchies have partially dissolved, so too can hierarchies of love. But on the other hand, she is a realist. The "lifelong" and "heterosexual" components of *lifelong heterosexual monogamy* are now negotiable, she acknowledges, but not *monogamy*. People can marry and divorce multiple times, or pursue unmarried serial monogamy, without incurring disdain. Divorcees are not socially ostracized, nor—in much of society—are gays and lesbians. But still today, polyamory inspires disgust and hatred, as Jenkins documents by sharing a vitriolic hate mail she received.[85]

Although Jenkins values personal autonomy as Woolf did, the polyamorous critique of amatonormativity is not a defense of solitude or of the "negativity" associated by Shelden with the modernist traditions she admires. It does not devalue sexual or emotional attachment any more than Clarissa's outburst against "love and religion" indicts *all imaginable* forms of love. But Woolf and Jenkins understand the destabilizing potential in their critiques. Woolf's celebration of Old Bloomsbury's "sexual variations" is echoed in Jenkins's assertion that "there is no single model of what women (or men) want."[86] In Bloomsbury's time, this appreciation of human variety and the burdens of compulsory marriage led Russell to advocate for "trial marriage."[87] In 2016, in a similar vein, Daniel Nolan advocated for the legal recognition of temporary marriage, pointing out that such arrangements are allowed in some cultural traditions.[88]

It is debatable to what degree Bloomsburian artistry in its time, and poly theory today, have destabilized heteroromantic and monogamous ideals. Arguably, changes in life-practices come first, and experimental storytelling and avant-garde theorizing come next, rationalizing them. Alternatively, artists and intellectuals can be seen as catalysts without whom new forms of consciousness and life would never emerge.

But terms like "destabilization" are loaded. I might instead ask whether Bloomsbury and its poly legatees have *created* and *modeled* new forms of psychosexual attachment, or given language to a wave of progress and liberation saturating the private and public spheres. Numerous thinkers about love today are historical optimists, however qualified their enthusiasm. As mentioned in Chapter 1, Eli Finkel anticipates "the most successful period of marital well-being that the world has ever seen,"[89] though he suspects that this utopia is available mostly to the socioeconomically advantaged. Jenkins "believes that we can, collectively, effect unimaginable changes to romantic love's social role," though she does not expect a "total replacement" of all the "characteristic features" of love as we know it.[90] Neither of these thinkers argues for a benign "arc" to the "universe" of people's sexual and platonic affections. But their accounts of where love has come from and where it is going hover between a *petit* and a *grand récit* and ring with hope.

Implications for Literary Form and Bloomsburian Legacies

What does this mean about Bloomsbury's relation to modernism? Modernist storytellers modeled post-Victorian narrative epistemologies, as modernist lovers (including Bloomsbury) modeled new forms of intimacy. Ironically, in life and art, these avant gardists may have challenged prevailing systems only to develop new ones—though if they are more inclusive and flexible than the old ones, the net gain has been substantial.

Future poly artists might fabricate new forms—perhaps spurred by Bloomsbury and modernism. Future poly novels might interweave multiple plot lines, such as Smith's *White Teeth* uses to depict multicultural London and Rushdie's *Midnight's Children* uses to depict multicultural Bombay. Poly TV shows might depict blended families, á la *The Brady Bunch*, except with a Mr. Smith in the household, along with Mr. and Mrs. Brady. Polyamorous lyric poetry might innovate in its own ways.

Literary scholars are beginning to develop polyamorous interpretive strategies. Imagining "polyamory" liberally, Christopher Nagle sees it in forms including free love, intentional cruelty, libertinism, second loves, and Orientalist fantasies of the harem. He even suggests, riffing on Harold Bloom's idea of "influence anxiety," that polyamorous relations inhere within and among texts.[91] Where progress in the private sphere is concerned, the eighteenth century's discourse of Sensibility has been seen as a modernism *avant la lettre*—a pluralistic attention to affective and erotic life and to formal experimentation. Women's expanding roles as readers and writers in this period likely contributed to these thematic foci.

* * *

Scholars who are "incredulous toward metanarratives" might find it intellectually "embarrassing"—to invoke Fussell—to invest faith in the march of social progress. They might doubt that post-Enlightenment love and friendship could be borne on a benevolent tide, *even if* public-sphere life improves over time. Finally, they might wonder how *literature that depicts intimacy as it evolves* could transform in anything but muddled ways.

But as Chapter 1 shows, multiple sources outside of literary criticism provide language for describing post-Enlightenment progress and analyzing intimacy in its light. Historians of marriage from Coontz to Finkel recognize that intimacy does not progress a linear way, that the future holds no guarantees, and that the fruits of progress are not enjoyed equally by privileged and underprivileged people. Nonetheless, their historiographies render despair at the current state of intimacy more *embarrassing* than Bloomsbury's relative sanguinity. They suggest that we already inhabit some sort of queer futurity, notwithstanding José Muñoz's assertion that, by definition, such a futurity is "not yet here."[92]

Bloomsburians drew on a rich archive of post-Enlightenment thought, including Carpenter's anticipation that love was "coming of age," in venturing hopeful ideas about sexual equality, androgyny, tolerance of queer sexualities, and future literature about intimacy. Bloomsbury's progeny, including Smith and Cunningham, have found inspiration in Forster's and Woolf's troubled hope—i.e., models for something other than "fashionable despair"[93] about civilization and the future prospects for Forster's cherished "personal relations."

If polyamorous values enrich future literature, art, and theory, this will likely redound to Bloomsbury's credit, although the group lacked the polyamorous self-awareness that has been available to lovers over the last thirty years. As mentioned, Cunningham sees writing as "by definition ... optimistic." Bloomsbury's lives and art radiate a similar light. They record hopeful attempts, some of them failed and many successful, to reanimate the ways that men and women can enjoy friendship and erotic love: their rich archive of the past offers visions of progress for the future.

Notes

1. "Tradition and the Individual Talent" 115.
2. Hardy and Easton 32.
3. *Women in Love* 352: 5.
4. Moffat 65.
5. *The Hours* 23.
6. Moffat 160.
7. Ibid. 95.
8. Forster, *Letters*. D. H. Lawrence to E. M. Forster, Wednesday [February 3] 1915: King's College Modern Archives, Cambridge University. Qtd. in Moffat 120.
9. Locked Diary, June 16, 1911; King's College Modern Archives. Qtd. in Armstrong, *Howards End* 275.
10. Moffat 116.
11. Ibid. 119.
12. *Howards End* 95.
13. *The Diaries of Virginia Woolf*, II: 171, March 12, 1922.
14. Moffat 31, 95, 97, 117, 204 for "disembodied," 205 for "gay and all embracing."
15. Ibid. 212.
16. Locked Diary, March 24, 1925, King's College Modern Archives. Qtd. in Moffat 211.
17. Moffat 96, 103, 111.
18. Ibid. 187.
19. Ibid. 148, 161, 166.
20. Ibid. 187.
21. The coming paragraphs on Forster draw on Moffat 220-32 and Roberts.
22. Moffat 223.
23. *Moments of Being* 194.
24. Ibid. 191-2.
25. Ibid. 196-7.
26. Ibid. 108.
27. The remainder of this paragraph draws on Forrester. See 19, 20, 26.
28. *Mrs Dalloway* 31, 8.
29. Sheff 55, 72-3.
30. Ibid. 2.
31. Hardy and Easton 7, Sheff x.
32. Sheff 46-7.
33. Hardy and Easton 12, Jenkins 180.
34. Sheff, 21, 126-7, 28, Schippers 26-7.
35. Sheff reports that, as of 2104, poly Internet sites estimated 1.2-9.8 million poly or nonmonogamous people in the United States (3).
36. Sheff 30-1. See Jenkins on how stigmas against polyamory give queer activists incentive to distance themselves from poly communities (135).
37. Sheff 36, Schippers 23, Hines. Brake (91) argues that communities of African-Americans, Latin Americans, unmarried urbanites, and seniors mirror some traits of poly life, such as significant friendships and shared child rearing.
38. Sheff (45-50) cites three "waves" of visible polyamorous life: nineteenth-century transcendentalism, 1960s-'70s counterculture, and the internet era.
39. Hardy and Easton 12. Also see Anapol 183.

40 Muncy discusses nineteenth-century utopian communities in America, including their brevity and limited membership (8, 13, etc.). Hardy and Easton also discuss utopian communities, including how, after they dissolve, their ideas about sex and love can influence mainstream culture (32, 81). Sheff provides a broader survey of poly communities in America, stretching from the nineteenth century until the present (45–80). Raphael discusses the fate of "womyn's lands": intentional communities founded in America since the 1960s, for women only.
41 Marler, "The Bloomsbury Love Triangle" 140.
42 Hardy and Easton 9, 39, 69, Sheff 15–16.
43 Sheff 17–18.
44 Hardy and Easton 25, 28, 14.
45 Jenkins 39.
46 Hardy and Easton 219–22, 215.
47 Freud, "The Sexual Enlightenment of Children" 132, Sheff 259–62.
48 Sheff 241–2, 252–4.
49 In addition to Sheff, see Anapol 183–94.
50 Sheff 276–8.
51 *Mrs Dalloway* 188.
52 Sheff 20, 279.
53 Avery, "Bloomsbury and Sexuality" 23, Marler, "The Bloomsbury Love Triangle" 145.
54 Sheff 79–80, 246–8.
55 Savage, *American Savage* 31, 35, 38, 104.
56 Helt and Detloff 5.
57 Marler 148.
58 Ibid. 147, Shone 15.
59 Ibid. 140, 144.
60 Ibid. 142.
61 Ibid. 145.
62 Ibid. 140, Helt and Detloff 9.
63 Helt 124, *A Room of One's Own* 101–2.
64 Rich.
65 Schippers 4–5, 13–14.
66 Ibid. 6, 33, Giddens 58.
67 *Howards End* 305.
68 *On Beauty* 110.
69 Dan Savage's essay "It's Never Okay to Cheat (Except When It Is)" argues that the taboo against sexual infidelity is irrational and harmful. Vandenberghe et al. reported in August 2019 that 75 percent of Americans consider extramarital sex "always wrong," a drop of eight points from a decade ago, but still a "vast majority."
70 Brake 88. The following discussion draws on Brake 88–102.
71 Ibid. 93, 97.
72 Ibid. 91.
73 Waite and Gallagher, Regnerus and Uecker, Douthat.
74 See Fisher.
75 Savage, "Three Things We Get Wrong about Love" 32:00–32:14.
76 Savage and Perel. 10:04–10:59.
77 I borrow this term from T. H. Huxley, who uses it to refer to an unhealthfully worshipful attitude toward women (194–6).
78 Hardy and Easton 17, Jenkins 98.

79 *Mrs Dalloway* 126.
80 Jenkins discusses these brain chemicals on 22, 28, 42, and 100.
81 *A Passage to India* 112.
82 Jenkins 154.
83 Russell, *Marriage and Morals* 123.
84 Shelden 57.
85 Jenkins 139–40, 173–4, 7, 69, 100, 175–6.
86 Ibid. 63.
87 Russell, *Marriage and Morals* 156–67.
88 See his essay "Temporary Marriage" in a collection edited by Brake.
89 Finkel 26.
90 Jenkins 176–7.
91 See Nagle.
92 Muñoz 185.
93 McEwan looks askance at this attitude. See "My Purple Scented Novel."

Appendices

Appendix A (Tables 1–5)

Marriage, Childbirth, Divorce, Female Empowerment

These tables offer a bird's-eye view of how marriage and intimacy have evolved over the last century and a half, and especially since the counterculture of the 1960s and '70s. In summation, Britons have become less likely to marry, more likely to divorce (though this practice peaked in the late twentieth century and has since declined), and more likely to have children out of wedlock. Women have become far more likely than men to seek and be granted divorce. In the early twentieth century, when men were more likely to do so, the annual divorce rate in England and Wales numbered merely in the hundreds. This difference is difficult to represent visually on Table A5, given that, by the 1980s, the numbers were so much higher, with over 100,000 divorces granted annually to women (more than twice the number granted to men).

Marriage

Tables 1–2 show that, for a century beginning in the Victorian era, the social convention of "mandatory marriage" kept marriage rates stable and high. But beginning circa 1970, thanks in part to the "sexual revolution," it has become less unusual for people to be unmarried for some length of time, or never to marry.

Childbirth

Table 3 shows the decoupling of marriage and childbirth in the contemporary era.

Divorce

Table 4 records the "divorce revolution" that was roughly concurrent with the end of mandatory marriage. The drop in the raw number of divorces since 1991 could be seen as evidence of a resurgence in traditional values, especially given that the drop in the raw number of marriages over the same period has not been as abrupt. But other evidence— including other tables in this appendix—warns against such an interpretation.

Female Empowerment

Table 5 shows that, as legislative changes have equalized the sexes' power to sue for divorce, and as women's economic self-sufficiency has increased, women have replaced men as the sex more commonly seeking divorce.

Table A1 Percentage of adults ever married (currently married, widowed, or divorced)

Year	Men	Women
1851	83.8%	83.7%*
1861	85.8	84.1
1871	86.3	84.4
1881	86.2	84.6
1891	85.3	83.6
1911	83.1	80.4
1921	85.0	80.8
1931	87.8	80.6
1941	88.8	82.7**
1946	88.1	83.6
1951	89.1	85.8
1956	89.7	89.5
1960	89.0	91.3

Table A2 Married couples as percentage of adult population (age 16 and over)***

Year	Percentage of population
1971	67
1981	64
1991	55
2001	50.7
2011	48.4

* In Table A1, for the years 1851–1931 (which cover the 35–44-year-old age group), see *Census 1931: General Tables, England and Wales*, "Table 21: Ages (grouped) and marital conditions at successive censuses (England and Wales)," 150. Tracking marriage rates by an age bracket, particularly one in the prime of life, is a standard method of tabulation. Data are uncertain before 1851, when the Census began recording marital status.

** In Table A1, for the years 1941–60 (which cover the 40–44-year-old age group), see Busfield and Paddon, Table 1:5. Proportion of persons ever married (out of 1,000) in England and Wales, 1881–"1960," 9.

*** Statistics for Table A2 are for England and Wales. See www.statistics.gov.uk/census2001/profiles/commentaries/family.asp and the Office for National Statistics.

Table A3 Illegitimacy rates (England and Wales)*

Year	Percentage of unmarried women (age 15–44) who gave birth	Illegitimate births per 100 legitimate births
1901	0.84%	4.1
1911	0.80%	4.5
1915		4.7
1918		6.7
1921	0.79%	4.8
1931	0.57%	4.7
1941		5.7
1945		10.3

Year			
1951	0.98%	5.1	
1961	1.66%	6.4	
1971	2.22%	9.2	
1981	1.99%	14.6	
1991	3.99%	43.3	
2001		66.8	
2011		89.2	

* Garrett 212–13. Also see Rothenbacher, Table EW.4: "Demographic developments, England and Wales 1850–1945," v.1, 734-7; Table EW.4A: "Demographic developments, England and Wales 1946–1995 (absolute figures and rates)," v.2, 880-3. For a graph of this data for the entire UK through 1991, see Figure UK.5: "Fertility and Legitimacy, United Kingdom 1864–1939," v.1, 711; Figure UK.5: "Fertility and Legitimacy, United Kingdom 1946–1995," v.2, 855. For the data on illegitimate births since 2001, see http://www.ons.gov.uk/ons/rel/vsob1/characteristics-of-Mother-1-england-and-wales/2011/sb-characteristics-of-mother-1.html. Accessed October 18, 2020.

Spikes in 1918 and 1945 reflect war-time "bumps" coincident with itinerant soldier populations.

Table A4 Divorce rates through Edwardian times and today

Year	Divorces per 100 marriages performed*	Raw # of divorces**	Raw # of marriages
	From the establishment of the Divorce Court through WWI		
1858	0.0	24	--
1861	0.1	196	--
1871	0.1	166	190,112
1881	0.2	311	197,290
1891	0.2	369	226,526
1901	0.2	477	259,400
1910	*Howards End* published		
1911	0.2	580	274,943
	From 1960 to the present		
1961	7.3	25,394	346,678
1971	18.4	74,437	404,737
1981	41.4	145,713	351,973
1991	51.7	158,745	306,756
2001	57.7	143,818	249,227
2005	*On Beauty* published		
2010***	49.6	119,589	241,100 (provisional)

* Derived from Rothenbacher, "Table EW.4: Demographic developments, England and Wales 1850–1945" (v.1, 734–7) and "Table EW.4A: Demographic developments, England and Wales 1946–1995 (absolute figures and rates)" (v.2, 880–1).

** *Marriage, Divorce, and Adoption Statistics*, Dataset PVH41: "Divorces: 1858–2002, Numbers of couples divorcing, by party petitioning/granted decree."

*** For 2010, see http://www.ons.gov.uk/ons/rel/vsob1/divorces-in-england-and-wales/2011/chd-figure-1-number-of-marriages-and-divorces—1931-to-2011.xls. Accessed October 18, 2020.

Table A5 Divorces granted by sex: England and Wales, 1900–2010

Source: Office for National Statistics, Dataset Name: PVH41; Divorce Statistics Historical Series, 2010. Statistical information is for England and Wales.

Historical Divorce Timeline:

- 1857—Matrimonial Causes Act allowed ordinary people to divorce. Women divorcing on the grounds of adultery had to prove unfaithfulness with additional circumstances, such as rape and incest.
- 1923—A Private Member's Bill made it easier for women to petition for divorce due to adultery.
- 1937—"Herbert Act," named for A. P. Herbert, allowed divorce on other grounds in addition to adultery, including drunkenness and abandonment.
- 1969—Divorce Reform Act allowed couples to divorce if they had been separated for two years (or five if only one party wanted the divorce). Neither party had to prove fault. (Adopted in 1971.)
- 1984—Matrimonial and Family Proceedings Act made divorce easier. Couples could split after only twelve months of separation.
- 1996—White v. White divorce case settled, in which House of Lords decided to split family earnings more evenly, instead of favoring the husband financially, as had been the practice.

Appendix B (Tables 1–5)

Immigration, interracial marriage, and public sentiment in the UK and US, 1664–present

These tables offer some support for optimistic, metanarrative readings of the UK's and US's multicultural societies, documenting such things as immigration and interracial-marriage trends and the increased tolerance with which they generally correlate. But the tables also capture ongoing public ambivalence toward racial mixing and the challenges that some interracial couples still encounter.

UK data: Tables B1–2
South Asian immigration to Britain

Table B1 measures this phenomenon over the last six decades.

Cultural and political responses

Table B2 records a post-Second World War history of ambivalence toward immigration in the UK, with the 1960s and '70s restricting the more open immigration policy enacted in the late 1940s.

US data: Tables B3–5
Black-white marriages

Table B3 records the growth of Black-white US marriages since 1980.

Attitudes toward interracial marriage

Table B4 measures public attitudes toward interracial marriages since 1972.

Legislative and cultural context

Table B5 provides a timeline pertaining to interracial marriage since colonial times.

TABLES B1–B2:

South Asian immigration and related events in the UK: 1947–2011

Table B1 Growth of the South Asian population of Great Britain, 1951–2011

Year	Indian	Pakistani	Bangladeshi	Total South Asian	Percent of population
1951	31,000	10,000	2,000	43,000	.1%
1961	81,000	25,000	6,000	112,000	.2%
1961	Salman Rushdie's parents send him from Bombay to attend Rugby School at age 13.				

1971	375,000	119,000	22,000	516,000	.9%
1981	676,000	296,000	65,000	1,037,000	1.8%
1991	840,000	477,000	163,000	1,480,000	2.7%
2001	1,000,000	747,000	280,000	2,027,000	4%
2011	1,412,958	1,124,511	447,200	2,984,669	5.3%

Sources: Figures for 1951–91 are taken from Ceri Peach, "Introduction," in Ceri Peach (ed), Ethnicity in the 1991 Census, Volume 2: The Ethnic Minority Populations of Great Britain (London: Office for National Statistics, 1996), p 9, Table 5; and Census of England and Wales 2001, Table S101. Census output is Crown copyright and is reproduced with the permission of the Controller of HMSO and the Queen's Printer for Scotland. Figures for "Percent of Population" 1951–2001 are taken from the 1951–2001 censuses of England and Wales County Report, Table 3. Accessed October 16, 2019.

Figures for 2011 from Table QS211EW 2011 Census: Ethnic group (detailed), England and Wales: http://www.ons.gov.uk/ons/rel/census/2011-census/key-statistics-and-quick-statistics-for-wards-and-output-areas-in-england-and-wales/rft—qs211ew-wm.xls. Accessed October 18, 2020.

Table B2 Timeline of post-Second World War immigration legislation and cultural events

- 1947—India receives independence from Britain, leading to mass immigration to UK.
- 1948—British Nationality Act 1948 passed, allowing 800 million subjects in British Empire to live and work in Britain without needing visas.
- 1962—Commonwealth Immigrants Act 1962 closes borders to immigrants, permitting only those with government-issued employment vouchers to settle.
- 1968—In his "Rivers of Blood" speech, Enoch Powell claims "We must be mad, literally mad, as a nation to be permitting the annual inflow of some 50,000 dependants …. It is like watching a nation busily engaged in heaping up its own funeral pyre."
- 1968—Commonwealth Immigrants Act 1968 restricts future right of entry to those born in the UK or who had a least one parent or grandparent born there.
- 1968—Race Relations Act 1968 makes it illegal to refuse housing, employment, or public services to a person on the grounds of color, race, and ethnic or national origins.
- 1971—Immigration Act 1971 restricts primary immigration.[1]
- 1972—President Idi Amin expels 55,000 Indian and Pakistani residents from Uganda; many immigrate to the UK.
- 1978—Margaret Thatcher quoted as saying that people in Britain feel "swamped" by immigrants from Pakistan.
- 1981—British Nationality Act (enacted 1983) requires that at least one parent of a child born in the UK must have British citizenship or be a permanent resident for the child to claim citizenship, effectively leaving hundreds of thousands of children "stateless."
- 1986—The Conservative politician Shreela Flather becomes Britain's first female Asian mayor, being elected to this office in Windsor and Maidenhead. In 1990, she became the first Asian woman to receive a peerage.

Notes

1. The movement of a family earner or unattached single man, who might later bring his family to join him in the new country (this would be "secondary immigration"), under family unification immigration law.
2. See http://civilliberty.about.com/od/raceequalopportunity/tp/Interracial-Marriage-Laws-History-Timeline.htm. Accessed October 18, 2020.

Tables B3–B5:

Laws, attitudes, and behavior patterns concerning interracial marriage in the United States, 1664–2010*

Table B3 Estimated number of Black-white US marriages, 1980–2010

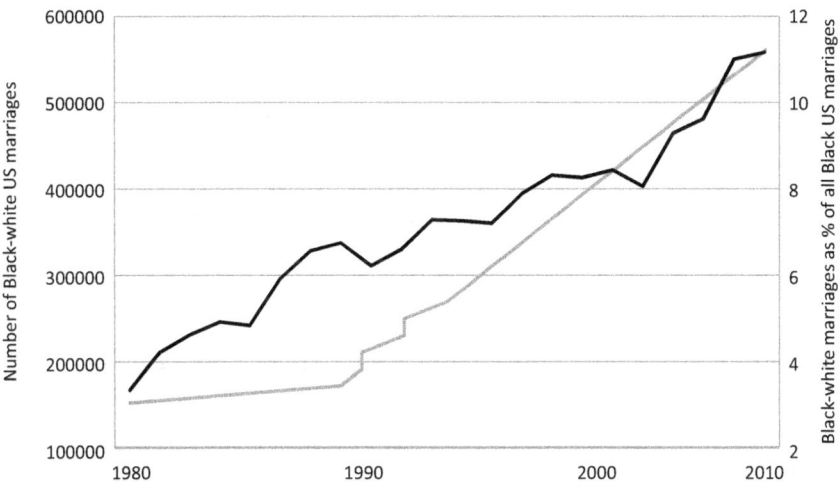

* Data on Interracial Marriages in the United States, where one partner is Black and one partner is white

(Data are taken from the US Census Bureau Table MS-1. Marital Status of the Population Fifteen Years Old and Over, by Sex, Race and Hispanic Origin and Table MS-3. Interracial Married Couples)

Table B4 US attitudes toward interracial marriage, 1972–2002

From the General Social Survey:
Question asked: Do you think there should be laws against marriages between Blacks and whites?

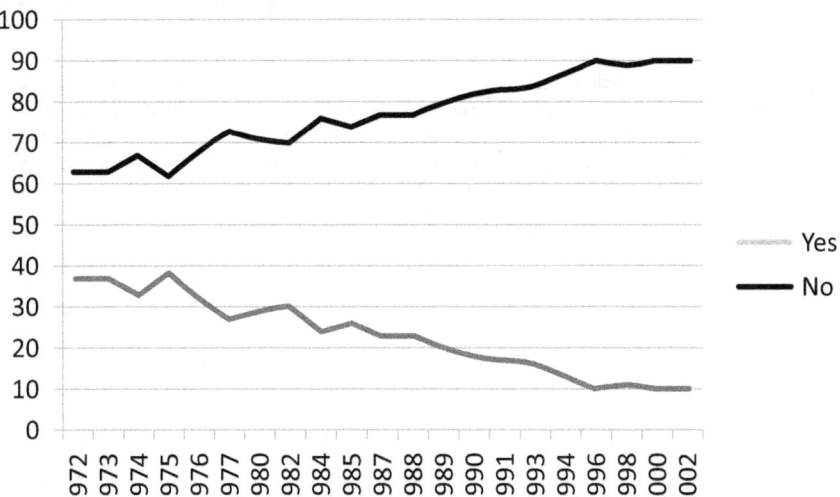

Table B5 US laws and culture pertaining to interracial marriage, 1664–1967[2]

British colonial anti-miscegenation laws

1664—Maryland law bans marriage between whites and Blacks, orders enslavement of white women who have married Black men.
1691—Virginia Commonwealth bans interracial marriage.

State-level repeal of such laws

1780—Pennsylvania repeals its 1725 law.
1843—Massachusetts repeals its 1705 law.

Attempts to amend the US Constitution to ban interracial marriage

1871, 1912, 1928—A Missouri congressman, a Georgia senator, and a South Carolina senator spearhead failed amendments.

Supreme Court rulings on state-level bans against interracial sex and marriage

1883—"Pace v. Alabama": unanimous ruling that state-level bans on interracial marriage do not violate the 14th Amendment.
1964—"McLaughlin v. Florida": unanimous ruling that laws banning interracial sex do violate the 14th Amendment.
1967—"Loving v. Virginia": unanimous overturning of "Pace v. Alabama" asserts that state-level bans on interracial marriage violate the 14th Amendment.

Cultural events

1967—The film *Guess Who's Coming to Dinner* portrays marriage between an educated Black man and a white woman in a positive light, winning Oscars for Best Actress (Katharine Hepburn) and Best Original Screenplay (by William Rose).
2005—Zadie Smith's *On Beauty* treats marriage between a less-educated Black woman and a Ph.D.-holding white man.
2011—In his book *Is Marriage for White People? How the African-American Marriage Decline Affects Everyone*, Ralph Richard Banks describes how, relative to Black men, Black women more frequently graduate from college and enter middle-class professions, yet are reluctant to "marry out" of their race, preferring instead to "marry down," i.e., partner with working-class Black men. Banks argues that this behavioral pattern lessens Black women's power in the "relationship market," and he therefore encourages Black women to be more open to interracial coupling.

Bibliography

Abel, Elizabeth. "(E)merging Identities: The Dynamics of Female Friendship in Contemporary Fiction by Women." *Signs* 6 (1981): 413–35.
Abel, Elizabeth. "Narrative Structure(s) and Female Development: The Case of *Mrs Dalloway*." In *The Voyage In: Fictions of Female Development*. Ed. Elizabeth Abel, Marianne Hirsch, and Elizabeth Langland. University Press of New England, 1983. 161–85.
Adams, Ann Marie. "Mr. McEwan and Mrs. Woolf: How a Saturday in February Follows 'This Moment of June.'" *Contemporary Literature* 53:3 (Fall 2012): 548–72.
Adams, Ann Marie. "A Passage to Forster: Zadie Smith's Attempt to 'Only Connect' to *Howards End*." *Critique* 52:4 (2011): 377–99.
Ahmed, Sarah. *The Promise of Happiness*. Durham: Duke University Press, 2010.
Ahmed, Sarah. *Queer Phenomenology*. Durham: Duke University Press, 2006.
Alexander, Jeffrey, Ron Eyerman, Berhnard Giesen, Neil J. Smelser, and Piotr Sztompka. *Cultural Trauma and Collective Identity*. Berkeley: U of California P, 2004.
Alley, Henry. "*Mrs Dalloway* and Three of Its Contemporary Children." *Papers on Language and Literature: A Journal for Scholars and Critics of Language and Literature* 42:4 (Fall 2006): 401–18.
Alt, Christina. *Virginia Woolf and the Study of Nature*. Cambridge University Press, 2010.
Alter, Robert. "Howard's End." Rev. of *On Beauty*, by Zadie Smith. *New Republic*: October 3, 2005. 29–32.
"An" and "a." http://en.wikipedia.org/wiki/Article_(grammar) Accessed October 18, 2020.
Anapol, Deborah M. *Polyamory in the Twenty-First Century: Love and Intimacy with Multiple Partners*. Lanham, MD: Rowman and Littlefield, 2010.
Anderson, Lydia. "Divorce Rate in the U.S.: Geographic Variation, 2015." https://www.bgsu.edu/ncfmr/resources/data/family-profiles/anderson-divorce-rate-us-geo-2015-fp-16-21.html. Accessed October 18, 2020.
Apstein, Barbara. "Ian McEwan's *Atonement* and 'The Techniques of Mrs. Woolf.'" *Virginia Woolf Miscellany* 64 (Fall–Winter 2003): 11–12.
Armstrong, Paul. "The Narrator in the Closet: The Ambiguous Narrative Voice in *Howards End*." *Modern Fiction Studies* 47 (2001): 306–28.
Arnett, Jeffrey. *Emerging Adulthood: The Winding Road from the Late Teens through the Twenties*. New York: Oxford University Press, 2004.
Avery, Todd. "Bloomsbury and Sexuality." *The Handbook to the Bloomsbury Group*. Ed. Derek Ryan and Stephen Ross. London: Bloomsbury Academic, 2018. 17–29.
Avery, Todd. "Nailed: Lytton Strachey's Jesus Camp." In *Queer Bloomsbury*. Ed. Brenda Helt and Madelyn Detloff. Edinburgh University Press, 2016. 172–88.
Axline, Virginia. *Dibs in Search of Self*. New York: Ballantine Books, 1986.
Banks, Ralph Richard. *Is Marriage for White People? How the African-American Marriage Decline Affects Everyone*. New York: Plume, 2012.
Barker, Pat. *The Eye in the Door*. New York: Plume, 1995.
Barker, Pat. *The Ghost Road*. New York: Plume, 1996.

Barker, Pat. Interview with Carolyn T. Hughes. "An Interview with Pat Barker." *Poets and Writers*, January–February 2004.

Barker, Pat. Interview with Rob Nixon. "An Interview with Pat Barker." *Contemporary Literature* 45:1 (2004): 1–21.

Barker, Pat. *Regeneration*. New York: Plume, 1993.

Barone, Joshua. "Review: An 'Orlando' Opera Is a Milestone, but No More, in Vienna." *The New York Times*. December 29, 2019. https://www.nytimes.com/2019/12/09/arts/music/orlando-vienna-opera-review.html. Accessed September 29, 2021.

Beer, Gillian. "Negation in *A Passage to India*." *Essays in Criticism: A Quarterly Journal of Literary Criticism*." 30 (1980): 151–66.

Begam, Richard. "Rushdie and the Art of Modernism." In *Modernism, Postcolonialism, and Globalism*. Ed. Richard Begam and Michael Valdez Moses. Oxford University Press, 2019. 125–43.

Begam, Richard and Michael Valdez Moses. "Introduction." In *Modernism, Postcolonialism, and Globalism*. Ed. Richard Begam and Michael Valdez Moses. Oxford University Press, 2019. 1–30.

Begam, Richard and Michael Valdez Moses, eds. *Modernism, Postcolonialism, and Globalism*. Oxford University Press, 2019.

Bell, Clive. *Art*. New York: Frederick A. Stopes, 1914.

Bell, David. "The Powerpoint Philosophe: Waiting for Steven Pinker's Enlightenment." *The Nation*. April 2, 2018. 27–31.

Benn Michaels, Walter. *The Trouble with Diversity: How We Learned to Love Identity and Ignore Inequality*. New York: Metropolitan Books, 2006.

Berlant, Lauren. *Cruel Optimism*. Durham: Duke University Press, 2011.

Bhabha, Homi. "Of Mimicry and Man: The Ambivalence of Colonial Discourse." In *The Location of Culture*. New York: Routledge, 1994. 121–31.

Bhabha, Homi. "The Other Question: Stereotype, Discrimination, and the Discourse of Colonialism." In *The Location of Culture*. London: Routledge, 1994. 94–120.

Blair, Elaine. "All Told: Rachel Cusk's Autobiographical Fictions." A review of *Outline*. *The New Yorker*. December 29, 2014. https://www.newyorker.com/magazine/2015/01/05/told-2. Accessed October 18, 2020.

Bloom, Harold. *The Anxiety of Influence: A Theory of Poetry*, 2nd ed. New York: Oxford University Press, 1997.

Bloom, Harold. *The Western Canon: The Books and School of the Ages*. New York: Riverhead Books, 1994.

Boileau, Nicolas Pierre. "'In Some Rare and Sacred Dead Time …, there is a Miracle of Silence,' On Not Lifting the Veil in McGregor's and Cusk's Novels." *L'Atelier* 7:2 (2015): 58–74. *HAL Open Access Archive*. Accessed October 23, 2018. hal-01304162.

Born, Daniel. "Private Gardens, Public Swamps: *Howards End* and the Revaluation of Liberal Guilt." In *Howards End*, by E. M. Forster. Ed Paul Armstrong. Norton: New York, 1998. 365–77.

Boulton, James T., ed. *The Letters of D. H. Lawrence, Vol. 1*. Cambridge University Press, 1979.

Bradbury, Malcolm and James McFarlane. "The Name and Nature of Modernism." In *Modernism: A Guide to European Literature, 1890–1930*. Ed. Bradbury and McFarlane. London: Penguin, 1991. 19–55.

Bradley, Arthur. "The New Atheist Novel: Literature, Religion, and Terror in Amis and McEwan." *Yearbook of English Studies* 39:1–2 (2009): 20–38.

Bradley, Arthur and Andrew Tate. *The New Atheist Novel: Fiction, Philosophy and Polemic After 9/11*. London: Continuum, 2010.

Brake, Elizabeth, ed. *After Marriage: Rethinking Marital Relationships*. New York: Oxford University Press, 2016.
Brake, Elizabeth. *Minimizing Marriage: Marriage, Morality, and the Law*. New York: Oxford University Press, 2012.
Brians, Paul. *Notes for Salman Rushdie: The Satanic Verses*. Version of February 13, 2004.
"Bromley contingent." http://en.wikipedia.org/wiki/Bromley_Contingent. Accessed November 26, 2019.
Brooks, David. "America Is Having a Moral Convulsion." *The Atlantic*. https://www.theatlantic.com/ideas/archive/2020/10/collapsing-levels-trust-are-devastating-america/616581/ October 5, 2020. Accessed October 6, 2020.
Brooks, David. "The Virtue of Radical Honesty." *New York Times*. February 22, 2018. https://www.nytimes.com/2018/02/22/opinion/steven-pinker-radical-honesty.htmlAccessed October 18, 2020.
Brooks, Peter. *Reading for the Plot: Design and Intention in Narrative*. New York: Knopf, 1984.
Brown, Dennis. "The *Regeneration* Trilogy: Total War, Masculinities, and the Talking Cure." In *Critical Perspectives on Pat Barker*, ed. Sharon Monteith, Margareta Jolly, Nahem Yousaf, and Ronald Paul. Columbia: University of South Carolina Press, 2005 187–202.
Brown, Jonathan. "Virginia Woolf's *Orlando*, theater review." *The Independent*. February 26, 2014. https://www.independent.co.uk/arts-entertainment/theatre-dance/reviews/virgina-woolf-s-orlando-theatre-review-9154751.html. Accessed September 29, 2021.
Brown, Richard. "Politics, the Domestic and the Uncanny Effects of the Everyday in Ian McEwan's *Saturday*." *Critical Survey* 20:1 (2008). 80–93.
Brunsma, David L. "Interracial Families and the Racial Identification of Mixed-Race Children: Evidence from the Early Childhood Longitudinal Study." *Social Forces* 84:2 (December 2005): 1131–57.
Burra, Peter. "Introduction to the Everyman Edition" (1934), reprinted in Appendix 2 of *A Passage to India*. Oliver Stallybrass, ed. Abinger Edition of E. M. Forster 6. New York: Abinger, 1983. 319–33.
Buss, David M. "Human Mate Selection: Opposites Are Sometimes Said to Attract, but in Fact We Are Likely to Marry Someone Who Is Similar to Us in Almost Every Variable." *American Scientist* 73:1 (January–February 1985): 47–51.
Canning, Richard. *Hear Us Out: Conversations with Gay Novelists*. New York: Columbia University Press, 2003.
Carpenter, Edward. *Love's Coming of Age*. Forgotten Books, 2008.
Castaneda, Vilma. "Reclaiming the Spectacle of Fright and Freaks in *Freak Orlando*." *Film Matters* 5:2 (Fall 2014): 5–10.
Chaudhuri, Nirad. "Passage to and From India." *Encounter* (June 2, 1954): 19–24.
Ciecko, Anne. "Transgender, Transgenre, and the Transnational: Sally Potter's *Orlando*." *The Velvet Light Trap* 41 (Spring 1998): 19–34.
Clarke, Colin. *River of Dissolution: D. H. Lawrence and English Romanticism*. London: Routledge, 1969.
Condorcet, Jean-Antoine-Nicolas de Caritat. *Sketch for a Historical Picture of the Progress of the Human Mind*. London: Noonday Press, 1955.
Cooke, Jennifer. "Intimacy, the Good Life, and Instructive Psychoanalytic Errors." *Textual Practice* 27:6 (October 2013): 943–60.
Cooke, Jennifer, ed. *Scenes of Intimacy*. London: Bloomsbury, 2014.

Coontz, Stephanie. *Marriage, a History: How Love Conquered Marriage*. New York: Penguin, 2006.

Coontz, Stephanie. "The Not-So-Good Old Days," *New York Times*. June 15, 2013. http://www.nytimes.com/2013/06/16/opinion/sunday/coontz-the-not-so-good-old-days.html. Accessed October 18, 2020.

Cooper, Marianne. *Cut Adrift: Families in Insecure Times*. University of California Press, 2014.

Coppola, Darlene and Carlo Coppola. "Salman Rushdie's *The Satanic Verses*: Some Freudian Aspects." *South Asian Review* 16:13 (1992): 84–91.

Craft-Fairchild, Catherine. "'Same Person … Just a Different Sex': Sally Potter's Construction of Gender in *Orlando*." *Woolf Studies Annual* 7 (2001): 23–48.

Crews, Frederick. *Unauthorized Freud: Doubters Confront a Legend*. New York: Viking, 1998.

Cunningham, Michael. *The Hours*. New York: Farrar, Straus, and Giroux, 1998.

Cusk, Rachel. *Arlington Park*. New York: Farrar, Straus, and Giroux, 2006.

Cusk, Rachel. *The Bradshaw Variations*. London: Faber and Faber, 2009.

Cusk, Rachel. "Introduction." In *The Rainbow*. Ed. D. H. Lawrence. London: Vintage, 2011. vii–xiii.

Cusk, Rachel. *Kudos*. New York: Farrar, Straus, and Giroux, 2018.

Cusk, Rachel. "Lions on Leashes." In *Coventry: Essays*. New York: Farrar, Straus, and Giroux, 2019. 88–107.

Cusk, Rachel. *Outline*. New York: Farrar, Straus, and Giroux, 2014.

Cusk, Rachel. "Shakespeare's daughters." *The Guardian*. December 11, 2009. https:/www.theguardian.com/books/2009/dec/12.rachel-cusk-women-writing-review. Accessed June 13, 2019.

Cusk, Rachel. *Transit*. New York: Farrar, Straus, and Giroux, 2017.

Dalleo, Raphael. "Colonization in Reverse: *White Teeth* as Caribbean Novel." In *Zadie Smith: Critical Essays*. Ed. Tracey L. Walters. New York: Peter Lang, 2008. 91–104.

Davies, Tony. "Introduction." In *A Passage to India: Theory in Practice*. Ed. Tony Davies and Nigel Wood. Buckingham: Open University Press, 1994. 1–22.

Dawkins, Richard. *The God Delusion*. London: Bantam, 2006.

Dennet, Daniel. *Breaking the Spell: Religion as a Natural Phenomenon*. London: Allen Lane, 2006.

Dereseiwicz, William. "A Man. A Woman. Just Friends?" *New York Times*. April 7, 2012. http://www.nytimes.com/2012/04/08/opinion/sunday/a-man-a-woman-just-friends.html?_r=2&nl=todaysheadlines&emc=edit_th_20120408&pagewanted=all. Accessed October 18, 2020.

DeSalvo, Louise. *Virginia Woolf: The Impact of Childhood Sexual Abuse on Her Life and Work*. Boston: Beacon Press, 1989.

Detloff, Madelyn. "Woolf and Crip Theory." In *A Companion to Virginia Woolf*. Ed. Jessica Berman. Massachusetts: Wiley Blackwell, 2016. 277–89.

Deudney, Daniel and G. John Ikenberry. "Liberal World: The Resilient Order." *Foreign Affairs* 97:4 (July/August 2018): 16–24.

D'hoker, Elke. "Confession and Atonement in Contemporary Fiction: J. M. Coetzee, John Banville, and Ian McEwan." *Critique: Studies in Contemporary Fiction* 48:1 (2006): 31–43.

Douthat, Ross. "Why Monogamy Matters." *New York Times*. https://www.nytimes.com/2011/03/07/opinion/07douthat.html?auth=login-email. Accessed October 18, 2020.

Dowling, David. *Bloomsbury Aesthetics and the Novels of Forster and Woolf.* New York: St. Martin's Press, 1985.
Driscoll, Lawrence. *Evading Class in Contemporary British Literature.* New York: Palgrave Macmillan, 2009.
Eagleton, Terry. *The Illusions of Postmodernism.* Massachusetts: Wiley-Blackwell, 1996.
Easterbrook, Gregg. *It's Better Than It Looks: Reasons for Optimism in an Age of Fear.* New York: Public Affairs, 2018.
Easton, Dossie and Janet W. Hardy. *The Ethical Slut: A Practical Guide to Polyamory, Open Relationships, & Other Adventures.* Berkeley: Celestial Arts, 2009.
Eliot, T. S. "The Metaphysical Poets." In *The Waste Land by T. S. Eliot: A Norton Critical Edition.* Ed. Michael North. New York: Norton, 2001. 121–7.
Eliot, T. S. "Tradition and the Individual Talent." In *The Waste Land by T. S. Eliot: A Norton Critical Edition.* Ed. Michael North. New York: Norton, 2001. 114–19.
Eliot, T. S. *The Waste Land: A Norton Critical Edition.* Ed. Michael North. New York: Norton, 2001.
Emmett, Martha. *I Love the Person You Were Meant to Be.* New York: Warner Books, 1976.
English, James and John Frow. "Literary Authorship and Celebrity Culture." In *A Concise Companion to Contemporary British Fiction.* Ed. James L. English. Blackwell, 2006. 39–57.
Fenichel, Otto. *The Psychoanalytic Theory of Neurosis.* Norton: New York, 1945.
Ferenczi, Sandor. "The Meaning of Introjection." 1912.
Ferraresi, Franco. *Threats to Democracy: The Radical Right in Italy after the War.* Princeton University Press, 1996.
Ferriss, Suzanne and Kathleen Waites. "Unclothing Gender: The Postmodern Sensibility in Sally Potter's *Orlando.*" *Literature/Film Quarterly* 27:2 (1999): 110–15.
Finkel, Eli J. *The All-or-Nothing Marriage: How the Best Marriages Work.* New York: Dutton, 2017.
Fischer, Susan Alice. "'Gimme Shelter': Zadie Smith's *On Beauty.*" In *Zadie Smith: Critical Essays.* Ed. Tracey L. Walters. New York: Peter Lang, 2008. 107–22.
Fisher, Helen. *Why We Love: The Nature and Chemistry of Romantic Love.* New York: Henry Holt, 2004.
Fisher, Michael Herbert. *Counterflows to Colonialism: Indian Travellers and Settlers in Britain 1600–1857.* Delhi: Permanent Black, 2004.
Flood, Allison. "New Bloomsbury Archive Casts Revealing Light on Virginia Woolf's Death." *The Guardian,* March 19, 2010. http://www.guardian.co.uk/books/2010/mar/19/bloomsbury-archive-virginia-woolf-death. Accessed October 18, 2020.
Fontana, Bianca Maria. "Just Look How Far We Have Come." *The Times Higher Education Supplement* Issue 2345 (2018): 54–5.
Forrester, Viviane. *Virginia Woolf: A Portrait.* Trans. Jody Gladding. New York: Columbia University Press, 2015.
Forster, E. M. *Aspects of the Novel.* London: Harcourt, 1955.
Forster, E. M. "The Challenge of Our Time." In *Two Cheers for Democracy.* Abinger Edition of E. M. Forster 11. London: Edward Arnold, 1972. 54–8.
Forster, E. M. *Howards End.* Ed. Oliver Stallybrass. Abinger Edition of E. M. Forster 4. London: Edward Arnold, 1973.
Forster, E. M. "A Magistrate's Figures." *The New Statesman and Nation* XLVI (October 31, 1953): 508–9.
Forster, E. M. *Maurice.* Toronto: Macmillan, 1971.

Forster, E. M. "Notes on the English Character." In *Abinger Harvest and England's Pleasant Land*. Abinger Edition of E. M. Forster 10. London: Andre Deutsch, 1996. 3–13.

Forster, E. M. *Passage to India*. Ed. Oliver Stallybrass. Abinger Edition of E. M. Forster 6. London: Edward Arnold, 1978.

Forster, E. M. "Terminal Note." In *Maurice*. Toronto: Macmillan, 1971. 249–55.

Forster, E. M. "What I Believe." In *Two Cheers for Democracy*. Ed. Oliver Stallybrass. Abinger Edition of E. M. Forster 11. London: Edward Arnold, 1972. 65–73.

Fowler, Brad. Talk Today (USATODAY.com). USA Today Book Club: Michael Cunningham. (Questions from Readers). January 21, 2005. http://www.usatoday.com/community/chat_03/2003-03-20-cunningham.htm. Accessed October 18, 2020.

Fraser, Kennedy. "Ghost Writer: Pat Barker's Haunted Imagination." *New Yorker*. March 10, 2008. http://www.newyorker.com/magazine/2008/03/17/ghost-writer. Accessed October 18, 2020.

Freud, Sigmund. *Analysis Terminable and Interminable*. Standard Edition XXIII. London: The Hogarth Press and The Institute of Psychoanalysis. 216–53.

Freud, Sigmund. *Beyond the Pleasure Principle*. Standard Edition XVIII 7–64.

Freud, Sigmund. "Case Histories: Frau Emmy von N." In *Studies on Hysteria*. Standard Edition II 48–105.

Freud, Sigmund. "Case Histories: Fraulein Elisabeth von R." In *Studies on Hysteria*. Standard Edition II 135–81.

Freud, Sigmund. *Fragment of an Analysis of a Case of Hysteria*. Standard Edition VII: 3–122.

Freud, Sigmund, and Josef Breuer. *The Interpretation of Dreams I and II*. Standard Edition IV and V: 339–625.

Freud, Sigmund, and Josef Breuer. *On the Psychical Mechanism of Hysterical Phenomena: Preliminary Communication*. Standard Edition II: 3–17.

Freud, Sigmund, and Josef Breuer. "The Psychotherapy of Hysteria." In *Studies on Hysteria*. Standard Edition II. London: The Hogarth Press and The Institute of Psychoanalysis. 255–305.

Freud, Sigmund, and Josef Breuer. *Recommendations to Physicians Practicing Psychoanalysis*. Standard Edition XII: 111–20.

Freud, Sigmund, and Josef Breuer. *Remembering, Repeating, and Working-Through*. Standard Edition XII. London: The Hogarth Press and The Institute of Psychoanalysis. 145–56.

Freud, Sigmund, and Josef Breuer. *The Sexual Enlightenment of Children*. Standard Edition IX: 131–9.

Friedan, Betty. *The Feminine Mystique*. New York: Norton, 1963.

Friedman, Susan. *Planetary Modernisms: Provocations on Modernity across Time*. New York: Columbia University Press, 2015.

Frim, Landon and Harrison Fluss. "Steven Pinker: False Friend of the Enlightenment." *Jacobin*. October 10, 2018. https://jacobinmag.com/2018/10/steven-pinker-enlightenment-now-review. Accessed October 18, 2020.

Frimmel, Wolfgang, Martin Halla, and Rudolf Winter-Ebmer. "Assortative Mating and Divorce: Evidence from Austrian Register Data." *Journal of the Royal Statistical Society. Series A (Statistics in Society)* 176:4 (October 2013): 907–29.

Fussell, Paul. *The Great War and Modern Memory*. New York: Oxford University Press, 2000.

Garner, Dwight. "An Appeal to Listen and Learn." A review of *Outline*. *New York Times*. January 6, 2015. https://www.nytimes.com/2015/01/07/books/outline-rachel-cusks-new-novel.html?ref=books&_r=0. Accessed October 18, 2020.

Garner, Dwight. "With 'Kudos,' Rachel Cusk Completes an Exceptional Trilogy." *New York Times*. May 21, 2018. https://www.nytimes.com/2018/05/21/books/review-kudos-rachel-cusk.html. Accessed October 18, 2020.

Garner, Dwight. "Rachel Cusk's 'Transit' Offers Transcendent Reflections." *New York Times*. January 17, 2017. https://www.nytimes.com/2017/01/17/books/review-rachel-cusk-transit.html. Accessed October 19, 2028.

Garnett, Angelica. *Deceived with Kindness: A Bloomsbury Childhood*. San Diego: Harcourt, 1985.

Gasiorek, Andrzej. "'A renewed sense of difficulty': E. M. Forster, Iris Murdoch and Zadie Smith on ethics and form." In *The Legacies of Modernism*. Ed. David James. Cambridge University Press, 2012. 170–86.

Gillis, John R. *For Better, for Worse: British Marriages: 1600 to the Present*. Oxford University Press, 1985.

Gilmore, David D. *Misogyny: The Male Malady*. Philadelphia: University of Pennsylvania Press, 2001.

Girard, Monica. "Virginia Woolf's *Mrs Dalloway*: Genesis and Palimpsests." In *Rewriting/Reprising: Plural Intertextualities*. Ed. Georges Letissier. Newcastle upon Tyne: Cambridge Scholars. 50–64.

Glab, Anna. "The Ethical Laboratory of Beauty in Zadie Smith's *On Beauty*." *Tulsa Studies in Women's Literature* 35:2 (Fall 2016): 491–512.

Gliatto, Michael F. and Anil K. Rai "Evaluation and Treatment of Patients with Suicidal Ideation." *American Family Physician* 59:6 (March 1999): 1500–6. March 15, 1999 Issue. https://www.aafp.org/afp/1999/0315/p1500.html Accessed October 18, 2020.

Goldin, Claudia. "A Grand Gender Convergence: Its Last Chapter." *American Economic Review* 104:4 (April 2014): 1091–119.

Goldman, Jane. "Forster and Women." In *The Cambridge Companion to E. M. Forster*. Ed David Bradshaw. Cambridge University Press, 2007. 120–37.

Gopnik, Alison. "A Cure for Contempt." *The Atlantic*. April 2018. 39–41.

Gottleib, Lori. "How to Land Your Kid in Therapy." *The Atlantic*. July/August 2011 Issue. https://www.theatlantic.com/magazine/archive/2011/07/how-to-land-your-kid-in-therapy/308555/ Accessed October 18, 2020.

Gray, J. A. "Beauty Is as Beauty Does." Rev. of *On Beauty*, by Zadie Smith. *First Things*: November, 2006. 48–53.

Gray, John. "Freud: The Last Great Enlightenment Thinker." *Prospect Magazine*. December 14, 2011. https://www.prospectmagazine.co.uk/magazine/freud-the-last-great-enlightenment-thinker. Accessed October 18, 2020.

Gray, John. "The Limits of Reason." *The New Statesman*. February 23–March 1, 2018. 42–4.

Grünbaum, Alfred. "Made-to-Order Evidence." In *Unauthorized Freud: Doubters Confront a Legend*. Ed. Frederick Crews. New York: Viking, 1998. 71–5.

Guillory, John. *Cultural Capital: The Problem of Literary Canon Formation*. Chicago: University of Chicago Press, 1993.

Hai, Ambreen. "'Marching in from the Peripheries': Rushdie's Feminized Artistry and Ambivalent Feminism." In *Critical Essays on Salman Rushdie*. Ed. M. Keith Booker. New York: G. K. Hall, 1999. 16–50.

Hale, Dorothy J. "*On Beauty* as Beautiful?: The Problem of Novelistic Aesthetics by Way of Zadie Smith." *Contemporary Literature* 53:4 (Winter 2012): 814–44.

Hale, Nathan. *The Rise and Crisis of Psychoanalysis in the United States 1917–85*. Oxford University Press, 1995.

Harris, Sam. *The End of Faith: Religion, Terror, and the Future of Reason*. New York: Norton, 2004.

Hart, Stephen and Wen-chin Ouyang, ed. *A Companion to Magical Realism*. Woodbridge, England: Tamesis, 2005.

Hegel, Georg Wilhelm. *Elements of the Philosophy of Right*. Tr. H. B. Nisbet. Cambridge Texts in the History of Political Thought. Ed. Allen Wood. Cambridge University Press, 1991.

Hegel, Georg Wilhelm. *Lectures on the Philosophy of World History*. Tr. H. B. Nisbet. Cambridge Studies in the History and Theory of Politics. Cambridge University Press, 1981.

Hegel, Georg Wilhelm. *The Letters*. Trans. Clark Butler and Christine Seiler with commentary by Clark Butler. Bloomington: Indiana University Press, 1984.

Helt, Brenda. "Passionate Debates on 'Odious Subjects': Bisexuality and Woolf's Opposition to Theories of Androgyny and Sexual Identity." In *Queer Bloomsbury*. Ed. Brenda Helt and Madelyn Detloff. Edinburgh University Press, 2016. 114–31.

Helt, Brenda and Madelyn Detloff. Introduction. *Queer Bloomsbury*. Edinburgh University Press, 2016. 1–12.

Helt, Brenda and Madelyn Detloff. *Queer Bloomsbury*. Edinburgh University Press, 2016.

Henke, Suzette. "Bloomsbury Blues: Virginia Woolf's *Moments* and Michael Cunningham's *Hours*." In *From Camera Lens to Critical Lens: A Collection of Best Essays on Film Adaptation*. Ed. Rebecca Housel. Newcastle: Cambridge Scholars Press, 2006. 9–20.

Hillis Miller, J. "Virginia Woolf's All Souls' Day: The Omniscient Narrator in *Mrs Dalloway*." In *The Shaken Realist*. Ed. Melvin J. Friedman and John B. Vickery. Baton Rouge: Louisiana State University Press, 1970. 100–27.

Hines, Alice. "Polyamory Works for Them." https://www.nytimes.com/2019/08/03/style/polyamory-nonmonogamy-relationships.html. Accessed October 18, 2020.

Hitchens, Christopher. *God Is Not Great: How Religion Poisons Everything*. New York: Twelve, 2007.

Hite, Molly. "Introduction." *The Waves*. London: Harcourt, 2006.

Hite, Molly. "Tonal Cues and Uncertain Values: Affect and Ethics in *Mrs Dalloway*." *NARRATIVE* 18:3 (October 2010): 249–75.

Hoberek, Andrew. "Introduction: After Postmodernism." *Twentieth-Century Literature* 53:3 (Fall 2007): 233–47.

Högberg, Elsa. *Virginia Woolf and the Ethics of Intimacy*. London: Bloomsbury Academic, 2020.

Holroyd, Michael. *Lytton Strachey: A Critical Biography*. 2 vols. New York: Holt, 1967.

Hoyle, Brian. "Intertextuality and Film: Sally Potter's *Orlando*." In *European Intertexts: Women's Writing in English in a European Context*. Berlin: Peter Lang, 2005. 193–214.

Hungerford, Amy. "On the Period Formerly Known as Contemporary." *American Literary History* 20:1–2 (Spring/Summer 2008): 410–19.

Hutcheon, Linda. *A Poetics of Postmodernism: History, Theory, Fiction*. New York: Routledge, 1988.

Hutcheon, Linda. *A Theory of Adaptation*. New York: Routledge, 2006.

Huxley, T. H. "Emancipation—Black and White." In *The Essence of T. H. Huxley: Selections from His Writings*. Ed Cyril Bibby. London: St. Martin's Press, 1967.

Huyssen, Andreas. "Introduction: Modernism after Postmodernity." *New German Critique*, No. 99, Modernism after Postmodernity (Fall 2006): 1–5.

Illouz, Eva. *Cold Intimacies: The Making of Emotional Capitalism*. Cambridge: Polity Press, 2007.
James, David. "Mapping Modernist Continuities." In *The Legacies of Modernism: Historicising Postwar and Contemporary Fiction*. Ed. David James. Cambridge University Press, 2011. 1–19.
James, David. *Modernist Futures*. Cambridge University Press, 2012.
James, David, and Urmila Seshagiri. "Metamodernism: Narratives of Continuity and Revolution." *PMLA* 129:1 (2014): 87–100.
Jameson, Frederic. "The Cultural Logic of Late Capitalism." In *Postmodernism, or, the Cultural Logic of Late Capitalism*. Durham: Duke University Press, 1991. 1–54.
Jameson, Frederic. "Postmodernism and Consumer Society." In *The Cultural Turn: Selected Writings on the Postmodern, 1983–1998*. London: Verso, 1998. 1–20.
Jay, Betty, ed. *E. M. Forster: A Passage to India: A Reader's Guide to Essential Criticism*. New York: Palgrave, 1998. Icon Guides. Series editor: Richard Beynon.
Jenkins, Carrie. *What Love Is: And What It Could Be*. New York: Basic Books, 2017.
Jones, Ernest. *The Life and Work of Sigmund Freud: Volume 3: The Last Phase: 1919–1939*. New York: Basic Books, 1957.
Jordan, Zbigniew A. *The Evolution of Dialectical Materialism: A Philosophical and Sociological Analysis*. London: Macmillan, 1967.
Joyce, James. "The Dead." In *Dubliners*. New York: Penguin, 2014. 151–94.
Joyce, James. *Dubliners*. New York: Penguin, 2014.
Joyce, James. *Ulysses: The Gabler Edition*. New York: Random House, 1986.
Julavitz, Heidi. "Rachel Cusk's 'Outline.'" January 7, 2015. https://www.nytimes.com/2015/01/11/books/review/rachel-cusks-outline.html. Accessed October 18, 2020.
Jussawalla, Feroza. "Rushdie's Dastan-E-Dilruba: *The Satanic Verses* as Rushdie's Love Letter to Islam." *Diacritics: A Review of Contemporary Criticism* 26:1 (Spring 1996): 50–73.
Kant, Immanuel. "What Is Enlightenment?" In *The Enlightenment: A Brief History with Documents*. Ed. Margaret C. Jacob. New York: Bedford/St. Martin's Press, 2001. 203–8.
Keller, Lynn. *Re-making It New: Contemporary American Poetry and the Modernist Tradition*. Cambridge University Press, 1988.
Kemp, Peter. "On Beauty by Zadie Smith." *The Sunday Times*. September 4, 2005. https://www.thetimes.co.uk/article/on-beauty-by-zadie-smith-tz8fzthrxgk. Accessed October 18, 2020.
Kern, Stephen. *The Culture of Love: Victorians to Moderns*. Cambridge: Harvard University Press, 1992.
Kern, Stephen. *The Culture of Time and Space 1880–1918*. Cambridge: Harvard University Press, 1983.
Keynes, John Maynard. "My Early Beliefs." In *The Collected Writings of John Maynard Keynes*. 30 Vols. London: Macmillan, 1971–89. Vol. 10: *Essays in Biography*. 433–50.
Krouse, Tonya. "The Politics of Nature in Woolf's *The Years*." *Virginia Woolf Miscellany* 81 (Spring 2012): 12–14.
Kyaga, Simon, Mikael Landén, Marcus Boman, Christina M. Hultman, Niklas Långström, and Paul Lichtenstein. "Mental Illness, Suicide, and Creativity: 40-Year Prospective Total Population Study." *Journal of Psychiatric Research* 47:1 (January 2013): 83–90.
Laird, Nick. http://www.thefullwiki.org/Nick_Laird.
Laplanche, Jean. *New Foundations for Psychoanalysis*. Tr. David Macey. Oxford: Basil Blackwell, 1989.

Lasch, Christopher. *The True and Only Heaven: Progress and Its Critics*. New York: Norton, 1991.
Latham, Monica. "Variations on *Mrs. Dalloway*: Rachel Cusk's *Arlington Park*." *Woolf Studies Annual* 19 (2013): 195-213.
Latham, Sean and Gayle Rogers. *Modernism: Evolution of an Idea*. New Modernisms Series. London: Bloomsbury Academic, 2015.
Lawrence, D. H. Foreword. "Morality and the Novel." In *Selected Literary Criticism*. Ed. Anthony Beal. New York: Viking, 1956. 108-13.
Lawrence, D. H. "Morality and the Novel." In *Selected Literary Criticism*. Ed. Anthony Beal. New York: Viking, 1956. 108-13.
Lawrence, D. H. Foreword. *Lawrence: Sex, Literature and Censorship*. Ed. Harry Moore. New York: Viking, 1959.
Lawrence, D. H. *Lawrence: Sex, Literature and Censorship*. Ed. Harry Moore. New York: Viking, 1959.
Lawrence, D. H. Foreword. *Women in Love*. Ed. David Farmer, Lindeth Vasey, and John Worthen. Cambridge Edition of the Letters and Works of D. H. Lawrence. Cambridge University Press, 1987.
Lawrence, D. H. *Women in Love*. Ed. David Farmer, Lindeth Vasey, and John Worthen. Cambridge Edition of the Letters and Works of D. H. Lawrence. Cambridge University Press, 1987.
Leavis, Queenie D. "Caterpillars of the Commonwealth Unite!" *Scrutiny* (September 1938): 203-14.
Lenin, Vladimir. *Imperialism, the Highest Stage of Capitalism: A Popular Outline*. New York: International Publishers, 1939.
Lewis, C. S. "De Descriptione Temporum." In *They Asked for a Paper*. London: Geoffrey Bles, 1962. 9-25.
Lewis, Matt. "Obama Loves Martin Luther King's Great Quote—But He Uses it Incorrectly." *The Daily Beast*. Updated 4-11-17. http://www.thedailybeast.com/obama-loves-martin-luther-kings-great-quotebut-he-uses-it-incorrectly. Accessed October 18, 2020.
Lewis, Pericles. *Religious Experience and the Modernist Novel*. Cambridge University Press, 2010.
Lopez, Alejandra. "Mixed-Race School-Age Children: A Summary of Census 2000 Data." *Educational Researcher* 32:6 (August–September 2003): 25-37.
Lubbock, Percy, ed. *The Letters of Henry James*. 2 vols, vol. 2. New York: Scribner's, 1920.
Luria, Alexander. *The Man with a Shattered World: The History of a Brain Wound*. New York: Basic Books, 1972.
Luria, Alexander. *The Mind of a Mnemonist: A Little Book about a Vast Memory*. New York: Basic Books, 1968.
Lyotard, Jean François. *The Postmodern Condition*. University of Minnesota Press, 1997.
Mackenzie, Compton. *Extraordinary Women: Theme and Variations*. London: Hogarth, 1986.
Majumdar, Saikat. *Prose of the World: Modernism and the Banality of Empire*. New York: Columbia University Press, 2013.
Malcolm, Janet. *Psychoanalysis: The Impossible Profession*. New York: Vintage, 1980.
Mann, Harveen Sachdeva. "'Being Born Across': Translation and Salman Rushdie's *The Satanic Verses*." *Criticism* 37:2 (Spring 1995): 281-302, n. 35.
Marcus, Laura. "Ian McEwan's Modernist Time: *Atonement* and *Saturday*." In *Ian McEwan*. Ed. Sebastian Groes. London: Bloomsbury, 2013. 83-98.

Marcus, Laura. "The Legacies of Modernism." In *The Cambridge Companion to the Modernist Novel*. Ed. Morag Shiach. Cambridge University Press, 2007. 82–98.

Marler, Regina. "The Bloomsbury Love Triangle." In *Queer Bloomsbury*. Ed. Brenda Helt and Madelyn Detloff. Edinburgh University Press, 2016. 135–51.

Marler, Regina. *Bloomsbury Pie: The Making of the Bloomsbury Boom*. New York: Henry Holt, 1997.

Martin, Robert. "Edward Carpenter and the Double Structure of *Maurice*." In *E. M. Forster*. Ed. Jeremy Tambling. New York: St. Martin's Press, 1995.

Martin, Ruth Lee. "Framing Ambiguity and Desire through Musical Means in Sally Potter's Film 'Orlando.'" *Music, Sound, and the Moving Image* 5:1 (Spring 2011): 25–37.

Marx, Karl and Friedrich Engels. *The German Ideology*. Moscow: Progress Publishers, 1976.

Mason, Wyatt. "White Knees: Zadie Smith's Novel Problems." Rev. of *On Beauty*, by Zadie Smith. *Harper's Magazine*. October 2005: 83–8.

Masson, J. M., ed. and trans. *The Complete Letters of Sigmund Freud to Wilhelm Fleiss 1887–1904*. Cambridge: Harvard University Press, 1985.

Matz, Jesse. *Modernist Time Ecology*. Baltimore: Johns Hopkins, 2019.

Matz, Jesse. "Pseudo-Impressionism?" *The Legacies of Modernism: Historicising Postwar and Contemporary Fiction*. Ed. David James. Cambridge University Press, 2012. 114–32.

Matz, Jesse. *The Modern Novel: A Short Introduction*. Malden, MA: Blackwell, 2004.

May, Brian. *The Modernist as Pragmatist: E. M. Forster and the Fate of Liberalism*. University of Missouri Press, 1997.

McCann, Colum. Foreword to *Dubliners*: "Splitting the Atom." New York: Penguin, 2014. ix–xv.

McEwan, Ian. *Atonement*. New York: Random House, 2001.

McEwan, Ian. *Enduring Love*. New York: Random House, 1997.

McEwan, Ian. Interview with Michael Silverblatt, *Bookworm*, KCRW, July 11, 2002.

McEwan, Ian. "My Purple Scented Novel." *The New Yorker*. March 21, 2016. https://www.newyorker.com/magazine/2016/03/28/my-purple-scented-novel-fiction-by-ian-mcewan. Accessed October 18, 2020.

McEwan, Ian. *Saturday*. New York: Random House, 2005.

McEwan, Ian. *Solar*. New York: Doubleday, 2010.

McHale, Brian. "Change of Dominant from Modernist to Postmodernist Writing." In *Approaching Postmodernism*. Ed. Fokkema Douwe and Hans Bertens. Amsterdam: Benjamins, 1986. 53–79.

Mendelson, Edward. "The Death of Mrs. Dalloway: Two Readings." In *Textual Analysis: Some Readers Reading*. Ed. Mary Ann Caws. New York: Modern Language Association of America, 1986. 272–80.

Meyers, Jeffrey. "The Politics of *A Passage to India*." *Journal of Modern Literature* 1 (1971): 329–38.

Miller, Claire Cain. "The Upshot: Modern Families. The Divorce Surge Is Over, but the Myth Lives on." December 2, 2014. https://www.nytimes.com/2014/12/02/upshot/the-divorce-surge-is-over-but-the-myth-lives-on.html Accessed October 18, 2020.

Mirze, Z. Esra. "Fundamental Differences in Zadie Smith's *White Teeth*." In *Zadie Smith: Critical Essays*. Ed. Tracey L. Walters. New York: Peter Lang, 2008. 187–200.

Moeyes, Paul. *Siegfried Sassoon: Scorched Glory*. Basingstoke, England: Palgrave Macmillan, 1997.

The Moody Bible Institute of Chicago. *The Ryrie Study Bible: King James Version*. Chicago: Moody Press, 1978.

Moffat, Wendy. *A Great Unrecorded History: A New Life of E. M. Forster*. New York: Farrar, Straus, and Giroux, 2010.

Moffat, Wendy. "*A Passage to India* and the Limits of Certainty." *Journal of Narrative Technique* 20 (1990): 331–41.

Moran, Jo Ann Hoeppner. "E. M. Forster's *A Passage to India*: What Really Happened in the Caves." *Modern Fiction Studies* 34 (1988): 596–604.

Moore, G. E. *Principia Ethica: Revised Edition*. Cambridge University Press, 2000.

Moore-Gilbert, Bart. "Introduction." In *Writing India 1757–1990*. Ed. Bart Moore-Gilbert. Manchester University Press, 1996. 1–29.

Moyn, Samuel. "Hype for the Best." In *The New Republic*. April 2018. 68–71.

Mufti, Aamir. "Reading the Rushdie Affair: 'Islam,' Cultural Politics, Form." In *Critical Essays on Salman Rushdie*. Ed. M. Keith Booker. New York: G. K. Hall and Co., 1999. 51–77.

Muncy, Raymond Lee. *Sex and Marriage in Utopian Communities: 19th-Century America*. Bloomington: Indiana University Press, 1973.

Muñoz, José. *Cruising Utopia: The Then and There of Queer Futurity*. New York University Press, 2009.

Murdoch, Iris. "Against Dryness." In *Existentialists and Mystics: Writings on Philosophy and Literature*. New York: Penguin, 1997. 287–95.

Murdoch, Iris. "On 'God' and 'Good.'" In *Existentialists and Mystics: Writings on Philosophy and Literature*. New York: Penguin, 1997. 337–62.

Murdoch, Iris. "The Idea of Perfection." In *Existentialists and Mystics: Writings on Philosophy and Literature*. Penguin 1997. 299–336.

Nagle, Christopher. "Teaching the Polyamorous (Long) Eighteenth Century." *Digital Defoe: Studies in Defoe and His Contemporaries* 1:3 (Fall 2011): 68–74.

Nancy, Jean-Luc. *The Inoperative Community*. Minneapolis: University of Minnesota Press, 1991.

Neuman, Shirley. "*Heart of Darkness*, Virginia Woolf, and the Specter of Domination." In *Virginia Woolf: New Critical Essays*. Ed. Patricia Clements and Isobel Grundy. New Jersey: Barnes and Noble, 1983. 57–76.

Nicholls, Peter. "Divergences: Modernism, Postmodernism, Jameson and Lyotard." *Critical Quarterly* 33:3 (Autumn 1991): 1–18.

Nolan, Daniel. "Temporary Marriage." In *After Marriage: Rethinking Marital Relationships*. Ed. Elizabeth Brake. New York: Oxford University Press, 2016. 180–203.

O'Neill, Joseph. *Netherland*. New York: Pantheon, 2008.

O'Neill, Nena and George O'Neill. *Open Marriage: A New Lifestyle for Couples*. New York: Evans, 1972.

Parashkevova, Vassilena. "'I Put Down Roots in the Women I Love': Migrant Stories/Cities and Cartographic Re-inscription of Gender and Sexuality in Salman Rushdie's *The Satanic Verses*." *Texts: English Studies in Italy* 23:2 (2010): 437–52.

Pastoor, Charles. "The Absence of Atonement in *Atonement*." *Renascence* 66:3 (Summer 2014): 203–15.

PBS Newshour. "Elizabeth Farnsworth. A Conversation with Michael Cunningham, Who Won the Pulitzer Prize in Fiction for His Novel." *The Hours*. April 20, 1999. http://www.pbs.org/newshour/bb/entertainment/jan-june99/pulitzer_4-13.html. Accessed May 9, 2014.

Peach, Ceri. *Ethnicity in the 1991 Census. Vol. 2, the Ethnic Minority Populations in Great Britain*. London: Office for National Statistic, 1996.

Penguin. Interview with Zadie Smith. http://www.us.penguingroup.com/static/rguides/us/on_beauty.html. Accessed October 30, 2012.

Phillips, Adam. *Monogamy*. New York: Pantheon Books, 1996.
Phillips, Adam. "Poetry and Psychoanalysis." In *Promises, Promises: Essays on Psychoanalysis and Literature*. New York: Basic Books, 2001. 1–34.
Phillips, Adam. "Promises, Promises." In *Promises, Promises: Essays on Psychoanalysis and Literature*. New York: Basic Books, 2001. 364–75.
Phillips, Kathy J. "Salman Rushdie's *The Satanic Verses* as a Feminist Novel." In *Constructions and Confrontations: Changing Representations of Women and Feminisms, East and West: Selected Essays*. Ed. Cristina Bacchilega and Cornelia Moore. Honolulu: University of Hawaii Press, 1996. 103–8.
Phillips, Roderick. *Untying the Knot: A Short History of Divorce*. Cambridge University Press, 1991.
Pinker, Steven. *The Blank Slate: The Modern Denial of Human Nature*. New York: Viking, 2002.
Pinker, Steven. *Enlightenment Now: The Case for Reason, Science, Humanism, and Progress*. New York: Viking, 2018.
Pipes, Daniel. *The Rushdie Affair: The Novel, the Ayatollah, and the West*. Milton: Talyor and Francis, 2017.
"Polyamory." https://www-oed.com.libproxy.csustan.edu/view/Entry/252745?redirectedFrom=polyamory#eid. Accessed August 13, 2019.
Poole, Roger. *The Unknown Virginia Woolf*, 3rd ed. Atlantic Highlands, NJ: Humanities Press. 1990.
Pugh, Allison. *The Tumbleweed Society: Working and Caring in an Age of Insecurity*. New York: Oxford University Press, 2015.
Purdon, James. Interview in *The Guardian*. "Tom McCarthy: 'To ignore the avant garde is akin to ignoring Darwin.'" https://www.theguardian.com/books/2010/aug/01/tom-mccarthy-c-james-purdon. Accessed March 19, 2019.
Racker, Heinrich. *Transference and Countertransference*. New York: International Universities Press, 1968.
Ranasinha, Ruvani. "The *fatwa* and Its Aftermath." In *The Cambridge Companion to Salman Rushdie*. Ed. Abdulrazak Gurnah. Cambridge University Press, 2007. 45–59.
Randall, Bryony. "A Day's Time: The One-Day Novel and the Temporality of the Everyday." *New Literary History* 47 (2016): 591–610.
Raphael, Rina. "Why Doesn't Anyone Want to Live in This Perfect Place?" *The New York Times*. https://www.nytimes.com/2019/08/24/style/womyns-land-movement-lesbian-communities.html Accessed October 18, 2020.
Rawlinson, Mark. *Pat Barker*. New British Fiction Series. Houndmills: Palgrave, 2010.
Reed, Christopher. *Bloomsbury Rooms: Modernism, Subculture, and Domesticity*. New Haven: Yale University Press, 2004.
Regan, Tom. *Bloomsbury's Prophet*. Philadelphia: Temple University Press, 1986.
Regnerus, Mark and Jeremy Uecker. *Premarital Sex in America: How Young Americans Meet, Mate, and Think about Marrying*. Oxford University Press, 2011.
Reisman, David. *The Lonely Crowd. A Study of the Changing American Character*. New Haven: Yale University Press, 1953.
Rich, Adrienne. "Compulsory Heterosexuality and Lesbian Experience." In *Powers of Desire: The Politics of Sexuality*. Ed. Ann Snitow, Christine Stansell, and Sharon Thompson. New York: Monthly Review Press, 1983. 177–205.
Ricoeur, Paul. *Freud and Philosophy*. Tr. Dennis Savage. New Haven: Yale University Press, 1970.
Rieff, Philip. "Introduction." In *Dora*. By Sigmund Freud. New York: Macmillan, 1963.

Roberts, Bethan. "E. M. Forster and his 'wondrous muddle.'" *The Guardian*. February 17, 2012. https://www.theguardian.com/books/2012/feb/17/e-m-forster-my-policeman. Accessed February 23, 2022.
Robinson, Paul. *The Freudian Left: Wilhelm Reich, Geza Roheim, Herbert Marcuse*. New York: Harper & Row Press, 1969.
Robinson, Richard. "The Modernism of Ian McEwan's *Atonement*." MFS 56:3 (2010): 473–95.
Rorty, Richard. "Freud and Moral Reflection." *Essays on Heidegger and Others: Philosophical Papers, Vol 2*. 143–63.
Rorty, Richard. "Introduction." In *Contingency, Irony, and Solidarity*. Cambridge University Press, 1989. viii–xvi.
Rosecrance, Barbara. *Forster's Narrative Vision*. Ithaca: Cornell University Press, 1982.
Rosling, Hans. *Factfulness: Ten Reasons We're Wrong about the World—and Why Things Are Better Than You Think*. New York: Flatiron Books, 2018.
Rushdie, Salman. "In God We Trust." In *Imaginary Homelands: Essays and Criticism 1981–1991*. New York: Penguin, 1992. 376–92.
Rushdie, Salman. "In Good Faith." In *Imaginary Homelands: Essays and Criticism 1981–1991*. New York: Penguin, 1992. 393–414.
Rushdie, Salman. "Influence." In *Step across This Line*. New York: Random House, 2002. 62–9.
Rushdie, Salman. "Is Nothing Sacred?" In *Imaginary Homelands: Essays and Criticism 1981–1991*. New York: Penguin, 1992. 415–29.
Rushdie, Salman. *Joseph Anton: A Memoir*. New York: Random House, 2013.
Rushdie, Salman. "May 2000: J. M. Coetzee." In *Step across This Line: Collected Nonfiction 1992-2002*. New York: Random House, 2002. 297–9.
Rushdie, Salman. *Midnight's Children*. New York: Random House, 2006.
Rushdie, Salman. *The Satanic Verses*. New York: Random House, 2008.
Rushdie, Salman. "V. S. Naipaul." In *Imaginary Homelands: Essays and Criticism 1981–1991*. New York: Penguin, 1992. 148–51.
Rushdie, Salman. *The Wizard of Oz*. London: British Film Institute, 1992.
Russell, Bertrand. *The Conquest of Happiness*. New York: Liveright, 2013.
Russell, Bertrand. *Marriage and Morals*. New York: Liveright, 1970.
Russo, Francine. "The Toxic Well of Loneliness." *Scientific American*. January 2018. 66–9.
Ryan, Derek and Stephen Ross. "Introduction." In *The Handbook to the Bloomsbury Group*. London: Bloomsbury Academic, 2018. 1–15.
Salih, Sabah. "The Space of the Woman in Salman Rushdie's *The Satanic Verses*." *Notes on Contemporary Literature* 32:3 (2002 May): 2–3.
Savage, Dan. *American Savage: Insights, Slights, and Fights on Faith, Sex, Love, and Politics*. New York: Penguin, 2013.
Savage, Dan. "It's Never Okay to Cheat (Except When It Is)." In *American Savage: Insights, Slights, and Fights on Faith, Sex, Love, and Politics*. New York: Penguin, 2013. 19–39.
Savage, Dan. "Three Things We Get Wrong about Love." *Mindvalley Talks*. October 2, 2017. https://www.youtube.com/watch?v=brZIb4MG8oA Accessed October 18, 2020.
Savage, Dan, and Esther Perel. "Love, Marriage, and Monogamy." Talks at Google. February 4, 2006. https://www.youtube.com/watch?v=s7E9ASb3LfE. Accessed October 18, 2020.
Scarry, Elaine. *On Beauty and Being Just*. The Tanner Lectures on Human Values. https://blogs.aalto.fi/researchinart/files/2012/10/scarryBEAUTY.pdf. Accessed June 13, 2019.

Schippers, Mimi. *Beyond Monogamy: Polyamory and the Future of Polyqueer Sexualities*. New York: NYU Press, 2016.

Schlack, Beverly Ann. "A Freudian Look at *Mrs Dalloway.*" *Literature and Psychology* 23 (1973): 49–58.

Schoene, Berthold. *The Cosmopolitan Novel*. Edinburgh University Press, 2009.

Schwartz, Joseph. *Cassandra's Daughter: A History of Psychoanalysis*. London: Penguin, 1999.

Scott, Bonnie Kime. *In the Hollow of the Wave: Virginia Woolf and Modernist Uses of Nature*. University of Virginia Press, 2012.

Scott, Paul. "India: A Post-Forsterian View." *Essays by Divers Hands*, vol. 36. Ed. Mary Stocks. Oxford University Press, 1970. 113–32.

Seshagiri, Urmila. "Encounters with Modernism: Ian McEwan, Jhumpa Lahiri, and the Ethics of Abstraction." *M/m Forums*. December 11, 2018. Volume 3, Cycle 4. https://doi.org/10.26597/mod.0079.

Sharpe, Jenny. "The Unspeakable Limits of Rape: Colonial Violence and Counter-Insurgency," *Genders* 10 (1991): 25–46.

Shaw, Andrea. "The Other Side of the Looking Glass: The Marginalization of Fatness and Blackness in the Construction of Gender Identity." *Social Semiotics* 15:2 (2005): 143–52.

Sheff, Elisabeth. *The Polyamorists Next Door: Inside Multiple-Partner Relationships and Families*. Maryland: Rowman and Littlefield, 2014.

Shelden, Ashley. *Unmaking Love: The Contemporary Novel and the Impossibility of Union*. New York: Columbia University Press, 2017.

Shermer, Michael. "Reason (and Science) for Hope." *Skeptic* 23:2: 58–9.

Shklovsky, Viktor: "Art as Device." In *Viktor Shklovsky: A Reader*. Ed. Alexandra Berlina. Bloomsbury 2017. 73–96.

Shone, Richard. *Bloomsbury Portraits*. Oxford: Phaidon, 1976.

Showalter, Elaine. *The Female Malady: Women, Madness, and English Culture, 1830–1980*. New York: Pantheon, 1985.

Silva, Jennifer. *Coming Up Short: Working-Class Adulthood in an Age of Uncertainty*. Oxford University Press, 2015.

Simawe, Saadi. "Rushdie's *The Satanic Verses* and Heretical Literature in Islam." *The Iowa Review* 20:1 (Winter 1990): 185–98.

Slobodin, Richard. *W. H. R. Rivers: Pioneer Anthropologist, Psychiatrist of* The Ghost Road. Gloucestershire: Sutton, 1997.

Smiley, Jane. "Trapped in English Suburbia." Review of *Arlington Park*. *Los Angeles Times*. http://articles.latimes.com/2006/dec/31/books/bk-smiley31. Accessed October 18, 2020.

Smith, Zadie. "Acknowledgements." *On Beauty*. New York: Penguin, 2005.

Smith, Zadie. *On Beauty*. New York: Penguin, 2005.

Smith, Zadie. "Brief Interviews with Hideous Men: The Difficult Gifts of David Foster Wallace." In *Changing My Mind: Occasional Essays*. New York: Penguin, 2009. 255–97.

Smith, Zadie. *Changing My Mind: Occasional Essays*. New York: Penguin, 2009. Foreword. xiii–xiv.

Smith, Zadie. "E. M. Forster, Middle Manager." In *Changing My Mind: Occasional Essays*. New York: Penguin, 2009. 14–28.

Smith, Zadie. "Fail Better" and "Read Better." *The Guardian*. January 13, 2007.

Smith, Zadie. "F. Kafka, Everyman." In *Changing My Mind: Occasional Essays*. New York: Penguin, 2009. 58–71.

Smith, Zadie. "Love, actually." *The Guardian*. https://www.theguardian.com/books/2003/nov/01/classics.zadiesmith. Accessed October 18, 2020.

Smith, Zadie. "*Middlemarch* and Everybody." *Changing My Mind: Occasional Essays*. New York: Penguin, 2009. 29–41.

Smith, Zadie. *NW*. New York: Penguin, 2012.

Smith, Zadie. "*Their Eyes Were Watching God*: What Does *Soulful* Mean?" In *Changing My Mind: Occasional Essays*. New York: Penguin, 2009. 1–13.

Smith, Zadie. "This Is How it Feels to Me." *The Guardian*. October 13, 2011. https://www.theguardian.com/books/2001/oct/13/fiction.afghanistan. Accessed October 18, 2020.

Smith, Zadie. "Two Directions for the Novel." In *Changing My Mind: Occasional Essays*. New York: Penguin, 2009. 72–96.

Smith, Zadie. *White Teeth*. New York: Vintage, 2000.

Sontag, Susan. "Against Interpretation." In *Against Interpretation and Other Essays*. New York: Dell, 1966. 3–14.

Sprengnether, Madelon. "Enforcing Oedipus: Freud and Dora." *In Dora's Case: Freud—Hysteria—Feminism*. Ed. Charles Bernheimer and Claire Kahane. New York: Columbia University Press, 1985. 254–75.

Spring, Justin. "Michael Cunningham." *BOMB* 66 (Winter 1999): 76–80.

Staff. "Author's Sister Writes Next Chapter in Kureishi Family Feud." *Poets & Writers*. March 11, 2008. https://www.pw.org/content/author039s_sister_writes_next_chapter_kureishi_family_feud. Accessed October 18, 2020.

Stepansky, Paul. *Psychoanalysis at the Margins*. New York: Other Press, 2009.

Stevenson, Sheryl. "With the Listener in Mind: Talking about the *Regeneration* Trilogy with Pat Barker." In *Critical Perspectives on Pat Barker*. Ed. Sharon Monteith, Margaretta Jolly, Nahem Yousaf, and Ronald Paul. Columbia: University of South Carolina Press, 2005. 175–84.

Stone, Wilfred. *The Cave and the Mountain: A Study of E. M. Forster*. Stanford University Press, 1966.

Strachey, James. Editor's Note to "Analysis Terminable and Interminable" by Sigmund Freud. Standard Edition XXIII: 211–15.

Strachey, James. Editor's Introduction to *Papers on Technique* by Sigmund Freud. Standard Edition XII: 85–8.

Stuckey, Lexi. "Red and Yellow, Black and White: Color Blindness as Disillusionment in Zadie Smith's 'Hanwell in Hell.'" In *Zadie Smith: Critical Essays*. Ed. Tracey L. Walters. New York: Peter Lang, 2008. 157–69.

Suleri, Sara. "Contraband Histories: Salman Rushdie and the Embodiment of Blasphemy." In *Reading Rushdie: Perspectives on the Fiction of Salman Rushdie*. Ed. M. D. Fletcher. Amsterdam: Rodopi, 1994. 221–35.

Szalai, Jennifer. "Steven Pinker Wants You to Know Humanity Is Doing Fine. Just Don'tAsk Individual Humans." *New York Times*. February 28, 2018. https://www.nytimes.com/2018/02/28/books/review-enlightenment-now-steven-pinker.html. Accessed October 18, 2020.

Tennyson, Alfred. *Tennyson's Poetry*. Ed. Robert W. Hill Jr. New York: Norton, 1971.

Thomas, D. M. "Author's Note." In *The White Hotel*. New York: Penguin, 1981. vii–viii.

Thomas, D. M. *The White Hotel*. New York: Penguin, 1981.

Timpanaro, Sebastiano. *The Freudian Slip: Psychoanalysis and Textual Criticism*. Tr. Kate Soper. London: NLB, 1976.

Todd, Pamela. *Bloomsbury at Home*. New York: H. N. Abrams, 1999.

Todd, Richard. "Literary Fiction and the Book Trade." In *A Concise Companion to Contemporary British Fiction*. Ed. James L. English. Blackwell, 2006. 19–38.
Tortorici, Dayna. "Zadie Smith's Dance of Ambivalence." *The Atlantic*. December 2016. 32–4.
Trilling, Lionel. *E. M. Forster: A Study*. New York: New Directions, 1943.
Trilling, Lionel. "Introduction." In *The Selected Letters of John Keats*. Ed. Lionel Trilling. New York: Farrar, Straus and Young, 1951. 3–41.
Tynan, Maeve. "'Only Connect': Intertextuality and Identity in Zadie Smith's." In *On Beauty. Zadie Smith: Critical Essays*. Ed. Tracey L. Walters. New York: Peter Lang, 2008. 73–90.
Vandenberghe, Betsy, Jeffrey P. Dew, and W. Bradford Wilcox. "Marriage and Fidelity in the Internet Age." *The National Review*. https://www.nationalreview.com/2019/08/marriage-fidelity-internet-age/ Accessed October 18, 2020.
Wachtel, Eleanor. "In Conversation with Zadie Smith." *Brick* 85 (June 2010): 115–23.
Waite, Linda and Maggie Gallagher. *The Case for Marriage: Why Married People Are Happier, Healthier, and Better off Financially*. New York: Doubleday, 2000.
Wally, Johannes. "Ian McEwan's *Saturday* as a New Atheist Novel? A Claim Revisited." *Anglia: Zeitschrift für Englische Philologie* 130:1 (2012): 95–119.
Walters, Tracey L. "Still Mammies and Hos: Stereotypical Images of Black Women in Zadie Smith's Novels." In *Zadie Smith: Critical Essays*. Ed. Tracey L. Walters. New York: Peter Lang, 2008. 123–39.
Wang, Joy. "Othello Revisited: Metropolitan Romance in Fanon's *Black Skin, White Masks* and Rushdie's *The Satanic Verses*." *Journal of Postcolonial Writing* 45:1 (March 2009): 49–59.
Watson, John B. *Psychological Care of Infant and Child*. New York: Arno Press, 1972.
Weigel, Moira. "I Have Multiple Loves." *The Chronicle of Higher Education*, February 3, 2017. Accessed September 15, 2018.
Wells, Juliette. "Shades of Austen in Ian McEwan's *Atonement*." *Persuasions: The Jane Austen Journal* 30 (2008): 101–12.
Westman, Karen. *Pat Barker's Regeneration: A Study Guide*. Continuum Contemporaries. New York: Continuum, 2001.
Whitehead, Anne. "Open to Suggestion: Hypnosis and History in the *Regeneration* Trilogy." In *Critical Perspectives on Pat Barker*. Ed. Sharon Monteith, Margareta Jolly, Nahem Yousaf, and Ronald Paul. Columbia: University of South Carolina Press, 2005. 203–18.
Whyte, L. L. *The Unconscious before Freud*. London: Tavistock, 1962.
Whitman, Walt. "Passage to India." In *Leaves of Grass: the 1892 Edition*. New York: Bantam, 1983. 328–36.
Williams, Raymond. "The Bloomsbury Fraction." In *Problems in Materialism and Culture: Selected Essays*. London: Verso, 1980. 148–69.
Wiegman, Robyn and Elizabeth Wilson. *Queer Theory without Antinormativity*. A Special Issue. *Differences: A Journal of Feminist Cultural Studies*.
Williamson, Kevin. "A Failed Quest for Meaning." *National Review*. March 1, 2018. https://www.nationalreview.com/magazine/2018/03/19/steven-pinker-enlightenment-now-review-failed-quest-meaning/ Accessed October 18, 2020.
Wilson, Anne. *Mixed-Race Children: A Study of Identity*. London: Allen and Unwin, 1987.
Wilson, Sloan. *The Man in the Gray Flannel Suit*. New York: Simon and Schuster, 1955.
Wittgenstein, Ludwig. *The Blue and Brown Books*. Oxford: Basil Blackwell, 1958.
Wolfe, Jesse. *Bloomsbury, Modernism, and the Reinvention of Intimacy*. Cambridge University Press, 2011.

Wolfe, Jesse. "Case Study: Edward Carpenter's Radical Integrity and Its Influence on E. M. Forster." In *The Handbook to the Bloomsbury Group*. Ed. Derek Ryan and Stephen Ross. London: Bloomsbury Academic, 2018. 30–44.

Wollstonecraft, Mary. *A Vindication of the Rights of Man*. Cambridge University Press, 1991.

Wollstonecraft, Mary. *A Vindication of the Rights of Woman: Norton Critical Edition*, 2nd ed. New York: Norton, 1988.

Wood, James. "Human, All Too Inhuman. On the Formation of a New Genre: Hysterical Realism." *The New Republic*. July 23, 2000. https://newrepublic.com/article/61361/human-inhuman. Accessed October 18, 2020.

Woolf, Leonard. *The Village in the Jungle*. Oxford University Press, 1981.

Woolf, Virginia. *Between the Acts*. New York: Harcourt, 1941.

Woolf, Virginia. *The Diaries of Virginia Woolf*. Ed. Anne Bell. 5 Vols. London: Harcourt, 1984.

Woolf, Virginia. *The Letters of Virginia Woolf*. Ed. Nigel Nicholson and Joanne Trautmann. San Diego: Harcourt, 1975–80.

Woolf, Virginia. "Modern Fiction." In *The Common Reader: First Series Annotated Edition*. New York: Harvest, 1984. 146–54.

Woolf, Virginia. *Moments of Being*. San Diego: Harcourt, 1985.

Woolf, Virginia. *Mr Bennet and Mrs Brown*. London: Hogarth, 1924.

Woolf, Virginia. *Mrs Dalloway*. New York: Harcourt, 1981.

Woolf, Virginia. "Old Bloomsbury." In *Moments of Being*. Ed. Jeanne Schulkind. San Diego: Harcourt, Brace, Jovanovich, 1985. 181–201.

Woolf, Virginia. *Orlando*. New York: Harcourt, 1928.

Woolf, Virginia. *A Room of One's Own*. New York: Harcourt, 1957.

Woolf, Virginia. *Three Guineas*. New York: Harcourt, 1938.

Woolf, Virginia. *The Years*. New York: Harcourt, 1937.

Wright, Richard. *Lawd Today*. New York: Walker and Company, 1963.

Young, Tory. *Michael Cunningham's The Hours: A Reader's Guide*. London: Continuum, 2003.

Index

Locators followed by "n." indicate endnotes.

Ackerley, J. R. 197–8
Adams, Anne Marie 24 n.60
Ahmed, Sarah 3–4, 43
    The Promise of Happiness 7, 43–4,
        53–4, 59
    Queer Phenomenology 43
AIDS 55, 179, 193 n.23
The Aliens Show 142
Alley, Henry 193 n.15
Alt, Christina 72 n.61
amatonormativity 11, 22, 202, 206,
    210–14
ambivalence 4, 7, 13, 16, 39, 75–6, 163,
    178, 201, 210–14, 223
"Angel of the House" 212
Anglophone culture 134
Anthropological Society 125 n.82
anti-metanarrative skepticism 97
anti-misogyny 144, 147. *See also* male
    malady, misogyny
antinormativity 8, 160, 189, 210
anti-realism 17, 89, 129–31, 162
antirelationality 7
The Apostles 31
Arlington Park (Cusk) 12, 17–18, 21, 44,
    49–74, 76, 152, 212
    Amanda Clapp 58–9, 64, 69
    Arlington Rise 57, 61, 66, 69–70
    Christine Lanham 50, 56–8, 63, 68–70
    clock time 60, 63–4
    dinner party 60, 66–9
    history of abuse 58
    Joe 56–7, 70
    Juliet Randall 44, 52–6, 58–9, 63–4, 69
    Larry 56–7
    loss of faith 52–3
    Maisie Carrington 56–9, 63–4, 68–9,
        185
    Matthew Milford 56

modernist paralysis and stretched-
    out present time 4, 17, 25, 49,
    53–61, 64, 70, 170
neo-modernist techniques 60
one-day structure 60, 64–6
ongoing crisis 54, 57
selfishness and greed 57
short-story cycle 60, 65
Solly Kerr-Leigh 50, 58, 63, 65–6
spousal relations 56, 69
Viv 56–7
weather 60–4
women's coldness 59, 61
Armstrong, Paul 148 n.21
asexual femininity 211
Atonement (McEwan) 18–20, 51, 60, 70,
    72 n.56, 75–96, 119
    accusatory letter 85
    Briony 81–2, 84–8, 93, 95 n.34, 96
        n.48, 96 n.63
    Christian/post-Christian attributes
        82
    manifest/latent divisions 84–8
    religious confession 81
    Robbie and Cecelia 70, 81, 85, 87–92,
        95 n.20, 96 n.48
    writing as hysteria, Briony's 88–91
Austen, Jane 3, 82, 89, 154–5, 158–9,
    209
    Austenian realism 87, 89
    Northanger Abbey 87, 93
    Pride and Prejudice 154–5, 158
avant garde 4, 52
    domestic 10
    prestige of 153–9
    and realism 158
    techniques 21, 26
Avery, Todd 10
Axline, Virginia 99
    Dibs in Search of Self 122 n.8

Ayesha 132, 143–5
Aziz (*A Passage to India*, Forster) 6, 20, 30–2, 76, 127, 129, 131–2, 135

Barker, Pat 3, 11–12, 49, 70, 78, 100, 102–4, 113, 115, 121, 122 n.10
  Another World 108
  The Eye in the Door 106, 120
  Ghost Road 100–1, 112, 118–21
  Life Class 108
  "The Passion of Rivers" 115
  Regeneration trilogy 18–20, 27, 76, 97–126
    paralysis, hysterical 103
    paralysis, spinal 103
  Toby's Room 108
Beard, Michael 19
Beckett, Samuel, *Texts for Nothing* 1
Begam, Richard, *Modernism, Postcolonialism, and Globalism* 24 n.46
Bell, Clive 10, 178, 201, 203, 205–6
Bell, Quentin 201
Bell, Vanessa 14
Bem, Sandra 40
Benjamin, Walter 109
Berlant, Lauren 25
  Cruel Optimism 7, 23 n.18, 53–5
  people's "incoherent mash" 54, 56
Bersani, Leo, *Homos* 7
Billimoria, Pimple 145
Billy Prior (*Regeneration* trilogy, Barker) 19, 99–100, 102–4, 106, 108, 111, 114–16, 119–20, 122, 123 n.24, 124 n.36
Birkin (*Women in Love*, Lawrence) 2, 6, 15, 31–2, 205, 207, 210
Black authenticity 153, 157
Bloom, Leopold 139
Bloomsbury/Bloomsburian 3, 50, 127, 153, 162, 195, 202, 204
  aesthetics 13–14, 51
  amatonormativity 11, 22, 202, 206, 210–14
  ambivalence and polyamorous challenge 210–14
  antinormativity 210
  "becoming together" 10–11
  belief in progress 10
  canonization and commercialization 175
  civilization 9–10, 17, 32
  compulsory coupledom, ambivalent challenges 207–10
  conviviality 10–11, 153
  dissident individualism 10
  domestic avant garde 10
  durability and polyaffectivity 204–5
  as forerunner to polyamory 195
  as forerunner to poly literature 40
  heteronormativity 11, 22, 202, 206, 208, 210
  housework 10
  legatees 3–4, 13, 15, 44, 49, 52, 170, 175, 208–10, 213–14
  melioristic musings 30–2
  modernism 11, 17, 70, 147, 192, 202–4, 214
  mononormativity 11, 22, 202, 206, 209–10, 211–13
  optimism and pessimism 32–5
  polyamory 11, 21–2, 40, 195–6, 198, 202–6, 215
  proto-polyamorous network 198
  proto-poly culture 196, 200, 202
  "requeering" the group 205–6
  sexual variations 200
Born, Daniel 173 n.102
Bovary, Emma 158, 187
Bowen, Elizabeth 85
Bradley, Arthur 81
The Brady Bunch (TV show) 215
Brake, Elizabeth 210–12, 216 n.37
break-ups, effects on people's lives 137, 167, 192, 211
Breuer, Josef 101–7. *See also* Freud, Sigmund
Brians, Paul 148 n.26
British Film Institute, "Film Classics" series 128
Brontë, Charlotte 31, 57
  Jane Eyre 57, 155
Brooks, David 46 n.37
Brooks, Peter 93–4 n.5, 108–9
Brown, Dan (*The Hours*, Cunningham) 188
Brown, Dennis 112, 122 n.10
Brown, Norman O. 123 n.15

Brown, Richard 24 n.60, 52, 55, 178, 182–3, 185, 188, 191
Browning, Robert, *The Ring and the Book* 131
Buckingham, Bob 40, 198–200, 203
Buckingham-Forster V 199
Bulgakov, Mikhail, *Master and Margarita* 131
Burns (*Regeneration*, Barker) 111, 114, 120–1
Butler, Judith, *Gender Trouble* 23 n.30
Byrne, Gabriel 122 n.8

capitalist society 53
Carpenter, Edward 27, 40, 42, 197–9, 215
    feminism and economic radicalism 27
    Intermediates 27–8
    Love's Coming of Age 27–8
    optimism 32, 42
Carpentier, Alejo, *Kingdom of This World* 131
Carrington, Dora 206
civilization 1–3, 9–12, 17, 19, 24 n.39, 25, 27, 32, 61, 69, 98, 112–13, 129–30, 134, 162, 215
civilized individualism 9
Cixous, Helene 123 n.15
Clarissa Vaughan (*The Hours*, Cunningham) 21, 52, 176, 178–9, 181–2, 185–6, 188–92
climate change 1, 5, 18–19, 33, 51
commonality of fatherless families 16
communal anxiety and rage 5
compersion (lovers) 41, 204, 209
compulsory heterosexuality 207, 209
Condorcet, Marquis de 26–7
    optimism 32
    Sketch for a Historical Picture of the Progress of the Human Mind 26
conversion 78–81. *See also* de-conversion
Cooke, Jennifer, *Scenes of Intimacy* 47 n.77
Coontz, Stephanie 36, 215
    gender roles 38
    Marriage: A History 34
    pre-modern husbands 37
countertransference 19, 24 n.61, 83–4, 99, 101–2, 113, 115, 120–2, 123 n.20. *See also* transference
Covid-19 5, 43

credulity and incredulity toward the idea of progress 5, 7, 16, 25, 58, 75–7, 99, 105, 113, 123, 129, 139, 155
Crews, Frederic 94 n.8
Criminal Law Amendment Act (1885). *See* Labouchere Amendment
Cunningham, Michael 12–13, 18, 30, 49, 51–2, 59, 152, 170, 175–94, 215
    homage to Virginia Woolf 17, 21, 51, 175–94 (*see also* homage)
    The Hours 21, 38–9, 44, 49, 52, 55, 64, 68, 72 n.56, 152, 154, 170, 175–94 196
    Kodak moments 179
    metamodernist strategies 49
    optimism 17
    queer theory without antinormativity 176
Cusk, Rachel 3, 30, 41, 49, 55, 151, 152, 170, 192, 212
    Arlington Park (*see Arlington Park* (Cusk))
    The Bradshaw Variations 49–50, 54
    Kudos 51
    "Lions on Leashes" 71 n.24
    loss of faith in progress 52–3
    Outline trilogy 3, 51, 60, 154
    pessimism 17
    sexual inequality and bias 50, 54
    Transit 51
Cyril Connolly (CC) rejection letter 84–7

Daldry, Stephen 177
Dawkins, Richard 81
death 59, 97, 101, 192
    of despair 5
    instinct 19, 101, 108–9, 112
    natural 109
    rates 33
    self-inflicted 183, 188
    sex and 36
de-conversion 77–81, 113, 145
Deresiewicz, William 41
despair 3, 6, 32–3, 53, 55, 67, 76, 98, 105, 110, 113, 116, 188–9, 191
    cultural 70
    deaths of 5
    fashionable 215
    ongoing sources of 5

precarity and 46 n.38
temporal dislocation 191
destabilization 214
Detloff, Madelyn, *Queer Bloomsbury* 10–11, 205
D'hoker, Elke 60, 81–2
Diagnostical Statistical Manual (DSM)-III 107
Diagnostical Statistical Manual (DSM)-IV 94 n.14
Dickinson, Goldsworthy Lowes 196
disbelief 132
   in coherence of human subject 1
   in historical progress 1, 55
   in love 1, 7, 69, 136, 213
   its philosophical limitations 3–5
   in realist narrative techniques 2
divorce 7, 38–9, 70, 152, 175, 205, 219
   divorcees 213
   historical timeline 222
   mass 1, 16, 51, 166
   poly-style 203
   rates 37, 42, 47 n.74, 219, 221–2
   revolution 219
Dora (Freud) 13, 18–19, 24 n.61, 79, 82–4, 88, 94 n.7, 95 n.32, 98–9, 123 n.15, 124 n.54
   Herr K. 83, 89–90, 106
   Ida Bauer 83, 93, 95 n.19
   reversal of affect 90–1
Driscoll, Lawrence 193 n.45

Easterbrook 33
Easton, Dossie 203, 204, 212–13, 217 n.40
Edelman, Lee 7–8, 23 n.30
el Adl, Mohammed 197–8
Eliot, George 3, 89, 112, 134, 153–4
Eliot, Thomas Stearns 32, 155, 195
   "High Church" 155
   The Waste Land 6
Emmett, Martha 99, 122 n.8
Eng, David 23 n.30
Engels, Friedrich 27
   The German Ideology 27
   The Origin of the Family, Private Property, and the State 27
Enlightenment 5–6, 9, 17, 27, 33, 77, 129, 153, 169. *See also* post-Enlightenment

internal logic 34–5
love revolution 22, 37–8, 42
rationalism 37, 140
theories of social change 26
Erikson, Erik 83
ethnonationalism 1, 5, 147
Euripides, *Medea* 71 n.24
exploratory behaviors 204

Felski, Rita, *The Limits of Critique* 7–8
feminism 27, 35, 38, 43–4, 51, 55, 57, 62, 66, 72 n.61, 143, 145, 167, 185, 210, 212. *See also* Wollstonecraft, Mary
   and anti-authoritarianism 62
   in *Arlington Park* (Cusk) 49, 50, 51, 54, 55, 57, 62, 66
   female empowerment 219
   female-female intimacy 65
   in *The Satanic Verses* (Rushdie) 128, 134, 143–5, 148 n.9
Ferdinand, Franz 124 n.38
Ferenczi, Sandor 95 n.32, 102
Fielding (*A Passage to India,* Forster) 6, 20, 30–2, 76, 127, 129, 131–2, 135, 140, 198, 212
Finkel, Eli (on marriage) 34–7, 42–3, 214–15
Firestone, Shulamith, *The Dialectic of Sex: The Case for Feminist Revolution* 27
First World War 1, 19, 25, 97–8, 101, 104, 107, 109, 114, 120, 140, 179, 193 n.23
Fontana, Bianca Maria 46 n.37
Forrester, Viviane 201
Forster, Edward Morgan 8–9, 11, 24 n.39, 26–7, 30–1, 34, 37, 39, 44, 49, 73 n.100, 127, 130, 139–40, 147, 148 n.21, 151, 154, 158–9, 162, 169–70, 175, 196–8, 200, 208, 215
   anti-realism 130–1
   epistemological multiplicity 20, 130–2
   friendship 32, 127, 168, 197–9
   Howards End (*see Howards End* (Forster))
   humanism 4, 21, 32, 147, 159, 170, 212
   "Love the Beloved Republic" 16, 135

"A Magistrate's Figures" 38
Maurice 27, 31–2, 196
"Notes on the English Character" 30
optimism 21, 49
A Passage to India 6, 8, 20, 26, 30–2, 76, 127–31, 135, 137, 140, 147, 148 n.9, 152, 157, 170, 196–7, 210, 212
"Person" 1, 3–4, 161
post-Freudian world 158
"Psychology" 2
sex and love life 197
sexual self-exploration 197
skepticism 20, 129–30
"What I Believe" 1–2, 15, 30, 161, 197, 210
Foucault, Michel 1, 34
History of Sexuality 23 n.30
Fraser, Kennedy 107
Freud, Sigmund 1, 3–4, 11–12, 17, 28, 43–4, 77–8, 93 n.5, 94 n.5, 121, 159, 201
civilizational despair 3
classical Freudian theory 87, 91, 94 n.14, 95 n.32, 102
Collected Writings 78
comparison of his to McEwan's techniques 83
concepts 29
countertransference 83–4
cure, methods of and ideas about 29, 40, 44, 77–81, 84, 88, 98, 102–12, 115
disturbance in the sphere of sexuality 89–90
Dora (see Dora (Freud))
epistemology 29, 88
Freud-bashing 92
Freudianism 79–82, 92, 95 n.15, 98
Freudian Left 14, 123 n.15
Freudian literature 82–4
Freudian metanarrative 29, 78, 89, 94 n.5, 97, 121
"Analysis Terminable and Interminable" 77, 80, 94 n.9, 95 n.30, 110–12, 115, 124 n.65
Beyond the Pleasure Principle 93 n.5, 108–10, 112
early childhood masturbation 78

Oedipal phase 78
pressure technique 102
remembering, repeating, and working-through 80, 104–8, 123 n.20, 136
strangulated affect 103
Studies on Hysteria 101–4, 106–7, 123 n.20
the unconscious 29, 78–9, 83, 88–9, 92, 94 n.9, 94 n.14, 101, 106, 110, 123 n.15, 159, 161
Freudian revisionism 94 n.8
humanistic program 78
interminable analysis 80, 119
The Interpretation of Dreams 124 n.54
and Josef Breuer 101–7
masterplot 93–4 n.5, 108–9
middle-class social order 204
psyche 29, 98, 107
psychodynamic model 43, 79–80, 84, 87, 94 n.14
re-evaluations of his legacy 78–81
seduction theory 104
skepticism and hope 18–20, 32
storytelling techniques 49
transformational ambitions 80
Friedan, Betty 17, 38, 184
The Feminine Mystique 38, 185
friendship 13–14, 26, 30, 56, 75, 137, 142, 152, 168, 206, 215, 216 n.37. *See also* love; marriages
and art 17
Forsterian 32, 127, 168, 197–9
same-sex 127
Froula, Christine 9–10, 67
Fry, Roger 14, 31, 206
Fussell, Paul 10, 97, 109, 215

Gandhi, Bhupen 149 n.58
Garnett, Angelica, *Deceived with Kindness* 40
Gasiorek, Andrzej 154
gay 19, 27, 31, 38, 40, 55, 100, 116, 179, 196–8, 200, 202–3, 213
gender 10, 13–14, 28, 38, 46 n.56, 49, 64, 153, 178–9, 212
differentiation 38
essentialism 55
grand convergence 40–2

and intimacy 169, 176
and marriage 207
performativity 23 n.30
politics 143, 167
Gerald (*Women in Love*, Lawrence) 31, 207
Giddens, Anthony 26, 152, 212–13
  intimacy as democracy 135, 141, 152, 169
  plastic sexuality 36
  pre-modern husbands 37
  pure relationship 36, 42, 213
  The Transformation of Intimacy 15–16, 34
Gilroy, Paul 10
Godbole (*A Passage to India*, Forster) 20, 131–2, 142
Goode, William 38, 42
Gopnik, Alison 46 n.37
Gottleib, Lori 170 n.11
Grafton Gallery (London) exhibition 31
grand recit 33, 35, 41, 77, 79, 97, 101, 108, 214
Grant, Duncan 14
Great White God 112, 116
Greenberg, Clement 10

Halberstam, Judith (Jack) 8
Hallet (*Ghost Road*, Barker) 118–22
Halperin, David, queer liberalism 23 n.30
Hamidullah (*A Passage to India*, Forster) 140, 142
Hardy, Janet 203–4, 212–13, 217 n.40
Hardy, Walter 189
Hare, David 177
HBO, *In Treatment* 99, 122 n.8
Head, Henry 113, 116–18
Hegel, Georg Wilhelm 26–7
Helt, Brenda 207
  Queer Bloomsbury 10–11, 205
Henke, Suzette 191
heterogeneous family systems 141, 152
heteronormativity 22, 176, 180, 183, 198, 202, 206, 208, 210
high modernism 5–6, 25, 51, 66, 70, 175
Hilda Doolittle 120
Hines, Alice 216 n.37
historical moods 17
  hope and apprehensiveness 4

optimism 3, 25–6, 179 (*see also* optimism)
pessimism 1, 8 (*see also* pessimism)
Hite, Molly, affective indeterminacy 67
Högberg, Elsa 3–4
homage 13, 17–18, 21, 41, 51–2, 151–94, 208
homicides 33
homoeroticism 130, 178
homophobia 7, 20, 31, 34, 38, 99, 120, 189, 196
  pre-Stonewall 38
  Victorian 195
homosexuality 30, 32, 52, 116, 196
Hortense Bowden (*White Teeth*, Smith) 168
Howards End (Forster) 5, 13, 15, 21, 26–8, 30, 32, 36, 39–41, 73 n.100, 131, 147, 151–3, 158, 160, 163, 165–6, 168–70, 172 n.80, 173 n.102, 197, 199, 208–9
  Helen Schlegel 131, 151, 153, 160, 163, 166, 197, 208–9
  Henry Wilcox 15, 28, 39, 41, 145, 152, 166, 208–9
  Leonard Bast 158, 160
  Margaret Schlegel 5, 15, 27–8, 30, 39–40, 52, 131, 145, 153, 163, 169, 173 n.102, 197, 208
  Ruth Wilcox 15, 39, 73 n.100, 168–9, 208–9
  Tibby 39, 153, 158
human sexual variety, awareness of 28, 79
Hunt, James 125 n.82
Hurston, Zora Neale 153, 172 n.96
  Their Eyes Were Watching God 157
Hutcheon, Linda, historiographic metafiction 176
Huxley, Thomas Henry 217 n.77

illegitimacy rates (England and Wales) 220–1
Illouz, Eva 44
  Cold Intimacies: The Making of Emotional Capitalism 43
  communication, ethos 43
India Independence Act (1947) 127
internalization 94 n.6

The International Journal of Psychoanalysis 124 n.38
interracial love 4, 26, 37, 135, 139, 152, 175, 213
intertextuality/intertextual modes 17, 24 n.46, 46 n.56, 59, 129, 171 n.36
intimacy/and progress 3–4, 11, 14, 25, 27, 30, 34, 78, 91, 133, 135, 140, 147, 179, 201, 215. *See also* love, historical progress of
  avoidance 204
  Bloomsbury's implications for 21–2
  as democracy 15, 135, 141, 152, 169
  equality in 42
  forms and tradition 206
  freedom 39, 76, 144, 147, 175–6
  higher-order 36
  in history 4, 13, 16, 20, 26, 32, 35, 37, 39, 41, 49, 52–3, 76, 151, 155, 166–70, 178, 182, 210
  post-Enlightenment 16–17, 22, 32, 34–5, 215
  radical theory and 43–4
  same-sex 6, 127, 152
  and selfhood 40
  and sexuality 50, 177, 202
  spousal and parent-child 151
intimate networks 40, 203
Irigaray, Luce 123 n.15

James, David 176, 195
  "Metamodernism" 12–13, 24 n.42
James, Henry 25, 98, 196
  end of belief in progress 98
  repressed homosexuality 196
Jameson, Frederic 52, 122 n.11
Jenkins, Carrie 211–14, 216 n.36
  What Love Is: And What It Could Be 40, 213
Jones, Ernest 108
Joyce, James 4, 12, 41, 55, 60–1, 69, 129, 154–6, 170
  "The Dead" 12, 61, 64–6
  Dubliners 6, 12, 17, 25, 55–6, 60
  Ulysses 12, 49, 64, 66, 154, 175
Jung, Carl 115

Kant, Immanuel 33, 36
Karenina, Anna 158, 185, 187

Keller, Lynn 2
Kermode, Frank, *The Sense of an Ending* 76
Keynes, John Maynard 10, 25, 30, 206
Khomeini, Ayatollah 128, 139, 144
Kinsey, Alfred 203
Krouse, Tonya 62

Labouchere, Henry 147 n.3, 200
Labouchere Amendment 127, 147 n.3, 196
Laird, Nick 151
Lanchester, John, *Mr Phillips* 72 n.56
Laplanche, Jean 75, 77
  psychoanalytic theory 77
Lasch, Christopher 76
Laura Brown (*The Hours*, Cunningham) 21, 38, 44, 68, 176–82, 184–8, 191, 193 n.18
Lawrence, David Herbert 2–3, 7, 12, 32, 34, 43–4, 49–50, 56, 61, 75–6, 151, 196, 207–8
  "Democracy" 15
  The Rainbow 49, 61, 207
  skepticism 3
  Sons and Lovers 6, 153
  Women in Love 1–2, 6, 15, 31, 50, 195, 205, 207–8, 210
lay religion 98
Leave it to Beaver 38
Leavis, Queenie 70
Le Corbusier 10
Lessing, Doris 185
Lewis, Pericles, *Religious Experience and the Modernist Novel* 76
LGBT community 10
liberalism 23 n.30, 33, 98, 171 n.37
lifelong heterosexual monogamy 213
Lippincott, Robin, *Mr Dalloway* 72 n.56
long-term monogamous/consensually non-monogamous 47 n.66
Lopez-Ropero, Lourdes 165, 171 n.36, 172 n.80
Lopokova, Lydia 206
love 4, 13–14, 26, 31, 37, 41, 75, 138, 152, 181, 192, 205, 212, 215. *See also* friendship; marriages
  disbelief in 1, 7, 69, 136, 213
  Forsterian faith in 2

historical progress of (Bloomsbury's time and present-day) 39–43
historical progress of (18th century) 35–7
historical retrenchments (1800s and 1950s) 37–8
and intimacy 16, 43, 202
and literary successes 151
lovers in urban poly hubs 203
and marriage 34
and religion 212
revolution 22, 35, 37–8, 42
and sexual exploration/sex 35, 205
as sickness 213
Lovelace, Richard 138
Loving v. Virginia 140–1, 213
Luard, Clarissa 141
Luria, Alexander 99, 122 n.8
Lyotard, Jean Francois 53, 77, 93 n.1, 100, 129, 139
incredulity toward metanarrative 5, 25, 75, 99, 129
modern subject 122 n.11
The Postmodern Condition 97, 99

Malcolm, Janet 83, 95 n.32
male malady 143, 146. *See also* anti-misogyny; misogyny
mandatory marriage, era of 1, 16, 219
Marcus, Laura 175
Marcuse, Herbert 34, 123 n.15
Marler, Regina 11, 205–6
"The Bloomsbury Love Triangle" 206
Marquez, Gabriel Garcia, *One Hundred Years of Solitude* 131
marriages 13, 16, 34–6, 38, 49, 55, 59, 166, 181, 187, 192, 198, 200–1, 206–7, 214, 219. *See also* friendship; love
and childbirth 43, 219
institution 39
interracial 52, 140, 223, 225–6
love 36, 192, 212
married couples 220
and motherhood/parenthood 55, 64–6
percentage of adults ever married 220
pragmatic 36–7
proponents 211
and sexuality 41

Marshall, Frances 206
Marshall, Paul 84–5, 87
Marx, Karl 26–7
economic history 29
The German Ideology 27
Marxism 98
metanarratives 29
Mary Krull (*The Hours,* Cunningham) 189–90
Maslow, Abraham
hierarchy 42
higher-order needs 35
Masood, Syed 140, 197–8
mass divorce, era 1, 16, 166
Matz, Jesse 176
time ecology 23 n.24, 45 n.7
McCarthy, Tom, *Remainder* 77, 155–8, 162
McEwan, Ian 7, 11–12, 17, 30, 49, 51, 60, 70, 78, 88–9, 92, 93 n.3, 104, 119
Atonement (*see Atonement* (McEwan))
comparison of his techniques to Freud's 83
conversation with modernism 85
Enduring Love 18
Saturday 18–19, 24 n.60, 72 n.56
Solar 18–19
McGregor, Jon, *If Nobody Speaks of Remarkable Things* 72 n.56
McHale, Brian 99, 176
change in the dominant 99
ontological preoccupations 122–3 n.12
Memoir Club 202
Meredith, Hugh Owen 196, 198, 200
Merrill, George 27–8, 197
meta-Bloomsbury 12–14, 195
metamodernism 176, 195
metanarrative 5, 9, 16, 20–1, 26–7, 29, 38, 53, 75, 77–9, 81–2, 88–9, 91, 94 n.5, 97–112, 116, 119, 121–2, 215, 223. *See also* Freud, Sigmund, Freudian metanarrative
MeToo movement 5
milieu therapy 123 n.15
misogyny 20, 128, 140, 143–7, 150 n.90, 161. *See also* anti-misogyny; male malady

modernism 2–5, 11–12, 17, 25–6, 32, 35, 51, 66–7, 70, 87, 93 n.1, 131, 176, 214
   avant la lettre 215
   "greening" of 72 n.61
   incredulity and 99
   legacies of 72 n.55, 147, 151, 155
   in relationship forms 202–4
Moffat, Wendy 24 n.39, 199
mononormativity 11, 22, 202, 206, 209–13
Moore, George Edward 17, 31, 163–4
   Principia Ethica 162, 168
Moore-Gilbert, Bart 20, 148 n.9
Morgan, Robin 199
Moses, Michael Valdez, *Modernism, Postcolonialism, and Globalism* 24 n.46
motherhood 37–8, 65–6, 181, 201
"The Mother Who Ran Away" (*McCall*) 38
Mozart, Wolfgang Amadeus, *Ave Verum Corpus* 160
Mrs Dalloway (Woolf) 2–3, 6, 12–13, 15, 17–19, 21, 24 n.60, 26, 39, 44, 55, 57, 59–60, 64–8, 99, 131, 170, 175–7, 179–82, 184, 186–9, 192, 201, 212
   Big Ben's chime 64, 175, 177
   Clarissa Dalloway 52, 55–6, 58–9, 68–9, 176, 178, 180, 182–4, 186–7, 189–91, 193 n.18, 193 n.23, 205, 210, 212
   Doris Kilman 189
   Peter Walsh 59, 65, 176, 185, 189–90, 201
   Richard Dalloway 213
   Septimus Smith 3, 19, 59, 64–5, 67, 177–8, 182–3, 185–8, 191, 193 n.23
muddle 9, 93, 158, 190
multiracial multiplicity 161
Muncy, Raymond Lee 217 n.40
Muñoz, José 215
   Cruising Utopia: The Then and There of Queer Futurity 8
Murdoch, Iris 89, 153–4, 162–3, 165, 168–9
   "Against Dryness" 156–7
   "The Idea of Perfection" 164
   Murdochian realism 155
Murdock, George Peter 38

Nagle, Christopher 215
Naipaul, Vidiadhar Surajprasad 136–7
   Enigma of Arrival 136
nationalism and cisnormativity 23 n.30, 139
natural death, concept 109
negative capability 158, 171 n.42
negative transference 102
negativity 7, 214
   romance 8
neo-modernist techniques 60
New Modernisms Series 12
Nicholls, Peter 93 n.1
Nietzsche, Friedrich 112, 160–1
Nixon, Rob 121
Njiru (*Ghost Road,* Barker) 101, 118–19, 121
Nolan, Daniel 214

Obergefell v. Hodges 213
Odysseus 133
Oedipal trauma 78
Oedipus Rex 84
On Beauty (Smith) 21, 28, 36, 39, 41, 49, 52, 76, 141, 147, 151–74, 208–9
   Black diversity 168
   cautious optimism 159
   extreme femininity 167
   heteroglossia 165
   Howard Belsey 41, 141, 152–3, 155, 160, 165–7, 209
   intimacy in history 166–70
   Kiki Belsey 28, 152, 159–63, 165–9, 172 n.96, 209
   liberal aesthetic 171 n.37
   liberal-humanist ethos 163
   postcolonial intertextuality 171 n.36
   reclaiming Howard's soul 159–66
O'Neill, Joseph, *Netherland* 155–7, 159, 162, 165
   authenticity 156
   Chuck Ramkissoon 156
optimism 3, 7, 17, 26, 32–5, 39, 42, 49, 54, 111, 187
   On Beauty (Smith) 159
   historical 3, 25–6, 179
   metanarrative 21, 88
   and pessimism 32–5, 110
Ottinger, Ulrike 39

Oxford English Dictionary 202
Ozzie and Harriet 38

Paradise Lost 133
Parsons, Talcott 38
Partridge, Ralph 206
Pastoor, Charles 77, 81, 93 n.3
    religiously hermeneutical approach 77
Patmore, Coventry 14
pessimism 17, 31–5, 42
    historical 1, 8
    optimism and 32–5, 110
    Woolfian 17–18
Phillips, Adam 80–1, 82, 92–3
philosophical skepticism 1
Picasso, Pablo
    analytical cubism 4
    Guernica 3
Pinker, Steven 32, 34, 43, 70
    Enlightenment Now: The Case for Reason, Science, Humanism, and Progress 33
Pipes, Daniel 148 n.26
plastic sexuality 36
political polarization 5
Pollyannaism 6, 16, 25, 119
polyaffectivity 205
polyamorous life 216 n.38
polyamorous theory 200
polyamory 4, 11, 21–2, 40, 202–3, 213, 215
    anti-essentialism 202, 204
    identity-forming effect 204
    sexual and social norms 22
polymorphous perversity 14, 88
polysexuality 204–5
poly-style divorce 203
positive transference 102
post-Bloomsburian horizons/fiction 9, 21, 77
post-Enlightenment 215
    intimacy 16–17, 22, 32, 35
    modernity 16
    revolution 9
postmodernism 25, 93 n.1, 122 n.11, 139, 176
poststructuralism 1, 160
Potter, Sally 39
private sphere 1, 5, 6–7, 15–16, 22, 26–7, 30, 32, 35, 44, 75, 214–15

psychiatric literature 178
psychic fluidity 37
psychoanalysis 20, 41, 43, 75, 78, 80–1, 92, 95 n.32, 106, 123 n.15
psychological femininity/masculinity 40
psychotherapeutic metanarrative 79
PTSD 107
public sphere 1, 5–6, 15–16, 32, 34–5, 37, 214–15
pure critiques 7, 25
Pynchon, Thomas 157

queer studies 7–8, 43
queer theory 8, 23 n.30
queer utopianism 8

radical dismay 7–9
radical modernism 25
radical theory and intimacy 43–4
Randall, Briony 72 n.56
Rank, Otto 110
Raphael, Dalleo 217 n.40
Rashomon (Kurosawa) 131
Rawlinson, Mark 107
Reed, Christopher 10
    Bloomsbury bashing 12
reflexivity 16, 26
Reich, Wilhelm 123 n.15
    "Orgone therapy" 102
Reisman, David, *The Lonely Crowd* 38
Rich, Adrienne, compulsory heterosexuality 207, 209
Rieff, Philip 123 n.15
Rivers, William Halse Rivers 18–19, 70, 76, 98–103, 111, 121, 123 n.24, 124 n.36, 125 n.82
    amazing freedom 116
    Anderson's neurosis 107
    Christ complex and interminable guilt 115–18, 122
    as Christ with small "c" 114–15
    countertransference neurosis 115
    de-throning (the idea of god) 116
    hypnosis 106
    Moffet's hysterical paralysis 103
    as postmodern hero 112–14, 122 n.10
    thinks *vs.* may unconsciously mean 117
    uncertain conscience 118–20

Rivers Centre in the Royal Edinburgh Hospital 107
Rorty, Richard 79
    "Freud and Moral Reflection" 94 n.12
Rosling, Hans, *Factfulness: Ten Reasons We're Wrong about the World-and Why Things Are Better Than You Think* 33
Rosner, Victoria, *Cambridge Companion to Bloomsbury* 11
Ross, Stephen, *Handbook to the Bloomsbury Group* 11
Ruhl, Sarah 39
Rushdie, Salman 4, 12, 17, 30, 49, 127–51, 213
    ambivalent feminism 150 n.88 (*see also* feminism, in *The Satanic Verses* (Rushdie))
    anti-Victorian methods 131
    "The Empire Writes Back with a Vengeance" 134
    historiography and question of progress 139–47
    "In God We Trust" 53, 139–40, 148 n.12
    "In Good Faith" 136, 142, 148 n.9, 148 n.30, 149 n.58
    Jahilian Hind 143
    Joseph Anton 147, 148 n.9
    magical realism 131–2
    Midnight's Children 128, 214
    non-linear conception of history 76
    on people's "essentially imaginative" response to the world 142, 146
    racial stereotypes 142
    rationalism 148 n.12, 149 n.58
    The Satanic Verses (see *The Satanic Verses* (Rushdie))
    The Wizard of Oz 128
Ruskinian socialism 27
Russell, Bertrand 40, 213
    The Conquest of Happiness 41
    trial marriage 214
    pessimism 42
Ryan, Derek, *Handbook to the Bloomsbury Group* 11

Sacks, Oliver 99, 122 n.8
Sackville-West, Vita 8, 180, 201

Saeed, Mirza 137, 144
Said, Edward 148 n.9
same-sex intimacy/love 6, 21, 26, 31, 65, 113–14, 127, 152, 175, 185, 200, 213
The Sampling Officials of the Drapers' Guild (Rembrandt) 164
Sassoon, Siegfried 19, 27, 99–100, 102, 107–8, 116, 118–20
    anti-war neurosis 100, 114
    The Memoirs of George Sherston 107
    "Soldier's Declaration" 114
The Satanic Verses (Rushdie) 20–1, 76, 121, 127–8, 148 n.9, 148 n.10, 148 n.12, 162, 213
    Allie Cone 129, 135–6, 143–6
    anti-absolutism and modernism 148 n.9
    Britishness and Islam 127, 129, 134–5, 147, 148 n.26
    Changez Chamchawalla 133, 136, 138–9
    "A City Visible but Unseen" 141
    Eugene Dumsday 137
    feminism (*see* feminism, in *The Satanic Verses* (Rushdie))
    Gibreel 20, 129–30, 131–3, 136–8, 140, 143–5
    Hal Valance 134, 137, 142
    Hind Sufyan 140, 145
    historical skepticism, narrative anti-realism 129–30
    magical-realist techniques and skepticism 162
    Mahound 130, 132, 136, 143
    Mimi Mamoulian 137
    mythical significance, circular design 132–3
    neophobia 133–9
    Otto Cone 129, 132, 144
    Pamela Lovelace 129, 133–5, 137–40, 142–3, 145–6, 162
    racism and misogyny 20, 128, 140–3, 146–7
    Saladin Chamcha 20, 53, 129–30, 132–43, 145–7, 162
    Schopenhauerian force 144
    Zeeny 134–6, 138–9, 142, 146–7

Savage, Dan 205, 211–12
    "It's Never Okay to Cheat (Except
        When It Is)" 217 n.69
    monogamish 205
Schippers, Mimi 207, 216 n.37
    *Beyond Monogamy: Polyamory and the
        Future of Polyqueer Sexualities* 40
schizophrenia 129, 132
Scott, Bonnie Kime 72 n.61
Second World War 1, 19, 25, 186
Sedgwick, Eve Kosofsky
    Epistemology of the Closet 23 n.30
    Touching Feeling 8
Seshagiri, Urmila 13, 85, 176
    "Metamodernism" 12, 195
sex addiction 204
sexism and heterosexism 210
sexual inequality 6, 50, 54–5
sexuality 10, 27, 31, 34, 36, 39–40, 56, 94
        n.7, 116, 152, 177, 180–1, 202–3
    plastic 36
    pre-moderns 36
    psychophysical capacity 10
    queer 14
sexual radicalism 35
sexual revolution 35, 42, 202, 219
sexual selfhood 12–13, 32, 37
shared child rearing 216 n.37
Shaw, Andrea 172 n.95
Sheff, Elisabeth 202, 216 nn.34–8,
        217 n.40
    polyaffectivity 205
    The Polyamorists Next Door 40
Shelden, Ashley 69, 213–14. *See also*
        negativity
    disbelief in love 1, 7, 69, 136, 213
    Unmaking Love 7, 70, 136
"shell shock" patients 98–9, 107, 177
Showalter, Elaine 99, 107, 114, 116
Simawe, Saadi 148 n.26
similarity-within-difference principle 101
singlehood 16, 34, 38, 207, 213
singlism 210
skepticism 1–3, 7, 58, 67, 77, 92, 97, 99,
        136, 156, 158, 160, 162, 209
    Freudian 18–20, 32
    historical (Rushdie) 129–30
    philosophical 1
    toward the idea of progress 25

Slobodin, Richard 114, 125 n.82
Smiley, Jane 55
Smith, Zadie 7–9, 12, 17, 30, 41, 51–2,
        127, 151–74, 209, 215
    aesthetics of alterity 154
    On Beauty (*see On Beauty* (Smith))
    Black Female Literary Tradition 168
    Changing My Mind 153, 157
    homage 163, 192
    ideological inconsistency 171 n.38
    miserabilism 70
    NW 154, 168
    optimism 170 n.8
    process of elimination 156
    self-expression 155
    Swing Time 154
    as theorist and critic 153–9
    "Two Directions for the Novel" 154–5,
        162, 165
    White Teeth 36, 157, 161, 167–8,
        170 n.8, 172 n.96, 214
social change 8, 13, 26
social progress 8, 35–7, 52, 142–3, 177,
        192, 215
society 3, 27, 29, 31, 34, 38–9, 51, 76, 92,
        100–1, 108, 116, 119, 141, 161,
        169, 179, 186–9, 208, 211, 213
    evolution 4
    and justice 14
    mechanization 53
    and psychosexuality 28
    rational 28
    whole 9, 123 n.15
sociological and psychological research
        140–1
sociological Bloomsbury 15–16
Sontag, Susan 92
The Sopranos 99
starvation economy 204
Stein, Gertrude 2
    Tender Buttons 3
Stephen, Leslie 200–1
Stevenson, Sheryl 79
Stonewall riots 127, 210
Strachey, Alix 11, 78, 206
Strachey, James 11, 78, 124 n.65, 176,
        206
Strachey, Lytton 10, 30, 204, 206
Stuckey, Lexi 170 n.8

suicide 5, 19, 34, 103, 129, 136, 148 n.3, 161, 176–84, 186–8, 198
Suleri, Sara 129, 132

Tate, Andrew 81
Tennyson, Alfred, *In Memoriam* 26
Textual Practice 47 n.77
therapeutic intimacy 98–101
Thomas, Carl 165
Tortorici, Dayna 158, 171 n.38
transference 19, 29, 78, 83, 99, 105, 115, 123 n.20. *See also* countertransference
   negative 102
   neurosis 105
   positive 102
The Trapped Housewife (CBS documentary) 38
Trilling, Lionel 3, 157, 159
Trumpism 34
Turing, Alan 147 n.3
Twain, Mark 97

United Kingdom (UK) 140
   illegitimacy rates 220–1
   interracial marriage 223, 225, 226
   Labouchere Amendment 147 n.3
   legislative and cultural context 223, 226
   post-Second World War history 223, 224
   South Asian immigration and events 223–4
United States (US) 211
   homicides 33
   immigration, interracial marriage, and public sentiment 223, 225
   poly/nonmonogamous people 216 n.35
   racism, sexism, and homophobia 34
Ursula (*Women in Love*, Lawrence) 2, 15, 31, 205, 207, 210
The U.S. Bureau of Labor Statistics 22 n.11

Vandenberghe, Betsy 217 n.69
van den Broek, Hans 155
van Gogh, Vincent 181
Victorian era 2–3, 6, 15, 26–7, 37–8, 76, 131, 140, 167, 219
   gender roles/segregation 28, 195, 207, 212
   homophobia 195

marriage model 13, 42, 207
meliorism 25
realism 60, 154, 175
sentimentality 37, 212
sexual Intermediates 42
society 31, 178
traits 159

Wallace, David Foster 157, 170 n.18
Walters, Tracey 167–8, 172 n.95
war-time psychotherapy 99
Watson, John 170 n.13
Weber, Max 76
When Harry Met Sally 41
Whitman, Walt 27
Wiegman, Robyn 8–10, 16, 23 n.30, 152, 160, 176, 189
   "Antinormativity's Queer Conventions" 8, 210
Wilde, Oscar 147 n.3
Williams, Raymond 9–10
Wilson, Anne, racial challenges (children) 141, 150 n.76
Wilson, Elizabeth 8–10, 16, 23 n.30, 152, 160, 176, 189
   "Antinormativity's Queer Conventions" 8, 210
Wilson, Robert 39
Wilson, Sloan, *The Man in the Gray Flannel Suit* 38
Winterson, Jeanette, *Lighthousekeeping* 72 n.56
Wittgenstein, Ludwig 79
Wolfe, Jesse, *Bloomsbury, Modernism, and the Reinvention of Intimacy* 13, 16
Wollstonecraft, Mary 22, 213
Vindication of the Rights of Man 35
Wood, James 127, 157
   "hysterical realism," critique of 157, 161
   "overblown, manic prose," critique of 157
Woolf, Leonard 11, 14, 78, 179–81, 188, 192, 193 n.32, 201, 205
Woolf, Virginia 2, 4, 9, 11–12, 14, 26, 30–2, 34, 39, 41, 44, 49–50, 52, 60, 70, 73 n.89, 78, 151, 155, 169, 176, 179, 186, 193 n.32, 208, 210, 215
Between the Acts 31

androgynous mind 40
anti-realism 17, 89
ecocriticism and feminism 72 n.61
Jacob's Room 51, 62, 154, 200
To the Lighthouse 6, 15, 60–2, 65–8, 73 n.105, 176, 212
   Charles Tansley 68
   Lily Briscoe 15, 68–9, 176
liking 32
"Modern Fiction" 2, 61
modernist autocritique 85
Mr Bennet and Mrs Brown 85
Mrs Dalloway (*see Mrs Dalloway* (Woolf))

Night and Day 15, 51
"Old Bloomsbury" 10, 200–2, 208, 214
optimism 21, 49, 187
Orlando 31, 39–40, 46 n.56
perspectivalism 89
pessimism 17–18
post-Woolfian technique 60–71
"Professions for Women" 6, 14
A Room of One's Own 6, 32, 57, 207
Three Guineas 6, 32
The Waves 2–3, 61–2, 65, 200
The Years 61–2

Yealland, Lewis 116

Plate 1 *The Walled Garden at Charleston* (1916), by Vanessa Bell. 46 × 35.5 cm. Oil on canvas. Courtesy Artists Rights Society.

Plate 2 Monk's House, dining room. Photograph courtesy of Howard Grey.

Plate 3 *The Sampling Officials of the Drapers' Guild* (1662), by Rembrandt van Rijn. 191.5 × 279 cm. Oil on canvas. Courtesy Rijksmuseum, Amsterdam.

Plate 4 *A Woman Bathing in a Stream* (1654), by Rembrandt van Rijn. 61.8 × 47 cm. Oil on panel. Courtesy National Gallery, London.

Plate 5 *The Hours*. Film. 2003.

Plate 6 *The Hours*. Film. 2003.

Plate 7 *The Hours*. Film. 2003.

Plate 8 *The Hours*. Film. 2003.

Plate 9 *The Hours*. Film. 2003.

Plate 10 *The Hours*. Film. 2003.

Plate 11 *The Hours.* Film. 2003.